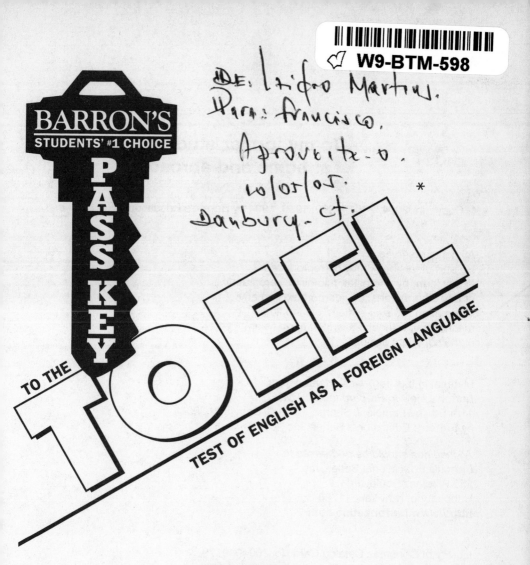

BARRON'S
STUDENTS' #1 CHOICE

PASS KEY

TO THE

TOEFL

TEST OF ENGLISH AS A FOREIGN LANGUAGE

De: Isidro Martins.
Para: Francisco.
Aproveite-o.
10/05/05.
Danbury-ct.

*

Fifth Edition

Pamela J. Sharpe, Ph.D.
The Ohio State University

BARRON'S EDUCATIONAL SERIES, INC.

To my former students at home and abroad

Material in this book was adapted from
Barron's *How to Prepare for the TOEFL*,
11th Ed., by Pamela J. Sharpe, Ph.D. © Copyright 2004
by Barron's Educational Series, Inc.

All inquiries should be addressed to:
Barron's Educational Series, Inc.
250 Wireless Boulevard
Hauppauge, New York 11788
http://www.barronseduc.com

Library of Congress Catalog Card No. 2004049779
ISBN-13: 978-0-7641-7585-5
ISBN-10: 0-7641-7585-8

Library of Congress Cataloging-in-Publication Data

Sharpe, Pamela J.
    Pass key to the TOEFL / Pamela J. Sharpe.—5th ed.
        p.   cm.
    ISBN 0-7641-7585-8 (book & audio compact disks)
    1. Test of English as a Foreign Language—Study guides.   2. English
language—Textbooks for foreign speakers.   3. English language—
Examinations—Study guides.   I. Title.

PE1128 .S523 2004
428′.0076—dc22   2004049779

PRINTED IN CANADA
9 8 7 6 5 4 3

CONTENTS

INTRODUCTION

QUESTIONS AND ANSWERS CONCERNING THE TOEFL

REVIEW OF LISTENING

PREVIEW OF SPEAKING

REVIEW OF STRUCTURE

REVIEW OF READING

REVIEW OF WRITING

TOEFL MODEL TESTS

ANSWER KEYS

EXPLANATORY ANSWERS AND AUDIO SCRIPTS

SCORE ESTIMATES

To the Student

Barron's Pass Key to the TOEFL is the concise version of the classic Barron's How to Prepare for the TOEFL. Small enough to put in your purse, backpack, or book bag, this convenient book can always be in the right place when you have a few minutes to study—on the bus, while you wait for an appointment, or on break at work or school.

This concise version, Pass Key to the TOEFL, 5th Edition, can be used to prepare for both the Supplemental Paper-Based TOEFL and for the Computer-Based TOEFL as well as the new Next Generation TOEFL. To make this book smaller, less expensive, and more convenient to carry with you, we have included four Model Tests in the book and the audio for three Model Tests on the compact disks. The larger version of this book, Barron's How to Prepare for the TOEFL, 11th Edition, includes nine Model Tests. The CD-ROM that supplements the larger book includes the audio and the computer screens for Computer-Assisted Model Tests as well as a Computer-Adaptive Model Test and a Next Generation Model Test.

Ideally, you would use these two books for two different purposes. You would use this book, Pass Key to the TOEFL, 5th Edition, to take the best advantage of your time while you are away from your computer or when you don't want to carry heavy materials. You would use the larger version of this book, Barron's How to Prepare for the TOEFL, 11th Edition, and the CD-ROM that supplements it, when you have access to your computer.

Study thoughtfully, and take the TOEFL with confidence. It may well be the most important examination of your academic career. And this book can be an essential pass key to your success.

To the Teacher

Rationale for a TOEFL Preparation Course

Although Barron's How to Prepare for the TOEFL was originally written as a self-study guide for students who were preparing to take the TOEFL, in the years since its first publication, I have received letters from ESL teachers around the world who are using the book successfully for classroom study. In fact, in recent years, many special courses have been developed within the existing ESL curriculum to accommodate TOEFL preparation.

I believe that these TOEFL preparation courses respond to three trends within the profession. First, there appears to be a greater recognition on the part of many ESL teachers that student goals must be acknowledged and addressed. For the engineer, the business person, the doctor, or the preuniversity student, a satisfactory score on the TOEFL is one of the most immediate goals; for many, without the required score, they cannot continue their professional studies or obtain certification to practice their professions. They may have other language goals as well, such as learning to communicate more effectively or improving their writing, but these goals do not usually exert the same kinds of pressure that the required TOEFL score does.

Second, teachers have recognized and recorded the damaging results of test anxiety. We have all observed students who were so frightened of failure that they have performed on the TOEFL at a level far below that which their performance in class would have indicated. The standardized score just didn't correspond with the score in the gradebook. In addition, teachers have become aware that for some students, the TOEFL represents their first experience in taking a computer-assisted test. The concepts of working within time limits, marking on a screen, and guessing to improve a score are often new and confusing to students, and they forfeit valuable points because they must concentrate on unfamiliar procedures instead of on language questions.

Third, teachers have observed the corresponding changes in student proficiency that have accompanied the evolutionary changes in ESL syllabus design. Since this book was first written, we have moved away from a grammatical syllabus to a communicative syllabus, and at this writing, there seems to be growing interest in a content-based syllabus. Viewed in terms of what has actually happened in classrooms, most of us have emphasized the facilitation of communication and meaning and de-emphasized the teaching of forms. As we did so, we noticed with pride the improvement in student fluency and with dismay the corresponding loss of accuracy. Some of our best, most fluent students received disappointing scores on the test that was so important to them.

Through these observations and experiences, teachers have concluded that (1) students need to work toward their own goals, (2) students need some time to focus on accuracy as well as on fluency, and (3) students need an opportunity to practice taking a standardized test in order to alleviate anxiety and develop test strategies. With the introduction of the Computer-Based TOEFL, the opportunity to gain experience taking a computer-assisted model test has also become important to student confidence and success. In short, more and more teachers have begun to support the inclusion of a TOEFL preparation course in the ESL curriculum.

Organization of a TOEFL Preparation Course

Organizing a TOEFL preparation course requires that teachers make decisions about the way that the course should be structured and the kinds of supplementary materials and activities that should be used.

Structuring

Some teachers have suggested that each review section in this book be used for a separate class; they are team teaching a TOEFL course. Other teachers direct their students to the language laboratory for independent study in listening comprehension three times a week, checking on progress throughout the term; assign reading and vocabulary study for homework; and spend class time on structure and writing. Still other teachers develop individual study plans for each student based on previous TOEFL part scores. Students with high listening and low reading scores concentrate their efforts in reading labs, while students with low listening and high reading scores spend time in listening labs.

Materials and Activities

Listening. Studies in distributive practice have convinced teachers of listening comprehension that a little practice every day for a few months is more valuable than a lot of practice concentrated in a shorter time. In addition, many teachers like to use two kinds of listening practice—intensive and extensive. Intensive practice consists of listening to problems like those in the review of listening in this book.

By so doing, the student progresses from short conversations through longer conversations to mini-talks, gaining experience in listening to simulations of the TOEFL examination. Extensive practice consists of watching a daytime drama on television, listening to a local radio program, or auditing a class. Creative teachers everywhere have developed strategies for checking student progress such as requiring a summary of the plot or a prediction of what will happen the following day on the drama; a one-sentence explanation of the radio program, as well as the name of the speaker, sponsor of the program, and two details; a copy of student notes from the audited class.

Speaking. One of the best ways to support students who are fearful of speaking is to address the issue of confidence. Developing a positive attitude toward the speaking tasks is a key to success on this section of the TOEFL.

Another important strategy is to make 60-second telephone assignments. The TOEFL Academic Speaking Test (TAST), which is a preliminary version of the Speaking Section on the Next Generation TOEFL, is currently administered by telephone. To prepare our students for this new experience, some of us are experimenting with phone-in speaking practice by using telephone answering machines to record our students when they call. In this way, the students can become accustomed to the telephone tasks and we can provide more realistic feedback for them.

Structure. Of course, the focus in a review of structure for the TOEFL will be on form. It is form that is tested on the TOEFL. It is assumed that students have studied grammar prior to reviewing for the TOEFL, and that they are relatively fluent. The purpose of a TOEFL review then is to improve accuracy. Because accuracy is directly related to TOEFL scores and because the scores are tied to student goals, this type of review motivates students to pay attention to detail that would not usually be of much interest to them.

Among ESL teachers, the debate rages on about whether students should ever see errors in grammar. But many teachers have recognized the fact that students *do* see errors all the time, not only in the distractors that are used on standardized tests like the TOEFL and teacher-made tests like the multiple-choice midterms in their grammar classes, but also in their own writing. They argue that students must be able to recognize errors, learn to read for them, and correct them.

The student preparing for the TOEFL will be required not only to recognize correct answers but also to eliminate incorrect answers, or distractors, as possibilities. The review of structure in this book supports recognition by alerting students to avoid certain common distractors. Many excellent teachers take this one step further by using student compositions to create personal TOEFL tests. By underlining four words or phrases in selected sentences, one phrase of which contains an incorrect structure, teachers encourage students to reread their writing. It has proven to be a helpful transitional technique for students who need to learn how to edit their own compositions.

Reading. One of the problems in a TOEFL preparation course is that of directing vocabulary study. Generally, teachers feel that encouraging students to collect words and develop their own word lists is the best solution to the problem of helping students who will be faced with the dilemma of responding to words from a possible vocabulary pool of thousands of words that may appear in context in the reading section. In this way, they will increase their vocabularies in an ordered and productive way, thereby benefiting even if none of their new words appears on the test that they take. Activities that support learning vocabulary in context are also helpful. In this edition, a "Glossary of Campus Vocabulary" supports comprehension of listening as well as of reading items that are, for the most part, campus based.

In order to improve reading, students need extensive practice in reading a variety of material, including newspapers and magazines as well as short excerpts from textbooks. In addition, students need to check their comprehension and time themselves carefully.

It is also necessary for students who are preparing for the Computer-Based TOEFL to practice reading from a computer screen. The skill of scrolling through text is different from the skill of reading a page in a book. To succeed on the TOEFL and after the TOEFL, students must develop new reading strategies for texts on screens. An English encyclopedia on CD-ROM is an inexpensive way to provide students with a huge amount of reading material from all the nonfiction content areas tested on the TOEFL. By reading on screen, students gain not only reading comprehension skills but also computer confidence. Again, it is well to advise students of the advantages of distributed practice. They should be made aware that it is better to read two passages every day for five days than to read ten passages in one lab period.

Writing. There are many excellent ESL textbooks to help students improve their writing. Because TOEFL topics include opinion, persuasion, and argument, some teachers tend to emphasize these types of topics in composition classes.

The extensive list of writing topics published in the *Information Bulletin* for the Computer-Based TOEFL and listed on the TOEFL web site offers teachers an opportunity to use actual TOEFL topics in class. In order to help students organize their thoughts, the topics can be used as conversation starters for class discussion. In this way, students will have thought about the topics and will have formed an opinion before they are presented with the writing task on the TOEFL.

It is also a good idea to time some of the essays that students write in class so that they can become accustomed to completing their work within thirty minutes.

Although teachers need to develop grading systems that make sense for their teaching situations, the scoring guide that is used for the essay on the TOEFL is general enough to be adapted for at least some of the assignments in an ESL composition class. By using the guide, teachers can inform students of their progress as it relates to the scores that they can expect to receive on the essay they will write for the TOEFL.

Staying Current

So many changes have been made in the design and content of the TOEFL over the years that one of the greatest challenges for teachers is to remain current and to help our students prepare for the format that they will see when they take the TOEFL. Now there are three TOEFL formats—the Paper-Based TOEFL, the Computer-Based TOEFL, and the Next Generation TOEFL—each of which requires slightly different preparation. In addition to the explanations and examples of each format that are provided in this book, the official TOEFL web site is a good resource for the most recent changes. Refer often to updates at *www.toefl.org*.

Networking with ESL Teachers

One of the many rewards of writing is the opportunity that it creates to exchange ideas with so many talented colleagues. At conferences, I have met ESL teachers who use or have used one of the previous editions of this book;

through my publisher, I have received letters from students and teachers from fifty-two nations. This preface and many of the revisions in this new edition were included because of comments and suggestions from those conversations and letters.

Thank you for your ideas. I hope that by sharing we can help each other and thereby help our students more. Please continue corresponding by mail or by e-mail.

Pamela Sharpe
1406 Camino Real
Yuma, Arizona 85364
sharpe@teflprep.com

Acknowledgments

With affection and deep appreciation I acknowledge my indebtedness to the friends, family, and colleagues who have been part of the TOEFL team for so many years:

The late Dr. Jayne Harder, former Director of the English Language Institute at the University of Florida
for initiating me into the science of linguistics and the art of teaching English as a second language;

Robert and Lillie Sharpe, my parents,
for their encouragement during the preparation of the manuscript and for their assistance in typing and proofreading previous editions;

The late Dr. Tom Clapp, former Dean of Continuing Education at the University of Toledo
for the maturity and confidence that I gained during our marriage because he believed in me;

Carole Berglie, former Editor at Barron's Educational Series
for her guidance in the first edition of the larger version of this book, and to all of the editors at Barron's for their contributions to later editions;

Marcy Rosenbaum, Project Editor at Barron's Educational Series
for her astute advice, direction, and support during the preparation and production of the book; she deserves much more credit and thanks than this small space permits;

Debby Becak, Production Manager at Barron's Educational Series
for the suggestions and designs, large and small, that have improved every
chapter;

Joan Franklin, President, and John Rockwell, Editor, at Cinema Sound
for casting and directing the talented voices and bringing the script to life;

Kathy Telford, Proofreader at Proofreader's Plus
for her skillful review of the pages, her attention to the important details in the
writing process, and her positive approach to errors;

*Roxanne Nuhaily, Associate Director of the English Language Program
at the University of California, San Diego*
for field testing the items for the computer adaptive model test on the
CD-ROM that supplements the larger version of this book;

*Dr. Sheri McCarthy-Tucker, Associate Professor at Northern Arizona
University*
for analyzing and calibrating the items for the adaptive model test;

*Karen McNiel, Reading Coordinator at Yuma High School and Dr. Jean
Zukowski-Faust, Professor at Northern Arizona University*
for reviewing the reading level and collaborating in the revision of selected
reading passages in the computer-based model tests;

Faye Chiu, Director at Test University
for managing the transformation from print to CD-ROM on all editions of the
larger version of this book;

John T. Osterman, my husband—a special thank you
for the unconditional love, the daily interest in and support for my writing
career; each revision of this book is better than the last, and every new and
revised year with John is the best year of my life.

Permissions

"Civilization"
From *Western Civilization, Comprehensive Volume, 4th Edition,* by Jackson J. Spielvogel ©2000. Reprinted with permission of Wadsworth, a division of Thomson Learning: *www.thomsonrights.com.*

"Scientific Method"
From *The Sciences—An Integrated Approach, 3rd Edition,* by James Trefill and Robert M. Hazen ©2001 John Wiley & Sons, Inc. This material is used by permission of John Wiley & Sons, Inc.

"Symbiotic Relationships"
From *Environmental Sciences, 8th Edition,* by Eldon D. Enger and Bradley F. Smith ©2002 McGraw-Hill Companies. This passage is used with the permission of the McGraw-Hill Companies.

Timetable for the TOEFL

THE THREE TOEFL FORMATS

	Paper-Based TOEFL	Computer-Based TOEFL	Next Generation TOEFL
Tutorial	No questions	Variable	Variable
Listening	50 questions	30–50 questions	33–34 questions
Speaking	No questions	No questions	6 questions
Listening/Speaking	No questions	No questions	Included
Structure	40 questions	20–25 questions	No questions
Reading	50 questions	45–55 questions	36–39 questions
Reading/Speaking	No questions	No questions	Included
Writing	1 question	1 question	2 questions
Listening/Writing	No questions	No questions	Included
Reading/Writing	No questions	No questions	Included
TIME	3 hours	4 hours, 30 minutes	4 hours

Note: The actual times will vary in accordance with the time the supervisor completes the preliminary work and begins the actual test. On the Computer-Based TOEFL and the Next Generation TOEFL, the time for the tutorial will vary from one person to another. Exact numbers of questions will also vary slightly from one test to another for statistical purposes. This is a good estimate.

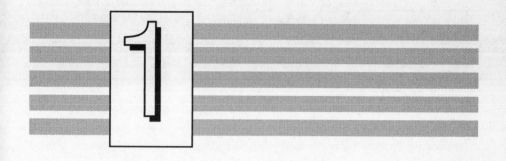

INTRODUCTION

Study Plan for the TOEFL

Many students do not prepare for the TOEFL. They do not even read the *Information Bulletin* that they receive from Educational Testing Service along with their registration forms. You have an advantage. Using this book, you have a study plan.

Barron's TOEFL Series

There are three books in the Barron's TOEFL series to help you prepare for the Test of English as a Foreign Language. Each book has a different purpose.

Barron's Practice Exercises for the TOEFL. A book for learners who need additional practice for the TOEFL. It includes a general preview of the TOEFL examination and almost one thousand exercises. Six separate audio CDs accompany the book to give you practice in listening and speaking. You may have used *Barron's Practice Exercises for the TOEFL* before using this book. Many students use *Barron's Practice Exercises for the TOEFL* as a workbook for the book you are using now.

Barron's How to Prepare for the TOEFL. A book for learners who need review and practice for the TOEFL. It includes questions and answers about the TOEFL examination, a detailed review for each section of the examination, and eight model tests similar to the Computer-Based TOEFL examination. Several sets of additional materials are available to supplement this book, including a separate package of cassette tapes, a separate package of audio compact disks, or the book may be accompanied by compact disks for audio only, or a CD-ROM for use with a computer. A computer-adaptive test like that of the Computer-Based TOEFL is found on the CD-ROM. In addition, Model Test 9 in the book and on the CD-ROM provides an opportunity to practice taking a Next Generation TOEFL test.

Barron's Pass Key to the TOEFL. A pocket-sized edition of *Barron's How to Prepare for the TOEFL.* It is for learners who need review and practice for the TOEFL and want to be able to carry a smaller book with them. It includes questions and answers about the TOEFL examination, basic tips on how to prepare for the TOEFL, and four model tests from *Barron's How to Prepare for the TOEFL*—three model tests for the Computer-Based TOEFL and one model test for the Next Generation TOEFL. Two audio CDs accompany the book to give you practice in listening and speaking.

More About This Book

In preparing to take the TOEFL or any other language examination, it is very important to review the language skills for each section of the examination and to have an opportunity to take model tests that are similar to the actual examination. Reviewing will help you recall some of the language skills you have studied in previous classes and other books. Taking model tests will give you the experience of taking a TOEFL before you take the actual examination. If you plan to take the Computer-Based TOEFL or the Next Generation TOEFL, it is very helpful for you to practice using the CD-ROM that supplements the larger version of this book.

Remember, the purpose of the book is to provide you with a concise review of the language skills for each section of the TOEFL examination and to provide you with opportunities to take model tests similar to the actual TOEFL examination. By studying this book, you should renew and sharpen your skills, increase your speed, and improve your score.

Planning to Take the TOEFL

Study Plan I—For Intermediate Level Learners
- First, use *Barron's Practice Exercises for the TOEFL* to begin your TOEFL preparation.
- Then use this book, *Barron's Pass Key to the TOEFL* for preparation at times when you do not have a computer available.
- Also use *Barron's How to Prepare for the TOEFL* with the CD-ROM for practice on computer-assisted tests.

Study Plan II—For High Intermediate Level or Advanced Learners
- Use *Barron's How to Prepare for the TOEFL* with the CD-ROM for practice on computer-assisted tests.
- Use *Barron's Pass Key to the TOEFL* for preparation at times when you do not have a computer available.

Study Plan III—For Advanced Learners
- Use this book, *Barron's Pass Key to the TOEFL* for the most concise study plan.

An Eight-Week Calendar

Week One
- Read Chapter 1, "Introduction."
- Read Chapter 2, "Questions and Answers Concerning the TOEFL."
- Request a copy of the TOEFL *Information Bulletin* or download it from the TOEFL web site.

- Register for your test date.
- Take Model Test 1 to determine which sections will be most challenging.

Week Two
- Focus on Listening.
- Refer to Chapter 3 and review the listening problems.
- Mark problems that you need to study.

Week Three
If you are taking the Next Generation TOEFL:
- Focus on Speaking.
- Refer to Chapter 4 and preview the speaking problems.
- Mark problems that you need to study.
If you are taking the Computer-Based TOEFL or the Paper-Based TOEFL:
- Use this time to review one of the other sections that you identified as challenging when you took Model Test 1.

Week Four
If you are taking the Computer-Based TOEFL or the Paper-Based TOEFL:
- Focus on Structure.
- Refer to Chapter 5 and review the structure problems.
- Mark problems that you need to study.
If you are taking the Next Generation TOEFL:
- Use this time to review one of the other sections that you identified as challenging when you took Model Test 1.

Week Five
- Focus on Reading and Writing.
- Refer to Chapter 6 and review the reading problems.
- Mark problems that you need to study.
- Refer to Chapter 7 and review the writing problems.
- Mark problems that you need to study.

Week Six
- Take Model Test 2.
- Refer to the Explanatory Answers in Chapter 10.
- Mark items that you need to review.

Week Seven
- Take Model Test 3.
- Refer to the Explanatory Answers in Chapter 10.
- Mark items that you need to review.

Week Eight
- Focus on the test format
If you are taking the Paper-Based TOEFL:

- Review all the items that you have marked in the model tests.

If you are taking the Computer-Based TOEFL:

- Review all the items that you have marked in the model tests.

If you are taking the Next Generation TOEFL:

- Take Model Test 4.
- Refer to the Explanatory Answers in Chapter 10.
- Mark items that you need to review and study them.

Adjusting the Calendar

Ideally, you will have eight weeks to prepare for the TOEFL. But, if you have a shorter time to prepare, follow the plan in the same order, adjusting the time to meet your needs.

Plan for Preparation

To improve your scores most, follow this plan:

- *First,* if you have taken the TOEFL before, you already know which section or sections are difficult for you. Look at the part scores on your score report. If your lowest score is on Listening, then you should spend more time reviewing Section 1. If your lowest score is on Section 2 or Section 3, then you should spend more time reviewing them.

- *Second,* spend time preparing every day for at least an hour instead of sitting down to review once a week for seven hours. Even though you are studying for the same amount of time, research shows that daily shorter sessions produce better results on the test.

- *Finally,* do not try to memorize questions from this or any other book. The questions on the test that you take will be very similar to the questions in this book, but they will not be exactly the same.

What you should try to do as you use this and your other books is learn how to apply your knowledge. Do not hurry through the practice exercises. While you are checking your answers to the model tests, *think* about the correct answer. Why is it correct? Can you explain the answer to yourself before you check the explanatory answer? Is the question similar to others that you have seen before?

Plan for Additional Preparation

Although this book should provide you with enough review material, some of you will want to do more in order to prepare for the TOEFL. Suggestions for each section follow.

- **To prepare for Listening.** Listen to radio and television newscasts and weather reports, television documentaries, lectures on educational television stations, and free lectures sponsored by clubs and universities. Attend movies in English. Try to make friends with speakers of American English and participate in conversations.

- **To prepare for Speaking.** Talk on the telephone in English with a friend. Ask each other your opinions about conversational topics. Use a timer to become accustomed to answering in 60 seconds.

- **To prepare for Structure.** Use an advanced grammar review book. If you are attending an English course, do not stop attending.

- **To prepare for Reading.** Read articles in English newspapers and magazines, college catalogs and admissions materials, travel brochures, and entries that interest you from American and English encyclopedias. Try to read a variety of topics—American history, culture, social science, and natural science.

- **To prepare for Writing.** Refer to the TOEFL *Information Bulletin* for the Computer-Based TOEFL or visit the TOEFL web site at *www.toefl.org*. Actual essay topics for the TOEFL are listed in the TOEFL *Information Bulletin* and on the web site. For a fee, the test developers will grade one of your practice essays. Click on "Score It Now."

A Good Start

Learn to relax. If you start to panic in the examination room, close your eyes and say "no" in your mind. Tell yourself, "I will not panic. I am prepared." Then take several slow, deep breaths, letting your shoulders drop in a relaxed manner as you exhale.

Concentrate on the questions. Do not talk. Concentrate your attention. Do not look at anything in the test room except the answers that correspond to the question you are working on. Do not think about your situation, the test in general, your score, or your future. If you do, force yourself to return to the question. If you do not understand a problem and you do not have a good answer, do your best. Then stop thinking about it. Be ready for the next problem.

Do not cheat. In spite of opportunity, knowledge that others are doing it, desire to help a friend, or fear that you will not make a good score, *do not cheat*. On the TOEFL, cheating is a very serious matter. If you are discovered, your test will not be scored. Legal action may be taken by Educational Testing Service (ETS).

Advice for Success

Your attitude will influence your success on the TOEFL examination. You must develop patterns of positive thinking. To help in developing a positive attitude, memorize the following sentences and bring them to mind after each study session. Bring them to mind when you begin to have negative thoughts.

I know more today than I did yesterday.
I am preparing.
I will succeed.

Remember, some tension is normal and good. Accept it. Use it constructively. It will motivate you to study. But don't panic or worry. Panic will cause loss of concentration and poor performance. Avoid people who panic and worry. Don't listen to them. They will encourage negative thoughts.

You know more today than you did yesterday.
You are preparing.
You will succeed.

There is more "Advice for Success" at the end of each review chapter. Please read and consider the advice as you continue your study plan.

QUESTIONS AND ANSWERS
CONCERNING THE TOEFL

The TOEFL is the Test of English as a Foreign Language.

Almost one million students from 180 countries register to take the TOEFL every year at test centers throughout the world. Some of them do not pass the TOEFL because they do not understand enough English. Others do not pass it because they do not understand the examination.

The following questions are commonly asked by students as they prepare for the TOEFL. To help you, they have been answered here.

TOEFL Programs

What is the purpose of the TOEFL?

Since 1963, the TOEFL has been used by scholarship selection committees of governments, universities, and agencies such as Fulbright, the Agency for International Development, AMIDEAST, Latin American Scholarship Programs, and others as a standard measure of the English proficiency of their candidates. Some professional licensing and certification agencies also use TOEFL scores to evaluate English proficiency.

The admissions committees of more than 4,400 colleges and universities in the United States, Canada, and many other countries worldwide require foreign applicants to submit TOEFL scores along with transcripts and recommendations in order to be considered for admission.

Many universities use TOEFL scores to fulfill the foreign language requirement for doctoral candidates whose first language is not English.

Which TOEFL testing programs are available now?

The official TOEFL examination is currently administered at test sites around the world in three different formats: the Paper-Based TOEFL (PBT), the Computer-Based TOEFL (CBT), and the Next Generation TOEFL. The same language proficiency skills are tested on every format, but they are tested in different ways.

In addition to the official TOEFL administrations, some schools and agencies administer the institutional TOEFL for their students and employees. The institutional TOEFL is usually the Paper-Based format.

What is the Computer-Based TOEFL program?

The CBT is a computer-adaptive test that is offered as an official standard for language proficiency worldwide. The CBT is also called the Official TOEFL.

The Computer-Based TOEFL has four sections: Listening, Structure, Writing, and Reading. The Writing is equivalent to the Test of Written English (TWE) on the Paper-Based TOEFL. The CBT is an adaptive test, which means that everyone who takes the TOEFL during the same administration may not see and answer the same questions. The computer selects questions for you at your level of proficiency. There are three subscores—Listening, Structure/Writing, and Reading. The total score is based on a scale of 0–300.

What is the Paper-Based TOEFL?

The PBT is a pencil and paper test that is offered for two purposes. One purpose of the PBT is for placement and progress evaluations. Colleges or other institutions use the PBT to test their students. The scores are not valid outside the place where they are administered, but the college or institution accepts the PBT that they administer as an official score. This PBT is also called an Institutional TOEFL.

The other purpose of the PBT is to supplement the official Computer-Based TOEFL in areas where computer-based testing is not possible. The scores are usually valid outside the place where they are administered. This PBT is also called a Supplemental TOEFL.

The Paper-Based TOEFL has three sections: Listening Comprehension, Structure and Written Expression, and Reading. In addition, the TWE is a required essay that provides a writing score. The PBT is a linear test, which means that everyone who takes the TOEFL during the same administration will see and answer the same questions. The total score is based on a scale of 310–677.

What is the Next Generation TOEFL?

The Next Generation TOEFL is a computer-assisted test that will be introduced in September 2005 worldwide. The Next Generation TOEFL has four sections: Listening, Speaking, Reading, and Writing. The Speaking Section was already introduced in 2003 as the TOEFL Academic Speaking Test (TAST) and can be taken and scored without the other sections. On the four-part Next Generation TOEFL, most of the questions are independent, but some of the questions are integrated. For example, you may be asked to listen to a lecture or read a text and then speak about it or write a response. The total score will be based on a scale of 0–120.

What is the Institutional TOEFL program?

More than 1,200 schools, colleges, universities, and private agencies administer the Institutional TOEFL. The Institutional TOEFL is the same length, format, and difficulty as the official Paper-Based TOEFL, but the dates and the purposes of the Institutional TOEFL are different from those of the official TOEFL.

The dates for the Institutional TOEFL usually correspond to the beginning of an academic session on a college or university calendar. The Institutional TOEFL is used for admission, placement, eligibility, or employment only at the school or agency that offers the test. If you plan to use your scores for a different college, university, or agency, you should take one of the official TOEFL tests. For more information about the Institutional TOEFL Program, contact the school or agency that administers the test.

How can I order an *Information Bulletin?*

There are three ways to order a TOEFL *Information Bulletin.*
Download	*www.toefl.org*
Phone	1-609-771-7100
Mail	TOEFL Services
	P.O. Box 6151
	Princeton, NJ 08541-6151
	U.S.A.

Many schools and educational advising centers also have copies of the TOEFL *Information Bulletin* in their counseling centers. If you order your TOEFL *Information Bulletin* by mail, it is correct to limit your correspondence to two sentences. For example:

REQUEST FOR THE TOEFL *INFORMATION BULLETIN*

> (write your address here)
> (write the date here)
>
> TOEFL Order Services
> P.O. 6151
> Princeton, NJ 08541-61561
> U.S.A.
>
> Dear TOEFL Representative:
>
>   Please send me a copy of the TOEFL *Information Bulletin*.
> Thank you for your earliest attention.
>
> Sincerely yours,
>
> (write your name here)

The TOEFL *Information Bulletin* is often available overseas in the U.S. embassies and advising offices of the United States Information Service, binational centers, IIE and AMIDEAST Counseling Centers, Fulbright offices, and ETS Regional Registration Centers as well as from international TOEFL representatives.

May I choose the format of my TOEFL—Computer-Based TOEFL, Paper-Based TOEFL, or Next Generation TOEFL?

When the Computer-Based TOEFL is phased in for the area where you will take your TOEFL, you must take the Computer-Based TOEFL. The TOEFL web site lists the areas where the Supplemental Paper-Based TOEFL has been reintroduced on a temporary basis. When the Next Generation TOEFL appears in 2005, the plan is to phase out the Computer-Based TOEFL and retain a minimum number of Supplemental Paper-Based TOEFL sites.

Which language skills are tested on the Computer-Based TOEFL?

In general, the same language skills are tested in all TOEFL formats. Some differences occur in the number of sections and the types of questions used to test the language skills, however. Charts that outline the differences are included in the Quick Comparisons in the review chapters for each section of the TOEFL. The chart below shows the four sections on the Computer-Based TOEFL.

Section 1   Listening
Section 2/4   Structure/Writing
Section 3   Reading

On the Computer-Based TOEFL, the essay counts 50 percent of the total score for Section 2.

Which language skills are tested on the Paper-Based TOEFL?

In general, the same language skills are tested in all TOEFL formats. Some differences occur in the number of sections and the types of questions used to test the language skills, however. Charts that outline the differences are included in the Quick Comparisons in the review chapters for each section of the TOEFL. The chart below shows the three sections on the Paper-Based TOEFL.

Section 1   Listening
Section 2   Structure
Section 3   Reading

Does the TOEFL have a Composition Section?

The Computer-Based TOEFL has a Writing Section. On the Writing Section and on the TWE (Test of Written English), you must write a short essay on an assigned topic. The essay should be about 300 words long. The topic is typical of academic writing requirements at colleges and universities in North America. You have 30 minutes to finish writing. Both the Writing Section and the TWE are described in greater detail in the Tutorial for the Writing Section.

The Paper-Based TOEFL does not have a Composition Section. However, you are also required to take the TWE. It is a short essay on an assigned topic. The essay should be 300-350 words long. The topic is usually an opinion question. You have 30 minutes to finish writing. The TWE rating is reported as a separate score from that of the TOEFL.

Does the TOEFL have a Speaking Section?

The Computer-Based TOEFL does not have a Speaking Section. Only the Next Generation TOEFL includes a Speaking Section.

A Speaking Section is planned for the Paper-Based TOEFL, but it has not been included in the test yet. It will probably be administered by telephone.

Are all the TOEFL tests the same length?

The forms for the TOEFL vary in length. Some items are included for research purposes and are not scored. On the Computer-Based TOEFL, items are selected by the computer based on the level of difficulty and the number of correct responses from previous items. Difficult items are worth more points than average or easy items.

All of the forms for the Paper-Based TOEFL are the same length—140 questions. Occasionally, additional questions are included for research purposes, but they are not included in the section scores.

How do the Paper-Based TOEFL and the Institutional TOEFL compare with the Computer-Based TOEFL?

The Paper-Based TOEFL and the Institutional TOEFL are different from the Computer-Based TOEFL for several reasons. First, taking a test with a pencil and paper is different from taking a test with a computer. Second, the test designs are different. The Paper-Based TOEFL and the Institutional TOEFL are linear tests. This means that all the questions appear in a row and everyone receives the same questions. The Computer-Based TOEFL has two sections, Listening and Structure, that are computer-adaptive. This means that only one question appears on the screen at a time, and everyone does not receive the same questions. Everyone begins with a question of average difficulty. If you answer it correctly, you are given a more difficult question. If you answer it incorrectly, you are given an easier question. You receive more points for answering difficult questions correctly than you do for answering average or easy questions correctly.

For a more detailed comparison of the Paper-Based TOEFL with the Computer-Based TOEFL, please refer to the Quick Comparisons in each review chapter of this book.

Is the Computer-Based TOEFL fair?

The Computer-Based TOEFL is fair because the computer is constantly adjusting the selection of items based on your previous responses. It allows you to achieve the maximum number of points that you are capable of based on your English language proficiency. In addition, everyone receives the same test content and the same proportion of question types—multiple-choice and computer-assisted.

What if I have little experience with computers?

The beginning of the official Computer-Based TOEFL has a Tutorial to help you become familiar with the computer before you begin your test. In the Tutorial, you will review how to use a mouse, how to scroll, and how to answer all the question types on the test. The Tutorials on the CD-ROM are similar. If you would like to work through the official Tutorial before the day of your Computer-Based TOEFL, you can download it at no charge from the TOEFL web site at *www.ets.org/cbt/cbtdemo.html*.

Registration

How do I register for the TOEFL?

There are three ways to register for the Computer-Based TOEFL. If you plan to pay by credit card—VISA, MasterCard, or American Express—you may register by phone. Call Candidate Services at 1-800-468-6335 to make an appointment for a test in the United States, or phone your Regional Registration Center to make an appointment for a test in another country. The phone numbers for the regional centers are listed in the TOEFL *Information Bulletin.* If you plan to pay by check, money order, or credit card, you may register by mail. To arrange a test in the United States, Canada, Puerto Rico, or a U.S. territory, return the voucher request form in your TOEFL *Information Bulletin,* along with your registration fee, to TOEFL Services in Princeton, New Jersey. A mailing label is provided in the TOEFL *Information Bulletin.* To arrange a test in all other locations where the Computer-Based TOEFL is offered, return the International Test Scheduling Form to your Regional Registration Center. Mailing labels are provided in the TOEFL *Information Bulletin.* Be sure to sign the form and include your registration fee. You may be asked to choose two days of the week and two months of the year as well as two test centers. If no appointments are available on the dates you have requested, you will be assigned a date close to the request you have made. To register online, visit *www.toefl.org.*

The *Information Bulletin* for the Paper-Based TOEFL has a registration form in it. Using the directions in the TOEFL *Information Bulletin,* fill out the form and mail it to the TOEFL Registration Office. Be sure to sign the form and include your registration fee. To register online, visit *www.toefl.org.*

When should I register for the TOEFL?

If you are taking the TOEFL as part of the application process for college or university admission, plan to take the test early enough for your score to be received by the admission office in time to be considered with your application. Usually, a test date at least two months before the admission application deadline allows adequate time for your scores to be considered with your admission application. Test centers often receive more requests than they can accommodate on certain dates. Try to schedule your appointment by phone or mail at least a month before the date you prefer to take the TOEFL, especially in October, November, December, April, and May. You must call at least three days before the appointment date that you are requesting.

What are the fees for the TOEFL?

In the United States, the registration fee for both the Computer-Based TOEFL and the Paper-Based TOEFL is $130 U.S. The fee may be paid by check, credit card, money order, bank draft, or U.S. postal money order. In Canada, the fee is $130 U.S. plus taxes. In other countries, the registration fee is also $130 U.S. However, because of exchange rates, the actual cost may vary from one country to another. For exact fees in local currency and options for payment, refer to the TOEFL *Information Bulletin.*

Which credit cards will be accepted?

Only MasterCard, VISA, and American Express may be used to pay for TOEFL registration fees and services.

May I pay by check or money order?

In order to pay for the Computer-Based TOEFL (CBT) by check or money order, you should complete a voucher request form and mail it to the TOEFL Office with your payment. This form and an envelope for it are bound in the middle of the TOEFL *Information Bulletin* for the Computer-Based TOEFL. You can also find these materials on the TOEFL web site. You will receive a CBT voucher by return mail.

In order to pay for the Paper-Based TOEFL by check or money order, include payment with your registration form. Checks, bank drafts, and money orders must be drawn on a bank in the U.S. Canadian checks will be subject to taxes. Do not send cash or demand drafts.

Which currencies will be accepted?

Payments at the current exchange rate for the U.S. dollar may be made in the following currencies:

Australian dollar, British pound, Canadian dollar, Danish krone, Euro, Hong Kong dollar, Japanese yen, New Zealand dollar, Norwegian kroner, Singapore dollar, Swedish krona, Swiss franc.

Is there a fast way to send mail to the TOEFL Office?

For the fastest delivery, use e-mail on the TOEFL web site. For rush mail delivery, use the express courier delivery address:
TOEFL Services (25-Q-310)
Distribution and Receiving Center
225 Phillips Blvd.
Ewing, NJ 08628-7435
U.S.A.

Will Educational Testing Service (ETS) confirm my registration?

If you register for the Computer-Based TOEFL, you will receive an appointment confirmation number. If you do not receive an appointment confirmation number or if you lose your appointment confirmation number, call 1-800-GOTOEFL (1-800-468-6335) in the United States or call your Regional Registration Center outside the United States. The phone numbers for regional registration centers are listed in the TOEFL *Information Bulletin*.

If you register for the Paper-Based TOEFL, you will receive an admission ticket. Your admission ticket is your confirmation. You must complete the ticket and take it with you to the test center on the day of the test along with your passport. If you have not received your admission ticket two weeks before the test, contact TOEFL Services.

May I change the date or cancel my registration?

In the United States, Canada, Puerto Rico, and U.S. territories, call Candidate Services at 1-800-468-6335. Be sure to call by noon, three business days before the date of your appointment, or you will not receive a partial reimbursement of your registration fee, usually $65. If you want to choose a different date, you may be asked to pay a rescheduling fee of $40. In all other locations, call your Regional Registration Center by noon, five business days before the date of your appointment, or you will not receive a partial reimbursement of your registration fee. If you want to choose a different date, you may be asked to pay a rescheduling fee of $40. You must provide your appointment confirmation number when you call. You will be given a cancellation number.

Test date changes are not permitted for the Paper-Based TOEFL; however, you may receive absentee credit. If you cancel your test, the refund request form and the unused admission ticket must arrive within 60 days of your test date for you to receive $65 cash or a $65 credit toward registration for a different date. Mail the form and the admission ticket to TOEFL Services or fax them to 1-609-771-7500. Allow ten weeks for the refund to arrive.

May I give my appointment to a friend?

Appointments cannot be reassigned or exchanged among friends.

How should I prepare the night before the TOEFL?

Don't go to a party the night before you take your TOEFL examination, but don't try to review everything that you have studied either. By going to a party, you will lose the opportunity to review a few problems that may add valuable points to your TOEFL score. By trying to review everything, though, you will probably get confused, and you may even panic. Instead, select a limited amount of material to review the night before you take the TOEFL. And remember, you are not trying to score 100 percent on the TOEFL examination. No one knows everything. If you answer 75 percent of the questions correctly, you will receive an excellent score.

May I register on the day of the TOEFL?

Registration of candidates on the day of the test is permitted for only the Computer-Based TOEFL, but most of the time there is no space. Candidates who arrive at the center are admitted only if a seat is available.

Registration is not available for the Paper-Based TOEFL on the day of the test administration.

Test Administration

Where are the test centers?

The most recent listing of the test centers for the TOEFL administrations worldwide is found in the current TOEFL *Information Bulletin* or on the TOEFL web site.

May I change my test center assignment?

You may go to another center on the date printed on your admission ticket, but you may or may not find a seat and test materials available.

What kind of room will be used for the TOEFL?

Rooms used for the Computer-Based TOEFL are small. They are like the study areas in a library or in a language laboratory. Usually only six to fifteen students are at individual computer stations. Each student has a headset.

Rooms used for the Paper-Based TOEFL tend to be large, but they vary greatly from one test site to another. The seats are usually school desks. It is a good idea to wear clothing that allows you to adjust to warm or cold room temperatures.

What should I take with me to the examination room?

For the Computer-Based TOEFL, take your appointment confirmation number and your official identification. Also take the institution and department codes for the schools or agencies to which you will report your scores. These codes can be found in the TOEFL *Information Bulletin.* You will not need a watch because the computer screen has a clock face on it. Books, dictionaries, tape recorders, cellular phones, pagers, highlighters, pens, and notes are not permitted in the examination room. Some centers will have lockers for you to store your possessions but it is really better not to take with you anything that you cannot take into the examination room.

For the Paper-Based TOEFL, take your admission ticket, photo identification form, and official photo identification with you. Taking three sharpened pencils and a watch would be helpful, although most examination rooms will have clocks. Books, dictionaries, tape recorders, cellular phones, pagers, highlighters, pens, and notes are not permitted in the examination room. Don't forget the institution and department codes for the schools or agencies to which you will report your scores.

What kind of identification is required?

In the United States, only your valid passport will be accepted for admission to the Computer-Based TOEFL examination. In other countries, your valid passport is still the best identification, but if you do not have a passport, you may refer to the TOEFL *Information Bulletin* for special directions. Your photograph will be taken at the test center and reproduced on all official score reports sent to institutions. Your identification will be checked against the new photograph. In addition, all Computer-Based TOEFL sessions will be videotaped. Be sure to use the same spelling and order of your name on your registration materials or phone registration, the test center log that you will sign when you enter the test area, the forms on the computer screens, and any correspondence that you may have with TOEFL Services, Candidate Services, or other local representatives.

The test center supervisor will not admit you to the Paper-Based TOEFL examination if you do not have official identification. In the United States, only your valid passport will be accepted. The supervisor will not allow you to enter with an expired passport or a photocopy of your passport. In other countries, your valid passport is still the best identification, but if you do not have a passport, you may refer to the TOEFL *Information Bulletin* for special directions. Be sure that your photo identification form and your passport picture look like you do on the day of the examination. If not, you may not be admitted to the examination room. Be sure to use the same spelling and order of your name on your registration materials, admission ticket, answer sheet, and any correspondence that you may have with either TOEFL Services or your Regional Registration Center.

Will I sign a confidentiality statement?

Before you begin the Computer-Based or Paper-Based TOEFL, you may be asked to sign a confidentiality statement. You will agree to keep confidential the content of all test questions. The purpose of this procedure is to protect the security of the test.

Where should I sit?

You will be assigned a seat. You may not select your own seat. It is usually better not to sit with friends anyway. If you do, you may find yourself looking at friends instead of concentrating on your test materials. You may even be accused of cheating if you appear to be communicating in some way.

What if I am late?

Report to the test center 30 minutes before the appointment for your TOEFL. You will need a half hour to check in. If you arrive late, you may not be admitted, and your fee may not be refunded.

How long is the testing session of the TOEFL?

The time for the Computer-Based TOEFL will vary, depending on your familiarity with computers. A computer Tutorial is offered at the beginning of the session for those who need some practice using the computer before taking the Computer-Based TOEFL. In general, the Computer-Based TOEFL takes between four hours and four hours and 30 minutes, including the Tutorial. When you finish, you may leave the room quietly.

The total time for the testing session of the Paper-Based TOEFL is three hours. Since the instructions are not included as part of the timed sections, the actual time that you will spend in the examination room will be about three hours and 30 minutes. When you finish, you must sit quietly until the supervisor dismisses the group.

How much time do I have to complete each of the sections?

Work as rapidly as possible without compromising accuracy. Check the Timetable for the TOEFL on page xiv for an estimate.

Are breaks scheduled during the TOEFL?

A 10-minute break is scheduled during the Computer-Based TOEFL. It usually occurs between the Structure and the Reading Sections.

No breaks are scheduled for the Paper-Based TOEFL.

Is there a place to eat lunch at the test centers?

Some of the testing centers are conveniently located near restaurants, but many, especially the mobile centers, are not. You may want to take a snack with you to eat before or after your test.

How can I complain about a test administration?

If you feel that the test situation was not fair, you have a right to register a complaint by mail or by fax. Within three days of the date of the test, write a letter to Test Administration Services. Their address appears on page 13. If you prefer to send a fax, the fax number is 1-609-771-7500. Mention the date of your test, the city, and the country. Explain why you feel that the test was not fair.

Examination

What kinds of questions are found on the TOEFL?

The majority of the questions on the Computer-Based TOEFL are multiple-choice. Some other types of questions are also on the Computer-Based TOEFL. These questions have special directions on the screen. You will have many examples of them in the Model Tests in this book.

All the questions on the Paper-Based TOEFL are multiple-choice.

How do I answer the test questions?

When you are presented with a multiple-choice question on the Computer-Based TOEFL, read the four possible answers on the screen, point the arrow, and click beside the answer that you choose. The oval will change from white to black. When you are presented with other types of questions, follow the directions on the screen.

To answer test questions on the Paper-Based TOEFL, read the four possible answers in your test book, and mark the corresponding space on the answer sheet.

How do I mark the answers?

MARKING THE ANSWER SCREEN: COMPUTER-BASED TOEFL

One question is shown on the computer screen. One answer is marked on the screen.

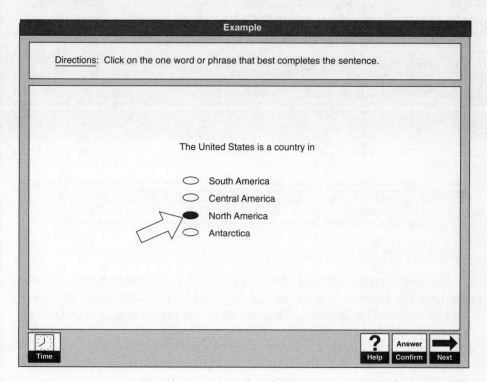

MARKING THE ANSWER SHEET: SUPPLEMENTAL PAPER-BASED TOEFL

One question is shown in the test book. One answer is marked on the answer sheet.

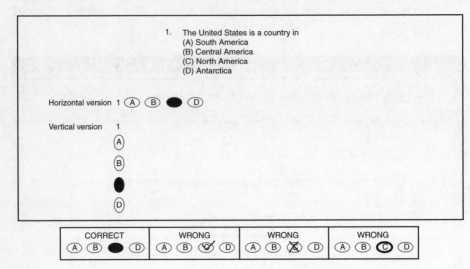

On the Computer-Based TOEFL, you will have an opportunity to practice marking the answers to questions on the computer screen before the examination begins. The Tutorial will include all the different types of questions on the Computer-Based TOEFL.

May I make notes in the test book or on the scratch paper?

There is no test book for the Computer-Based TOEFL. All the questions and the answer options are presented on the computer screen. You may not use the scratch paper for your essay to make notes for any other section of the test.

You are not allowed to make marks in your test book for the Paper-Based TOEFL. You may not underline words or write notes in the margins of the test book. Doing so is considered cheating.

May I change an answer?

On the first two sections of the Computer-Based TOEFL, Listening and Structure, you can change your answer by clicking on the new answer. You can change your answer as many times as you wish until you click on the **Confirm Answer** button. When you click on **Confirm Answer**, you move to the next question, and you cannot go back to a previous question. On the third section of the Computer-Based TOEFL, Reading, you can change your answer as many times as you wish. You may go on to the next question and back to the previous questions. The CD-ROM that supplements this book will provide you with practice in choosing and changing answers on the computer screen.

You may erase an answer on the answer sheet of the Paper-Based TOEFL if you do so carefully and completely. Stray pencil marks may cause inaccurate scoring by the test-scoring machine.

If I am not sure of an answer, should I guess?

Try to answer every question on the Computer-Based TOEFL. Your score will be based not only on the difficulty of the questions but also on the number of questions answered.

If you are not sure of an answer on the Paper-Based TOEFL, you should guess. The number of incorrect answers is not subtracted from your score. Your score is based only on the number of correct answers. Do not mark more than one answer for each question. Do not leave any questions blank on your answer sheet.

How should I guess?

In the first two sections of the Computer-Based TOEFL, Listening and Structure, eliminate the incorrect answers, then guess, but do not use a "guess answer" to finish these sections quickly. You will probably receive a lower score for random guessing. On the third section, Reading, try to manage your time so that you can finish all of the questions. If you have only a minute or two left, try to answer all of the remaining questions. Use a "guess answer." Pace yourself so that you can finish as much of the test as possible. On the first two sections, Listening and Structure, you will be scored based on the number of questions answered, the number of correct answers you have submitted, and the level of difficulty of the questions that you have answered. On the third section, Reading, you will be scored on the number of questions you have answered and the number of correct answers you have submitted.

For the Paper-Based TOEFL, first eliminate all the possibilities that you know are NOT correct. Then, if you are almost sure of an answer, guess that one. If you have no idea of the correct answer for a question, choose one letter and use it for your "guess answer" throughout the entire examination. The "guess answer" is especially useful for finishing a section quickly. If the supervisor tells you to stop working on a section before you have finished it, answer all the remaining questions with the "guess answer."

What should I do if I discover that I have marked my answers incorrectly?

Marking your screen incorrectly on the Computer-Based TOEFL is not possible because the computer program will present only one question on each screen. If you change your mind after you have confirmed a response on the Listening or Structure sections, the computer will not allow you to return to a previous question on these two sections, and you will not be able to change the answer that you have confirmed. As you see, it is very important to be sure of the answer before you click on **Confirm Answer**.

Do not panic if you have marked an answer incorrectly on the Paper-Based TOEFL. Notify the supervisor immediately. If you have marked one answer in the wrong space on the answer sheet, the rest of the answers will be out of sequence. Ask for time at the end of the examination to correct the sequence. The TOEFL test supervisor may or may not allow you to do this. To save time finding the number on the answer sheet that corresponds to the problem you are reading, to avoid mismarking, and to save space on your desk, use your test book as a marker on your answer sheet. As you advance, slide the book down underneath the number of the question that you are marking on the answer sheet.

May I choose the order of the sections on my TOEFL?

You may not choose the order. Listening, Structure, and Reading are tested in that order on both the Computer-Based TOEFL and the Paper-Based TOEFL. The essay is written last. When you have finished with a section, you may not work on any other section of the test.

What if I cannot hear the tape for the Listening Section?

You have your own headset for the Computer-Based TOEFL. Before the Listening Section begins, you will have an opportunity to adjust the volume yourself. Be careful to adjust the volume when you are prompted to do so. If you wait until the test begins, you may not be able to adjust it.

The supervisor for the Paper-Based TOEFL has the responsibility of making sure that everyone is able to hear the tape. If you cannot hear it well, raise your hand and ask the supervisor to adjust the volume.

May I keep my test?

TOEFL Services publishes copies of TOEFL tests and makes them available for purchase. Visit the TOEFL web site for more information. If you try to keep or copy TOEFL tests from your test administration, the TOEFL Office may take legal action.

What can I do if I do not appear to take the test?

There is a $65 refund for the Computer-Based TOEFL if you cancel your test five business days before the date of your appointment.

If you do not appear to take the Paper-Based TOEFL test without canceling your appointment, you cannot request a refund. If you cancel your appointment, then you are entitled to a refund of $65. Write to TOEFL Services to make your request. You must contact them within 60 days of the date of the TOEFL administration that you have missed.

Score Reports

How is my TOEFL scored?

Total Computer-Based TOEFL scores range from 0–300. First, each of the sections of the TOEFL is graded on a scale from 0–30. Then the scores from the sections are added together. Finally, the sum is multiplied by 10 and divided by 3.

For example, the following scores were received on the sections:

Listening	23
Structure and Writing	25
Reading	<u>27</u>
	75

$75 \times 10 = 750 \div 3 = 250$ Total TOEFL Score

Total Paper-Based TOEFL scores range from 310–677. First, each of the three sections of the TOEFL is graded on a scale from 31–68. Then the scores from the three sections are added together. Finally, the sum is multiplied by 10 and divided by 3.

For example, the following scores were received on the three sections:

Listening Comprehension	52
Structure and Written Expression	48
Vocabulary and Reading Comprehension	<u>50</u>
	150

150 × 10 = 1,500 ÷ 3 = 500 Total TOEFL Score

The Test of Written English (TWE) rating is reported as a separate score on a scale from 1–6.

How are the Structure and Writing scores combined on the Computer-Based TOEFL?

The Structure score counts half of the section score on the Computer-Based TOEFL, and the essay counts half of the score. The rating scale of 1–6 for the essay is converted to a statistical equivalent of the points in the Structure Section.

How do I interpret my score?

There are no passing or failing scores on either the Computer-Based TOEFL or the Paper-Based TOEFL. Each agency or university will evaluate the scores according to its own requirements. Even at the same university, the requirements may vary for different programs of study, levels of study (graduate or undergraduate), and degrees of responsibility (student or teaching assistant).

The following summary of admissions policies are typical of U.S. universities. This assumes, of course, that the applicant's documents other than English proficiency are acceptable.

TYPICAL ADMISSIONS POLICIES OF AMERICAN UNIVERSITIES

Paper-Based TOEFL Score	Policy	Computer-Based TOEFL Score
650 or more	admission assured for graduate students	280 or more
600–649	admission assured for undergraduate students	250–279
550–599	admission probable for graduate students	213–249
500–549	admission probable for undergraduate students	173–212
450–499	individual cases reviewed	133–172
449 or less	referral to English language program probable	132 or less

Refer to the TOEFL *Information Bulletin* or web site for a detailed chart of percentile ranks for total TOEFL scores. This will help you interpret your score relative to the scores of others taking the examination.

How do the scores on the Supplemental Paper-Based TOEFL compare with those on the Computer-Based TOEFL?

A concordance table is a table that shows comparisons. A concordance table for the Paper-Based TOEFL and the Computer-Based TOEFL has been mailed to all institutions that use TOEFL scores for admissions decisions. A copy of the concordance table is printed in the TOEFL *Information Bulletin* and posted on the TOEFL web site. A shorter version of the table follows:

Paper-Based TOEFL	Computer-Based TOEFL
677	300
650	280
600	250
550	213
500	173
450	133
400	97

If I score very poorly on one part of the TOEFL, is it still possible to receive a good total score?

If you feel that you have done very poorly on one part of a section, do not despair. You may receive a low score on one part of a section and still score well on the total examination if your scores on the other parts of that section and the other sections are good.

When can I see my scores?

After you complete your Computer-Based TOEFL, you can view your estimated score on the screen. You will be able to see section scores for both Listening and Reading as well as for the multiple-choice part of the Structure Section. However, the essay, which is included as half of the Structure score, will not have been graded. The estimated score that you will see shows a total score range based on a very poorly written essay or on a very well written essay. For example, your score range might be 150–220.

You are entitled to five copies of your test results, including one personal copy for yourself and four official score reports. Your official scores for all sections will be mailed to you about two to five weeks after you take your Computer-Based TOEFL. However, you will have a very good idea of how you performed on the test after you see the estimate.

For the Paper-Based TOEFL, you are entitled to five copies of your test results, including one personal copy for yourself and four official score reports. You will receive your copy four or five weeks after you take the test.

How can I know my scores sooner?

If your essay is typed instead of handwritten, your scores will be mailed sooner. If you would like to know your score on the same day that the report is mailed, you may use the TOEFL phone service. Using a touch-tone phone, call the TOEFL Office. You will hear prompts to enter your appointment number, your test date, your date of birth, and a credit card number. The fee to hear your scores by phone is $10 plus any long-distance charges that apply.

To call toll-free from the United States or Canada, touch 1-888-TOEFL-44, which is 1-888-863-3544. To call with long-distance charges from all other locations, touch 1-609-771-7267.

What can I do if I want to register a complaint?

For the Computer-Based TOEFL, submit your complaint in writing to:

CBT Administration
Computer-Based Testing Network Group
Educational Testing Service
Mail Stop 16-2
Rosedale Road
Princeton, NJ 08541
U.S.A.

Occasionally, on the Paper-Based TOEFL, the computer will score an answer sheet incorrectly because of the way you have marked it. If you feel your score is much, much lower than you expected, you have a right to register a complaint. To do so, submit your complaint in writing to:

CBT Administration
Paper-Based Testing
Educational Testing Service
Mail Stop 16-2
Rosedale Road
Princeton, NJ 08541
U.S.A.

May I cancel my scores?

After you view your score on the screen, you will be given the option to report or cancel your scores for the Computer-Based TOEFL. If you choose to report your scores, you will then choose four institutions to receive your score report. All of this is arranged by responding to questions on the computer screen.

If you do not want your Paper-Based TOEFL scores to be reported, you have a right to cancel them. To cancel your test scores, you must complete the score cancellation section of your TOEFL answer sheet, or you must write, e-mail, call, or fax TOEFL Services. If a signed request is received at TOEFL Services within seven days of the date of the test, your scores will not be reported.

How will the agencies or universities of my choice be informed of my score?

Two to five weeks after the Computer-Based TOEFL testing, your official score reports will be forwarded directly to the agencies and/or universities that you designated on the information section on the computer screen the day of the examination. Personal copies of score reports are not accepted by institutions without confirmation by TOEFL Services. Scores more than two years old are not considered valid on the Computer-Based TOEFL.

Four or five weeks after the Paper-Based TOEFL testing, your official score reports will be forwarded directly to the agencies and/or universities that you designated on an information section at the top of the TOEFL answer sheet the day of the examination. Personal copies of score reports are not accepted by institutions without confirmation by TOEFL Services. Scores more than two years old are not considered valid on the Paper-Based TOEFL.

How can I send additional reports?

You can use a form in the TOEFL *Information Bulletin* to have official score reports for the Computer-Based TOEFL sent to institutions that were not listed on your computer screen. If you use the form, do not send a letter because correspondence will cause a delay. If you prefer, the TOEFL Office offers a telephone service for additional score reports. To use the service, you will need a touch-tone phone. Call 1-888-TOEFL-44 in the U.S. or 1-609-771-7267 from all other locations. For the Computer-Based TOEFL, you will be asked to provide your appointment confirmation number, a credit card number, your test date, and both the institution and department codes for the schools you wish to add to your score report list. You will use the numbers on your touch-tone phone to enter the numbers for all of the dates and codes. The fee for this service is $12 per call and $12 for each report. Official score reports will be mailed the same day as your telephone request.

You can use a form in the TOEFL *Information Bulletin* to have official score reports for the Paper-Based TOEFL sent to institutions that were not listed on your answer sheet. If you use the form, do not send a letter because correspondence will cause a delay. You may also request official score reports by phone for the Paper-Based TOEFL. To use this service, you must have your admission ticket, a credit card, and a touch-tone phone. Use the same telephone numbers that appear above for the CBT. Call from six in the morning to ten at night, New York time. The fee for this service is a $12 charge to your credit card per call, a $12 charge per score report, plus a charge to your telephone bill for the long-distance call. Official score reports will be mailed three days after your telephone request.

May I take the TOEFL more than one time?

You may not take the Computer-Based TOEFL more than once a month. For example, if you take the Computer-Based TOEFL in July, you must wait until August to take it again.

You may take the Paper-Based TOEFL as many times as you wish in order to score to your satisfaction.

If I have already taken the TOEFL, how will the first score or scores affect my new score?

TOEFL scores are considered valid for two years. If you have taken the TOEFL more than once but your first score report is dated more than two years ago, TOEFL Services will not report your first score. If you have taken the TOEFL more than once in the past two years, TOEFL Services will report the score for the test date you request on your score request form.

Is there a direct correspondence between proficiency in English and a good score on the TOEFL?

There is not always a direct correspondence between proficiency in English and a good score on the TOEFL. Many students who are proficient in English are not proficient in how to approach the examination. That is why it is important to prepare by using this book.

What is the relationship between my score on the Model Tests and my score on the TOEFL?

Calculating an exact TOEFL score from a score that you might receive on a Model Test is not possible. This is so because the actual TOEFL examination has a wider variety of problems.

The Model Tests have been especially designed to help you improve your total TOEFL score by improving your knowledge of the types of problems that most often appear on the TOEFL. These problem types are repeated throughout the Model Tests so that you will have practice in recognizing and answering them.

By improving your ability to recognize and correctly answer those types of problems that most often appear on the TOEFL, you will improve your total TOEFL score.

Can I estimate my TOEFL score after I have prepared?

To estimate your TOEFL score after you complete each of the Model Tests, use the Score Estimates in Chapter 11 of this book. After you complete the Computer Adaptive Test on the CD-ROM that supplements this book, you will see an estimate of your TOEFL score.

Will I succeed on the TOEFL?

You will receive from your study what you give to your study. The information is here. Now, it is up to you to devote the time and effort. Thousands of other students have succeeded by using *Barron's How to Prepare for the TOEFL*. You can be successful, too.

The Next Generation TOEFL

When will the Next Generation TOEFL be administered?

The Next Generation TOEFL will be phased in. There will be three stages:

2003	The Speaking Section will be offered by telephone for practice. To purchase a practice test, visit the official TOEFL web site at *www.toefl.org* on the Internet. Click on the TAST (TOEFL Academic Speaking Test). The cost is $30 U.S.
2004	Several full-length forms of the Next Generation TOEFL will be made available on the Internet at no cost. Visit *www.toefl.org* and follow the directions to take advantage of this opportunity.
2005	The Next Generation TOEFL will replace the Computer-Based TOEFL (CBT) worldwide as the official TOEFL examination. In some remote areas, the Paper-Based TOEFL will be offered. A telephone version of the Speaking Section is planned to supplement the Paper-Based TOEFL.

Which language skills are tested on the Next Generation TOEFL?

In general, the same language skills are tested in all TOEFL formats. Some differences occur in the number of sections and the types of questions used to test the language skills, however. Charts that outline the differences are included in the Quick Comparisons in the review chapters for each section of the TOEFL. The chart below shows the four sections on the Next Generation TOEFL.

Section 1   Reading
Section 2   Listening
Section 3   Speaking
Section 4   Writing

Does the Next Generation TOEFL have a Composition Section?

The Next Generation TOEFL has a Writing Section that includes both independent writing and integrated writing. The independent writing is a response to a question that asks your opinion about a familiar topic. You have 30 minutes to complete the independent writing task. The integrated writing is a response to a question about the content of a short reading passage and a short lecture. You have 20–30 minutes to complete the integrated writing task.

Does the Next Generation TOEFL have a Speaking Section?

The Next Generation TOEFL has a Speaking Section that includes both independent speaking and integrated speaking. The independent speaking is a response to a question that asks for your opinion about a familiar topic. You have 15 seconds to prepare and 45 seconds to respond. The integrated writing is a response to a question about the content of a short reading passage, a short lecture, or both. You have 20–30 seconds to prepare and 60 seconds to respond. You may use notes while you speak.

Are all the Next Generation TOEFL tests the same length?

All of the forms for the Next Generation TOEFL are about the same length. It is not an adaptive test.

How do I register for the Next Generation TOEFL?

The *Information Bulletin* for the Next Generation TOEFL will have a registration form in it. Using the directions in the TOEFL *Information Bulletin*, fill out the form and mail it to the TOEFL Registration Office. Be sure to sign the form and include your registration fee. To register online, visit *www.toefl.org*.

What are the fees for the Next Generation TOEFL?

The fees for the Next Generation TOEFL have not been determined. However, they will be about the same as those for the Computer-Based TOEFL.

Where are the test centers?

The test centers for the Next Generation TOEFL will be announced on the TOEFL web site *www.toefl.org*. Many test centers are being planned at school sites throughout the world.

How long is the testing session of the TOEFL?

The total time for the testing session of the Next Generation TOEFL is about four hours.

How much time do I have to complete each of the sections?

Work as rapidly as possible without compromising accuracy. Refer to page xiv to see the Timetable for the Next Generation TOEFL.

What kinds of questions are found on the TOEFL?

The majority of the questions on the Next Generation TOEFL are multiple-choice. Some other types of questions are also on the Next Generation TOEFL. These questions will have special directions on the screen. You will have examples of them in Model Test 9.

How do I answer the test questions?

When you are presented with a multiple-choice question on the Next Generation TOEFL, read the four possible answers on the screen, point the arrow, and click beside the answer that you choose. The oval will change from white to black. When you are presented with other types of questions, follow the directions on the screen. This is similar to the way that the test questions on the Computer-Based TOEFL are answered.

May I make notes in the test book or on the scratch paper?

You are allowed to take notes and use them to answer questions on the Next Generation TOEFL. You will be given paper for that purpose when you go into the test room.

May I change an answer?

On the Listening Section of the Next Generation TOEFL, you can change your answer by clicking on the new answer. You can change your answer as many times as you wish until you click on the **Confirm Answer** button. When you click on **Confirm Answer**, you move to the next question, and you cannot go back to a previous question. On the Speaking Section, you will be cued with a beep to begin and end speaking. Everything that you say during the recording time will be submitted. You cannot change an answer. On the Reading Section, you can change your answer by clicking on the new answer. You can change your answer as many times as you wish, and you can go back to previous answers on the same reading passage. When you begin a new reading passage, you may not return to the previous passage to change answers. On the Writing Section, you can revise your essays as much as you wish until the clock indicates that no time is remaining. If you submit your essays before time is up, you cannot return to them. The CD-ROM that supplements the larger version of this book will provide you with practice in choosing and changing answers on the computer screen.

If I am not sure of an answer, should I guess?

If you are not sure of an answer, you should guess. The number of incorrect answers is not subtracted from your score. Your score is based on only the number of correct answers.

How should I guess?

First, eliminate all of the possibilities that you know are NOT correct. Then, if you are almost sure of an answer, guess that one. If you have no idea of the correct answer for a question, choose one letter and use it for your "guess answer" throughout the entire examination. The "guess answer" is especially useful for finishing a section quickly. If the supervisor tells you to stop working on a section before you have finished it, answer all the remaining questions with the "guess answer."

How is the Next Generation TOEFL scored?

The Next Generation TOEFL will have section scores for each of the four sections. The range for each section score will be 0–25. Then the scores for the four sections will be added together. Although final scoring has not been determined, the total score range for the Next Generation TOEFL will probably be 0–120. Check the TOEFL web site at *www.toefl.org* for the latest information about the scoring scale.

How do I interpret my score?

Admissions policies have not yet been decided by American universities. For the latest information about scoring, visit *www.toefl.org* on the Internet.

How do scores on the Next Generation TOEFL compare with those on the Computer-Based TOEFL?

A concordance table comparing the two tests is not yet available from the test developers. However, the TOEFL formats have been carefully calibrated so that scores on one format equate with scores on another format. If you score well on the Computer-Based TOEFL, for example, you should score well on the Next Generation TOEFL also.

When can I see my scores?

After you complete your Next Generation TOEFL, you can view your estimated score on the screen. You will be able to see section scores for both Listening and Reading, but the Speaking and Writing Sections will require additional time to evaluate. The estimated score that you will see shows a total score range based on a very low score on the Speaking and Writing Sections and a very high score on the Speaking and Writing Sections.

You will be entitled to five copies of your test results, including one personal copy for yourself and four official score reports. You will receive your copy about five weeks after you take the test, but you will have an idea of how you performed on the test after you see the estimate.

How can I know my scores sooner?

You may be able to use the TOEFL phone service to receive your report on the same day that it is mailed. Watch the *www.toefl.org* web site for more information about this option.

May I take the TOEFL more than one time?

You may take the Next Generation TOEFL as many times as you wish in order to score to your satisfaction. There may be a limit to the number of times that you may take the test in a one-month time period. More information about these limits will be published at a later date.

Updates

Visit the TOEFL web site at *www.toefl.org* or my web site at *www.teflprep.com* for the latest information about the TOEFL.

This web site helps students and professionals prepare for the Test of English as a Foreign Language (TOEFL®). You are invited to practice with the types of questions that appear on the TOEFL, visit the TEFL Prep Center Bookstore, and ask Dr. Pamela Sharpe questions about her books. The TEFL Prep Center web site also has information about scholarships and news about the TOEFL.

Welcome	The Practice Page	The TEFL Center Bookstore	TOEFL News	Scholarship Opportunities	Dear Dr. Sharpe

If you are not seeing images or if the page is loading improperly, you may want to use these links to download Netscape Navigator or Internet Explorer, available at no cost.

TOEFL is a registered trademark of Educational Testing Service.
The TEFLPREP Center bears sole responsibility for this web site's content
and is not connected with the Educational Testing Service.

REVIEW OF LISTENING

Overview of the Listening Section

QUICK COMPARISON—LISTENING
PAPER-BASED TOEFL,
COMPUTER-BASED TOEFL, AND NEXT GENERATION TOEFL

Paper-Based TOEFL	*Computer-Based TOEFL*	*Next Generation TOEFL*
Three types of questions are presented in three separate parts. Part A has short conversations; Part B has long conversations and class discussions; Part C has mini-talks and lectures.	Three types of questions are presented in three sets. The first set has short conversations; the second set has longer conversations and class discussions; the third set has lectures.	Two types of questions are presented in six sets. The first sets each have a long conversation. The next sets each have one lecture.
The talks and lectures are about 2 minutes long.	The lectures are about 3 minutes long.	The lectures are about 5 minutes long.
Everyone taking the TOEFL answers the same questions.	The computer selects questions based on your level of language proficiency.	Everyone taking the same form of the TOEFL answers the same questions.
There are no pictures or visual cues.	Each short conversation begins with a picture to provide orientation. There are several pictures and visual cues with longer conversations and lectures.	Each conversation and lecture begins with a picture to provide orientation. There are several pictures and visual cues with lectures.
You hear the questions, but they are not written out for you to read.	The questions are written out on the computer screen for you to read while you hear them.	The questions are written out on the computer screen for you to read while you hear them.
Everyone taking the TOEFL proceeds at the same pace. You cannot pause the tape.	You may control the pace by choosing when to begin the next conversation or lecture.	You may control the pace by choosing when to begin the next conversation or lecture.
The section is timed. At the end of the tape, you must have completed the section.	The section is timed. A clock on the screen shows the time remaining for you to complete the section.	The section is timed. A clock on the screen shows the time remaining for you to complete the section.
You may not replay any of the conversations or lectures.	You may not replay any of the conversations or lectures.	You may not replay any of the conversations or lectures.
All of the questions are multiple-choice.	Most of the questions are multiple-choice, but some of the questions have special directions.	Most of the questions are multiple-choice, but some of the questions have special directions.
Every question has only one answer.	Some of the questions have two or more answers.	Some of the questions have two or more answers.

Paper-Based TOEFL	Computer-Based TOEFL	Next Generation TOEFL
You answer on a paper answer sheet, filling in ovals marked Ⓐ, Ⓑ, Ⓒ, and Ⓓ.	You click on the screen in the oval that corresponds to the answer you have chosen, or you follow the directions on the screen.	You click on the screen in the oval that corresponds to the answer you have chosen, or you follow the directions on the screen.
You can return to previous questions, erase, and change answers on your answer sheet.	You cannot return to previous questions. You can change your answer before you click on **Confirm Answer**. After you click on **Confirm Answer**, you cannot go back.	You cannot return to previous questions. You can change your answer before you click on **OK**. After you click on **OK**, you cannot go back.
You may NOT take notes.	You may NOT take notes.	You may take notes while you listen to the conversations and lectures.

Review of Problems and Questions for the Listening Section

This Review can be used to prepare for the Supplemental Paper-Based TOEFL, the Computer-Based TOEFL, and the Next Generation TOEFL. For the most part, the same types of problems are tested on all three forms; however, questions on Informal Conversations and Tours are found only on the Paper-Based TOEFL and are not addressed in this book.

Most of the questions are multiple-choice. Some of the questions on the Computer-Based TOEFL and the Next Generation TOEFL are computer-assisted. The computer-assisted questions have special directions on screen.

Although the computer-assisted questions in this book are numbered, and the answer choices are lettered A, B, C, D, the same questions on the CD-ROM that supplements the larger version of this book are not numbered and lettered. You need the numbers and letters in the book to refer to the Answer Key, the Explanatory Answers, and the Audio Script for the Listening Section. On the CD-ROM, you can refer to other chapters by clicking on the screen. The computer-assisted questions have special directions on the screen.

Types of Problems in Short Conversations

 Details

Details are specific facts stated in a conversation.

In some short conversations, you will hear all of the information that you need to answer the problem correctly. You will NOT need to draw conclusions.

When you hear a conversation between two speakers, you must remember the details that were stated.

EXAMPLE

Man: Front desk. How may I help you?
Woman: I'd like to arrange a wake-up call for tomorrow morning at seven o'clock, please.

Narrator: When does the woman want to get up tomorrow?
Answer: Seven o'clock in the morning.

 Idiomatic expressions

Idiomatic expressions are words and phrases that are characteristic of a particular language with meanings that are usually different from the meanings of each of the words used alone.

In some short conversations, you will hear idiomatic expressions, such as "to kill time," which means to *wait*.

When you hear a conversation between two speakers, you must listen for the idiomatic expressions. You will be expected to recognize them and restate the idiom or identify the feelings or attitudes of the speaker.

It will help you if you study a list of common idioms as part of your TOEFL preparation.

EXAMPLE

Man:	I'm single. In fact, I've never been married.
Woman:	No kidding!
Narrator:	What does the woman mean?
Answer:	She is surprised by the man's statement.

3   Suggestions

A *suggestion* is a recommendation.

In some short conversations, you will hear words and phrases that make a suggestion, such as "you should," "why don't you," or "why not."

When you hear the words and phrases that introduce a suggestion, you must be able to recognize and remember what the speaker suggested, and who made the suggestion.

EXAMPLE

Woman:	Oh, no. Dr. Thompson's class is closed.
Man:	Already?
Woman:	I know. This is only the first day of registration.
Man:	Well, it's offered every term. Why don't you just take it next semester?
Narrator:	What does the man suggest that the woman do?
Answer:	Wait until next semester to take Dr. Thompson's class.

4   Assumptions

An *assumption* is a statement accepted as true without proof or demonstration.

In some short conversations, an assumption is proven false, and the speaker or speakers who had made the assumption express surprise.

When you hear a conversation between two speakers, you must be able to recognize remarks that register surprise, and draw conclusions about the assumptions that the speaker may have made.

EXAMPLE

| Woman: | Let's just e-mail our response to Larry instead of calling. |
| Man: | *Larry* has an e-mail address? |

| Narrator: | What had the man assumed about Larry? |
| Answer: | He would not have an e-mail address. |

5   Predictions

A *prediction* is a guess about the future based on evidence from the present.

In some short conversations, you will be asked to make predictions about the future activities of the speakers involved.

When you hear a conversation between two speakers, you must listen for evidence from which you may draw a logical conclusion about their future activities.

EXAMPLE

| Man: | Could you please book me on the next flight out to Los Angeles? |
| Woman: | I'm sorry, sir. Continental doesn't fly into Los Angeles. Why don't you try Northern or Worldwide? |

| Narrator: | What will the man probably do? |
| Answer: | He will probably get a ticket for a flight on Northern or Worldwide Airlines. |

6   Implications

Implied means suggested, but not stated. In many ways, implied conversations are like prediction conversations.

In some short conversations, you will hear words and phrases or intonations that will suggest how the speakers felt, what kind of work or activity they were involved in, or where the conversation may have taken place.

When you hear a conversation between two speakers, you must listen for information that will help you draw a conclusion about the situation.

EXAMPLE

Woman:	Where's Anita? We were supposed to go to the library to study.
Man:	Well, here is her coat, and her books are over there on the chair.
Narrator:	What does the man imply about Anita?
Answer:	Anita has not left for the library yet.

7   Problems

A *problem* is a situation that requires discussion or solution.

In some short conversations, you will hear the speakers discuss a problem.

When you hear a discussion between two speakers, you must be able to identify what the problem is. This may be more difficult because different aspects of the problem will also be included in the conversation.

EXAMPLE

Woman:	It only takes two hours to get to New York, but you'll have a six-hour layover between flights.
Man:	Maybe you could try routing me through Philadelphia or Boston instead.
Narrator:	What is the man's problem?
Answer:	His flight connections are not very convenient.

8   Topics

A *topic* is a main theme in a conversation or in a piece of writing.

In some short conversations, the speakers will discuss a particular topic.

When you hear a conversation, you must be able to identify the main topic from among several secondary themes that support the topic.

EXAMPLE

Man: Tell me about your trip to New York.
Woman: It was great! We saw the Statue of Liberty and the Empire
            State Building and all of the tourist attractions the first day,
            then we saw the museums the second day and spent the
            rest of the time shopping and seeing shows.
Narrator: What are the man and woman talking about?
Answer: The woman's trip.

Types of Problems in Longer Conversations

9   Academic Conversations

Academic conversations are conversations between students and professors or other academic personnel on a college or university campus.

In some longer conversations, you will hear an academic conversation between two speakers.

When you hear a conversation, you must be able to summarize the main ideas. You may also be asked to recall important details.

EXAMPLE

Joe: Hi, Dr. Watkins. Are you busy?
Dr. Watkins: Oh, hello, Joe. Come in.
Joe: Thanks. You've probably graded our midterms.
Dr. Watkins: Just finished them. Frankly, I was surprised that you didn't
              do better on it.

Joe:	I know. I had two midterms on the same day, and I didn't organize my time very well. I spent too much time studying for the first one, and then I ran out of time to study for yours.
Dr. Watkins:	I see.
Joe:	So I was wondering whether I could do a project for extra credit to bring my grade back up. I'm sure I have a B or even a C after that midterm, but before that I had a solid A.
Dr. Watkins:	Did you have anything in mind for your project?
Joe:	Well, I was thinking that I could develop a reading list, using the main topics from the midterm. And then, if the list looks okay to you, I could write a summary of each of the readings. But, if you don't like that idea, I'd be happy to do any project you would approve.
Dr. Watkins:	Actually, that sounds like a good plan. In fact, I have a reading list that might work for you.
Joe:	Better yet.
Dr. Watkins:	Good. If you do summaries for all of these articles, the extra points should put you back on track for an A.
Joe:	Thanks. Thanks a lot.

Question:	What is Joe's problem?
Answer:	His grade in the course is low because of his midterm.

Question:	Why didn't Joe do better on the midterm?
Answer:	He spent too much time studying for a midterm for another class.

Question:	What does Joe want to do?
Answer:	He wants to complete some additional assignments to earn extra points.

Question:	How does Professor Watkins respond to Joe's proposal?
Answer:	She is helpful.

Types of Problems in Talks and Lectures

10   Class Discussions

Class discussions are conversations that occur in classrooms.

In some talks, you will hear a class discussion between two, three, or more speakers.

When you hear a discussion, you must be able to summarize the important ideas. You will usually NOT be required to remember small details.

It will help you to audit some college classes.

EXAMPLE

Miss Richards:	Good morning. My name is Miss Richards, and I'll be your instructor for Career Education 100. Before we get started, I'd appreciate it if you would introduce yourselves and tell us a little bit about why you decided to take this class. Let's start here. . . .
Bill:	I'm Bill Jensen, and I'm a sophomore this term, but I still haven't decided what to major in. I hope that this class will help me.
Miss Richards:	Good, I hope so, too. Next.
Patty:	I'm Patty Davis, and I'm majoring in foreign languages, but I'm not sure what kind of job I can get after I graduate.
Miss Richards:	Are you a sophomore, too, Patty?
Patty:	No. I'm a senior. I wish I'd taken this class sooner, but I didn't know about it until this term.
Miss Richards:	Didn't your advisor tell you about it?
Patty:	No. A friend of mine took it last year, and it helped her a lot.
Miss Richards:	How did you find out about the course, Bill?
Bill:	The same way Patty did. A friend of mine told me about it.
Question:	In what class does this discussion take place?
Answer:	Career Education.

| Question: | What are the two students talking about? |
| Answer: | They are introducing themselves. |

| Question: | Why is the woman taking the course? |
| Answer: | To help her find a job after graduation. |

| Question: | How did the students find out about the course? |
| Answer: | From friends who had taken it. |

11   Academic Talks

Academic talks are short talks that provide orientation to academic courses and procedures.

In some talks, you will hear academic talks on a variety of college and university topics.

When you hear a talk, you must be able to summarize the main ideas. You must also be able to answer questions about important details. You will usually not be asked to remember minor details.

EXAMPLE

Since we'll be having our midterm exam next week, I thought I'd spend a few minutes talking with you about it. I realize that none of you has ever taken a class with me before, so you really don't know what to expect on one of my exams.

First, let me remind you that I have included a very short description of the midterm on the syllabus that you received at the beginning of the semester. So you should read that. I also recommend that you organize and review your notes from all of our class sessions. I'm not saying that the book is unimportant, but the notes should help you to identify those topics that we covered in greatest detail. Then, you can go back to your book and reread the sections that deal with those topics. I also suggest that you take another look at the articles on reserve in the library. They have information in them that is not in the book, and although we didn't talk much about them in class, I do feel that they are important, so you can expect to see a few questions from the articles on the exam. Oh, yes, I almost forgot. Besides the twenty-five objective questions, there will be five essay questions, and you must choose three.

EXAMPLE

Question: What does the speaker mainly discuss?
Answer: The midterm exam.

Question: When will the students take the exam?
Answer: Next week.

Question: According to the professor, what should the
           students do to prepare?
Answer: Study their notes, the articles on reserve, and
           appropriate sections of the book.

Question: What is the format of the exam?
Answer: Twenty-five objective questions and five essay questions.

12   Lectures

Lectures are short talks that provide information about academic subjects. They are like short lectures that might be heard in a college classroom.

In some talks, you will hear academic information in a short lecture.

When you hear a lecture, you must be able to summarize the important ideas. You must also be able to answer questions that begin with the following words: *who, what, when, where, why?*

It will help you to listen to documentary programs on radio and television. Programs on educational broadcasting networks are especially helpful. Listen carefully. Ask yourself questions to test your ability to remember the information.

EXAMPLE

The vast array of fruits presents a challenge for scientists who try to classify them, but they are usually classified into several types according to the origin of their development. Simple fruits are derived from flowers with just one pistil. Here is a diagram of a simple fruit. Some of the most obvious examples include cherries, peaches, and plums, but coconuts are also simple fruits.

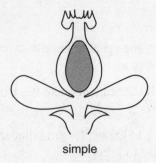

simple

As you can see, the second classification of fruits, aggregate fruits, differs from simple fruits in that each flower has several pistils. Examples of aggregate fruits are blackberries, raspberries, and strawberries. Now, let's look at a diagram of an aggregate fruit.

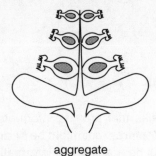

aggregate

The third type, a multiple fruit, develops from a group of flowers that grow in clusters. When the walls of the pistils thicken, then they bond and become incorporated into a single fruit. The classic example of this type is the pineapple, but figs are also classified as multiple fruits. Here is a diagram of a multiple fruit for comparison with the other two types.

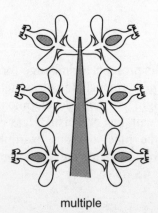

multiple

Selective breeding creates new varieties of fruit, usually larger, juicier, and more appealing than the smaller natural fruits. However, even laboratory fruits seem to adhere to this general typology.

Okay, I'm going to put some specimens into the lab for you to examine. There will be three trays—the first with samples of simple fruits, the second with samples of aggregate fruits, and the third with samples of multiple fruits. Please examine both the flowers and the fruits themselves, and this is important—please look at the three trays in this order—simple fruits, aggregate fruits, and multiple fruits.

TYPES OF QUESTIONS

Multiple-Choice Questions

Paper-Based TOEFL

1. What is the lecture mainly about?
    - Ⓐ Laboratory assignments with fruit
    - Ⓑ Selective breeding of fruit
    - Ⓒ Basic classifications of fruit
    - Ⓓ A definition of fruit

2. Which of the fruits is an example of a multiple fruit?
    - Ⓐ Pineapples
    - Ⓑ Cherries
    - Ⓒ Strawberries
    - Ⓓ Blackberries

Computer-Based TOEFL

What is the lecture mainly about?
- ○ Laboratory assignments with fruit
- ○ Selective breeding of fruit
- ● Basic classifications of fruit
- ○ A definition of fruit

Which of the fruits is an example of a multiple fruit?
- ● Pineapples
- ○ Cherries
- ○ Strawberries
- ○ Blackberries

3. What distinguishes laboratory
    fruits from natural fruits?
    - Ⓐ They do not taste as sweet
      as natural fruits.
    - Ⓑ Laboratory fruits tend to be
      larger.
    - Ⓒ They are not classified the
      same way as natural fruits.
    - Ⓓ Laboratory fruits are bred
      with more pistils.

What distinguishes laboratory
fruits from natural fruits?
- ○ They do not taste as sweet
  as natural fruits.
- ● Laboratory fruits tend to be
  larger.
- ○ They are not classified the
  same way as natural fruits.
- ○ Laboratory fruits are bred
  with more pistils.

4. Which of the following fruits will
    NOT be placed into the first tray in
    the lab?
    - Ⓐ Coconuts
    - Ⓑ Plums
    - Ⓒ Peaches
    - Ⓓ Raspberries

Which of the following fruits will
NOT be placed into the first tray in
the lab?
- ○ Coconuts
- ○ Plums
- ○ Peaches
- ● Raspberries

Answer Sheet

1. Ⓐ Ⓑ ● Ⓓ
2. ● Ⓑ Ⓒ Ⓓ
3. Ⓐ ● Ⓒ Ⓓ
4. Ⓐ Ⓑ Ⓒ ●

Computer-Assisted Questions

Two-Answer Questions. On some of the computer-assisted questions, you will be asked to select two answers. Both answers must be correct to receive credit for the question.

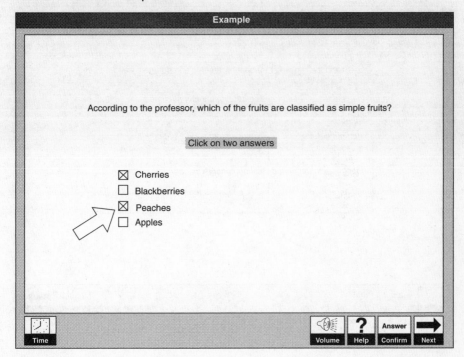

Visual Questions. On some of the computer-assisted questions, you will be asked to select a visual. The visual may be a picture, a drawing, or a diagram.

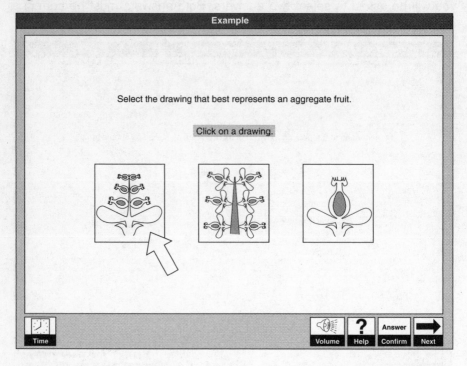

Sequencing Questions. On some of the computer-assisted questions, you will be asked to sequence events in order. The events could be historical events or the steps in a scientific process.

All answers must be sequenced correctly to receive credit for the question.

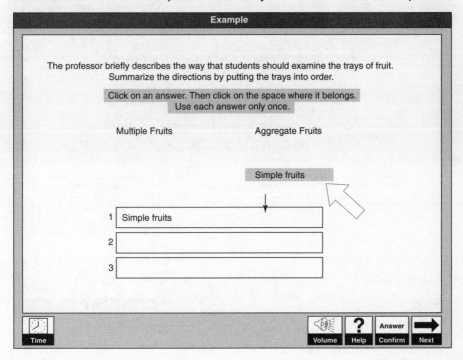

Classification Questions. On some of the computer-assisted questions, you will be asked to classify information by organizing it in categories.

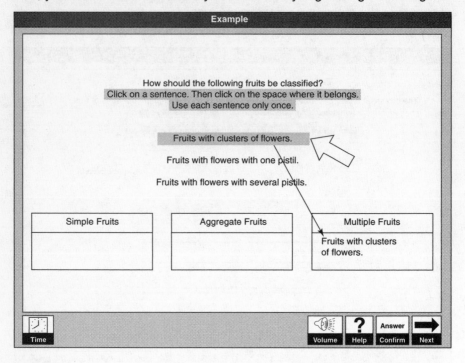

Computer Tutorial for the Listening Section

In order to succeed on the Computer-Based TOEFL, you must understand the computer vocabulary used for the test, and you must be familiar with the icons on the computer screens that you will see on the test. First, review the vocabulary. Then study the computer screens in this Tutorial.

Testing Tools: Vocabulary, Icons, and Keys

General Vocabulary for the Computer-Based TOEFL

Mouse   A small control with one or two buttons on it.

Mouse Pad   A rectangular pad where you move the *mouse*.

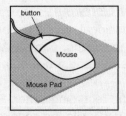

Arrow	A marker that shows you where you are moving on the computer screen. Move the *mouse* on the *mouse pad* to move the **Arrow** on the screen.
Click	To depress the button on the *mouse* is to **Click** the *mouse*. **Click** the *mouse* to make changes on the computer screen.
Icon	A small picture or a word or a phrase in a box. Move the *arrow* to the **Icon** and *click* on the **Icon** to tell the computer what to do.

Icons for the Computer-Based TOEFL

Dismiss Directions	An example of an *icon*. *Click* on **Dismiss Directions** to tell the computer to remove the directions from the screen.
Oval	The *icon* beside the answers for the multiple-choice test questions. Move the *arrow* to the **Oval** and *click* on one of the **Ovals** to choose an answer.
Next	An example of an *icon*. To see the next question on the screen, *click* on **Next** first and then *click* on **Confirm Answer**.
Confirm Answer	An example of an *icon*. *Click* on **Confirm Answer** after you *click* on **Next** to see the next question on the screen. Remember, *click* on **Next**, **Confirm Answer** in that order.
Help	An example of an *icon*. *Click* on the question mark to see a list of the *icons* and directions for the section.
Time	An *icon* of a clock in the bottom left corner of the screen. *Click* on the clock face to hide or show the time you have left to finish the section of the test you are working on. Five minutes before the end of each section of the test, the clock will appear automatically. Remember, the time appears in numbers at the top of the screen, not on the clock face. You cannot use the clock during the recording.

Specific Vocabulary for Listening

Volume One additional *icon* at the bottom of the screen in the Listening section. *Click* on **Volume** to go to a screen with an *up arrow* and a *down arrow*. *Click* on the *up arrow* to make the recording louder. *Click* on the *down arrow* to make the recording softer. Remember, you can change the volume while the speaker is giving directions, but not after the directions have concluded.

COMPUTER SCREENS FOR THE COMPUTER-BASED TOEFL

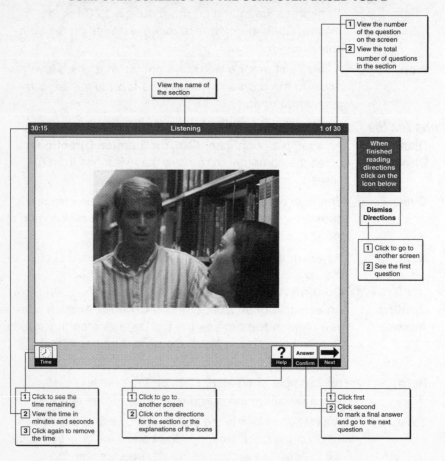

TIP: When the icons are black, you can click on them. When they are gray, they are not functioning. For example, **Confirm Answer** is gray until you click on **Next**. Then **Confirm Answer** is black. Remember the order to click on these two icons.

Computer Screens for Listening

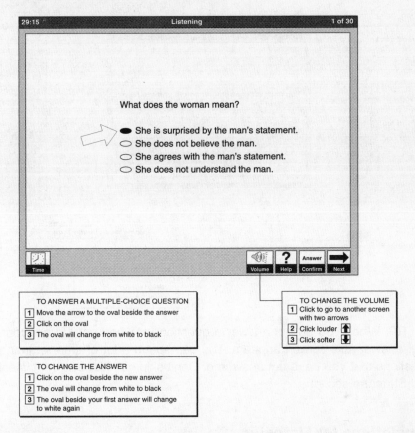

TO ANSWER A MULTIPLE-CHOICE QUESTION
1. Move the arrow to the oval beside the answer
2. Click on the oval
3. The oval will change from white to black

TO CHANGE THE VOLUME
1. Click to go to another screen with two arrows
2. Click louder
3. Click softer

TO CHANGE THE ANSWER
1. Click on the oval beside the new answer
2. The oval will change from white to black
3. The oval beside your first answer will change to white again

TIP: Most of the questions on the Computer-Based TOEFL are multiple-choice. When you learn to move the arrow to the oval and click on the oval, you will be able to answer most of the questions.

TIP: When you do not answer a question, or when you do not confirm your answer, this screen appears. You can spend a lot of time returning to questions that you have not answered. Don't skip questions in the Listening and Structure sections.

Simulations for Listening

In order to prepare for the experience that you will have on the Computer-Based TOEFL, use the CD-ROM that supplements the larger version of this book; *Barron's How to Prepare for the TOEFL*. Locate the Listening section on the Model Tests. The computer will simulate features of the Listening section on the Computer-Based TOEFL. These Model Tests are computer-assisted.

As part of your study plan, be sure to review all of the questions in all of the Model Tests. Use the Explanatory Answers on the CD-ROM or on pages 395–490. Finally, take the Cumulative Model Test on the CD-ROM. This test is computer-adaptive, which means that the computer will select questions for you at your level of language proficiency.

If you choose not to purchase the larger version of this book, or you do not have a computer, you can still simulate some of the features of the Computer-Based TOEFL. In Section 1 of the Model Tests in Chapter 8, the questions are written out for you to read while you listen to them. This is different from the Paper-Based TOEFL. Instead of the CD-ROM, you may be using either an audio compact disk or a cassette. Pause the tape or compact disk occasionally to give yourself more control of the time for each question. But be careful not to pause too often or you will not be able to complete all of the questions within the total time allowed for the section.

Preview of Listening on the Next Generation TOEFL

The Next Generation TOEFL will include comprehension passages with natural speech at a rate that is normal for native speakers and a style that is appropriate for campus conversations and academic classroom interactions.

Chapter 12 of this book includes a "Glossary of Campus Vocabulary" to help you understand the campus context. The next edition of this book will include a new, revised Listening Chapter to provide you with strategies to comprehend natural speech in academic situations.

Watch for *Barron's How to Prepare for the TOEFL, 12th Edition* to be published when the Next Generation TOEFL is introduced.

Advice for the Listening Section

Be sure to adjust the volume before you begin. Before you begin the Listening section, you will have an opportunity to adjust the volume on your headset. Be sure to do it before you dismiss the directions and begin the test. After the test has begun, you may not adjust the volume.

Do not let the visuals of people distract you from listening to the short conversations. We all respond in different ways to pictures. If you become too involved in looking at the pictures, you may pay less attention to the recording. For the most part, the pictures of people are for orientation to the short conversation. After you look briefly at the picture, give your full concentration to the conversation. If you take the Model Tests on the CD-ROM that supplements the larger version of this book, *Barron's How to Prepare for the TOEFL*, first practice by watching the screen during the short conversation and then by closing your eyes or looking away during the conversation. Find the best way for you to listen to this part of the test.

Focus on the visuals of objects, art, specimens, maps, charts, and drawings in the talks. In general, the pictures of people are for orientation to the talks, whereas the visuals of objects, art, specimens, maps, charts, and drawings support the meaning of the talks. Do not focus on the pictures of people. Do focus on the other visuals that appear during the talks. They could reappear in a question. When you take the Model Tests, practice selective attention. Disregard the pictures of the lecturer and the students, and be alert to the other visuals.

Be sure to read the question while you are hearing it. The questions will be shown on the screen while you are hearing them. If you find that it is to your advantage to close your eyes or look away during the short conversations, be sure to give your full attention to the screen again while the question is being asked. During the questions for longer conversations and talks, watch the screen carefully. By using the Model Tests, you will be able to develop a rhythm for interacting with the screen that is to your advantage.

Advice for Success

This advice from Dr. Charles Swindell is framed on the wall of my office near my computer so that I can see it every day. I am happy to share it with you:

"The longer I live, the more I realize the impact of attitude on life. Attitude to me is more important than facts. It is more important than the past, than education, than money, than circumstances, than failures, than successes, than what other people think or say or do. It is more important than appearance, giftedness, or skill. The remarkable thing is, we have a choice every day regarding the attitude we will embrace for that day. We cannot change our past . . . we cannot change the fact that people may act in a certain way. We cannot change the inevitable. The only thing we can do is play on the one string we have, and that is our attitude. I am convinced that life is 10 percent what happens to me and 90 percent how I react to it. And so it is with you. We are in charge of our attitudes."

Henry Ford said it another way:

"If you think you can or you think you can't, you are probably right."

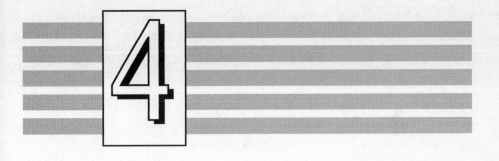

PREVIEW OF SPEAKING

Overview of the Speaking Section

QUICK COMPARISON—SPEAKING
PAPER-BASED TOEFL,
COMPUTER-BASED TOEFL, AND NEXT GENERATION TOEFL

Paper-Based TOEFL	*Computer-Based TOEFL*	*Next Generation TOEFL*
There is NO speaking section.	There is NO speaking section.	Three types of questions are presented in six sets. The first two sets have a general question; other sets have questions about campus and academic topics.
		After you see and hear the general questions, you will have 15 seconds to prepare your answers and 45 seconds to record them.
		After you hear the campus and academic questions, you will have 20–30 seconds to prepare each answer and 60 seconds to record it.

Directions and Examples for Speaking Questions

The Speaking Section of the TOEFL tests your ability to speak in English about a variety of general and academic topics. The Speaking Section is not included in either the Paper-Based TOEFL or the Computer-Based TOEFL. It is included in the Next Generation TOEFL.

Paper-Based TOEFL (PBT)

There is no Speaking Section on the current format of the Paper-Based TOEFL; however, there are plans for a telephone administration of speaking for future tests.

Computer-Based TOEFL (CBT)

There is no Speaking Section on the current format of the Computer-Based TOEFL.

Next Generation TOEFL

There are usually six questions in two parts on the Speaking Section of the Next Generation TOEFL. The questions are presented only one time. You may take notes. The topics are both general and academic. There are two types of tasks included in the Speaking Section: two independent speaking tasks and four integrated speaking tasks.

Independent Speaking

Directions: In the independent speaking tasks, you will hear questions about familiar topics. You can use your personal experience and general knowledge to answer. After each question, you have 15 seconds to prepare your answer, and 45 seconds to record it.

This is an example of an independent speaking question:

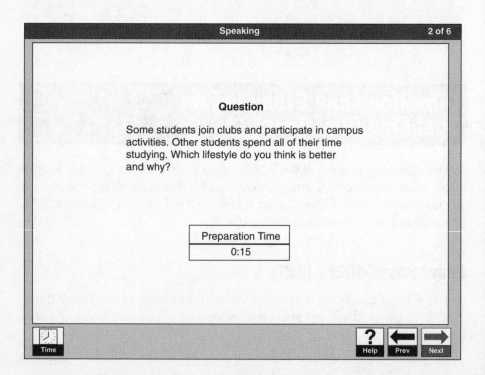

This is an example of an answer that receives an excellent rating:

"When I go to college, I plan to join at least one club and participate in some of the activities. Being part of a club is a good way to make friends because . . . you have something in common, and . . . and if I can make friends with Americans, I'll probably improve my English. And activities are also a good way to relax. Studying all the time is uh stressful, and breaks are good for your health. Um . . . another reason to participate in activities is to demonstrate that you lead a balanced life. Some of the scholarship committees are looking for additional qualities, like leadership or community service as well as high grades, and when you have extra . . . extra-curricular activities on your application, it can help you get a scholarship or admission to graduate school. So I think students who study all the time . . . they miss out on a lot of opportunities for friendship and maybe even for a scholarship."

Checklist for Independent Speaking
- ☑ The talk answers the topic question.
- ☑ The point of view or position is clear.
- ☑ The talk is direct and well-organized.
- ☑ The sentences are logically connected to each other.
- ☑ Details and examples support the main idea.
- ☑ The speaker expresses complete thoughts.
- ☑ The meaning is easy for the listener to comprehend.
- ☑ A wide range of vocabulary is used.
- ☑ There are only minor errors in grammar and idioms.
- ☑ The talk is within a range of 125–150 words.

Integrated Speaking

Directions: In the integrated speaking tasks, you will hear a lecture or read a passage about an academic topic, or you may listen to a lecture and read a related passage about an academic topic. You can take notes to prepare your answer. After each lecture or reading passage, you will hear a question that requires you to respond by speaking. You will have 20–30 seconds to prepare your answer, and 60 seconds to record it.

This is an example of a lecture:

(professor) Okay. Let's continue our discussion about the way that psychologists gather information. First, let me remind you that many of us reject the idea that the social sciences can be studied with the same methods that scientists use in the natural or physical sciences. We believe that human behavior is contextualized, that is, that the behavior is intensely personal and subjective, and must always be studied within the natural context of the behavior, not in an artificial, experimental setting. So, that said, let me talk about a couple of methods that we use.

One of the most useful methods is the interview. Unlike surveys that contain set answers from which the subject must select, the interview allows us to ask open-ended questions. This gives subjects the option of explaining why they hold a certain opinion and that can be very useful in understanding what motivates people and what would be likely to change their behaviors. Of course the problem is that it is extremely time consuming as compared with something more quantitative, like say, the survey.

So, one way to interview a larger number of people more efficiently is to bring them together in a focus group. Focus groups are situations in which groups of people are brought together with a researcher to focus on a topic not only to articulate their opinions but also to explain them to each other. The researcher learns by listening to the group and draws conclusions from their interactions. The advantages are obvious—focus groups provide data from a group much more quickly and cost effectively than would be possible if each individual were interviewed separately, and they provide a way for researchers to follow up and clarify responses that may be stated in an ambiguous way.

This is an example of an integrated speaking question:

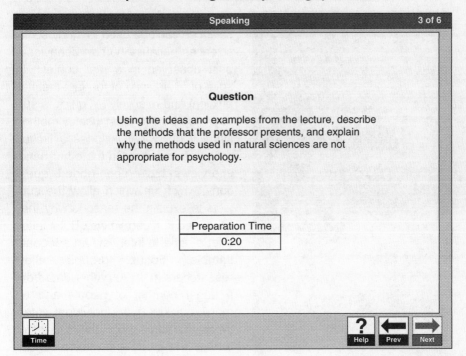

Question

Using the ideas and examples from the lecture, describe
the methods that the professor presents, and explain
why the methods used in natural sciences are not
appropriate for psychology.

Preparation Time
0:20

Time   Help Prev Next

Here is an example of an answer that receives an excellent rating:

"The methods used to study natural sciences can't be used to study social sciences because human behavior is best observed in a real context. In spite of . . . in spite of the fact that it is efficient and relatively . . . quick, a survey may be the least useful method since it uh . . . it includes a limited range of answers. On the other hand, interviews have open-ended questions, which uh which allow the subjects to explain the reasons why they answered in a certain way. But it takes a lot of time to interview an adequate sample. Focus groups allow researchers to . . . to gather data from a larger number of people and uh more quickly than individual interviews. In a focus group, the researcher listens to a group and makes conclusions about their opinions uh . . . following up and clarifying comments. The way subjects interact is also interesting to the researcher. So a focus group is probably the best option for gathering data."

Checklist for Integrated Speaking
- ☑ The talk answers the topic question.
- ☑ There are only minor inaccuracies in the content.
- ☑ The talk is direct and well-organized.
- ☑ The sentences are logically connected to each other.
- ☑ Details and examples support the main idea.
- ☑ The speaker expresses complete thoughts.
- ☑ The meaning is easy for the listener to comprehend.
- ☑ A wide range of vocabulary is used.
- ☑ The speaker paraphrases, using his or her own words.
- ☑ The speaker credits the lecturer with wording when necessary.
- ☑ There are only minor errors in grammar and idioms.
- ☑ The talk is within a range of 125–150 words.

Preview of Problems and Questions for the Speaking Section

Introduced as the TOEFL Academic Speaking Test (TAST)

This preview can be used to prepare for the Next Generation TOEFL Speaking Section or the TOEFL Academic Speaking Test (TAST). The TAST was introduced in 2003 as a first version of the TOEFL Speaking Section. Although minor modifications will be made in the second version of the TAST when it is included in the Next Generation TOEFL, this preview will be a good way to begin your preparation.

The Next Generation TOEFL Speaking Section, like the TAST, will measure your ability to speak in English about a variety of general and academic topics. There are six questions. The total time is 20 minutes. Although the administration is currently by telephone, the plan is to design a Speaking Section on the Internet.

There is no Speaking Section on the current format of the Paper-Based TOEFL or the Computer-Based TOEFL. However, there are plans for a telephone administration of speaking for future Paper-Based administrations.

TYPES OF QUESTIONS IN THE SPEAKING SECTION

Questions like those in this Preview of Speaking appear on the TOEFL Academic Speaking Test, soon to be reintroduced as the Next Generation TOEFL Speaking Section.

1 Experiences
2 Preferences
3 Reports
4 Examples
5 Problems
6 Summaries

Question 1—Experiences

In this question, you will be asked to speak about a personal experience. This may be a place, a person, a possession, a situation, or an occasion. After you hear the question, you will make a choice from your experience and then explain why you made that choice. You will have 15 seconds to prepare and 45 seconds to speak.

EXAMPLE QUESTION

Where would you like to study in the United States?

Task
• Describe your experience
• Explain the reasons for your choice

Directions
Read Question 1, the Example Notes, and the Example Answer. Use the Checklist to learn how to rate a speaking response for this type of question.

EXAMPLE NOTES

Washington, D.C.
• Family in area—advice, help
• International city—food, stores
• Tours—sites, trains to other cities
• Universities—excellent, accepted at one

SCRIPT FOR EXAMPLE ANSWER

I'd like to study at a university in Washington, D.C. because I have family in the area, and . . . and it would be nice to have them close by so I could visit them on holidays and in case I need advice or help. I've been to Washington several times, and I like it there. It's an international city, and there are restaurants and stores where I can buy food and other things from my country while uh I'm living abroad. And Washington is an exciting place. I've gone on several tours, but I still have many places on my list of sites to see. Also, um . . . there are trains to New York and Florida so I could take advantage of my free time to see other cities in the United States. Um . . . as for the universities, there are several excellent schools in Washington, and . . . and I'd probably be accepted at one of them.

Checklist

✔ The talk answers the topic question.

✔ The point of view or position is clear.

✔ The talk is direct and well-organized.

✔ The sentences are logically connected to each other.

✔ Details and examples support the main idea.

✔ The speaker expresses complete thoughts.

✔ The meaning is easy for the listener to comprehend.

✔ A wide range of vocabulary is used.

✔ There are only minor errors in grammar.

✔ The talk is within a range of 125–150 words.

Question 2—Preferences

In this question, you will be asked to speak about a personal preference. This may be a situation, an activity, or an event. After you hear the question, you will make a choice between two options presented and then explain why you made that choice. You will have 15 seconds to prepare and 45 seconds to speak.

EXAMPLE QUESTION

Some students live in dormitories on campus. Other students live in apartments off campus. Which living situation do you think is better and why?

Task
- Choose between two options
- Explain the reasons for your preference

Directions
Read Question 2 and the Example Answer. Use the Checklist to learn how to rate a speaking response for this type of question.

EXAMPLE NOTES

Dormitories
- More interaction—practice English, study
- Less responsibility—meals, laundry, cleaning
- Better location—library, recreation, classroom buildings

SCRIPT FOR EXAMPLE ANSWER

A lot of my friends live off campus, but I think that living in a dormitory is a better situation uh especially for the first year at a new college. Dormitories are structured to provide opportunities for interaction and for making friends. As a foreign student, it would be an advantage to be in a dormitory to practice English with other residents and even to find study groups in the dormitory. And dorm students have . . . uh have less responsibility for meals, laundry, and . . . and cleaning since there are meal plans and services available as part of the fees. Besides, there's only one check to write, so the bookkeeping's minimal. And the dormitory offers an ideal location near the library and um all the recreational facilities and . . . and classroom buildings.

Checklist

✔ The talk answers the topic question.
✔ The point of view or position is clear.
✔ The talk is direct and well-organized.
✔ The sentences are logically connected to each other.
✔ Details and examples support the main idea.
✔ The speaker expresses complete thoughts.
✔ The meaning is easy for the listener to comprehend.
✔ A wide range of vocabulary is used.
✔ There are only minor errors in grammar.
✔ The talk is within a range of 125–150 words.

Question 3—Reports

In this question, you will be asked to listen to a speaker and read a short passage on the same topic. The topic usually involves a campus situation, and the speaker's opinion about it. After you hear the question, you will be asked to report the speaker's opinion and relate it to the reading passage. You will have 30 seconds to prepare and 60 seconds to speak.

EXAMPLE QUESTION

The man expresses his opinion of the proposal in the announcement. Report his opinion and explain the reasons he gives for having that opinion.

Task
• Summarize a situation and an opinion about it
• Explain the reason or the background
• Connect listening and reading passages

Directions
Read the Announcement in 45 seconds. Then read the Conversation followed by the Example Answer. Use the Checklist to learn how to rate a speaking response for this type of question.

Reading

> Announcement concerning a proposal for a branch campus
> The university is soliciting state and local funding to build a branch campus on the west side of the city where the I-19 expressway crosses the 201 loop. This location should provide convenient educational opportunities for students who live closer to the new campus as well as for those students who may choose to live on the west side once the campus is established. The city plan for the next ten years indicates that there will be major growth near the proposed site, including housing and shopping areas. By building a branch campus, some of the crowding on the main campus may be resolved.

Talk
I understand that a branch campus on the city's west side would be convenient for students who live near the proposed site and might attract more local students, but I oppose the plan because it will redirect funds from the main campus where several classroom buildings need repair. Hanover Hall for one. And uh a lot of the equipment in the chemistry and physics labs should be replaced. In my lab classes, we don't do some of the experiments because uh because we don't have enough equipment. And we need more teachers on the main campus. I'd like to see the branch campus funding allocated for teachers' salaries in order to decrease the student-teacher ratios. Most of the freshman classes are huge, and there's very little interaction with professors. Um . . . a branch campus would be a good addition but not until some of the problems on the main campus have been taken care of.

EXAMPLE NOTES

Plans to open a branch campus
• Convenient for students near
• Might attract more students

But will redirect funds from main campus
• Buildings need repair
• Equipment should be replaced
• More teachers—smaller classes

SCRIPT FOR EXAMPLE ANSWER

The man concedes that the branch campus might be advantageous for students living close to the new location, but he's concerned that the funding for a branch campus will affect funding on main campus for . . . for important capital improvements such as classroom buildings that are in need of repair. Um . . . and equipment in the science labs is getting old, so it needs to be replaced. And he also points out that more teachers are needed for the main campus in order to reduce student-teacher ratios, which . . . which would improve the quality of the teaching and interaction in classes. So the man feels that more attention should be given to the main campus and funding should be allocated to improve the main campus before a branch campus is considered.

Checklist

✔ The talk summarizes the situation and the opinion.
✔ The point of view or position is clear.
✔ The talk is direct and well-organized.
✔ The sentences are logically connected to each other.
✔ Details and examples support the opinion.
✔ The speaker expresses complete thoughts.
✔ The meaning is easy for the listener to comprehend.
✔ A wide range of vocabulary is used.
✔ There are only minor errors in grammar.
✔ The talk is within a range of 125–150 words.

Question 4—Examples

In this question, you will be asked to listen to a speaker and read a short passage on the same topic. The topic usually involves a general concept, and a specific example of it. Sometimes the speaker provides a contradictory point of view. After you hear the question, you will be asked to explain the example and relate it to the concept. You will have 30 seconds to prepare and 60 seconds to speak.

EXAMPLE QUESTION

Explain the Wug experiment and why the results supported the basic theory of child language acquisition.

Task
• Explain how an example supports a concept
• Connect listening and reading passages

Directions

Read the Textbook Passage in 45 seconds. Then read the Lecture followed by the Example Answer. Use the Checklist to learn how to rate a speaking response for this type of question.

Reading

> The telegraphic nature of early sentences in child language is a result of the omission of grammatical words such as the article *the* and auxiliary verbs *is* and *are* as well as word endings such as *-ing*, *-ed*, or *-s*. By the end of the third year, these grammatical forms begin to appear in the speech of most children. It is evident that a great deal of grammatical knowledge is required before these structures can be used correctly, and errors are commonly observed. The correction of grammatical errors is a feature of the speech of preschoolers four and five years old. The study of the errors in child language is interesting because it demonstrates when and how grammar is acquired.

Lecture

English uses a system of about a dozen word endings to express grammatical meaning—the *-ing* for present time, *-s* for possession and plurality, and . . . the *-ed* for the past, to mention only a few. But uh how and when do children learn them? Well, in a classic study by Berko in the 1950s, investigators . . . they elicited a series of forms that required the target endings. For example, a picture was shown of a bird, and . . . and the investigator identified it by saying, "This is a Wug." Then the children were shown two similar birds um to . . . to elicit the sentence, "There are two ——." So . . . if the children completed the sentence by saying, "Wugs," then it was inferred that they had learned the *-s* ending. Okay. Essential to the study was the use of nonsense words like "Wug" since the manipulation of the endings could have been supported by words that the children...had already heard. In any case, charts were developed to demonstrate the uh the gradual nature of grammatical acquisition. And the performance by children from 18 months to four years confirmed the basic theory of child language that the . . . the gradual reduction of grammatical errors . . . these are evidence of language acquisition.

EXAMPLE NOTES

Word endings—grammatical relationships
- *-ed* past
- *-s* plural

Wug experiment—Berko
- Nonsense words—not influenced by familiar
- Manipulate endings
- Data about development

SCRIPT FOR EXAMPLE ANSWER

In English, there are several important word endings that express grammatical relationships, for example, the -ed ending that signals that the speaker's talking about the past and the -s ending that means "more than one" uh when it's used at the end of a noun. So, when children learn English, they um . . . they make errors in these endings, but they gradually refine their use until they master them. In the Wug experiment, Berko developed nonsense words to get children to use endings . . . so . . . so the researchers could uh follow their development. It was important not to use *real* words because the children might have been influenced by a word they'd heard before. So this experiment provided data about the time it takes and the age when endings are learned. It supported the basic theory of child language that um . . . sorting out grammatical errors is a feature of the speech of . . . of four year olds and a stage in language acquisition.

Checklist
✔ The talk relates an example to a concept.
✔ There are only minor inaccuracies in the content.
✔ The talk is direct and well-organized.
✔ The sentences are logically connected to each other.
✔ Details and examples support the talk.
✔ The speaker expresses complete thoughts.
✔ The meaning is easy for the listener to comprehend.
✔ A wide range of vocabulary is used.
✔ The speaker paraphrases, using his or her own words.
✔ The speaker credits the lecturer with wording.
✔ There are only minor errors in grammar.
✔ The talk is within a range of 125–150 words.

Question 5—Problems

In this question, you will be asked to listen to a conversation and explain a problem and the solutions that are proposed. You will have 20 seconds to prepare and 60 seconds to speak.

EXAMPLE QUESTION

Describe the woman's budgeting problem and the two suggestions that the man makes. What do you think the woman should do and why?

Task
- Describe a problem and several recommendations
- Express an opinion about the better solution
             or
- Propose an alternative solution

Directions
Read Question 5 and the Example Answer. Then read the Conversation. Use the Checklist to learn how to rate a speaking response for this type of question.

Conversation

Woman:	Did your scholarship check come yet?
Man:	Yeah, it came last week. Didn't yours?
Woman:	No. That's the problem. And everything's due at the same time—tuition, my dorm fee, and let's not forget about books. I need about 400 dollars just for books.
Man:	Well, do you have any money left from last semester, in your checking account, I mean?
Woman:	Some, but not nearly enough. The check won't be here until the end of the month, and I won't get paid at work for two more weeks . . . I don't know what I'm going to do.
Man:	How about your credit card? Could you use that?
Woman:	Maybe, but I'm afraid I'll get the credit card bill before I get the scholarship check, then I'll be in worse trouble because of, you know, the interest rate for the credit card on top of everything else.
Man:	I see your point. Still, the check might come before the credit card bill. You might have to gamble, unless . . .
Woman:	I'm listening.
Man:	Well, unless you take out a student loan. A short-term loan. They have them set up at the Student Credit Union. Isn't that where you have your checking account?

Woman:	Umhum.
Man:	So you could take out a short-term loan and pay it off on the day that you get your check. It wouldn't cost that much for interest because it would probably be only a few weeks. That's what I'd do.

EXAMPLE NOTES

Problem—not enough money
• Books
• Tuition
• Dorm

Solutions
• Use credit card
• Take out a student loan

SCRIPT FOR EXAMPLE ANSWER

The woman doesn't have enough money for her expenses. Um . . . she has to pay tuition, and her dorm fee is due at the same time. Besides, she needs to buy books. So the problem is everything has to be paid now, and she won't get her scholarship check until the end of the month, and she won't be paid at work for two weeks. The man suggests that she use her credit card because she won't have to pay it off until the end of the month, but the problem is . . . the . . . the interest would be substantial if the scholarship check is delayed. The other idea—to take out a student loan—that seems better because the loan could be paid off on the day the check arrives instead of a fixed date, and it wouldn't cost much to get a short-term loan at the Student Credit Union. So . . . I support applying for a student loan.

Checklist
✔ The talk summarizes the problem and recommendations.
✔ The speaker's point of view or position is clear.
✔ The talk is direct and well-organized.
✔ The sentences are logically connected to each other.
✔ Details and examples support the opinion.
✔ The speaker expresses complete thoughts.
✔ The meaning is easy for the listener to comprehend.
✔ A wide range of vocabulary is used.
✔ There are only minor errors in grammar.
✔ The talk is within a range of 125–150 words.

Question 6—Summaries

In this question, you will be asked to give a summary of an academic lecture. You will have 20 seconds to prepare and 60 seconds to speak.

EXAMPLE QUESTION

Using examples from the lecture, describe two general types of irrigation systems. Then explain the disadvantages of each type.

Task
- Comprehend part of an academic lecture
- Summarize the main points

Directions
Read Question 6, the Lecture, and the Example Answer. Use the Checklist to learn how to rate a speaking response for this type of question.

Lecture
Two types of irrigation methods that are used worldwide are mentioned in your book. Flood irrigation . . . that has been a method in use since ancient times . . . and we still use it today where water is cheap. Basically, canals connect a water supply like a river or a reservoir to the fields where ditches are constructed with valves uh valves that allow farmers to siphon water from the canal, sending it down through the ditches. So that way the field can be totally flooded, or smaller, narrow ditches along the rows can be filled with water to irrigate the crop. But, this method does have quite a few disadvantages. Like I said, it's contingent upon cheap water because it isn't very efficient, and the flooding isn't easy to control, I mean, the rows closer to the canal usually receive much more water, and of course, if the field isn't flat, then the water won't be evenly distributed. Not to mention the cost of building canals and ditches and maintaining the system. So let's consider the alternative—the sprinkler system. In this method of irrigation, it's easier to control the water and more efficient since the water is directed only on the plants. But, in hot climates, some of the water can evaporate in the air. Still, the main problem with the sprinklers is the expense for installation and maintenance because there's a very complicated pipe system and that usually involves a lot more repair and even replacement of parts, and of course, we have to factor in the labor costs in feasibility studies for sprinklers.

EXAMPLE NOTES

Flood
- Not efficient
- Difficult to control—flat fields
- Initial expense to build canals, ditches
- Requires maintenance

Sprinkler
- Complicated pipe system
- Expensive to install, maintain—repair, replace
- Labor cost

SCRIPT FOR EXAMPLE ANSWER

Two methods of irrigation were discussed in the lecture. First, flood irrigation. It involves the release of water into canals and drainage ditches that flow into the fields. The disadvantages of the flood method . . . um . . . well, it isn't very efficient since more water is used in flooding than the crops actually...uh, need, and also it isn't easy to control. Another problem is the initial expense for the construction of the canals and the connecting ditches as well as . . . as maintenance. And besides that, if the fields aren't flat, the water doesn't— I mean, it isn't distributed evenly. The second method is sprinkler irrigation which uses less water and provides better control, but there is some evaporation, and the pipe system's complicated and can be expensive to install and maintain, and there's usually a lot more labor cost because the equipment must be repaired and replaced more often than a canal system.

Checklist
✔ The talk summarizes a short lecture.
✔ There are only minor inaccuracies in the content.
✔ The talk is direct and well-organized.
✔ The sentences are logically connected to each other.
✔ Details and examples support the main idea.
✔ The speaker expresses complete thoughts.
✔ The meaning is easy for the listener to comprehend.
✔ A wide range of vocabulary is used.
✔ The speaker paraphrases, using his or her own words.
✔ The speaker credits the lecturer with wording.
✔ There are only minor errors in grammar.
✔ The talk is within a range of 125–150 words.

Computer Tutorial for the Speaking Section

The Speaking Section of the Next Generation TOEFL is being introduced as a telephone test. It is called the TAST (TOEFL Academic Speaking Test). Later, the TAST will be integrated into the Next Generation TOEFL as the Speaking Section, and it will be administered on the Internet. For now, dial the telephone number that you receive when you register. Then, follow the directions that you hear. You will be told when to prepare each answer and when to begin speaking. It is important to speak directly into the telephone. Speak up. If your voice is too soft, the rater will not be able to grade your answers.

Advice for the Speaking Section

Become familiar with the types of questions you will be asked. If you are listening to the kinds of questions that you expect to hear, you will be more prepared to organize your answers. That is why it is so important to study using the preview section in this book, and to practice using the model test.

Develop a sense of timing for the short speaking answers. You will be speaking for only 45–60 seconds, and that isn't very long to develop a complete answer. When you are answering the practice questions in this book, set a kitchen timer for 60 seconds and begin speaking. When the bell rings, stop. Did you complete your thought, or did you have more to say? Always use the timer when you are practicing. Soon you will develop a sense of the timing for the questions, and you will know how much you can say in a short answer.

Practice using the telephone to speak. Call a friend to practice some of the speaking questions by phone. Speak directly into the phone. Ask your friend to confirm that you are speaking at a good volume to be heard clearly.

Maintain a positive attitude toward the experience. It is natural to be a little anxious about speaking in a second language, but it is important not to become negative and frightened. Negative thoughts can interfere with your concentration, and you may not hear the questions correctly. Take some deep breaths before each question, and say this in your mind, "I am a good speaker. I am ready to speak." If you begin to have negative thoughts during the test, take another deep breath, and think "confidence" as you breathe in. Focus on listening to the questions. Focus on taking notes.

Choose a quiet place to take your test. Choose a room with a telephone where you can be alone. Close the door. Make a sign for the door asking friends and family not to enter while you are taking your test. Turn off pagers and cell phones. Eliminate other distracting noises. If you are disturbed while you are taking your test, you will not hear the questions, and you will lose valuable preparation time. Gather the materials that you need for the test. Always have an extra pencil in case you need it. Then, clear the desk or table that you will use for taking notes. If you see only the questions and your notes, you will focus more easily.

Advice for Success

Do you talk to yourself? Of course you do. Maybe not aloud, but all of us have mental conversations with ourselves. So the question is *how* do you talk to yourself?

Negative Talk	Positive Talk
I can't study all of this.	I am studying every day.
My English is poor.	My English is improving.
I won't get a good score.	I will do my best.
If I fail, I will be so ashamed.	If I need a higher score, I can try again.

How would you talk to good friends to encourage and support them? Be a good friend to yourself. When negative talk comes to mind, substitute positive talk. Encourage yourself to learn from mistakes.

REVIEW OF STRUCTURE

Overview of the Structure Section

QUICK COMPARISON—STRUCTURE
PAPER-BASED TOEFL,
COMPUTER-BASED TOEFL, AND NEXT GENERATION TOEFL

Paper-Based TOEFL	*Computer-Based TOEFL*	*Next Generation TOEFL*
Two types of questions are presented in separate parts. Part A has incomplete sentences, and Part B has sentences with underlined words and phrases.	Two types of questions are presented at random in one continuous section. You may see two incomplete sentences, one sentence with underlined words and phrases, another incomplete sentence, and so forth.	There is NO Structure Section.
All of the questions are multiple-choice.	All of the questions are multiple-choice.	
Everyone taking the TOEFL answers the same questions.	The computer will select questions based on your level of proficiency.	
Every question has only one answer.	Every question has only one answer.	
You have twenty-five minutes to complete the section.	You may control the pace by choosing when to begin the next question, but the section is timed. A clock on the screen shows the time remaining for you to complete the section.	
You answer on a paper Answer Sheet, filling in ovals marked Ⓐ, Ⓑ, Ⓒ, and Ⓓ.	You click on the screen either in the oval or on the underlined word or phrase.	
You can return to previous questions, erase, and change answers on your Answer Sheet.	You cannot return to previous questions. You can change your answer before you click on **Confirm Answer**. After you click on **Confirm Answer**, you will see the next question. You cannot go back.	
The score on the Structure Section is not combined with the score on the essay in the Test of Written English (TWE).	The score on the Structure Section is combined with the score on the essay in the Writing Section.	

Review of Problems and Questions for the Structure Section

This Review can be used to prepare for both the Supplemental Paper-Based TOEFL and the Computer-Based TOEFL. For the most part, the same types of problems are tested on both the Paper-Based TOEFL and the Computer-Based TOEFL. All of the questions on both the Paper-Based TOEFL and the Computer-Based TOEFL are multiple-choice.

Strategies and Symbols for Review

Strategies

How will this Review of Structure help you?

It won't teach you every rule of English grammar, but it will provide you with a review of the problems in structure and written expression that are most commonly tested on the TOEFL.

Use this review to study and to check your progress. Follow three easy steps for each problem.

1. *Review the generalization.* First, read the explanation and study the word order in the chart. Then, close your eyes, and try to see the chart in your mind.
2. *Study the examples.* Focus on the examples. First, read them silently, noting the difference between the correct and incorrect sentences. Then, read the underlined parts of the correct sentences aloud.
3. *Check your progress.* First, complete the exercise. Each exercise has two questions—one similar to Part A and the other similar to Part B on the Structure and Written Expression section of the TOEFL. Then, check your answers, using the Answer Key in Chapter 9 of this book.

If you are studying in an English program, use this review with your grammar book. After your teacher presents a grammar rule in class, find it in this review (see pages 98–208). Refer to the generalization, study the examples, and check your progress by completing the exercise.

When you go to your next grammar class, you will be more prepared. When you go to your TOEFL examination, you will be more confident. With preparation, you can succeed in school and on the TOEFL.

Symbols

In order for you to use the patterns and rules of style in this review, you must understand five kinds of symbols.

Abbreviations. An abbreviation is a shortened form. In the patterns, five abbreviations, or shortened forms, are used: *S* is an abbreviation for *Subject*, *V* for *Verb*, *V Ph* for *Verb Phrase*, *C* for *Complement*, and *M* for *Modifier*.

Small Letters. Small letters are lowercase letters. In the patterns, a verb written in small (lowercase) letters may not change form. For example, the verb *have* may not change to *has* or *had* when it is written in small letters.

Capital Letters. Capital letters are uppercase letters. In the patterns, a verb written in capital (uppercase) letters may change form. For example, the verb *HAVE* may remain as *have,* or may change to *has* or *had,* depending upon agreement with the subject and choice of tense.

Parentheses. Parentheses are curved lines used as punctuation marks. The following punctuation marks are parentheses: ( ). In the patterns, the words in parentheses give specific information about the abbreviation or word that precedes them. For example, *V (present)* means that the verb in the pattern must be a present tense verb. *N (count)* means that the noun in the pattern must be a countable noun.

Alternatives. Alternatives are different ways to express the same idea. In the patterns, alternatives are written in a column. For example, in the following pattern, there are three alternatives:

had would have could have	participle

The alternatives are *had, would have,* and *could have.* Any one of the alternatives may be used with the participle. All three alternatives are correct.

PATTERNS

Patterns are the parts of a sentence. In some books, *patterns* are called *structures.* In *patterns,* the words have the same order most of the time.

Some of the most important patterns are summarized in this review section. Remember, the generalizations in the charts and explanations for each pattern refer to the structure in the examples. There may be similar structures for which these generalizations are not appropriate.

Missing Main Verb

Remember that every English sentence must have a subject and a main verb.

S	V	
The sound of the dryer	bothers	my concentration

Avoid using an *-ing* form, an infinitive, an auxiliary verb, or another part of speech instead of a main verb.

EXAMPLES

INCORRECT: The prettiest girl in our class with long brown hair and brown eyes.

CORRECT: The prettiest girl in our class <u>has</u> long brown hair and brown eyes.

INCORRECT: In my opinion, too soon to make a decision.

CORRECT: In my opinion, <u>it is</u> too soon to make a decision.

INCORRECT: Do you know whether the movie that starts at seven?

CORRECT: Do you know whether the movie that starts at seven <u>is</u> good?

or

Do you know whether the movie <u>starts</u> at seven?

INCORRECT: Sam almost always a lot of fun.

CORRECT: Sam <u>is</u> almost always a lot of fun.

INCORRECT: The book that I lent you having a good bibliography.
  CORRECT: The book that I lent you <u>has</u> a good bibliography.

EXERCISES

Part A: Choose the correct answer.

Arizona _____ a very dry climate.
  (A) has
  (B) being
  (C) having
  (D) with

Part B: Choose the incorrect word or phrase and correct it.

Venomous snakes <u>with</u> modified teeth connected to
                        (A)
<u>poison glands</u> <u>in which</u> the venom <u>is secreted</u> and stored.
       (B)   (C)   (D)

2   Verbs that Require an Infinitive in the Complement

Remember that the following verbs require an infinitive for a verb in the complement.

agree	decide	hesitate	need	refuse
appear	demand	hope	offer	seem
arrange	deserve	intend	plan	tend
ask	expect	learn	prepare	threaten
claim	fail	manage	pretend	wait
consent	forget	mean	promise	want

S	V	C (infinitive)	M
We	had planned	to leave	day before yesterday

Avoid using an *-ing* form after the verbs listed. Avoid using a verb word after *want*.

EXAMPLES

INCORRECT: He wanted speak with Mr. Brown.
 CORRECT: He <u>wanted</u> <u>to speak</u> with Mr. Brown.

INCORRECT: We demand knowing our status.
 CORRECT: We <u>demand</u> <u>to know</u> our status.

INCORRECT: I intend the inform you that we cannot approve your
            application.
 CORRECT: I <u>intend</u> <u>to inform</u> you that we cannot approve your
            application.

INCORRECT: They didn't plan buying a car.
 CORRECT: They didn't <u>plan</u> <u>to buy</u> a car.

INCORRECT: The weather tends improving in May.
 CORRECT: The weather <u>tends</u> <u>to improve</u> in May.

EXERCISES

Part A: Choose the correct answer.

One of the least effective ways of storing information is learning
_____ it.
   (A) how repeat
   (B) repeating
   (C) to repeat
   (D) repeat

Part B: Choose the incorrect word or phrase and correct it.

Representative democracy seemed <u>evolve</u> <u>simultaneously</u>
                                  (A)   (B)
<u>during</u> the eighteenth and nineteenth centuries in Britain,
  (C)
Europe, and <u>the United States</u>.
                  (D)

Verbs that Require an *-ing* Form in the Complement

Remember that the following verbs require an *-ing* form for a verb in the complement:

admit	enjoy	recall
appreciate	finish	recommend
avoid	keep	regret
complete	mention	risk
consider	miss	stop
delay	postpone	suggest
deny	practice	tolerate
discuss	quit	understand

S	V	C (-ing)	M
He	enjoys	traveling	by plane

Avoid using an infinitive after the verbs listed.

Forbid may be used with either an infinitive or an *-ing* complement, but *forbid from* is not idiomatic.

EXAMPLES

INCORRECT: She is considering not to go.
  CORRECT: She is <u>considering</u> not <u>going</u>.

INCORRECT: We enjoyed talk with your friend.
  CORRECT: We <u>enjoyed</u> <u>talking</u> with your friend.

INCORRECT: Hank completed the writing his thesis this summer.
  CORRECT: Hank <u>completed</u> <u>writing</u> his thesis this summer.

INCORRECT: I miss to watch the news when I am traveling.
  CORRECT: I <u>miss</u> <u>watching</u> the news when I am traveling.

INCORRECT: She mentions stop at El Paso in her letter.
  CORRECT: She <u>mentions</u> <u>stopping</u> at El Paso in her letter.

EXERCISES

Part A: Choose the correct answer.

Strauss finished _____ two of his published compositions before his tenth birthday.
(A) written
(B) write
(C) to write
(D) writing

Part B: Choose the incorrect word or phrase and correct it.

<u>Many</u> people have stopped <u>to smoke</u> <u>because</u> they are afraid
 (A)   (B)   (C)
that it <u>may be</u> harmful to their health.
         (D)

4   Verb Phrases that Require an *-ing* Form in the Complement

Remember that the following verb phrases require an *-ing* form for a verb in the complement:

approve of	*do not mind*	*keep on*
be better off	*forget about*	*look forward to*
can't help	*get through*	*object to*
count on	*insist on*	*think about*
		think of

S	V Ph	C (-ing)	M
She	forgot about	canceling	her appointment

Avoid using an infinitive after the verb phrases listed. Avoid using a verb word after *look forward to* and *object to*. (Refer to pages 104 and 105 for more on verb words.)

Remember that the verb phrase BE *likely* does not require an *-ing* form but requires an infinitive in the complement.

EXAMPLES

INCORRECT: She is likely knowing.
  CORRECT: She <u>is likely</u> <u>to know.</u>

INCORRECT: Let's go to the movie when you get through to study.
  CORRECT: Let's go to the movie when you <u>get through</u> <u>studying</u>.

INCORRECT: We can't help to wonder why she left.
  CORRECT: We <u>can't help</u> <u>wondering</u> why she left.

INCORRECT: I have been looking forward to meet you.
  CORRECT: I have been <u>looking forward to</u> <u>meeting</u> you.

INCORRECT: We wouldn't mind to wait.
  CORRECT: We <u>wouldn't mind</u> <u>waiting</u>.

EXERCISES

Part A: Choose the correct answer.

Many modern architects insist on _____ materials native to the region that will blend into the surrounding landscape.

(A) use
(B) to use
(C) the use
(D) using

Part B: Choose the incorrect word or phrase and correct it.

During Jackson's administration, those <u>who</u> did not approve of
                                          (A)
<u>permit</u> common people in the White House <u>were shocked</u> by
 (B)   (C)
the president's insistence that they <u>be invited</u> into the mansion.
                                        (D)

5 Irregular Past Forms

Remember that past forms of the following irregular verbs are not the same as the participles:

Verb Word	Past Form	Participle
be	was/were	been
beat	beat	beaten
become	became	become
begin	began	begun

Verb Word	Past Form	Participle
bite	bit	bitten
blow	blew	blown
break	broke	broken
choose	chose	chosen
come	came	come
do	did	done
draw	drew	drawn
drink	drank	drunk
drive	drove	driven
eat	ate	eaten
fall	fell	fallen
fly	flew	flown
forget	forgot	forgotten
forgive	forgave	forgiven
freeze	froze	frozen
get	got	gotten or got
give	gave	given
go	went	gone
grow	grew	grown
hide	hid	hidden
know	knew	known
ride	rode	ridden
run	ran	run
see	saw	seen
shake	shook	shaken
show	showed	shown

Verb Word	*Past Form*	*Participle*
shrink	shrank	shrunk
sing	sang	sung
speak	spoke	spoken
steal	stole	stolen
swear	swore	sworn
swim	swam	swum
take	took	taken
tear	tore	torn
throw	threw	thrown
wear	wore	worn
weave	wove	woven
withdraw	withdrew	withdrawn
write	wrote	written

S	V (past)	M
The concert	began	at eight o'clock

Avoid using a participle instead of a past for simple past statements.

EXAMPLES

INCORRECT: They done it very well after they had practiced.
  CORRECT: They <u>did</u> it very well after they had practiced.

INCORRECT: Before she run the computer program, she had checked it out with her supervisor.
  CORRECT: Before she <u>ran</u> the computer program, she had checked it out with her supervisor.

INCORRECT: We eat dinner in Albuquerque on our vacation last year.
  CORRECT: We <u>ate</u> dinner in Albuquerque on our vacation last year.

INCORRECT: My nephew begun working for me about ten years ago.
  CORRECT: My nephew <u>began</u> working for me about ten years ago.

INCORRECT: I know that you been forty on your last birthday.
  CORRECT: I know that you <u>were</u> forty on your last birthday.

EXERCISES

Part A: Choose the correct answer.

Before the Angles and the Saxons _____ to England, the Iberians had lived there.

(A) coming
(B) come
(C) came
(D) did come

Part B: Choose the incorrect word or phrase and correct it.

When Columbus <u>seen</u> the New World, he <u>thought</u> that he
        (A)   (B)

<u>had reached</u> the East Indies <u>by way of</u> a Western route.
   (C)   (D)

6   Factual Conditionals—Absolute, Scientific Results

Remember that *absolute conditionals* express scientific facts. *Will* and a verb word expresses the opinion that the result is absolutely certain.

CONDITION			RESULT		
If	S	V (present) ,	S	V (present)	
If	a catalyst	is used ,	the reaction	occurs	more rapidly

or

CONDITION			RESULT		
If	S	V (present) ,	S	will	verb word
If	a catalyst	is used ,	the reaction	will	occur	more rapidly

Avoid using *will* and a verb word instead of the present verb in the clause beginning with *if*. Avoid using the auxiliary verbs *have*, *has*, *do*, and *does* with main verbs in the clause of result.

EXAMPLES

INCORRECT: If water freezes, it has become a solid.
CORRECT: If <u>water freezes, it</u> <u>becomes</u> a solid.

or

If <u>water freezes, it</u> <u>will become</u> a solid.

INCORRECT: If children be healthy, they learn to walk at about eighteen months old.
CORRECT: If <u>children</u> <u>are</u> healthy, <u>they</u> <u>learn</u> to walk at about eighteen months old.

or

If <u>children</u> <u>are</u> healthy, <u>they</u> <u>will learn</u> to walk at about eighteen months old.

INCORRECT: If orange blossoms are exposed to very cold temperatures, they withered and died.
CORRECT: If <u>orange blossoms</u> <u>are exposed</u> to very cold temperatures, <u>they</u> <u>wither and die.</u>

or

If <u>orange blossoms</u> <u>are exposed</u> to very cold temperatures, <u>they</u> <u>will wither and die.</u>

INCORRECT: If the trajectory of a satellite will be slightly off at launch, it will get worse as the flight progresses.
CORRECT: If <u>the trajectory</u> of a satellite <u>is</u> slightly off at launch, <u>it</u> <u>gets</u> worse as the flight progresses.

or

If <u>the trajectory</u> of a satellite <u>is</u> slightly off at launch, <u>it</u> <u>will get</u> worse as the flight progresses.

INCORRECT: If light strikes a rough surface, it diffused.
CORRECT: If <u>light</u> <u>strikes</u> a rough surface, <u>it</u> <u>diffuses.</u>

or

If <u>light</u> <u>strikes</u> a rough surface, <u>it</u> <u>will diffuse.</u>

EXERCISES

Part A: Choose the correct answer.

If water is heated to 212 degrees F. _____ as steam.
    (A) it will boil and escape
    (B) it is boiling and escaping
    (C) it boil and escape
    (D) it would boil and escape

Part B: Choose the incorrect word or phrase and correct it.

If a live sponge is <u>broken</u> into pieces, each piece <u>would turn</u>
           (A)   (B)

into a new sponge <u>like</u> <u>the original one</u>.
                   (C)   (D)

7   Factual Conditionals—Probable Results for the Future

Remember that *will* and a verb word expresses the opinion that the results are absolutely certain. In order of more to less probable, use the following modals: *will, can, may.*

If	S	V (present)		,	S	will can may	verb word	
If	we	find	her address	,	we	will	write	her

S	will can may	verb word		if	S	V (present)	
We	will	write	her	if	we	find	her address

Avoid using the present tense verb instead of a modal and a verb word in the clause of result.

EXAMPLES

INCORRECT: If you put too much water in rice when you cook it, it got sticky.

CORRECT: <u>If you put</u> too much water in rice when you cook it, <u>it will get</u> sticky.

               or

It <u>will get</u> sticky <u>if you put</u> too much water in rice when you cook it.

INCORRECT:	If they have a good sale, I would have stopped by on my way home.
CORRECT:	If <u>they have</u> a good sale, <u>I will stop</u> by on my way home.

or

I <u>will stop</u> by on my way home <u>if they have</u> a good sale.

INCORRECT:	We will wait if you wanted to go.
CORRECT:	<u>We will wait if you want</u> to go.

or

<u>If you want</u> to go, <u>we will wait</u>.

INCORRECT:	If you listen to the questions carefully, you answer them easily.
CORRECT:	If <u>you listen</u> to the questions carefully, <u>you will answer</u> them easily.

or

<u>You will answer</u> them easily <u>if you listen</u> to the questions carefully.

INCORRECT:	If we finished our work a little early today, we'll attend the lecture at the art museum.
CORRECT:	If <u>we finish</u> our work a little early today, <u>we'll attend</u> the lecture at the art museum.

or

<u>We'll attend</u> the lecture at the art museum <u>if we finish</u> our work a little early today.

EXERCISES

Part A: Choose the correct answer.

If services are increased, taxes _____.
   (A) will probably go up
   (B) probably go up
   (C) probably up
   (D) going up probably

Part B: Choose the incorrect word or phrase and correct it.

If you don't <u>register</u> before <u>the last day</u> of regular registration,
         (A)   (B)
you <u>paying a late fee</u>.
   (C)   (D)

8 Contrary-to-Fact Conditionals— Change in Conditions *Unless*

Remember that there is a subject and verb that determines the change in conditions after the connector *unless.*

S	V	unless	S	V	
Luisa	won't return	unless	she	gets	a scholarship

Avoid deleting *unless* from the sentence; avoid deleting either the subject or the verb from the clause after *unless.*

EXAMPLES

INCORRECT: I can't go I don't get my work finished.
 CORRECT: I can't go <u>unless</u> I <u>get</u> my work finished.

INCORRECT: They are going to get a divorce unless he stopping drugs.
 CORRECT: They are going to get a divorce <u>unless</u> <u>he</u> <u>stops</u> taking drugs.

INCORRECT: You won't get well unless you are taking your medicine.
 CORRECT: You won't get well <u>unless</u> <u>you</u> <u>take</u> your medicine.

INCORRECT: Dean never calls his father unless needs money.
 CORRECT: Dean never calls his father <u>unless</u> <u>he</u> <u>needs</u> money.

INCORRECT: We can't pay the rent unless the scholarship check.
 CORRECT: We can't pay the rent <u>unless the scholarship check</u> <u>comes</u>.

EXERCISES

Part A: Choose the correct answer.

Football teams don't play in the Super Bowl championship
_____ either the National or the American Conference.
    (A) unless they win
    (B) but they win
    (C) unless they will win
    (D) but to have won

Part B: Choose the incorrect word or phrase and correct it.

Usually <u>boys</u> cannot <u>become</u> Boy Scouts <u>unless completed</u>
     (A)   (B)   (C)
<u>the fifth grade</u>.
     (D)

9   Importance—Subjunctive Verbs

Remember that the following verbs are used before *that* and the verb word clause to express importance.

ask	*propose*
demand	*recommend*
desire	*request*
insist	*require*
prefer	*suggest*
	urge

S	V	that	S	verb word	
Mr. Johnson	prefers	that	she	speak	with him personally

Avoid using a present or past tense verb instead of a verb word. Avoid using a modal before the verb word.

Note: The verb *insist* may be used in nonsubjunctive patterns in the past tense. For example: *He* insisted *that I* was *wrong*.

EXAMPLES

INCORRECT: The doctor suggested that she will not smoke.
CORRECT: The doctor <u>suggested</u> that she not <u>smoke</u>.

INCORRECT: I propose that the vote is secret ballot.
CORRECT: I <u>propose</u> that the vote <u>be</u> secret ballot.

INCORRECT: The foreign student advisor recommended that she studied
                more English before enrolling at the university.
CORRECT: The foreign student advisor <u>recommended</u> that she <u>study</u>
                more English before enrolling at the university.

INCORRECT: The law requires that everyone has his car checked at least once a year.

CORRECT: The law <u>requires</u> that everyone <u>have</u> his car checked at least once a year.

INCORRECT: She insisted that they would give her a receipt.

CORRECT: She <u>insisted</u> that they <u>give</u> her a receipt.

EXERCISES

Part A: Choose the correct answer.

Less moderate members of Congress are insisting that changes in the Social Security System _____ made.

(A) will
(B) are
(C) being
(D) be

Part B: Choose the incorrect word or phrase and correct it.

<u>Many</u> architects prefer that a dome <u>is used</u> to roof buildings that
 (A)   (B)
need <u>to conserve</u> <u>floor space</u>.
         (C)   (D)

10 Importance—Impersonal Expressions

Remember that the following adjectives are used in impersonal expressions.

essential
imperative
important
necessary

it is	adjective	infinitive	
It is	important	to verify	the data

or

it is	adjective	that	S	verb word	
It is	important	that	the data	be	verified

Avoid using a present tense verb instead of a verb word. Avoid using a modal before the verb word.

EXAMPLES

INCORRECT: It is not necessary that you must take an entrance examination to be admitted to an American university

CORRECT: It is not necessary to take an entrance examination to be admitted to an American university.

or

It is not necessary that you take an entrance examination to be admitted to an American university.

INCORRECT: It is imperative that you are on time.

CORRECT: It is imperative to be on time.

or

It is imperative that you be on time.

INCORRECT: It is important that I will speak with Mr. Williams immediately.

CORRECT: It is important to speak with Mr. Williams immediately.

or

It is important that I speak with Mr. Williams immediately.

INCORRECT: It is imperative that your signature appears on your identification card.

CORRECT: It is imperative to sign your identification card.

or

It is imperative that your signature appear on your identification card.

INCORRECT: It is essential that all applications and transcripts are filed no later than July 1.

  CORRECT: It is essential <u>to file</u> all applications and transcripts no later than July 1.

or

It is essential <u>that</u> <u>all applications and transcripts</u> <u>be</u> filed no later than July 1.

EXERCISES

Part A: Choose the correct answer.

It is necessary _____ the approaches to a bridge, the road design, and the alignment in such a way as to best accommodate the expected traffic flow over and under it.

(A) plan
(B) to plan
(C) planning
(D) the plan

Part B: Choose the incorrect word or phrase and correct it.

It is essential that vitamins <u>are</u> supplied either by foods <u>or</u>
                       (A)   (B)
<u>by supplementary tablets</u> for normal growth <u>to occur</u>.
         (C)   (D)

11   Purpose—Infinitives

Remember that an infinitive can express purpose. It is a short form of *in order to.*

S	V	C	infinitive (purpose)	
Laura She	jogs takes	 vitamins	to stay to feel	fit better

Avoid expressing purpose without the word *to* in the infinitive. Avoid using *for* instead of *to*.

EXAMPLES

INCORRECT: Wear several layers of clothing for keep warm.
  CORRECT: Wear several layers of clothing to keep warm.

INCORRECT: David has studied hard the succeed.
  CORRECT: David has studied hard to succeed.

INCORRECT: Don't move your feet when you swing for play golf well.
  CORRECT: Don't move your feet when you swing to play golf well.

INCORRECT: Virginia always boils the water twice make tea.
  CORRECT: Virginia always boils the water twice to make tea.

INCORRECT: Wait until June plant those bulbs.
  CORRECT: Wait until June to plant those bulbs.

EXERCISES

Part A: Choose the correct answer.

In the Morrill Act, Congress granted federal lands to the states
_____ agricultural and mechanical arts colleges.
   (A) for establish
   (B) to establish
   (C) establish
   (D) establishment

Part B: Choose the incorrect word or phrase and correct it.

Papyrus was used for to make not only paper but also sails,
              (A)   (B)   (C)
baskets, and clothing.
         (D)

12   Passives—Word Order

Remember that in a passive sentence the actor is unknown or not important. The subject is not the actor.

Passive sentences are also common in certain styles of scientific writing.

S	BE	participle	
State University	is	located	at the corner of College and Third

Avoid using a participle without a form of the verb BE.

EXAMPLES

INCORRECT: My wedding ring made of yellow and white gold.
CORRECT: My wedding ring <u>is made</u> of yellow and white gold.
            (It is the *ring*, not the person who made the ring, that is
            important.)

INCORRECT: If your brother invited, he would come.
CORRECT: If your brother <u>were invited</u>, he would come.
            (It is your *brother*, not the person who invited him, that is
            important.)

INCORRECT: Mr. Wilson known as Willie to his friends.
CORRECT: Mr. Wilson <u>is known</u> as Willie to his friends.
            (It is *Mr. Wilson*, not his friends, that is important.)

INCORRECT: References not used in the examination room.
CORRECT: References <u>are not used</u> in the examination room.
            (It is *references*, not the persons using them, that are
            important.)

INCORRECT: Laura born in Iowa.
CORRECT: Laura <u>was born</u> in Iowa.
            (It is *Laura*, not her mother who bore her, that is important.)

EXERCISES

Part A: Choose the correct answer.

In the stringed instruments, the tones _____ by playing a bow across a set of strings that may be made of wire or gut.

(A) they produce
(B) producing
(C) are produced
(D) that are producing

Part B: Choose the incorrect word or phrase and correct it.

<u>Work</u> <u>is</u> often <u>measure</u> in units <u>called</u> foot pounds.
 (A) (B)   (C)   (D)

13   Belief and Knowledge—Anticipatory *It*

Remember that an anticipatory *it* clause expresses belief or knowledge. Anticipatory means before. Some *it* clauses that go before main clauses are listed below:

It is believed
It is hypothesized
It is known
It is said
It is thought
It is true
It is written

Anticipatory *it*	that	S	V	
It is believed	that	all mammals	experience	dreams

Avoid using an *-ing* form, a noun, or an infinitive instead of a subject and verb after an anticipatory *it* clause.

EXAMPLES

INCORRECT: It is hypothesized that the subjects in the control group not to score as well.

CORRECT: It is hypothesized that the subjects in the control group will not score as well.

INCORRECT: It is generally known that she leaving at the end of the year.
CORRECT: It is generally known that she is leaving at the end of the year.

INCORRECT: It is said that a buried treasure near here.
CORRECT: It is said that a buried treasure was hidden near here.

INCORRECT: It is believed that a horseshoe bringing good luck.
CORRECT: It is believed that a horseshoe brings good luck.

INCORRECT: It is thought that our ancestors building this city.
CORRECT: It is thought that our ancestors built this city.

EXERCISES

Part A: Choose the correct answer.

_____ Giant Ape Man, our biggest and probably one of our first human ancestors, was just about the size of a male gorilla.
(A) It is believed that
(B) That it is
(C) That is believed
(D) That believing

Part B: Choose the incorrect word or phrase and correct it.

That it is believed that most of the earthquakes in the world
          (A)   (B)
occur near the youngest mountain ranges—the Himalayas, the
          (C)   (D)
Andes, and the Sierra Nevadas.

14   Predictions—*Will Have* + Participle

Remember that *will have* followed by a participle and a future adverb expresses a prediction for a future activity or event.

adverb (future)	S	will	have	participle	
By the year 2010,	researchers	will	have	discovered	a cure for cancer

Avoid using *will* instead of *will have*.

EXAMPLES

INCORRECT: You will finished your homework by the time the movie starts.

CORRECT: You <u>will</u> <u>have</u> <u>finished</u> your homework <u>by the time the movie starts</u>.

INCORRECT: Jan will left by five o'clock.

CORRECT: Jan <u>will</u> <u>have</u> <u>left</u> by five o'clock.

INCORRECT: Before school is out, I have returned all of my library books.

CORRECT: <u>Before school is out</u>, I <u>will</u> <u>have</u> <u>returned</u> all of my library books.

INCORRECT: We have gotten an answer to our letter by the time we have to make a decision.

CORRECT: We <u>will</u> <u>have</u> <u>gotten</u> an answer to our letter <u>by the time we have to make a decision</u>.

INCORRECT: Before we can tell them about the discount, they will bought the tickets.

CORRECT: <u>Before we can tell them</u> about the discount, they <u>will</u> <u>have</u> <u>bought</u> the tickets.

EXERCISES

Part A: Choose the correct answer.

By the middle of the twenty-first century, the computer _____ a necessity in every home.

(A) became

(B) becoming

(C) has become

(D) will have become

Part B: Choose the incorrect word or phrase and correct it.

It is believed that by 2010 immunotherapy have succeeded in

     (A)   (B)   (C)

curing a number of serious illnesses.

     (D)

15   Missing Auxiliary Verb—Active

Remember that some main verbs require auxiliary verbs.

	BE	*-ing*	
Mom	is	watering	her plants

	HAVE	participle	
Mom	has	watered	her plants

	MODAL	verb word	
Mom	should	water	her plants

Avoid using *-ing* forms without BE, participles without HAVE, and verb words without modals when *-ing*, a participle, or a verb word function as a main verb.

EXAMPLES

INCORRECT: The party is a surprise, but all of her friends coming.
  CORRECT: The party is a surprise, but all of her friends
                   <u>are coming</u>.

INCORRECT: She read it to you later tonight.
  CORRECT: She <u>will read</u> it to you later tonight.

INCORRECT: The sun shining when we left this morning.
  CORRECT: The sun <u>was shining</u> when we left this morning.

INCORRECT: We gone there before.
  CORRECT: We <u>have gone</u> there before.

INCORRECT: I can't talk with you right now because the doorbell ringing.
  CORRECT: I can't talk with you right now because the doorbell <u>is</u>
                   <u>ringing</u>.

EXERCISES

Part A: Choose the correct answer.

The giraffe survives in part because it _____ the vegetation in the
high branches of trees where other animals have not grazed.
   (A) to reach
   (B) can reach
   (C) reaching
   (D) reach

Part B: Choose the incorrect word or phrase and correct it.

<u>According to</u> some scientists, the earth <u>losing</u> <u>its</u> outer
      (A)   (B) (C)
atmosphere <u>because of</u> pollutants.
                  (D)

16   Missing Auxiliary Verb—Passive

Remember that the passive requires an auxiliary BE verb.

S		BE	participle
The plants		are	watered
The plants	have	been	watered
The plants	should	be	watered

Avoid using a passive without a form of BE.

EXAMPLES

INCORRECT: The phone answered automatically.
  CORRECT: The phone is answered automatically.

INCORRECT: They have informed already.
  CORRECT: They have been informed already.

INCORRECT: These books should returned today.
  CORRECT: These books should be returned today.

INCORRECT: The plane delayed by bad weather.
  CORRECT: The plane was delayed by bad weather.

INCORRECT: My paper has not typed.
  CORRECT: My paper has not been typed.

EXERCISES

Part A: Choose the correct answer.

Hydrogen peroxide _____ as a bleaching agent because it effectively whitens a variety of fibers and surfaces.

   (A) used
   (B) is used
   (C) is using
   (D) that it uses

Part B: Choose the incorrect word or phrase and correct it.

If a rash <u>occurs</u> within twenty-four hours <u>after taking</u> a new
      (A)   (B)
<u>medication</u>, the treatment <u>should discontinued</u>.
     (C)   (D)

17   Object Pronouns after Prepositions

Remember that personal pronouns used as the object of a preposition should be object case pronouns.

	preposition	pronoun (object)
I would be glad to take a message	for	her

Remember that the following prepositions are commonly used with object pronouns:

among   of
between   to
for   with
from

Avoid using a subject pronoun instead of an object pronoun after a proposition.

EXAMPLES

INCORRECT: The experiment proved to my lab partner and I that prejudices about the results of an investigation are often unfounded.

CORRECT: The experiment proved <u>to</u> my lab partner and <u>me</u> that prejudices about the results of an investigation are often unfounded.

INCORRECT: Of those who graduated with Betty and he, Ellen is the only
             one who has found a good job.

  CORRECT: Of those who graduated <u>with</u> Betty and <u>him</u>, Ellen is the only
             one who has found a good job.

INCORRECT: Among we men, it was he who always acted as the
             interpreter.

  CORRECT: <u>Among us</u> men, it was he who always acted as the interpreter.

INCORRECT: The cake is from Jan, and the flowers are from Larry and we.

  CORRECT: The cake is from Jan, and the flowers are <u>from</u> Larry and <u>us</u>.

INCORRECT: Just between you and I, this isn't a very good price.

  CORRECT: Just <u>between</u> you and <u>me</u>, this isn't a very good price.

EXERCISES

Part A: Choose the correct answer.

Since the Earth's crust is much thicker under the continents, equipment
would have to be capable of drilling through 100,000 feet of rock to
investigate the mantle _____.
- (A) beneath them
- (B) beneath their
- (C) beneath its
- (D) beneath they

Part B: Choose the incorrect word or phrase and correct it.

According to Amazon legends, men <u>were forced</u> <u>to do</u> all of the
                                    (A)   (B)
household tasks for the women warriors <u>who</u> governed and
                                       (C)
protected the cities <u>for they</u>.
                        (D)

Relative Pronouns that Refer to Persons and Things

Remember that *who* is used to refer to persons, and *which* is used to refer to things.

	someone	who	
She is	the secretary	who	works in the international office

Avoid using *which* instead of *who* in reference to a person.

	something	which	
This is	the new typewriter	which	you ordered

Avoid using *who* instead of *which* in reference to a thing.

EXAMPLES

INCORRECT: The people which cheated on the examination had to leave the room.

  CORRECT: The people who cheated on the examination had to leave the room.

INCORRECT: There is someone on line two which would like to speak with you.

  CORRECT: There is someone on line two who would like to speak with you.

INCORRECT: Who is the man which asked the question?
  CORRECT: Who is the man who asked the question?

INCORRECT: The person which was recommended for the position did not fulfill the minimum requirements.

  CORRECT: The person who was recommended for the position did not fulfill the minimum requirements.

INCORRECT: The student which receives the highest score will be awarded a scholarship.

  CORRECT: The student who receives the highest score will be awarded a scholarship.

Exercises

Part A: Choose the correct answer.

Charlie Chaplin was a comedian _____ was best known for his work in silent movies.
- (A) who
- (B) which
- (C) whose
- (D) what

Part B: Choose the incorrect word or phrase and correct it.

Absolute zero, the temperature at <u>whom</u> <u>all substances</u> have
                            (A)   (B)

zero thermal energy and thus, <u>the lowest</u> possible temperatures,
                                    (C)

<u>is</u> unattainable in practice.
(D)

19   Count Nouns

Remember that *count nouns* have both singular and plural forms. Plural numbers can precede *count nouns* but not *noncount* nouns.

There are several categories of *count nouns* that can help you organize your study. Some of them are listed here.

1. Names of persons, their relationships, and their occupations:

one boy	*two boys*
one friend	*two friends*
one student	*two students*

2. Names of animals, plants, insects:

one dog	*two dogs*
one flower	*two flowers*
one bee	*two bees*

3. Names of things with a definite, individual shape:
one car	*two cars*
one house	*two houses*
one room	*two rooms*

4. Units of measurement:
one inch	*two inches*
one pound	*two pounds*
one degree	*two degrees*

5. Units of classification in society:
one family	*two families*
one country	*two countries*
one language	*two languages*

6. Containers of noncount solids, liquids, pastes, and gases:
one bottle	*two bottles*
one jar	*two jars*
one tube	*two tubes*

7. A limited number of abstract concepts:
one idea	*two ideas*
one invention	*two inventions*
one plan	*two plans*

Number (plural)	Noun (count-plural)
sixty	years

Avoid using a singular *count noun* with a plural number.

EXAMPLES

INCORRECT: We have twenty dollar left.
 CORRECT: We have <u>twenty dollars</u> left.

INCORRECT: I hope that I can lose about five pound before summer.
 CORRECT: I hope that I can lose about <u>five pounds</u> before summer.

INCORRECT: Several of the people in this class speak three or four language.
 CORRECT: Several of the people in this class speak <u>three or four languages</u>.

INCORRECT: The temperature has risen ten degree in two hours.
 CORRECT: The temperature has risen <u>ten degrees</u> in two hours.

INCORRECT: The teacher has ordered two book, but they aren't in at the bookstore.

CORRECT: The teacher has ordered <u>two books,</u> but they aren't in at the bookstore.

EXERCISES

Part A: Choose the correct answer.

A desert receives less than twenty-five _____ of rainfall every year.
(A) centimeter
(B) a centimeter
(C) centimeters
(D) of centimeters

Part B: Choose the incorrect word or phrase and correct it.

<u>In 1950</u> it was <u>naively</u> predicted that <u>eight or ten computer</u>
  (A)   (B)   (C)
would be sufficient <u>to handle</u> all of the scientific and business
                                (D)
needs in the United States.

20   Noncount Nouns

Remember that *noncount* nouns have only one form. They are used in agreement with singular verbs. The word *the* does not precede them.

There are categories of *noncount* nouns that can help you organize your study. Some of them are listed here.

1. Food staples that can be purchased in various forms:
   bread
   meat
   butter

2. Construction materials that can change shape, depending on what is made:
   wood
   iron
   grass

3. Liquids that can change shape, depending on the shape of the container:
   oil
   tea
   milk

4. Natural substances that can change shape, depending on natural laws:
   steam, water, ice
   smoke, ashes
   oxygen

5. Substances with many small parts:
   rice
   sand
   sugar

6. Groups of things that have different sizes and shapes:
   clothing   *(a coat, a shirt, a sock)*
   furniture   *(a table, a chair, a bed)*
   luggage   *(a suitcase, a trunk, a box)*

7. Languages:
   Arabic
   Japanese
   Spanish

8. Abstract concepts, often with endings *-ness, -ance, -ence, -ity*:
   beauty
   ignorance
   peace

9. Most *-ing* forms:
   learning
   shopping
   working

noun (noncount)	verb (singular)	
Friendship	is	important

Avoid using *the* before a *noncount* noun. Avoid using a plural verb with a noncount noun.

EXAMPLES

INCORRECT: The happiness means different things to different people.
  CORRECT: <u>Happiness</u> means different things to different people.

INCORRECT: Toshi speaks the Japanese at home.
  CORRECT: Toshi speaks <u>Japanese</u> at home.

INCORRECT: Bread are expensive in the grocery store on the corner.
  CORRECT: <u>Bread is</u> expensive in the grocery store on the corner.

INCORRECT: I like my tea with the milk.
  CORRECT: I like my tea with <u>milk</u>.

INCORRECT: If you open the door, airs will circulate better.
  CORRECT: If you open the door, <u>air</u> will circulate better.

EXERCISES

Part A: Choose the correct answer.

_____ at 212 degrees F. and freezes at 32 degrees F.
  (A) Waters boils
  (B) The water boils
  (C) Water boils
  (D) Waters boil

Part B: Choose the incorrect word or phrase and correct it.

<u>The religion</u> attempts <u>to clarify</u> <u>mankind's</u> relationship with a
   (A)   (B)   (C)
<u>superhuman power</u>.
     (D)

21 Nouns with Count and Noncount Meanings

Remember that some nouns may be used as *count* or as *noncount* nouns depending on their meanings. Materials and abstract concepts are *noncount* nouns, but they may be used as *count* nouns to express specific meanings.

Count noun	Specific meaning	Noncount noun	General meaning
an agreement agreements	an occasion or a document	agreement	abstract concept all agreements
a bone bones	a part of a skeleton	bone	construction material
a business businesses	a company	business	abstract concept all business transactions
a cloth cloths	a piece of cloth	cloth	construction material
a decision decisions	an occasion	decision	abstract concept all decisions
an education educations	a specific person's	education	abstract concept all education
a fire fires	an event	fire	material
a glass glasses	a container	glass	construction material
a history histories	a historical account	history	abstract concept all history
an honor honors	an occasion or an award	honor	abstract concept all honor
a language languages	a specific variety	language	abstract concept all languages
a life lives	a specific person's	life	abstract concept all life
a light lights	a lamp	light	the absence of darkness
a noise noises	a specific sound	noise	abstract concept all sounds
a pain pains	a specific occasion	pain	abstract concept all pain

a noise noises	a specific sound	noise	abstract concept all sounds
a pain pains	a specific occasion	pain	abstract concept all pain
a paper papers	a document or sheet	paper	construction material
a pleasure pleasures	a specific occasion	pleasure	abstract concept all pleasure
a silence silences	a specific occasion	silence	abstract concept all silence
a space spaces	a blank	space	the universe
a stone stones	a small rock	stone	construction material
a success successes	an achievement	success	abstract concept all success
a thought thoughts	an idea	thought	abstract concept all thought
a time times	a historical period or moment	time	abstract concept all time
a war wars	a specific war	war	the general act of war all wars
a work works	an artistic creation	work	employment abstract concept all work

	a document	
I have	a paper	due Monday

	construction material	
Let's use	paper	to make the present

Avoid using *count* nouns with specific meanings to express the general meanings of *noncount* nouns.

EXAMPLES

INCORRECT: Dr. Bradley will receive special honor at the graduation.
  CORRECT: Dr. Bradley will receive <u>a special honor</u> at the graduation.
              (an award)

INCORRECT: She needs to find a work.
  CORRECT: She needs to find <u>work</u>.
              (employment)

INCORRECT: My neighbor dislikes a noise.
  CORRECT: My neighbor dislikes <u>noise</u>.
              (all sounds)

INCORRECT: We need glass for the juice.
  CORRECT: We need <u>a glass</u> for the juice.
                        or
              We need <u>glasses</u> for the juice.
              (containers)

INCORRECT: A war is as old as mankind.
  CORRECT: <u>War</u> is as old as mankind.
              (the act of war)

EXERCISES

Part A: Choose the correct answer.

It is generally believed that an M.B.A. degree is good preparation for a career in _____.
  (A) a business
  (B) business
  (C) businesses
  (D) one business

Part B: Choose the incorrect word or phrase and correct it.

<u>A space</u> <u>is</u> the last frontier for <u>man</u> <u>to conquer</u>.
  (A) (B)   (C)   (D)

22 Noncount Nouns that Are Count Nouns in Other Languages

Remember, many nouns that are *count* nouns in other languages may be *noncount* nouns in English. Some of the most troublesome have been listed for you on the following page.

advice	*homework*	*money*	*poetry*
anger	*ignorance*	*music*	*poverty*
courage	*information*	*news*	*progress*
damage	*knowledge*	*patience*	
equipment	*leisure*	*permission*	
fun	*luck*		

	Ø	Noun (noncount)
Did you do your		homework?

Avoid using *a* or *an* before *noncount* nouns.

EXAMPLES

INCORRECT: Do you have an information about it?
CORRECT: Do you have <u>information</u> about it?

INCORRECT: Counselors are available to give you an advice before you register for your classes.
CORRECT: Counselors are available to give you <u>advice</u> before you register for your classes.

INCORRECT: George had a good luck when he first came to State University.
CORRECT: George had good <u>luck</u> when he first came to State University.

INCORRECT: A news was released about the hostages.
CORRECT: <u>News</u> was released about the hostages.

INCORRECT: Did you get a permission to take the placement test?
CORRECT: Did you get <u>permission</u> to take the placement test?

EXERCISES

Part A: Choose the correct answer.

Fire-resistant materials are used to retard _____ of modern aircraft in case of accidents.
  (A) a damage to the passenger cabin
  (B) that damages to the passenger cabin
  (C) damage to the passenger cabin
  (D) passenger cabin's damages

Part B: Choose the incorrect word or phrase and correct it.

A progress has been made toward finding a cure for AIDS.
  (A)   (B)   (C)   (D)

23 Singular and Plural Expressions of Noncount Nouns

Remember that the following singular and plural expressions are idiomatic:

a piece of advice	two pieces of advice
a piece of bread	two pieces of bread
a piece of equipment	two pieces of equipment
a piece of furniture	two pieces of furniture
a piece of information	two pieces of information
a piece of jewelry	two pieces of jewelry
a piece of luggage	two pieces of luggage
a piece of mail	two pieces of mail
a piece of music	two pieces of music
a piece of news	two pieces of news
a piece of toast	two pieces of toast
a loaf of bread	two loaves of bread
a slice of bread	two slices of bread
an ear of corn	two ears of corn
a bar of soap	two bars of soap
a bolt of lightning	two bolts of lightning
a clap of thunder	two claps of thunder
a gust of wind	two gusts of wind

	a	singular	of	noun (noncount)
A folk song is	a	piece	of	popular music

	number	plural	of	noun (noncount)
I ordered	twelve	bars	of	soap

Avoid using the noncount noun without the singular or plural idiom to express a singular or plural.

EXAMPLES

INCORRECT: A mail travels faster when the zip code is indicated on the envelope.

CORRECT: <u>A piece of mail</u> travels faster when the zip code is indicated on the envelope.

INCORRECT: There is a limit of two carry-on luggages for each passenger.

CORRECT: There is a limit of <u>two pieces of carry-on luggage</u> for each passenger.

INCORRECT: Each furniture in this display is on sale for half price.

CORRECT: <u>Each piece of furniture</u> in this display is on sale for half price.

INCORRECT: I'd like a steak, a salad, and a corn's ear with butter.

CORRECT: I'd like a steak, a salad, and <u>an ear of corn</u> with butter.

INCORRECT: The Engineering Department purchased a new equipment to simulate conditions in outer space.

CORRECT: The Engineering Department purchased <u>a new piece of equipment</u> to simulate conditions in outer space.

EXERCISES

Part A: Choose the correct answer.

Hybrids have one more _____ per plant than the other varieties.
    (A) corns
    (B) ear of corn
    (C) corn ears
    (D) corn's ears

Part B: Choose the incorrect word or phrase and correct it.

A few tiles on *Skylab* were the only equipments that failed
 (A)   (B)   (C)
to perform well in outer space.
 (D)

24   Infinitive and *-ing* Subjects

Remember that either an infinitive or an *-ing* form may be used as the subject of a sentence or a clause.

S (infinitive)	V	
To read a foreign language	is	even more difficult

S (*-ing*)	V	
Reading quickly and well	requires	practice

Avoid using a verb word instead of an infinitive or an *-ing* form in the subject. Avoid using *to* with an *-ing* form.

EXAMPLES

INCORRECT: To working provides people with personal satisfaction as well as money.

CORRECT: To work provides people with personal satisfaction as well as money.

or

Working provides people with personal satisfaction as well as money.

INCORRECT: The sneeze spreads germs.

CORRECT: To sneeze spreads germs.

or

Sneezing spreads germs.

INCORRECT: Shoplift is considered a serious crime.
CORRECT: <u>To shoplift</u> is considered a serious crime.
or
<u>Shoplifting</u> is considered a serious crime.

INCORRECT: The rest in the afternoon is a custom in many countries.
CORRECT: <u>To rest</u> in the afternoon is a custom in many countries.
or
<u>Resting</u> in the afternoon is a custom in many countries.

INCORRECT: To exercising makes most people feel better.
CORRECT: <u>To exercise</u> makes most people feel better.
or
<u>Exercising</u> makes most people feel better.

EXERCISES

Part A: Choose the correct answer.

_____ trees is a custom that many people engage in to celebrate Arbor Day.
(A) The plant
(B) Plant
(C) Planting
(D) To planting

Part B: Choose the incorrect word or phrase and correct it.

<u>Spell</u> <u>correctly</u> is easy with the aid of a number of
(A)   (B)
<u>word processing</u> programs for personal <u>computers</u>.
    (C)   (D)

25   Nominal *That* Clause

Remember that sometimes the subject of a verb is a single noun. Other times it is a long noun phrase or a long noun clause.

One example of a long noun clause is the *nominal that* clause. Like all clauses, the *nominal that* clause has a subject and verb. The *nominal that* clause functions as the main subject of the main verb which follows it.

Nominal *that* clause S	V	
That vitamin C prevents colds	is	well known

EXAMPLES

INCORRECT: That it is that she has known him for a long time influenced her decision.

CORRECT: <u>That she has known him for a long time</u> <u>influenced</u> her decision.

INCORRECT: It is that we need to move is sure.

CORRECT: <u>That we need to move</u> <u>is</u> sure.

INCORRECT: Is likely that the library is closed.

CORRECT: <u>That the library is closed</u> <u>is</u> likely.

INCORRECT: She will win is almost certain.

CORRECT: <u>That she will win</u> <u>is</u> almost certain.

INCORRECT: That is not fair seems obvious.

CORRECT: <u>That it is not fair</u> <u>seems</u> obvious.

EXERCISES

Part A: Choose the correct answer.

_____ migrate long distances is well documented.

(A) That it is birds

(B) That birds

(C) Birds that

(D) It is that birds

Part B: Choose the incorrect word or phrase and correct it.

That <u>it is</u> the moon influences only <u>one kind</u> of tide is not
    (A)   (B)

<u>generally</u> <u>known</u>.
   (C)   (D)

26 Noncount Nouns with Qualifying Phrases—*The*

Remember, *the* is used with count nouns. You have also learned that *the* can be used before an *-ing* noun that is followed by a qualifying phrase.

In addition, *the* can be used before a noncount noun with a qualifying phrase.

The	noncount noun	Qualifying Phrase	
The	art	of the Middle Ages	is on display

EXAMPLES

INCORRECT:	Poetry of Carl Sandburg is being read at the student union on Friday.
CORRECT:	The poetry of Carl Sandburg is being read at the student union on Friday.
INCORRECT:	Poverty of people in the rural areas is not as visible as that of people in the city.
CORRECT:	The poverty of people in the rural areas is not as visible as that of people in the city.
INCORRECT:	Science of genetic engineering is not very old.
CORRECT:	The science of genetic engineering is not very old.
INCORRECT:	History of this area is interesting.
CORRECT:	The history of this area is interesting.
INCORRECT:	Work of many people made the project a success.
CORRECT:	The work of many people made the project a success.

EXERCISES

Part A: Choose the correct answer.

_____ of Country-Western singers may be related to old English ballads.

(A) The music
(B) Music
(C) Their music
(D) Musics

Part B: Choose the incorrect word or phrase and correct it.

Philosophy of the ancient Greeks has been preserved in the
   (A)   (B)

scholarly writing of Western civilization.
    (C)   (D)

27 *No* Meaning *Not Any*

Remember that *no* means *not any*. It may be used with a singular or plural count noun or with a noncount noun.

no	noun (count singular) noun (count plural)	verb (singular) verb (plural)
No	tree	grows above the tree line
No	trees	grow above the tree line

no	noun (noncount)	verb (singular)	
No	art	is	on display today

Avoid using the negatives *not* or *none* instead of *no*. Avoid using a singular verb with a plural count noun.

EXAMPLES

INCORRECT: There is not reason to worry.
  CORRECT: There is <u>no reason</u> to worry.

INCORRECT: None news is good news.
  CORRECT: <u>No news</u> is good news.

INCORRECT: We have not a file under the name Wagner.
  CORRECT: We have <u>no file</u> under the name Wagner.

INCORRECT: None of cheating will be tolerated.
  CORRECT: <u>No cheating</u> will be tolerated.

INCORRECT: Bill told me that he has none friends.
  CORRECT: Bill told me that he has <u>no friends</u>.

EXERCISES

Part A: Choose the correct answer.

At Woolworth's first five-and-ten-cent store, _____ more than a dime.

    (A) neither items cost
    (B) items not cost
    (C) items none costing
    (D) no item costs

Part B: Choose the incorrect word or phrase and correct it.

Some religions <u>have</u> <u>none</u> deity but <u>are</u> philosophies that
           (A) (B)   (C)
function <u>instead of religions</u>.
          (D)

28   *Almost All of the* and *Most of the*

Remember that *almost all of the* and *most of the* mean all except a few, but *almost all of the* includes more.

almost all (of the) most (of the)	noun (count—plural)	verb (plural)	
Almost all (of the) Most (of the)	trees in our yard trees	are are	oaks oaks

almost all (of the) most (of the)	noun (noncount)	verb (singular)
Almost all (of the) Most (of the)	art by R. C. Gorman art by R. C. Gorman	is expensive is expensive

Avoid using *almost* without *all* or *all of the*. Avoid using *most of* without *the*.

EXAMPLES

INCORRECT: Almost the states have a sales tax.

  CORRECT: <u>Almost all of the</u> <u>states</u> have a sales tax.

or

Almost all states have a sales tax.

or

Most of the states have a sales tax.

or

Most states have a sales tax.

INCORRECT: Most of teachers at State University care about their students' progress.

  CORRECT: <u>Almost all of the</u> <u>teachers</u> at State University care about their students' progress.

or

Almost all teachers at State University care about their students' progress.

or

Most of the <u>teachers</u> at State University care about their students' progress.

or

Most <u>teachers</u> at State University care about their students' progress.

INCORRECT: My cousin told me that most of people who won the lottery got only a few dollars, not the grand prize.

CORRECT: My cousin told me that <u>almost all of the people</u> who won the lottery got only a few dollars, not the grand prize.

or

My cousin told me that <u>almost all people</u> who won the lottery got only a few dollars, not the grand prize.

or

My cousin told me that <u>most of the people</u> who won the lottery got only a few dollars, not the grand prize.

or

My cousin told me that <u>most people</u> who won the lottery got only a few dollars, not the grand prize.

INCORRECT: Most the dictionaries have information about pronunciation.

CORRECT: <u>Almost all of the dictionaries</u> have information about pronunciation.

or

<u>Almost all dictionaries</u> have information about pronunciation.

or

<u>Most of the dictionaries</u> have information about pronunciation.

or

<u>Most dictionaries</u> have information about pronunciation.

INCORRECT: Is it true that most Americans watches TV every night?

CORRECT: It is true that <u>almost all of the Americans</u> watch TV every night?

or

Is it true that <u>almost all Americans</u> watch TV every night?

or

Is it true that <u>most of the Americans</u> watch TV every night?

or

Is it true that <u>most Americans</u> watch TV every night?

EXERCISES

Part A: Choose the correct answer.

_____ fuel that is used today is a chemical form of solar energy.
(A) Most of
(B) The most
(C) Most
(D) Almost the

Part B: Choose the incorrect word or phrase and correct it.

<u>Almost</u> the plants <u>known to us</u> are made up of
  (A)   (B)
<u>a great many cells</u>, specialized <u>to perform</u> different tasks.
        (C)   (D)

29 Nouns that Function as Adjectives

Remember that when two nouns occur together, the first noun describes the second noun; that is, the first noun functions as an adjective. Adjectives do not change form, singular or plural.

	noun	noun
All of us are foreign	language	teachers

Avoid using a plural form for the first noun even when the second noun is plural. Avoid using a possessive form for the first noun.

EXAMPLES

INCORRECT: May I borrow some notebooks paper?
  CORRECT: May I borrow some <u>notebook paper</u>?

INCORRECT: All business' students must take the Graduate Management
             Admission Test.
  CORRECT: All <u>business students</u> must take the Graduate Management
             Admission Test.

INCORRECT: I forgot their telephone's number.
CORRECT: I forgot their <u>telephone number</u>.

INCORRECT: There is a sale at the shoes store.
CORRECT: There is a sale at the <u>shoe store</u>.

INCORRECT: Put the mail on the hall's table.
CORRECT: Put the mail on the <u>hall table</u>.

EXERCISES

Part A: Choose the correct answer.

_____ is cheaper for students who maintain a B average because they are a better risk than average or below-average students.

(A) Automobile's insurance
(B) Insurance of automobiles
(C) Automobile insurance
(D) Insurance automobile

Part B: Choose the incorrect word or phrase and correct it.

<u>Sex's education</u> is instituted to help the student <u>understand</u> the
   (A)   (B)
process of maturation, <u>to eliminate anxieties</u> <u>related</u> to
                          (C)   (D)
development, to learn values, and to prevent disease.

30   Hyphenated Adjectives

Remember that it is common for a number to appear as the first in a series of hyphenated adjectives. Each word in a hyphenated adjective is an adjective and does not change form, singular or plural.

	a	adjective	—	adjective	noun	
Agriculture 420 is	a	five	—	hour	class	

a	adjective	—	adjective	—	adjective	noun	
A	sixty	—	year	—	old	employee	may retire

Avoid using a plural form for any of the adjectives joined by hyphens even when the noun that follows is plural.

EXAMPLES

INCORRECT: A three-minutes call anywhere in the United States costs less than a dollar when you dial it yourself.

CORRECT: A three-minute call anywhere in the United States costs less than a dollar when you dial it yourself.

INCORRECT: They have a four-months-old baby.
CORRECT: They have a four-month-old baby.

INCORRECT: Can you make change for a twenty-dollars bill?
CORRECT: Can you make change for a twenty-dollar bill?

INCORRECT: A two-doors car is cheaper than a four-doors model.
CORRECT: A two-door car is cheaper than a four-door model.

INCORRECT: I have to write a one-thousand-words paper this weekend.
CORRECT: I have to write a one-thousand-word paper this weekend.

EXERCISES

Part A: Choose the correct answer.

The evolution of vertebrates suggests development from a very simple heart in fish to a _____ in man.
  (A) four-chamber heart
  (B) four-chambers heart
  (C) four-chamber hearts
  (D) four-chamber's heart

Part B: Choose the incorrect word or phrase and correct it.

The MX is a four-stages rocket with an 8000-mile range,
      (A)   (B)   (C)

larger than that of the Minuteman.
(D)

31 Cause-and-Result—So

Remember that *so* is used before an adjective or an adverb followed by *that*. The *so* clause expresses cause. The *that* clause expresses result.

CAUSE				RESULT			
S	V	so	adverb adjective	that	S	V	
She	got up	so	late	that	she	missed	her bus
The music	was	so	loud	that	we	couldn't talk	

Avoid using *as* or *too* instead of *so* in clauses of cause. Avoid using *as* instead of *that* in clauses of result.

EXAMPLES

INCORRECT: He is so slow as he never gets to class on time.
CORRECT: He is <u>so slow that</u> he never gets to class on time.

INCORRECT: This suitcase is as heavy that I can hardly carry it.
CORRECT: This suitcase is <u>so heavy that</u> I can hardly carry it.

INCORRECT: We arrived so late as Professor Baker had already called the roll.
CORRECT: We arrived <u>so late that</u> Professor Baker had already called the roll.

INCORRECT: He drives so fast as no one likes to ride with him.
CORRECT: He drives <u>so fast that</u> no one likes to ride with him.

INCORRECT: Preparing frozen foods is too easy that anyone can do it.
CORRECT: Preparing frozen foods is <u>so easy that</u> anyone can do it.

EXERCISES

Part A: Choose the correct answer.

Oil paints are _____ they have become the most popular painter's colors.

    (A) so versatile and durable that
    (B) so versatile and durable than
    (C) such versatile and durable as
    (D) such versatile and durable

Part B: Choose the incorrect word or phrase and correct it.

<u>By the mid-nineteenth century</u>, land was <u>such expensive</u> in
          (A)   (B)

large cities that architects began to <u>conserve</u> space <u>by designing</u>
                              (C)   (D)

skyscrapers.

32   Exact Similarity—*the Same as* and *the Same*

Remember that *the same as* and *the same* have the same meaning, but *the same as* is used between the two nouns compared, and *the same* is used after the two nouns or a plural noun.

noun		the same as	noun
This coat	is	the same as	that one

noun		noun		the same
This coat	and	that one	are	the same

noun (plural)		the same
These coats	are	the same

Avoid using *to* and *like* instead of *as*. Avoid using *the same* between the two nouns compared.

EXAMPLES

INCORRECT:	That car is almost the same like mine.
CORRECT:	That car is almost <u>the same as</u> mine.
	or
	That car and mine are almost <u>the same</u>.

INCORRECT:	My briefcase is exactly the same that yours.
CORRECT:	My briefcase is exactly <u>the same as</u> yours.
	or
	My briefcase and yours are exactly <u>the same</u>.

INCORRECT:	Is your book the same to mine?
CORRECT:	Is your book <u>the same as</u> mine?
	or
	Are your book and mine <u>the same</u>?

INCORRECT:	Are this picture and the one on your desk same?
CORRECT:	Are this picture and the one on your desk <u>the same</u>?
	or
	Is this picture <u>the same as</u> <u>the one</u> on your desk?

INCORRECT:	The teacher gave Martha a failing grade on her composition because it was the same a composition he had already read.
CORRECT:	The teacher gave Martha a failing grade on her composition because it was <u>the same as</u> <u>a composition</u> he had already read.
	or
	The teacher gave Martha a failing grade on her composition because it and a composition he had already read were <u>the same</u>.

EXERCISES

Part A: Choose the correct answer.

Although we often use "speed" and "velocity" interchangeably, in a technical sense, "speed" is not always _____ "velocity."
(A) alike
(B) the same as
(C) similar
(D) as

Part B: Choose the incorrect word or phrase and correct it.

When two products are <u>basically</u> <u>the same as</u>, <u>advertising</u> can
                      (A)   (B)   (C)
<u>influence</u> the public's choice.
   (D)

33   General Similarity—*Like* and *Alike*

Remember that *like* and *alike* have the same meaning, but *like* is used between the two nouns compared, and *alike* is used after the two nouns or a plural noun.

noun		like	noun
This coat	is	like	that one

noun		noun		alike
This coat	and	that one	are	alike

noun (plural)		alike
These coats	are	alike

Avoid using *as* instead of *like*. Avoid using *like* after the two nouns compared.

EXAMPLES

INCORRECT: The weather feels as spring.
  CORRECT: The weather feels <u>like</u> <u>spring</u>.

INCORRECT: These suits are like.
  CORRECT: This suit is <u>like</u> <u>that suit</u>.
                    or
            These suits are <u>alike</u>.

INCORRECT: Your recipe for chicken is like to a recipe that my mother has.
  CORRECT: Your recipe for chicken is <u>like</u> <u>a recipe</u> that my mother has.
                    or
            Your recipe for chicken and a recipe that my mother has are <u>alike</u>.

INCORRECT: I want to buy some shoes same like the ones I have on.
CORRECT: I want to buy some shoes <u>like</u> <u>the ones</u> I have on.
or
The shoes I want to buy and the shoes I have on are <u>alike</u>.

INCORRECT: Anthony and his brother don't look like.
CORRECT: Anthony doesn't look <u>like</u> <u>his brother</u>.
or
Anthony and his brother don't look <u>alike</u>.

EXERCISES

Part A: Choose the correct answer.

Although they are smaller, chipmunks are _____ most other ground squirrels.

(A) like to
(B) like as
(C) like
(D) alike

Part B: Choose the incorrect word or phrase and correct it.

<u>The first</u> living structures <u>to appear</u> on Earth thousands of years
   (A)   (B)
<u>ago</u> were <u>alike</u> viruses.
(C)   (D)

34   General Difference—*to Differ from*

Remember that *differ* is a verb and must change forms to agree with the subject.

	DIFFER	from	
This one	differs	from	the rest

Avoid using BE with *differ*. Avoid using *than*, *of*, or *to* after *differ*.

EXAMPLES

INCORRECT: Sharon is different of other women I know.
  CORRECT: Sharon <u>is different from</u> other women I know.
                        or
             Sharon <u>differs from</u> other women I know.

INCORRECT: Do you have anything a little different to these?
  CORRECT: Do you <u>have</u> anything a little <u>different from</u> these?
                        or
             Do you have anything that <u>differs</u> a little <u>from</u> these?

INCORRECT: The campus at State University different from that of City
             College.
  CORRECT: The campus at State University <u>differs from</u> that of City
             College.
                        or
             The campus at State University <u>is different from</u> that of City
             College.

INCORRECT: Jayne's apartment is very differs from Bill's even though they
             are in the same building.
  CORRECT: Jayne's apartment <u>is</u> very <u>different from</u> Bill's even though
             they are in the same building.
                        or
             Jayne's apartment <u>differs from</u> Bill's even though they are in
             the same building.

INCORRECT: Customs differ one region of the country to another.
  CORRECT: Customs <u>differ from</u> one region of the country to another.
                        or
             Customs <u>are</u> <u>different from</u> one region of the country to
             another.

EXERCISES

Part A: Choose the correct answer.

Modern blimps like the famous Goodyear blimps _____ the first
ones in that they are filled with helium instead of hydrogen.
   (A) differ from
   (B) different from
   (C) is different from
   (D) different

Part B: Choose the incorrect word or phrase and correct it.

Crocodiles <u>different from</u> alligators in that they have
   (A)   (B)
<u>pointed snouts</u> and long lower teeth that stick out when their
     (C)
mouths <u>are closed</u>.
         (D)

PROBLEM 35   Comparative Estimates— Multiple Numbers

Remember that the following are examples of multiple numbers:

half	four times
twice	five times
three times	ten times

	multiple	as	much many	as	
Fresh fruit costs	twice	as	much	as	canned fruit
We have	half	as	many	as	we need

Avoid using *so* instead of *as* after a multiple. Avoid using *more than* instead of *as much as* or *as many as*. Avoid using the multiple after *as much* and *as many*.

EXAMPLES

INCORRECT: This one is prettier, but it costs twice more than the other one.
CORRECT: This one is prettier, but it costs <u>twice as much as</u> the other one.

INCORRECT: The rent at College Apartments is only half so much as you pay here.
CORRECT: The rent at College Apartments is only <u>half as much as</u> you pay here.

INCORRECT:	Bob found a job that paid as much twice as he made working at the library.
CORRECT:	Bob found a job that paid <u>twice as much as</u> he made working at the library.
INCORRECT:	The price was very reasonable; I would gladly have paid three times more than he asked.
CORRECT:	The price was very reasonable; I would gladly have paid <u>three times as much as</u> he asked.
INCORRECT:	We didn't buy the car because they wanted as much twice as it was worth.
CORRECT:	We didn't buy the car because they wanted <u>twice as much as</u> it was worth.

EXERCISES

Part A: Choose the correct answer.

After the purchase of the Louisiana Territory, the United States had
_____ it had previously owned.

(A) twice more land than
(B) two times more land than
(C) twice as much land as
(D) two times much land than

Part B: Choose the incorrect word or phrase and correct it.

With American prices for sugar at three times <u>as much</u> the
                                              (A)
world price, manufacturers <u>are</u> beginning <u>to use</u> fructose
                           (B)   (C)
blended with pure sugar, <u>or</u> sucrose.
                         (D)

36 Comparative Estimates— *More Than* and *Less Than*

Remember that *more than* or *less than* is used before a specific number to express an estimate that may be a little more or a little less than the number.

	more than	number	
Steve has	more than	a thousand	coins in his collection

	less than	number	
Andy has	less than	a dozen	coins in his pocket

Avoid using *more* or *less* without *than* in estimates. Avoid using *as* instead of *than*.

EXAMPLES

INCORRECT: More one hundred people came to the meeting.
CORRECT: <u>More than one hundred</u> people came to the meeting.

INCORRECT: We have lived in the United States for as less than seven years.
CORRECT: We have lived in the United States for <u>less than seven</u> years.

INCORRECT: The main library has more as one million volumes.
CORRECT: The main library has <u>more than one million</u> volumes.

INCORRECT: A new shopping center on the north side will have five hundred shops more than.
CORRECT: A new shopping center on the north side will have <u>more than five hundred</u> shops.

INCORRECT: There are most than fifty students in the lab, but only two computers.
CORRECT: There are <u>more than fifty</u> students in the lab, but only two computers.

Exercises

Part A: Choose the correct answer.

In the Great Smoky Mountains, one can see _____ 150 different kinds of trees.
   (A) more than
   (B) as much as
   (C) up as
   (D) as many to

Part B: Choose the incorrect word or phrase and correct it.

Pelé scored <u>more as</u> 1280 goals <u>during his career</u>, <u>gaining</u> a
            (A)   (B)   (C)
reputation as <u>the best</u> soccer player of all time.
             (D)

37   Comparative Estimates—*As Many As*

Remember that *as many as* is used before a specific number to express an estimate that does not exceed the number.

	as many as	number	
We should have	as many as	five hundred	applications

Avoid using *as many* instead of *as many as*. Avoid using *much* instead of *many* before a specific number.

Note: Comparative estimates with *as much as* are also used before a specific number that refers to weight, distance, or money. For example, *as much as* ten pounds, *as much as* two miles, or *as much as* twenty dollars.

Examples

INCORRECT: We expect as much as thirty people to come.
  CORRECT: We expect <u>as many as</u> <u>thirty</u> people to come.

INCORRECT: There are as many fifteen thousand students attending summer school.

CORRECT: There are <u>as many as</u> <u>fifteen thousand</u> students attending summer school.

INCORRECT: The children can see as much as twenty-five baby animals in the nursery at the zoo.

CORRECT: The children can see <u>as many as</u> <u>twenty-five</u> baby animals in the nursery at the zoo.

INCORRECT: Many as ten planes have sat in line waiting to take off.

CORRECT: <u>As many as</u> <u>ten</u> planes have sat in line waiting to take off.

INCORRECT: State University offers as much as two hundred major fields of study.

CORRECT: State University offers <u>as many as</u> <u>two hundred</u> major fields of study.

EXERCISES

Part A: Choose the correct answer.

It has been estimated that _____ one hundred thousand men participated in the gold rush of 1898.

(A) approximate
(B) until
(C) as many as
(D) more

Part B: Choose the incorrect word or phrase and correct it.

It is generally accepted that the common cold <u>is caused</u> <u>by</u>
                                       (A)   (B)

<u>as much as</u> forty strains of viruses <u>that</u> may be present in the air
  (C)   (D)

at all times.

38 Degrees of Comparison—
Superlative Adjectives

Remember that superlatives are used to compare more than two.

	the	most (least) adjective (two + syllables) adjective -*est* (one syllable) adjective -*est* (two + syllables ending in -*y*)
An essay test is	the	most difficult
An essay test is	the	hardest
An essay test is	the	trickiest

Avoid using a comparative -*er* form when three or more are compared.

EXAMPLES

INCORRECT: She is more prettier than all of the girls in our class.
CORRECT: She is the prettiest of all of the girls in our class.

INCORRECT: New York is the larger of all American cities.
CORRECT: New York is the largest of all American cities.

INCORRECT: Of all of the candidates, Alex is probably the less qualified.
CORRECT: Of all of the candidates, Alex is probably the least qualified.

INCORRECT: Although there are a number of interesting findings, a most significant results are in the abstract.
CORRECT: Although there are a number of interesting findings, the most significant results are in the abstract.

INCORRECT: In my opinion, the more beautiful place in Oregon is Mount Hood.
CORRECT: In my opinion, the most beautiful place in Oregon is Mount Hood.

EXERCISES

Part A: Choose the correct answer.

The blue whale is _____ known animal, reaching a length of more than one hundred feet.
(A) the large
(B) the larger
(C) the largest
(D) most largest

Part B: Choose the incorrect answer and correct it.

<u>The</u> <u>more</u> important theorem of all in plane geometry <u>is</u>
(A) (B)   (C)
<u>the</u> Pythagorean Theorem.
(D)

39   Degrees of Comparison—Irregular Adjectives

Remember that some very common adjectives have irregular forms. Some of them are listed here for you.

Adjective	Comparative— to compare two	Superlative— to compare three or more
bad	worse	the worst
far	farther	the farthest
	further	the furthest
good	better	the best
little	less	the least
many	more	the most
much	more	the most

	irregular comparative	than	
This ice cream is	better	than	the other brands

	irregular superlative	
This ice cream is	the best	of all

Avoid using a regular form instead of an irregular form for these adjectives.

EXAMPLES

INCORRECT: The lab is more far from the bus stop than the library.
CORRECT: The lab is <u>farther from</u> the bus stop than the library.
or
The lab is <u>further from</u> the bus stop than the library.

INCORRECT: The badest accident in the history of the city occurred last night on the North Freeway.
CORRECT: <u>The worst</u> accident in the history of the city occurred last night on the North Freeway.

INCORRECT: These photographs are very good, but that one is the better of all.
CORRECT: These photographs are very good, but that one is <u>the best</u> of all.

INCORRECT: Please give me much sugar than you did last time.
CORRECT: Please give me <u>more</u> sugar than you did last time.

INCORRECT: This composition is more good than your last one.
CORRECT: This composition is <u>better</u> than your last one.

EXERCISES

Part A: Choose the correct answer.

_____ apples are grown in Washington State.
(A) Best
(B) The most good
(C) The best
(D) The better

Part B: Choose the incorrect word or phrase and correct it.

<u>Because</u> a felony is <u>more bad</u> than a misdemeanor, the
  (A)   (B)

punishment is <u>more severe</u>, and often includes a jail sentence
                        (C)

<u>as well as</u> a fine.
  (D)

40   Double Comparatives

Remember that when two comparatives are used together, the first comparative expresses cause and the second comparative expresses result. A comparative is *more* or *less* with an adjective, or an adjective with *-er*.

CAUSE				RESULT			
The	comparative	S	V,	the	comparative	S	V
The	more	you	review,	the	easier	the patterns	will be

Avoid using *as* instead of *the*. Avoid using the **incorrect** form $\boxed{lesser}$. Avoid omitting *the*. Avoid omitting *-er* from the adjective.

EXAMPLES

INCORRECT: The more you study during the semester, the lesser you have to study the week before exams.

CORRECT: <u>The more</u> you study during the semester, <u>the less</u> you have to study the week before exams.

INCORRECT: The faster we finish, the soon we can leave.

CORRECT: <u>The faster</u> we finish, <u>the sooner</u> we can leave.

INCORRECT: The less one earns, the lesser one must pay in income taxes.

CORRECT: <u>The less</u> one earns, <u>the less</u> one must pay in income taxes.

INCORRECT: The louder he shouted, less he convinced anyone.

CORRECT: <u>The louder</u> he shouted, <u>the less</u> he convinced anyone.

INCORRECT: The more you practice speaking, the well you will do it.

CORRECT: <u>The more</u> you practice speaking, <u>the better</u> you will do it.

EXERCISES

Part A: Choose the correct answer.

It is generally true that the lower the stock market falls, _____.
  (A) higher the price of gold rises
  (B) the price of gold rises high
  (C) the higher the price of gold rises
  (D) rises high the price of gold

Part B: Choose the incorrect word or phrase and correct it.

The higher the solar activity, <u>the intense</u> <u>the auroras</u> or polar
                               (A)   (B)
light displays in the skies <u>near</u> <u>the Earth's geomagnetic poles</u>.
                            (C)   (D)

41   Illogical Comparatives—General Similarity and Difference

Remember that comparisons must be made with logically comparable nouns. You can't compare *the climate* in the North with *the South*. You must compare *the climate* in the North with *the climate* in the South.

Remember that *that of* and *those of* are used instead of repeating a noun to express a logical comparative. An example with *different from* appears below.

noun (singular)		different	from	that	
Football in the U.S.	is	different	from	that	in other countries

noun (plural)		different	from	those	
The rules	are	different	from	those	of soccer

Avoid omitting *that* and *those*. Avoid using *than* instead of *from* with *different*.

EXAMPLES

INCORRECT: The food in my country is very different than that in the
United States.

CORRECT: The food in my country is very <u>different from that</u> in the
United States.

INCORRECT: The classes at my university are very different from State
University.

CORRECT: The classes at my university are very <u>different from those</u> at
State University.

INCORRECT: The English that is spoken in Canada is similar to the United
States.

CORRECT: The English that is spoken in Canada is <u>similar to that</u> of the
United States.

INCORRECT: Drugstores here are not like at home.

CORRECT: Drugstores here are not <u>like those</u> at home.

INCORRECT: The time in New York City differs three hours from Los
Angeles.

CORRECT: The time in New York City <u>differs</u> three hours <u>from that</u> of
Los Angeles.

EXERCISES

Part A: Choose the correct answer.

One's fingerprints are _____.

(A) different from those of any other person

(B) different from any other person

(C) different any other person

(D) differs from another person

Part B: Choose the incorrect word or phrase and correct it.

Perhaps the colonists were <u>looking for</u> a climate <u>like England</u>,
                         (A)   (B)

when they decided <u>to settle</u> the North American continent
                       (C)

<u>instead of</u> the South American continent.
  (D)

42   Addition—*Besides*

Remember that *besides* means *in addition to*. *Beside* means *near*.

besides	noun adjective	
Besides	our dog,	we have two cats and a canary
Besides	white,	we stock green and blue

	beside	noun
We sat	beside	the teacher

Avoid using *beside* instead of *besides* to mean *in addition*.

EXAMPLES

INCORRECT: Beside Marge, three couples are invited.
  CORRECT: <u>Besides</u> Marge, three couples are invited.

INCORRECT: Beside Domino's, four other pizza places deliver.
  CORRECT: <u>Besides</u> Domino's, four other pizza places deliver.

INCORRECT: To lead a well-balanced life, you need to have other interests
              beside studying.
  CORRECT: To lead a well balanced life, you need to have other interests
              <u>besides</u> studying.

INCORRECT: Beside taxi service, there isn't any public transportation in
              town.
  CORRECT: <u>Besides</u> taxi service, there isn't any public transportation in
              town.

INCORRECT: Janice has lots of friends beside her roommate.
  CORRECT: Janice has lots of friends <u>besides</u> her roommate.

EXERCISES

Part A: Choose the correct answer.

_____ a mayor, many city governments employ a city manager.
(A) Beside
(B) Besides
(C) And
(D) Also

Part B: Choose the incorrect word or phrase and correct it.

<u>To receive</u> a degree from an American university, one must take
  (A)

many courses <u>beside</u> <u>those</u> in <u>one's</u> major field.
     (B)   (C)   (D)

43 Cause—*Because of* and *Because*

Remember that *because of* is a prepositional phrase. It introduces a noun or a noun phrase. *Because* is a conjunction. It introduces a clause with a subject and a verb.

	because	S	V
They decided to stay at home	because	the weather	was bad

or

	because of	noun
They decided to stay at home	because of	the weather

Avoid using *because of* before a subject and verb. Avoid using *because* before a noun which is not followed by a verb.

EXAMPLES

INCORRECT: Classes will be canceled tomorrow because a national holiday.
CORRECT: Classes will be canceled tomorrow <u>because it is</u> a national holiday.
                or
           Classes will be canceled tomorrow <u>because of</u>
           <u>a national holiday</u>.

INCORRECT: She was absent because of her cold was worse.
  CORRECT: She was absent <u>because</u> <u>her cold was</u> worse.

or

She was absent <u>because of</u> <u>her cold.</u>

INCORRECT: John's family is very happy because his being awarded a scholarship.
  CORRECT: John's family is very happy <u>because</u> <u>he has been awarded</u> a scholarship.

or

John's family is very happy <u>because of</u> <u>his being awarded</u> a scholarship.

INCORRECT: She didn't buy it because of the price was too high.
  CORRECT: She didn't buy it <u>because</u> <u>the price was</u> too high.

or

She didn't buy it <u>because of</u> <u>the price.</u>

INCORRECT: It was difficult to see the road clearly because the rain.
  CORRECT: It was difficult to see the road clearly <u>because</u> <u>it was raining</u>.

or

It was difficult to see the road clearly <u>because of</u>
<u>the rain.</u>

EXERCISES

Part A: Choose the correct answer.

_____ in the cultivation of a forest, trees need more careful planning than any other crop does.
  (A) Because the time and area involved
  (B) For the time and area involving
  (C) Because of the time and area involved
  (D) As a cause of the time and area involved

Part B: Choose the incorrect word or phrase and correct it.

Many roads and railroads <u>were built</u> in the 1880s <u>because of</u> the
                         (A)   (B)   (C)
industrial cities needed a network <u>to link</u> them with sources of
                                     (D)
supply.

44 Correlative Conjunctions—Inclusives
not only . . . but also

Remember that *not only . . . but also* are correlative conjunctions. They are used together to include two parallel structures (two nouns, adjectives, verbs, adverbs).

	not only	parallel structure	but also	parallel structure
One should take	not only	cash	but also	traveler's checks
Checks are	not only	safer	but also	more convenient

Avoid using *only not* instead of *not only*. Avoid using *but* instead of *but also*.

Avoid using the incorrect pattern:

not only	parallel structure	but	parallel structure	also
not only	cash safer	but but	traveler's checks more convenient	also also

EXAMPLES

INCORRECT: The program provides only not theoretical classes but also practical training.

CORRECT: The program provides <u>not only</u> theoretical classes <u>but also</u> practical training.

INCORRECT: The new models are not only less expensive but more efficient also.

CORRECT: The new models are <u>not only</u> less expensive <u>but also</u> more efficient.

INCORRECT: The objective is not to identify the problem but also to solve it.

CORRECT: The objective is <u>not only</u> to identify the problem <u>but also</u> to solve it.

INCORRECT: Not only her parents but her brothers and sisters also live in Wisconsin.

CORRECT: Not only her parents but also her brothers and sisters live in Wisconsin.

INCORRECT: To complete his physical education credits, John took not only swimming also golf.

CORRECT: To complete his physical education credits, John took not only swimming but also golf.

EXERCISES

Part A: Choose the correct answer.

Amniocentesis can be used not only to diagnose fetal disorders _____ the sex of the unborn child with 95 percent accuracy.

(A) but determining
(B) but also determining
(C) but to determine
(D) but also to determine

Part B: Choose the incorrect word or phrase and correct it.

The deadbolt is the best lock for entry doors because it is not only
           (A)   (B)   (C)
inexpensive but installation is easy.
                   (D)

45   Future Result—*When*

Remember that *when* introduces a clause of condition for future result.

RESULT		CONDITION		
S	V (present) V (will + verb word)	when	S	V (present)
The temperature	drops	when	the sun	sets
The temperature	will drop	when	the sun	sets

Avoid using *will* instead of a present verb after *when*.

EXAMPLES

INCORRECT: I will call you when I will return from my country.
  CORRECT: I will call you <u>when</u> I <u>return</u> from my country.

INCORRECT: Marilyn plans to work in her family's store when she will get her M.B.A.
  CORRECT: Marilyn plans to work in her family's store <u>when</u> <u>she</u> <u>gets</u> her M.B.A.

INCORRECT: He will probably buy some more computer software when he will get paid.
  CORRECT: He will probably buy some more computer software <u>when</u> <u>he</u> <u>gets</u> paid.

INCORRECT: She will feel a lot better when she will stop smoking.
  CORRECT: She will feel a lot better <u>when</u> <u>she</u> <u>stops</u> smoking.

INCORRECT: When Gary will go to State University, he will be a teaching assistant.
  CORRECT: <u>When</u> <u>Gary</u> <u>goes</u> to State University, he will be a teaching assistant.

EXERCISES

Part A: Choose the correct answer.

Bacterial spores germinate and sprout _____ favorable conditions of temperature and food supply.
  (A) when encountering of
  (B) when they encounter
  (C) when they will encounter
  (D) when the encounter of

Part B: Choose the incorrect word or phrase and correct it.

In <u>most states</u> insurance agents <u>must pass</u> an examination
     (A)   (B)
<u>to be licensed</u> when they <u>will complete</u> their training.
     (C)   (D)

46 Indirect Questions

Remember that question words can be used as conjunctions. Question words introduce a clause of indirect question.

Question words include the following:

who	*why*
what	*how*
what time	*how long*
when	*how many*
where	*how much*

S	V	question word	S	V
I	don't remember	what	her name	is

V	S		question word	S	V
Do	you	remember	what	her name	is?

Avoid using *do*, *does*, or *did* after the question word. Avoid using the verb before the subject after the question word.

EXAMPLES

INCORRECT:	I didn't understood what did he say.
CORRECT:	I didn't understand <u>what</u> he <u>said</u>.

INCORRECT:	Do you know how much do they cost?
CORRECT:	Do you know <u>how much</u> they <u>cost</u>?

INCORRECT:	I wonder when is her birthday.
CORRECT:	I wonder <u>when</u> her birthday <u>is</u>.

INCORRECT:	Could you please tell me where is the post office?
CORRECT:	Could you please tell me <u>where</u> the post office <u>is</u>?

INCORRECT:	Can they tell you what time does the movie start?
CORRECT:	Can they tell you <u>what time</u> the movie <u>starts</u>?

EXERCISES

Part A: Choose the correct answer.

Recently, there have been several outbreaks of disease like Legionnaire's syndrome, and doctors don't know _____.
(A) what is the cause
(B) the cause is what
(C) is what the cause
(D) what the cause is

Part B: Choose the incorrect word or phrase and correct it.

In Ground Control Approach, <u>the air traffic controller</u> <u>informs</u>
                                     (A)   (B)
the pilot how far <u>is the plane</u> from <u>the touchdown point</u>.
                       (C)   (D)

47 Negative Emphasis

Remember that negatives include phrases like *not one, not once, not until, never, never again, only rarely*, and *very seldom*. Negatives answer the question, *how often?* They are used at the beginning of a statement to express emphasis. Auxiliaries must agree with verbs and subjects.

negative	auxiliary	S	V	
Never	have	I	seen	so much snow

Avoid using a subject before the auxiliary in this pattern.

EXAMPLES

INCORRECT: Never again they will stay in that hotel.
  CORRECT: <u>Never again will they stay</u> in that hotel.

INCORRECT: Only rarely an accident has occurred.
  CORRECT: <u>Only rarely has an accident occurred.</u>

INCORRECT: Very seldom a movie can hold my attention like this one.
  CORRECT: <u>Very seldom</u> <u>can</u> <u>a movie</u> <u>hold</u> my attention like this one.

INCORRECT: Not one paper she has finished on time.
  CORRECT: <u>Not one</u> paper <u>has</u> <u>she</u> <u>finished</u> on time.

INCORRECT: Not once Steve and Jan have invited us to their house.
  CORRECT: <u>Not once</u> <u>have</u> <u>Steve and Jan</u> <u>invited</u> us to their house.

EXERCISES

Part A: Choose the correct answer.

Not until the Triassic Period _____.
   (A) the first primitive mammals did develop
   (B) did the first primitive mammals develop
   (C) did develop the first primitive mammals
   (D) the first primitive mammals develop

Part B: Chose the incorrect word or phrase and correct it.

<u>Only</u> rarely <u>wins the same major league baseball team</u> the
 (A)   (B)
World Series <u>two years</u> <u>in a row</u>.
               (C)   (D)

48   Duration—*For* and *Since*

Remember that *for* is used before a quantity of time. *For* expresses duration. *For* answers the question, *how long? Since* is used before a specific time. *Since* expresses duration too, but *since* answers the question, *beginning when?*

Remember that a quantity of time may be several days—a month, two years, etc. A specific time may be Wednesday, July, 1960, etc. You will notice that the structure *HAVE* and a participle is often used with adverbs of duration.

S	HAVE	participle		for	quantity of time
She	has	been	in the U.S.	for	six months

S	HAVE	participle		since	specific time
She	has	been	in the U.S.	since	June

Avoid using *for* before specific times. Avoid using *before* after HAVE and a participle.

EXAMPLES

INCORRECT: Mary has been on a diet since three weeks.
  CORRECT: Mary has been on a diet <u>for three weeks.</u>

INCORRECT: She has been living here before April.
  CORRECT: She has been living here <u>since April.</u>

INCORRECT: We haven't seen him since almost a year.
  CORRECT: We haven't seen him <u>for almost a year</u>.

INCORRECT: We have known each other before 1974.
  CORRECT: We have known each other <u>since 1974</u>.

INCORRECT: He has studied English since five years.
  CORRECT: He has studied English <u>for five years</u>.

EXERCISES

Part A: Choose the correct answer.

Penguins, the most highly specialized of all aquatic birds, may live _____ twenty years.
    (A) before
    (B) since
    (C) for
    (D) from

Part B: Choose the incorrect word or phrase and correct it.

Because national statistics on crime have only been kept
<u>for 1930,</u> <u>it</u> is not possible <u>to make</u> judgments about crime
    (A)   (B)   (C)
<u>during the early years</u> of the nation.
          (D)

49   Generalization—*As a Whole* and *Wholly*

Remember that *as a whole* means generally. *Wholly* means completely. *As a whole* is often used at the beginning of a sentence or a clause. *Wholly* is often used after the auxiliary or main verb.

generally as a whole	S	V	
As a whole	the news	is	correct

S	V	completely wholly	
The news	is	wholly	correct

Avoid using *wholly* instead of *as a whole* at the beginning of a sentence or clause to mean generally. Avoid using *as whole* instead of *as a whole.*

EXAMPLES

INCORRECT: Wholly, we are in agreement.
  CORRECT: As a whole, we are in agreement.
        (generally)

INCORRECT: The house and all of its contents was as a whole consumed by the fire.
  CORRECT: The house and all of its contents was wholly consumed by the fire.
        (generally)

INCORRECT: The teams are not rated equally, but, wholly, they are evenly matched.
  CORRECT: The teams are not rated equally, but, as a whole, they are evenly matched.
        (generally)

INCORRECT: Wholly, Dan's operation proved to be successful.
  CORRECT: As a whole, Dan's operation proved to be successful.
        (generally)

INCORRECT: As whole, people try to be helpful to tourists.
  CORRECT: <u>As a whole,</u> people try to be helpful to tourists.
         (generally)

EXERCISES

Part A: Choose the correct answer.

_____ the Gulf Stream is warmer than the ocean water surrounding it.
(A) Wholly
(B) Whole
(C) As a whole
(D) A whole as

Part B: Choose the incorrect word or phrase and correct it.

Although <u>there are</u> exceptions, <u>as whole,</u> the male of the bird
           (A)   (B)
species is <u>more</u> <u>brilliantly</u> colored.
           (C)   (D)

50 Sentences and Clauses

Remember that a main clause, also called an independent clause, can function as a separate sentence. A subordinate clause, also called a dependent clause, must be attached to a main clause. A dependent clause is often marked with the clause marker *that*.

SENTENCE		
Main Clause (Sentence)	Clause Marker - - - - - - - - - - - Dependent Clause	
We were glad	that	the box came

Avoid using the clause marker with dependent clauses as sentences. Avoid using the clause marker *that* with a sentence that has no dependent clause following it.

EXAMPLES

INCORRECT: Utensils and condiments that are found on the table by the door.

CORRECT: <u>Utensils and condiments</u> <u>are found</u> on the table by the door.

INCORRECT: During final exam week, that the library when opening all night.

CORRECT: During final exam week, <u>the library</u> <u>is open</u> all night.

INCORRECT: The weather that is very rainy this time of year.

CORRECT: <u>The weather</u> <u>is</u> very rainy this time of year.

INCORRECT: All of the dorms that are located on East Campus.

CORRECT: All of the <u>dorms</u> <u>are located</u> on East Campus.

INCORRECT: During our vacation, that we suspended the newspaper delivery.

CORRECT: During our vacation, <u>we</u> <u>suspended</u> the newspaper delivery.

EXERCISES

Part A: Choose the correct answer.

Of all the cities in Texas, _____.
   (A) that San Antonio is probably the most picturesque
   (B) San Antonio is probably the most picturesque
   (C) probably San Antonio the most picturesque
   (D) the most picturesque probably that San Antonio

Part B: Choose the incorrect word or phrase and correct it.

<u>Thunder</u> <u>that</u> is audible from distances as far away <u>as</u> ten <u>miles</u>.
   (A)   (B)   (C)   (D)

STYLE

Style is a general term that includes elements larger than a single grammatical pattern or structure. In most grammar books, *style* means *sentence structure*—that is, how the parts of a sentence relate to each other.

Some of the most important elements of style are summarized in this review section.

Point of View—Verbs

In all patterns, maintain a point of view, either present or past.

Avoid changing from present to past tense, or from past to present tense in the same sentence.

EXAMPLES

INCORRECT: He was among the few who want to continue working on the project.

CORRECT: He <u>is</u> among the few who <u>want</u> to continue working on the project.

or

He <u>was</u> among the few who <u>wanted</u> to continue working on the project.

INCORRECT: It is an accepted custom for a man to open the door when he accompanied a woman.

CORRECT: It <u>is</u> an accepted custom for a man to open the door when he <u>accompanies</u> a woman.

or

It <u>was</u> an accepted custom for a man to open the door when he <u>accompanied</u> a woman.

INCORRECT: She closed the door and hurries away to class.

CORRECT: She <u>closes</u> the door and <u>hurries</u> away to class.

or

She <u>closed</u> the door and <u>hurried</u> away to class.

INCORRECT: We receive several applications a day and with them had been copies of transcripts and degrees.

CORRECT: We <u>receive</u> several applications a day and with them <u>are</u> copies of transcripts and degrees.

or

We <u>received</u> several applications a day and with them <u>were</u> copies of transcripts and degrees.

INCORRECT: Mr. Davis tried to finish his research, but he found only part of the information that he needs.

CORRECT: Mr. Davis <u>tries</u> to finish his research, but he <u>finds</u> only part of the information that he <u>needs</u>.

or

Mr. Davis <u>tried</u> to finish his research, but he <u>found</u> only part of the information that he <u>needed</u>.

EXERCISES

Part A: Choose the correct answer.

The first transistor was basically a small chip made of germanium onto one surface of which two pointed wire contacts _____ side by side.

(A) are made
(B) made
(C) were made
(D) making

Part B: Choose the incorrect word or phrase and correct it.

<u>Because</u> early balloons were at the mercy of <u>shifting</u> winds,
   (A)   (B)

they <u>are</u> not considered a practical means of transportation
     (C)

<u>until the 1850s</u>.
     (D)

2   Point of View—Verbs and Adverbs

In all patterns, avoid using past adverbs with verbs in the present tense.

EXAMPLES

INCORRECT:	Between one thing and another, Charles does not finish typing his paper last night.
CORRECT:	Between one thing and another, Charles <u>did</u> not finish typing his paper <u>last</u> <u>night</u>.
INCORRECT:	In 1990, according to statistics from the Bureau of Census, the population of the United States is 250,000,000.
CORRECT:	<u>In 1990,</u> according to statistics from the Bureau of Census, the population of the United States <u>was</u> 250,000,000.
INCORRECT:	We do not receive mail yesterday because it was a holiday.
CORRECT:	We <u>did</u> not receive mail <u>yesterday</u> because it <u>was</u> a holiday.
INCORRECT:	Mary does not finish her homework in time to go with us to the football game yesterday afternoon.
CORRECT:	Mary <u>did</u> not finish her homework in time to go with us to the football game <u>yesterday afternoon</u>.
INCORRECT:	Although there are only two hundred foreign students studying at State University in 1990, there are more than five hundred now.
CORRECT:	Although there <u>were</u> only two hundred foreign students studying at State University <u>in 1990,</u> there are more than five hundred now.

EXERCISES

Part A: Choose the correct answer.

Iron _____ for weapons and tools in the Bronze Age following the Stone Age.

(A) is generally used
(B) generally used
(C) was generally used
(D) used generally

Part B: Choose the incorrect word or phrase and correct it.

The <u>Nineteenth Amendment</u> to the Constitution <u>gives</u> women
　　　　　(A)　　　　　　　　　　　　　　　　　　(B)
the right <u>to vote</u> in <u>the elections</u> of 1920.
　　　　　(C)　　　　　(D)

Agreement—Modified Subject and Verb

In all patterns, there must be agreement of subject and verb.

Avoid using a verb that agrees with the modifier of a subject instead of with the subject itself.

EXAMPLES

INCORRECT:　His knowledge of languages and international relations aid him in his work.

CORRECT:　His <u>knowledge</u> of languages and international relations <u>aids</u> him in his work.

INCORRECT:　The facilities at the new research library, including an excellent microfilm file, is among the best in the country.

CORRECT:　The <u>facilities</u> at the new research library, including an excellent microfilm file, <u>are</u> among the best in the country.

INCORRECT:　All trade between the two countries were suspended pending negotiation of a new agreement.

CORRECT:　All <u>trade</u> between the two countries <u>was</u> suspended pending negotiation of a new agreement.

INCORRECT:　The production of different kinds of artificial materials are essential to the conservation of our natural resources.

CORRECT:　The <u>production</u> of different kinds of artificial materials <u>is</u> essential to the conservation of our natural resources.

INCORRECT:　Since the shipment of supplies for our experiments were delayed, we will have to reschedule our work.

CORRECT:　Since the <u>shipment</u> of supplies for our experiments <u>was</u> delayed, we will have to reschedule our work.

EXERCISES

Part A: Choose the correct answer.

Groups of tissues, each with its own function, _____ in the human body.

    (A) it makes up the organs

    (B) make up the organs

    (C) they make up the organs

    (D) makes up the organs

Part B: Choose the incorrect word or phrase and correct it.

The Zoning Improvement Plan, <u>better known as</u> zip codes,

                              (A)

<u>enable</u> postal clerks <u>to speed</u> the routing of <u>an</u> ever-increasing

 (B)   (C)   (D)

volume of mail.

4   Agreement—Subject with Appositive and Verb

Remember that there must be agreement of subject and verb. An appositive is a word or phrase that follows a noun and defines it. An appositive usually has a comma before it and a comma after it.

In all patterns, avoid using a verb that agrees with words in the appositive after a subject instead of with the subject itself.

EXAMPLES

INCORRECT: The books, an English dictionary and a chemistry text, was on the shelf yesterday.

  CORRECT: <u>The books,</u> an English dictionary and a chemistry text, <u>were</u> on the shelf yesterday.

INCORRECT: Three swimmers from our team, Paul, Ed, and Jim, is in competition for medals.

  CORRECT: <u>Three swimmers</u> from our team, Paul, Ed, and Jim, <u>are</u> in competition for medals.

INCORRECT: Several pets, two dogs and a cat, needs to be taken care of while we are gone.

CORRECT: <u>Several pets,</u> two dogs and a cat, <u>need</u> to be taken care of while we are gone.

INCORRECT: State University, the largest of the state-supported schools, have more than 50,000 students on main campus.

CORRECT: <u>State University,</u> the largest of the state-supported schools, <u>has</u> more than 50,000 students on main campus.

INCORRECT: This recipe, an old family secret, are an especially important part of our holiday celebrations.

CORRECT: <u>This recipe,</u> an old family secret, <u>is</u> an especially important part of our holiday celebrations.

EXERCISES

Part A: Choose the correct answer.

Cupid, one of the ancient Roman gods, _____.
- (A) were a little winged child
- (B) representing as a little winged child
- (C) was represented as a little winged child
- (D) a little winged child

Part B: Choose the incorrect word or phrase and correct it.

Columbus, Ohio, the capital of the state, <u>are</u> not only <u>the largest</u>
                                        (A)   (B)

city in Ohio <u>but also</u> a typical metropolitan area, often <u>used</u> in
               (C)   (D)

market research.

5 Agreement—Verb-Subject Order

There and *here* introduce verb-subject order. The verb agrees with the subject following it.

there	V	S
There	are	the results of the election

here	V	S
Here	is	the result of the election

Avoid using a verb that does not agree with the subject.

EXAMPLES

INCORRECT: There was ten people in line already when we arrived.
  CORRECT: There <u>were</u> <u>ten people</u> in line already when we arrived.

INCORRECT: There have been very little rain this summer.
  CORRECT: There <u>has been</u> <u>very little rain</u> this summer.

INCORRECT: Here are their house.
  CORRECT: Here <u>is</u> <u>their house</u>.

INCORRECT: There has been several objections to the new policy.
  CORRECT: There <u>have been</u> <u>several objections</u> to the new policy.

INCORRECT: I think that there were a problem.
  CORRECT: I think that there <u>was</u> <u>a problem</u>.

EXERCISES

Part A: Choose the correct answer.

In a suspension bridge _____ that carry one or more flexible cables firmly attached at each end.
    (A) there is two towers on it
    (B) there are two towers
    (C) two towers there are
    (D) towers there are two

Part B: Choose the incorrect word or phrase and correct it.

<u>There is</u> about 600 schools <u>in the United States</u> that <u>use</u> the
   (A)   (B)   (C)
Montessori method <u>to encourage</u> individual initiative.
                             (D)

6   Agreement—Noun and Pronoun

In all patterns, there must be agreement of noun and pronoun.
Avoid using a pronoun that does not agree in number with the noun to which it refers.

EXAMPLES

INCORRECT: If you want to leave a message for Mr. and Mrs. Carlson, I will be glad to take them.

CORRECT: If you want to leave <u>a message</u> for Mr. and Mrs. Carlson, I will be glad to take <u>it</u>.

INCORRECT: Al is interested in mathematics and their applications.

CORRECT: Al is interested in <u>mathematics</u> and <u>its</u> applications.

INCORRECT: It is easier to talk about a problem than to resolve them.

CORRECT: It is easier to talk about <u>a problem</u> than to resolve <u>it</u>.

INCORRECT: Although their visas will expire in June, they can have it extended for three months.

CORRECT: Although <u>their visas</u> will expire in June, they can have <u>them</u> extended for three months.

INCORRECT: In spite of its small size, these cameras take very good pictures.

CORRECT: In spite of <u>their</u> small size, <u>these cameras</u> take very good pictures.

EXERCISES

Part A: Choose the correct answer.

A college bookstore that sells used textbooks stocks _____ along with the new ones on the shelf under the course title.

(A) its
(B) their
(C) a
(D) them

Part B: Choose the incorrect word or phrase and correct it.

Magnesium, <u>the lightest</u> of our structural metals, has an
         (A)

important place <u>among</u> common engineering materials
         (B)

<u>because of</u> <u>their</u> weight.
  (C)   (D)

7   Agreement—Subject and Possessive Pronouns

In all patterns, there must be agreement of subject pronoun and possessive pronouns that refer to the subject.

Subject Pronouns	Possessive Pronouns
I	*my*
you	*your*
he	*his*
she	*her*
it	*its*
we	*our*
you	*your*
they	*their*

Remember that *it* refers to a small baby. Avoid using *it's* instead of *its* as a possessive pronoun. *It's* means *it is*.

EXAMPLES

INCORRECT: Those of us who are over fifty years old should get their blood pressure checked regularly.

CORRECT: <u>Those of us</u> who are over fifty years old should get <u>our</u> blood pressure checked regularly.

INCORRECT: Our neighbors know that when they go on vacation, we will get its mail for them.

CORRECT: Our neighbors know that when <u>they</u> go on vacation, we will get <u>their</u> mail for them.

INCORRECT: A mother who works outside of the home has to prepare for emergencies when she cannot be there to take care of your sick child.

CORRECT: A mother who works outside of the home has to prepare for emergencies when <u>she</u> cannot be there to take care of <u>her</u> sick child.

INCORRECT: Wine tends to lose their flavor when it has not been properly sealed.

CORRECT: Wine tends to lose <u>its</u> flavor when <u>it</u> has not been properly sealed.

INCORRECT: Optional equipment on a car can add several hundred dollars to it's resale value when you trade it in.

CORRECT: Optional equipment on a car can add several hundred dollars to <u>its</u> resale value when you trade <u>it</u> in.

EXERCISES

Part A: Choose the correct answer.

The television programs we allow _____ to watch influence their learning.

    (A) a children
    (B) our children
    (C) our child
    (D) their childs

Part B: Choose the incorrect word or phrase and correct it.

Although maple trees are <u>among</u> the most colorful varieties
(A)

<u>in the fall</u>, they lose <u>its</u> leaves <u>sooner than</u> oak trees.
(B)   (C)   (D)

8   Verbal Modifiers— *-ing* and *-ed* Forms

-ing forms and *-ed* forms may be used as verbals. Verbals function as modifiers.

An introductory verbal modifier with *-ing* or *-ed* should immediately precede the noun it modifies. Otherwise, the relationship between the noun and the modifier is unclear, and the sentence is illogical.

Avoid using a noun immediately after an introductory verbal phrase which may not be logically modified by the phrase.

EXAMPLES

INCORRECT: After graduating from City College, Professor Baker's studies were continued at State University, where he received his Ph.D. in English.

  CORRECT: <u>After graduating</u> from City College, <u>Professor Baker</u> continued his studies at State University, where he received his Ph.D. in English.

INCORRECT: Returning to her room, several pieces of jewelry were missing.

  CORRECT: <u>Returning</u> to her room, <u>she</u> found that several pieces of jewelry were missing.

INCORRECT: Having been delayed by heavy traffic, it was not possible for her to arrive on time.

  CORRECT: <u>Having been delayed</u> by heavy traffic, <u>she</u> arrived late.

INCORRECT: Accustomed to getting up early, the new schedule was not difficult for him to adjust to.

  CORRECT: <u>Accustomed to getting up</u> early, <u>he</u> had no difficulty adjusting to the new schedule.

INCORRECT: After finishing his speech, the audience was invited to ask questions.

CORRECT: <u>After finishing</u> his speech, <u>he</u> invited the audience to ask questions.

EXERCISES

Part A: Choose the correct answer.

_____ air traffic controllers guide planes through conditions of near zero visibility.
(A) They talk with pilots and watch their approach on radar,
(B) Talking with pilots and watching their approach on radar,
(C) Talk with pilots and watch their approach on radar,
(D) When they talked with pilots and watched their approach on radar,

Part B: Choose the incorrect word or phrase and correct it.

<u>Have designed</u> his own plane, *The Spirit of St. Louis*, Lindbergh
   (A)

<u>flew</u> from Roosevelt Field in New York across the ocean <u>to</u> Le
 (B)   (C)

Bourget Field <u>outside Paris</u>.
     (D)

9   Verbal Modifiers—Infinitives of Purpose to Introduce Instructions

An infinitive that expresses purpose may be used as an introductory verbal modifier. Remember that a verb word follows the infinitive. The verb word expresses a manner to accomplish the purpose.

Avoid using a noun or *to* with an *-ing* form instead of the infinitive of purpose. Avoid using an *-ing* form or a passive construction after an introductory verbal modifier.

EXAMPLES

INCORRECT: To protect yourself from dangerous exposure to the sun's rays, using a sunscreen.

CORRECT: To protect yourself from dangerous exposure to the sun's rays, use a sunscreen.

INCORRECT: Prepare for the TOEFL, study thirty minutes every day for several months.

CORRECT: To prepare for the TOEFL, study thirty minutes every day for several months.

INCORRECT: In order to take advantage of low air fares, to buy your tickets well in advance.

CORRECT: In order to take advantage of low air fares, buy your tickets well in advance.

INCORRECT: To taking action pictures, always use a high-speed film.

CORRECT: To take action pictures, always use a high-speed film.

INCORRECT: The send letters and packages from the United States overseas, use Global Mail or DHL Delivery.

CORRECT: To send letters and packages from the United States overseas, use Global Mail or DHL Delivery.

EXERCISES

Part A: Choose the correct answer.

To relieve pressure in the skull, _____ into the blood.
(A) you will inject a strong solution of pure glucose
(B) to inject a strong solution of pure glucose
(C) a strong solution of glucose will inject purely
(D) inject a strong solution of pure glucose

Part B: Choose the incorrect word or phrase and correct it.

To estimate how much it will cost to build a home, finding the
                             (A)   (B)   (C)
total square footage of the house and multiply by cost per
                                                 (D)
square foot.

10   Parallel Structure—In a Series

In all patterns, ideas of equal importance should be expressed by the same grammatical structure.

Avoid expressing ideas in a series with different structures.

EXAMPLES

INCORRECT: Jane is young, enthusiastic, and she has talent.
CORRECT: Jane is <u>young,</u> <u>enthusiastic,</u> and <u>talented.</u>

INCORRECT: We learned to read the passages carefully and underlining the main ideas.
CORRECT: We learned <u>to read</u> the passages carefully and <u>to underline</u> the main ideas.

INCORRECT: The duties of the new secretary are to answer the telephone, to type letters, and bookkeeping.
CORRECT: The duties of the new secretary are <u>to answer</u> the telephone, <u>to type</u> letters, and <u>to do</u> the bookkeeping.

INCORRECT: The patient's symptoms were fever, dizziness, and his head hurt.
CORRECT: The patient's symptoms were <u>fever,</u> <u>dizziness,</u> and <u>headaches</u>.

INCORRECT: Professor Williams enjoys teaching and to write.
CORRECT: Professor Williams enjoys <u>teaching</u> and <u>writing</u>.

EXERCISES

Part A: Choose the correct answer.

In a hot, sunny climate, man acclimatizes by eating less, drinking more liquids, wearing lighter clothing, and _____.
    (A) skin changes that darken
    (B) his skin may darken
    (C) experiencing a darkening of the skin
    (D) darkens his skin

Part B: Choose the incorrect word or phrase and correct it.

The aims of the European Economic Community <u>are</u> to
(A)

eliminate tariffs between member countries; <u>developing</u>
(B)

common policies for agriculture, labor, welfare, trade, and

<u>transportation</u>; and <u>to abolish</u> trusts and cartels.
     (C)   (D)

11 Parallel Structure—After Correlative Conjunctions

Remember that ideas of equal importance are introduced by correlative conjunctions:

both . . . and
not only . . . but also

Avoid expressing ideas after correlative conjunctions with different structures.

EXAMPLES

INCORRECT: She is not only famous in the United States but also abroad.
 CORRECT: She is famous not only <u>in the United States</u> but also <u>abroad</u>.

INCORRECT: The exam tested both listening and to read.
 CORRECT: The exam tested both <u>listening</u> and <u>reading</u>.

INCORRECT: He is not only intelligent but also he is creative.
 CORRECT: He is not only <u>intelligent</u> but also <u>creative</u>.

INCORRECT: Flying is not only faster but also it is safer than traveling by car.
 CORRECT: Flying is not only <u>faster</u> but also <u>safer</u> than traveling by car.

INCORRECT: John registered for both Electrical Engineering 500 and to study Mathematics 390.

CORRECT: John registered for both <u>Electrical Engineering</u> 500 and <u>Mathematics</u> 390.

EXERCISES

Part A: Choose the correct answer.

Both historically and _____, Ontario is the heartland of Canada.
(A) in its geography
(B) geographically
(C) also its geography
(D) geography

Part B: Choose the incorrect word or phrase and correct it.

The cacao bean <u>was cultivated</u> <u>by the Aztecs</u> not only to drink
　　　　　　　　　(A)　　　　　　　(B)

<u>but also</u> <u>currency</u>.
　(C)　　　(D)

12   Redundancy—Unnecessary Phrases

In all patterns, prefer simple, direct sentences to complicated, indirect sentences. Find the Subject-Verb-Complement-Modifier, and determine whether the other words are useful or unnecessary.

S	V	C	M
Lee	learned	English	quickly

Avoid using an adjective with such phrases as *in character* or *in nature*.

Avoid using the redundant pattern instead of an adverb such as *quickly.*

in a	adjective	manner
in a	quick	manner

Examples

INCORRECT: The key officials who testified before the Senate committee responded in a manner that was evasive.

CORRECT: <u>The key officials</u> who testified before the Senate committee <u>responded evasively</u>.

INCORRECT: Mr. Davis knows a great deal in terms of the condition of the situation.

CORRECT: <u>Mr. Davis knows a great deal about the situation</u>.

INCORRECT: It was a problem which was very difficult in character and very delicate in nature.

CORRECT: <u>The problem was difficult and delicate</u>.

INCORRECT: The disease was very serious in the nature of it.

CORRECT: <u>The disease was very serious.</u>

INCORRECT: Mary had always behaved in a responsible manner.

CORRECT: <u>Mary had always behaved responsibly</u>.

Exercises

Part A: Choose the correct answer.

Waitresses and waiters who serve _____ deserve at least a 20 percent tip.

(A) in a courteous manner
(B) courteously
(C) with courtesy in their manner
(D) courteous

Part B: Choose the incorrect word or phrase and correct it.

Hummingbirds move <u>their</u> wings so <u>rapid a way</u> that they
               (A)   (B)

appear <u>to be hanging</u> <u>in the air</u>.
      (C)   (D)

Redundancy—Repetition of Words with the Same Meaning

In all patterns, avoid using words with the same meaning consecutively in a sentence.

EXAMPLES

INCORRECT: The money that I have is sufficient enough for my needs.
CORRECT: The money that I have is <u>sufficient</u> for my needs.

INCORRECT: Bill asked the speaker to repeat again because he had not heard him the first time.
CORRECT: Bill asked the speaker <u>to repeat</u> because he had not heard him the first time.

INCORRECT: The class advanced forward rapidly.
CORRECT: The class <u>advanced</u> rapidly.

INCORRECT: She returned back to her hometown after she had finished her degree.
CORRECT: She <u>returned</u> to her hometown after she had finished her degree.

INCORRECT: I am nearly almost finished with this chapter.
CORRECT: I am <u>nearly</u> finished with this chapter.
            or
            I am <u>almost</u> finished with this chapter.

EXERCISES

Part A: Choose the correct answer.

Famous for his _____ punctuation, typography, and language, Edward Estlin Cummings published his collected poems in 1954.

(A) new innovations for
(B) innovations in
(C) newly approached
(D) innovations newly approached in

Part B: Choose the incorrect word or phrase and correct it.

The idea of a submarine is <u>an old ancient one</u>, dating from
                            (A)

<u>as early as</u> <u>the fifteenth century</u> when Drebbel and Da Vinci
   (B)   (C)

<u>made</u> preliminary drawings.
   (D)

14   Redundancy—Repetition of Noun by Pronoun

In all patterns, avoid using a noun and the pronoun that refers to it con-secutively in a sentence. Avoid using a pronoun after the noun it refers to, and *that.*

EXAMPLES

INCORRECT: My teacher he said to listen to the news on the radio in order to practice listening comprehension.

CORRECT: <u>My teacher</u> <u>said</u> to listen to the news on the radio in order to practice listening comprehension.

INCORRECT: Steve he plans to go into business with his father.
CORRECT: <u>Steve</u> <u>plans</u> to go into business with his father.

INCORRECT: My sister she found a store that imported food from our country.

CORRECT: <u>My sister</u> <u>found</u> a store that imported food from our country.

INCORRECT: Hospitalization that it covers room, meals, nursing, and additional hospital expenses such as lab tests, X-rays, and medicine.

CORRECT: <u>Hospitalization</u> <u>covers</u> room, meals, nursing, and additional hospital expenses such as lab tests, X-rays, and medicine.

INCORRECT: Anne she wants to visit Washington, D.C., before she goes home.

CORRECT: <u>Anne</u> <u>wants</u> to visit Washington, D.C., before she goes home.

EXERCISES

Part A: Choose the correct answer.

A perennial is _____ for more than two years, such as trees and shrubs.

(A) any plant that it continues to grow
(B) any plant it continuing to grow
(C) any plant that continues to grow
(D) any plant continuing growth

Part B: Choose the incorrect word or phrase and correct it.

Advertising <u>it</u> <u>provides</u> <u>most of the income</u> for magazines,
      (A)   (B)   (C)

newspapers, radio, and television <u>in the United States</u> today.
                                 (D)

15   Transitive and Intransitive Verbs— *Raise* and *Rise*

A transitive verb is a verb that takes a complement. An intransitive verb is a verb that does not take a complement.

The following pairs of verbs can be confusing. Remember that *raise* is a transitive verb; it takes a complement. *Rise* is an intransitive verb; it does not take a complement.

Transitive		
Verb word	*Past*	*Participle*
raise	raised	raised

Intransitive		
Verb word	*Past*	*Participle*
rise	rose	risen

Remember that *to raise* means to move to a higher place or to cause to rise. *To rise* means to go up or to increase.

Raise and rise are also used as nouns. A *raise* means an increase in salary. A *rise* means an increase in price, worth, quantity, or degree.

S	RAISE	C	M
Heavy rain Heavy rain	raises raised	the water level of the reservoir the water level of the reservoir	every spring last week

S	RISE	C	M
The water level The water level	rises rose		when it rains every spring when it rained last week

EXAMPLES

INCORRECT: The cost of living has raised 3 percent in the past year.
CORRECT: The cost of living <u>has risen</u> 3 percent in the past year.

INCORRECT: The flag is risen at dawn by an honor guard.
CORRECT: The flag <u>is raised</u> at dawn <u>by an honor guard</u>.
(An honor guard <u>raises</u> the flag.)

INCORRECT: Kay needs to rise her grades if she wants to get into graduate school.
CORRECT: <u>Kay needs to raise her grades</u> if she wants to get into graduate school.

INCORRECT: The landlord has risen the rent.
CORRECT: The landlord <u>has raised</u> the rent.

INCORRECT: The smoke that is raising from that oil refinery is black.
CORRECT: The <u>smoke</u> that <u>is rising</u> from that oil refinery is black.

EXERCISES

Part A: Choose the correct answer.

The average elevation of the Himalayas is twenty thousand feet, and Mount Everest _____ to more than twenty-nine thousand feet at its apex.
(A) raises
(B) rises
(C) roses
(D) arises

Part B: Choose the incorrect word or phrase and correct it.

When the temperature is <u>risen</u> to <u>the burning point</u> without a
                       (A)   (B)
source of escape <u>for the heat</u>, spontaneous combustion <u>occurs</u>.
              (C)   (D)

16 Transitive and Intransitive Verbs— *Lay* and *Lie*

Remember that *lay* is a transitive verb; it takes a complement. *Lie* is an intransitive verb; it does not take a complement.

Transitive

Verb word	Past	Participle
lay	laid	laid

Intransitive

Verb word	Past	Participle
lie	lay	lain

Remember that *to lay* means to put, to place, or to cause to lie. *To lie* means to recline or to occupy a place.

The past form of the verb *to lie* is *lay*.

S	LAY	C	M
The postman	lays	the mail	on the table every day
The postman	laid	the mail	on the table yesterday

S	LIE	C	M
He	lies		on the sofa to rest every day after work
He	lay		on the sofa to rest yesterday after work

EXAMPLES

INCORRECT: Her coat was laying on the chair.
  CORRECT: <u>Her coat</u> <u>was lying</u> on the chair.

INCORRECT: I have lain your notebook on the table by the door so that you won't forget it.
  CORRECT: <u>I have laid</u> <u>your notebook</u> on the table by the door so that you won't forget it.

INCORRECT: Key West lays off the coast of Florida.
  CORRECT: <u>Key West</u> <u>lies</u> off the coast of Florida.

INCORRECT: Why don't you lay down for awhile?
  CORRECT: Why don't <u>you</u> <u>lie</u> down for awhile?

INCORRECT: Linda always forgets where she lies her glasses.
  CORRECT: Linda always forgets where <u>she</u> <u>lays</u> <u>her glasses</u>.

EXERCISES

Part A: Choose the correct answer.

The geographic position of North America, _____ in the early days of the European settlement.
   (A) laying between the Atlantic and the Pacific Oceans, isolating it
   (B) isolating it as it laid between the Atlantic and the Pacific Oceans
   (C) lying between the Atlantic and the Pacific Oceans, isolated it
   (D) isolating it between the Atlantic and the Pacific Oceans as it was layed

Part B: Choose the incorrect word or phrase and correct it.

Melanin, a pigment that <u>lays</u> under the skin, <u>is</u> responsible for
                 (A)   (B)
skin color, including the variations that <u>occur</u> <u>among</u> different
                                 (C)   (D)
races.

Transitive and Intransitive Verbs—
Set and *Sit*

Remember that *set* is a transitive verb; it takes a complement. *Sit* is an intransitive verb; it does not take a complement.

	Transitive	
Verb word	*Past*	*Participle*
set	set	set

	Intransitive	
Verb word	*Past*	*Participle*
sit	sat	sat

Remember that *to set* means to put, to place, or to cause to sit. *To sit* means to occupy a place on a chair or a flat surface.

S	SET	C	M
The students	set	the lab equipment	on the table every class
The students	set	the lab equipment	on the table last class period

S	SIT	C	M
The equipment	sits		on the table every class
The equipment	sat		on the table last class period

EXAMPLES

INCORRECT: Please sit the telephone on the table by the bed.
  CORRECT: Please <u>set the telephone</u> on the table by the bed.

INCORRECT: Won't you set down?
  CORRECT: Won't <u>you sit</u> down?

INCORRECT: Their house sets on a hill overlooking a lake.
 CORRECT: Their <u>house sits</u> on a hill overlooking a lake.

INCORRECT: Let's sit your suitcases out of the way.
 CORRECT: Let's <u>set your suitcases</u> out of the way.

INCORRECT: Terry has set there waiting for us for almost an hour.
 CORRECT: <u>Terry has sat</u> there waiting for us for almost an hour.

EXERCISES

Part A: Choose the correct answer.

When Jacqueline Kennedy was first lady, she collected many beautiful antiques and _____ them among the original pieces in the White House.
  (A) sat
  (B) set
  (C) sit
  (D) sits

Part B: Choose the incorrect word or phrase and correct it.

Hyde Park, the family estate <u>of Franklin D. Roosevelt,</u> <u>sets</u> on
                                            (A)   (B)

top of a bluff <u>overlooking</u> <u>the Hudson River</u>.
                    (C)   (D)

Similar Verbs—*Make* and *Do*

Verb word	Past	Participle
do	*did*	*done*

Verb word	Past	Participle
make	*made*	*made*

Remember that *to do* and *to make* have similar meanings, but *do* is often used before complements that describe work and chores. *To make* is often used before complements that are derived from verbs.

DO an assignment	MAKE an agreement	(to agree)
the dishes	an announcement	(to announce)
a favor	an attempt	(to attempt)
homework	a decision	(to decide)
the laundry	a discovery	(to discover)
a paper	an offer	(to offer)
research	a profit	(to profit)
work	a promise	(to promise)

S	DO	C	M
We	do	our homework	before class every day
We	did	our homework	before class yesterday

S	MAKE	C	M
We	make	an agreement	with each other every semester
We	made	an agreement	with each other last semester

EXAMPLES

INCORRECT: I really don't mind making the homework for this class.
CORRECT: I really don't mind <u>doing the homework</u> for this class.

INCORRECT: Did you do a mistake?
CORRECT: Did you <u>make</u> <u>a mistake</u>?

INCORRECT: Please make me a favor.
CORRECT: Please <u>do</u> me <u>a favor</u>.

INCORRECT: Are they doing progress on the new road?
CORRECT: Are they <u>making</u> <u>progress</u> on the new road?

INCORRECT: Have you done any interesting discoveries while you were doing your research?
CORRECT: Have you <u>made</u> any interesting <u>discoveries</u> while you were <u>doing</u> your <u>research?</u>

EXERCISES

Part A: Choose the correct answer.

The president usually _____ unless his press secretary approves it.

(A) doesn't do a statement
(B) doesn't make a statement
(C) doesn't statement
(D) no statement

Part B: Choose the incorrect word or phrase and correct it.

A <u>one hundred-horsepower tractor</u> <u>can</u> <u>make</u> the work of
          (A)   (B) (C)
<u>a large number</u> of horses.
     (D)

19 Prepositional Idioms

Prefer these idioms	Avoid these errors
accede to	accede on, by
according to	according
approve of	approve for
ashamed of	ashamed with
bored with	bored of
capable of	capable to
compete with	compete together
composed of	composed from
concerned with	concerned of
conscious of	conscious for
depend on	depend in, to
effects on	effects in
equal to	equal as
except for	excepting for
from now on	after now on
from time to time	for, when time to time
frown on	frown to
glance at, through	glance
incapable of	incapable to
in conflict	on conflict
inferior to	inferior with
in the habit of	in the habit to
in the near future	at the near future
knowledge of	knowledge on
near; next to	near to
of the opinion	in opinion
on top of	on top
opposite	opposite over
prior to	prior
regard to	regard of
related to	related with
respect for	respect of
responsible for	responsible
similar to	similar as
since	ever since
until	up until
with regard to	with regard of

EXAMPLES

INCORRECT: Excepting for the Gulf Coast region, most of the nation will have very pleasant weather tonight and tomorrow.
CORRECT: <u>Except for</u> the Gulf Coast region, most of the nation will have very pleasant weather tonight and tomorrow.

INCORRECT: In recent years, educators have become more concerned of bilingualism.
CORRECT: In recent years, educators have become more <u>concerned with</u> bilingualism.

INCORRECT: He always does what he pleases, without regard of the rules and regulations.
CORRECT: He always does what he pleases, without <u>regard to</u> the rules and regulations.

INCORRECT: The bank opposite over the university isn't open on Saturdays.
CORRECT: The bank <u>opposite</u> the university isn't open on Saturdays.

INCORRECT: The customs of other countries are not inferior with those of our own country.
CORRECT: The customs of other countries are not <u>inferior to</u> those of our own country.

EXERCISES

Part A: Choose the correct answer.

_____ discovery of insulin, it was not possible to treat diabetes.
(A) Prior to the
(B) Prior
(C) The prior
(D) To prior

Part B: Choose the incorrect word or phrase and correct it.

<u>The price</u> of gold <u>depends in</u> <u>several factors</u>, including supply
  (A)   (B)   (C)
and demand <u>in relation to</u> the value of the dollar.
         (D)

20   Parts of Speech

Although it is usually very easy to identify the parts of speech, word families can be confusing. Word families are groups of words with similar meanings and spellings. Each word in the family is a different part of speech. For example, *agreement* is a noun; *agreeable* is an adjective; to *agree* is a verb. The endings of words can help you identify the parts of speech.

Nouns Derived from Verbs

Verb	Ending	Noun
store	*-age*	*storage*
accept	*-ance*	*acceptance*
insist	*-ence*	*insistence*
agree	*-ment*	*agreement*
authorize	*-sion/-tion*	*authorization*

Nouns Derived from Adjectives

Adjective	Ending	Noun
convenient	*-ce*	*convenience*
redundant	*-cy*	*redundancy*
opposite	*-tion*	*opposition*
soft	*-ness*	*softness*
durable	*-ty*	*durability*

Adjectives Derived from Nouns

Noun	Ending	Adjective
possibility	*-able/-ible*	*possible*
intention	*-al*	*intentional*
distance	*-ant*	*distant*
frequency	*-ent*	*frequent*
juice	*-y*	*juicy*

Adverbs Derived from Adjectives

Adjective	Ending	Adverb
efficient	*-ly*	*efficiently*

EXAMPLES

INCORRECT: The agreeing is not legal unless everyone signs his name.
CORRECT: The <u>agreement</u> is not legal unless everyone signs his name.

INCORRECT: Even young children begin to show able in mathematics.
CORRECT: Even young children begin to show <u>ability</u> in mathematics.

INCORRECT: Arranging have been made for the funeral.
CORRECT: <u>Arrangements</u> have been made for the funeral.

INCORRECT: A free educating is guaranteed to every citizen.
CORRECT: A free <u>education</u> is guaranteed to every citizen.

INCORRECT: The develop of hybrids has increased yields.
CORRECT: The <u>development</u> of hybrids has increased yields.

EXERCISES

Part A: Choose the correct answer.

Unless protected areas are established, the Bengal tiger, the blue whale, and the California condor face _____ of extinction.
   (A) possible
   (B) the possibility
   (C) to be possible
   (D) possibly

Part B: Choose the incorrect word or phrase and correct it.

<u>Because</u> blood from different individuals may <u>different</u> in the
   (A)   (B)
type of antigen on the surface of the red cells and the type of antibody
in the plasma, a dangerous reaction <u>can occur</u> between
                                         (C)
the donor <u>and</u> recipient in a blood transfusion.
           (D)

TYPES OF QUESTIONS

Multiple-Choice Questions

All of the questions on both the Paper-Based TOEFL and the Computer-Based TOEFL are multiple-choice. There are no computer-assisted questions with special directions.

Although the structure questions in this book are numbered, and the answer choices are lettered A, B, C, and D, the same questions on the CD-ROM that supplements the larger version of the book; *Barron's How to Prepare the TOEFL*, are not numbered and lettered. You need the numbers and letters in the book to refer to the Answer Key, the Explanatory Answers, and the Audio Script for the Listening Section. On the CD-ROM, you can refer to other chapters by clicking on the screen. The questions on the CD-ROM are like those on the Computer-Based TOEFL.

Paper-Based TOEFL

1. If water is heated to 121 degrees F, _____ as steam.
   - (A) it will boil and escape
   - (B) it is boiling and escaping
   - (C) it boil and escape
   - (D) it would boil and escape

2. If <u>water</u> freezes, <u>it</u> <u>has become</u> <u>a</u> solid.
      (A)   (B)   (C)   (D)

Answer Sheet

1. ●   Ⓑ   Ⓒ   Ⓒ
2. Ⓐ   Ⓑ   ●   Ⓓ

Computer-Based TOEFL

If water is heated to 121 degrees F, _____ as steam.

- ● it will boil and escape
- ○ it is boiling and escaping
- ○ it boil and escape
- ○ it would boil and escape

If <u>water</u> freezes, <u>it</u> <u>has become</u>

a solid.

Computer Tutorial for the Structure Section

In order to succeed on the Computer-Based TOEFL, you must understand the computer vocabulary used for the test, and you must be familiar
with the icons on the computer screens that you will see on the test. First,
review the vocabulary that you learned in the Tutorial for the Listening
Section on pages 62–64. The same vocabulary is used for the Structure
Section. Then study the computer screens in this Tutorial.

Testing Tools: Review of Vocabulary, Icons, and Keys

The following words are from the list of general vocabulary for the Computer-
Based TOEFL introduced in the previous chapter. Using the word list, fill in
the blanks in the ten sentences.

Arrow	**Mouse**
Click	**Mouse Pad**
Confirm Answer	**Next**
Dismiss Directions	**Oval**
Help (Question mark)	**Time (Clock)**
Icon	

1. A _____ is a small control with a button on it.

2. A _____ is a rectangular pad where you move the mouse.

3. An _____ is a marker on the screen that shows you where
   you are moving on the computer.

4. To _____ is to depress the button on the mouse. You
   _____ the mouse to make changes on the screen.

5. An _____ is a small picture or word or phrase in a box. Move
   the arrow to the _____ to tell the computer what to do.

6. Click on _____ to remove the directions from the screen.

7. Click on an _____ to choose an answer to one of the
   multiple-choice questions.

8. Click on _____, then click on _____ to see the next
   question.

9. Click on _____ to see a list of the icons and directions.

10. Click on _____ to hide or show the time you have left to finish the section of the test you are working on.

Computer Screens for Structure

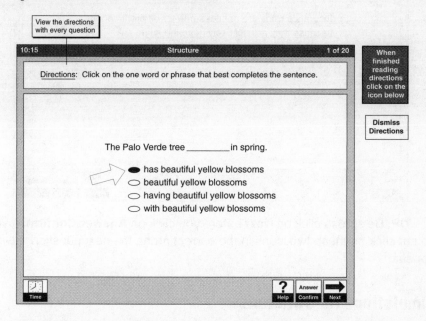

TIP: There are only two types of questions in the Structure Section. After you have read and understood the directions for both types of questions in this Tutorial, you will not need to read the top part of the screen every time.

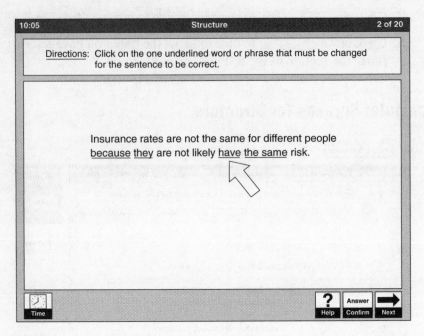

Directions: Click on the one underlined word or phrase that must be changed for the sentence to be correct.

Insurance rates are not the same for different people because they are not likely have the same risk.

Time
? Help   Answer Confirm   Next

TIP: Be sure to click on **Next** before you click on **Answer Confirm.** If you do not click on these two icons in the correct order, the next question will not appear.

Simulations for Structure

In order to prepare for the experience that you will have on the Computer-Based TOEFL, you can use the CD-ROM that supplements the larger version of this book, *Barron's How to Prepare for the TOEFL.* Locate the Structure Section on the Model Tests. The computer will simulate the Structure Section on the Computer-Based TOEFL. These Model Tests are computer-assisted.

As part of your study plan, be sure to review all of the questions in all of the Model Tests. Use the Explanatory Answers on the CD-ROM or in Chapter 10. Refer to the Review of Structure on the CD-ROM or on pages 93–208 of this book. Finally, if you have the CD-ROM, take the Cumulative Model Test. This test is computer-adaptive, which means that the computer will select questions for you at your level of language proficiency.

If you choose not to purchase the larger version of this book, or you do not have a computer, you can still simulate some of the features of the Computer-Based TOEFL. The Structure Section in the Model Tests in Chapter 8 of this book presents both types of questions randomly. This is different from the Paper-Based TOEFL. You can become accustomed to making a quick decision about the kind of answer required—completion or correction.

Preview of Structure on the Next Generation TOEFL

There is no Structure Section on the Next Generation TOEFL. However, proficiency and accuracy in grammar are factored into the scores on the Speaking and Writing Sections.

Chapter 5 of this book is a grammar reference. The next edition of this book will include a new, revised Structure Chapter to help you identify the most common structure errors that students make when they speak and write in response to tasks on the Next Generation TOEFL.

Watch for *Barron's How to Prepare for the TOEFL, 12th Edition* to be published when the Next Generation TOEFL is introduced.

Advice for the Structure Section

Become familiar with the directions. The two types of questions will appear at random. If you forget how to answer, look at the top of the screen. Directions will appear at the top of every screen for each question. To save time, learn to recognize the format for each question type, and be ready to respond without looking at the directions.

Move efficiently through the questions. In order to go to the next question, you must click on **Next** and then **Confirm Answer**. If you only click on **Next**, you will not be able to move to the next question. A screen will remind you to return to the previous question. You must enter an answer before you go to the next question. Click on **Return to Question** to move back to the question that you did not answer. Try to answer all questions without being referred to the **Return to Question** screen.

Change your answer before you confirm it. After you click on your answer and see the dark oval or dark box, you can still change your answer. Just click on a different choice. But remember that you cannot change your answer after you click on **Confirm Answer**. This means that you cannot go back to previous questions and change the answers. You must choose your answer, click on your choice, click on **Next**, click on **Confirm Answer**, and move to the next question.

Do your best. The computer will select the questions on this section of the test based on your responses. You will begin with questions that are considered of average difficulty. You will receive easier questions if you are not able to answer the average questions. You will receive more difficult questions if you are able to answer the average questions. You receive more points for the more difficult questions. Just do your best, and you will receive the most points for your level of structure ability.

Understand the **Help** *screen.* The **Help** screen has a question mark on it. It is mostly designed to repeat directions. Be careful. You can waste a lot of time on this screen. If you click on **Help** and you want to go back to the question you were answering, look at the box in the bottom right corner. Click on **Return to Where I Was.**

Get help from the test administrator. If you think that your computer is not performing correctly, notify one of the test administrators immediately. There should be several in the room. They cannot help you with the answers on the TOEFL, but they can help you use the computer. That is why they are there. Tell the administrator, "Excuse me. My computer won't _____." Show the administrator the problem on the computer.

Stay focused. There is only one test question on the screen at any time. Focus on it. If you need to rest your eyes or your neck muscles, don't look around at other people. Look down at your lap with your eyes closed. Then look up at the ceiling with your eyes closed. Then return to the question. Remember that you cannot return to previous questions, so give each question your full attention while it is on the screen. Then, get ready to focus on the next question.

Advice for Success

Perspective means "the way you view experiences." Have you heard the story about the teacup? Two people sit down at a table. There is only enough tea for one cup so they each have half a cup of tea to drink. One person looks at the cup and says, "Oh my, the cup is half empty." The other person looks at the cup and says, "Oh look, the cup is half full." Which kind of person are you?

At this point in your review, it is easy to become discouraged. However, if you choose the "half full" perspective, you will have more energy to continue your studies. Yes, there is certainly a lot to review. If you know half of the problems, you have a choice. You can say, "Oh my, I know only half of this." Instead you can say, "Oh look, I already know half of this!" You choose.

My advice is *believe in yourself.* Don't look at the long distance yet to travel. Celebrate the long distance that you have already traveled. Then you will have the energy and the courage to keep going.

REVIEW OF READING

Overview of the Reading Section

QUICK COMPARISON—READING
PAPER-BASED TOEFL,
COMPUTER-BASED TOEFL, AND NEXT GENERATION TOEFL

Paper-Based TOEFL	Computer-Based TOEFL	Next Generation TOEFL
There are five reading passages with an average of 10 questions after each passage.	There are three to six reading passages with an average of 6 to 10 questions after each passage.	There are three reading passages with an average of 12–13 questions after each passage.
The passages are about 250–300 words in length.	The passages are about 350–450 words in length.	The passages are about 700–800 words in length.
Everyone taking the TOEFL answers the same questions.	You will have the same questions as others who take the same form of the test.	You will answer the same questions as others who take the same form of the test.
There are no pictures or visual cues.	There may be pictures in the text and questions that refer to the content of the reading passage.	There may be pictures in the text and questions that refer to the content of the reading passage.
All of the questions are multiple-choice.	Most of the questions are multiple-choice, but some of the questions have special directions on the screen.	Most of the questions are multiple-choice, but some of the questions have special directions.
Every question has only one answer.	Some of the questions have two or more answers.	Some of the questions have two or more answers.
You answer on a paper Answer Sheet, filling in ovals marked Ⓐ, Ⓑ, Ⓒ, and Ⓓ.	You click on the screen in the oval that corresponds to the answer you have chosen, or you follow the directions on the screen.	You click on the screen in the oval that corresponds to the answer you have chosen, or you follow the directions on the screen.
You can return to previous passages and questions, erase, and change answers on your answer sheet.	You can return to previous passages and questions, change answers, and answer questions you have left blank.	You can return to previous questions, change answers, and answer questions you have left blank, but you cannot return to a previous passage.
There is NO glossary.	There is NO glossary.	There may be a glossary of technical terms.
You may not take notes.	You may not take notes.	You may take notes while you read.

Review of Problems and Questions for the Reading Section

This Review can be used to prepare for the Supplemental Paper-Based TOEFL, the Computer-Based TOEFL, and the Next Generation TOEFL. For the most part, the same types of problems are tested on all three forms. Most of the questions are multiple-choice.

Some of the questions on the Computer-Based TOEFL and the Next Generation TOEFL are computer-assisted. Although the computer-assisted questions in this book are numbered, and the answer choices are lettered A, B, C, and D, the same questions on the CD-ROM that supplements the larger version of this book, *Barron's How to Prepare for the TOEFL*, are not numbered and lettered. You need the numbers and letters in the book to refer to the Answer Key, the Explanatory Answers, and the Audio Script for the Listening Section. On the CD-ROM, you can refer to other chapters by clicking on the screen. The computer-assisted questions have special directions on the screen.

PROBLEM 1 Previewing

Research shows that it is easier to understand what you are reading if you begin with a general idea of what the passage is about. Previewing helps you form a general idea of the topic in your mind.

To preview, read the first sentence of each paragraph and the last sentence of the passage. You should do this as quickly as possible. Remember, you are not reading for specific information, but for an impression of the *topic*.

EXERCISE

DIRECTIONS: Preview the following passage. Focus on the first sentence in each paragraph and the last sentence of the passage. Can you identify the topic? Check your answer using the key on page 381.

A black hole is a region of space created by the total gravitational collapse of matter. It is so intense that nothing, not even light or radiation, can escape. In other words, it is a one-way surface through which matter can fall inward but cannot emerge.

Some astronomers believe that a black hole may be formed when a large star collapses inward from its own weight. So long as they are emitting heat and light into space, stars support themselves against their own gravitational pull with the outward thermal pressure generated by heat from nuclear reactions deep in their interiors. But if a star eventually exhausts its nuclear fuel, then its unbalanced gravitational attraction could cause it to contract and collapse. Furthermore, it could begin to pull in surrounding matter, including nearby comets and planets, creating a black hole.

2 Reading for Main Ideas

By previewing, you can form a general idea of what a reading passage is about; that is, you identify the *topic*. By reading for main ideas, you identify the point of view of the author—that is, what the writer's *thesis* is. Specifically, what does the author propose to write about the topic? If you could reduce the reading to one sentence, what would it be?

Questions about the main idea can be worded in many ways. For example, the following questions are all asking for the same information: (1) What is the main idea? (2) What is the subject? (3) What is the topic? (4) What would be a good title?

EXERCISE

DIRECTIONS: The main idea usually occurs at the beginning of a reading passage. Look at the first two sentences in the following passage. Can you identify the main idea? What would be a good title for this passage? Check your answers using the key on page 381.

For more than a century, despite attacks by a few opposing scientists, Charles Darwin's theory of evolution by natural selection has stood firm. Now, however, some respected biologists are beginning to question whether the theory accounts for major developments such as the shift from water to land habitation. Clearly, evolution has not proceeded steadily but has progressed by radical advances. Recent research in molecular biology, particularly in the study of DNA, provides us with a new possibility. Not only environmental change but also genetic codes in the underlying structure of DNA could govern evolution.

3   Using Contexts for Vocabulary

Before you can use a context, you must understand what a context is. In English, a context is the combination of vocabulary and grammar that surrounds a word. Context can be a sentence or a paragraph or a passage. Context helps you make a general *prediction* about meaning. If you know the general meaning of a sentence, you also know the general meaning of the words in the sentence.

Making predictions from contexts is very important when you are reading a foreign language. In this way, you can read and understand the meaning of a passage without stopping to look up every new word in a dictionary. On an examination like the TOEFL, dictionaries are not permitted in the room.

EXERCISE

DIRECTIONS: Read the following passage, paying close attention to the underlined words. Can you understand their meanings from the context without using a dictionary? Check your answers using the key on page 381.

At the age of sixty-six, Harland Sanders had to <u>auction</u> off everything he owned in order to pay his debts. Once the successful <u>proprietor</u> of a large restaurant, Sanders saw his business suffer from the construction of a new freeway that bypassed his establishment and rerouted the traffic that had <u>formerly</u> passed.

With an income of only $105 a month in Social Security, he packed his car with a pressure cooker, some chickens, and sixty pounds of the seasoning that he had developed for frying chicken. He stopped at restaurants, where he cooked chicken for owners to <u>sample</u>. If they liked it, he offered to show them how to cook it. Then he sold them the seasoning and collected a <u>royalty</u> of four cents on each chicken they cooked. The rest is history. Eight years later, there were 638 Kentucky Fried Chicken franchises, and Colonel Sanders had sold his business again—this time for over two million dollars.

4   Scanning for Details

After reading a passage on the TOEFL, you will be expected to answer six to ten questions. Most of them are multiple-choice. First, read a question and find the important content words. Content words are usually nouns, verbs, or adjectives. They are called content words because they contain the content or meaning of a sentence.

Next, let your eyes travel quickly over the passage for the same content words or synonyms of the words. This is called *scanning*. By scanning, you can find a place in the reading passage where the answer to a question is found. Finally, read those specific sentences carefully and choose the answer that corresponds to the meaning of the sentences you have read.

EXERCISE

DIRECTIONS: First, read the following passage. Then, read the questions after the reading passage, and look for the content words. Finally, scan the passage for the same words or synonyms. Can you answer the questions? Check your answers using the key on page 382.

> To prepare for a career in engineering, a student must begin planning in high school. Mathematics and science should form the core curriculum. For example, in a school where sixteen credit hours are required for high school graduation, four should be in mathematics, one each in chemistry, biology, and physics. The remaining credits should include four in English and at least three in the humanities and social sciences. The average entering freshman in engineering should have achieved at least a 2.5 grade point average on a 4.0 scale in his or her high school. Although deficiencies can be corrected during the first year, the student who needs additional work should expect to spend five instead of four years to complete a degree.

1. What is the average grade point for an entering freshman in engineering?

2. When should a student begin planning for a career in engineering?

3. How can a student correct deficiencies in preparation?

4. How many credits should a student have in English?

5. How many credits are required for a high school diploma?

5   Making Inferences

Sometimes, in a reading passage, you will find a direct statement of fact. That is called evidence. But other times, you will not find a direct statement. Then you will need to use the evidence you have to make an inference. An *inference* is a logical conclusion based on evidence. It can be about the passage itself or about the author's viewpoint.

EXERCISE

DIRECTIONS: First, read the following passage. Then, read the questions after the passage, and make inferences. Can you find the evidence for your inference in the reading passage? Check your answers using the key on pages 382–383.

> When an acid is dissolved in water, the acid molecule divides into two parts, a hydrogen ion and another ion. An ion is an atom or a group of atoms that has an electrical charge. The charge can be either positive or negative. If hydrochloric acid is mixed with water, for example, it divides into hydrogen ions and chlorine ions.
>
> A strong acid ionizes to a great extent, but a weak acid does not ionize so much. The strength of an acid, therefore, depends on how much it ionizes, not on how many hydrogen ions are produced. It is interesting that nitric acid and sulfuric acid become greatly ionized whereas boric acid and carbonic acid do not.

1. What kind of acid is sulfuric acid?

2. What kind of acid is boric acid?

6   Identifying Exceptions

After reading a passage on the TOEFL, you will be asked to select from four possible answers the one that is NOT mentioned in the reading.

Use your scanning skills to locate related words and phrases in the passage and the answer choices.

EXERCISE

DIRECTIONS: First, read the following passage. Then, read the question after the reading passage. Last, scan the passage again for related words and phrases. Try to eliminate three of the choices. Check your answer using the key on page 383.

All music consists of two elements—expression and design. Expression is inexact and subjective and may be enjoyed in a personal or instinctive way. Design, on the other hand, is exact and must be analyzed objectively in order to be understood and appreciated. The folk song, for example, has a definite musical design that relies on simple repetition with a definite beginning and ending. A folk song generally consists of one stanza of music repeated for each stanza of verse.

Because of their communal, and usually uncertain origin, folk songs are often popular verse set to music. They are not always recorded and tend to be passed on in a kind of musical version of oral history. Each singer revises and perfects the song. In part as a consequence of this continuous revision process, most folk songs are almost perfect in their construction and design. A particular singer's interpretation of the folk song may provide an interesting expression, but the simple design that underlies the song itself is stable and enduring.

1. All of the following are true of a folk song EXCEPT
   (A) there is a clear start and finish
   (B) the origin is often not known
   (C) the design may change in the interpretation
   (D) simple repetition is characteristic of its design

7   Locating References

After reading a passage on the TOEFL, you will be asked to find the antecedent of a pronoun. An antecedent is a word or phrase to which a pronoun refers. Usually, you will be given a pronoun such as "it," "its," "them," or "their," and you will be asked to locate the reference word or phrase in the passage.

First, find the pronoun in the passage. Then read the sentence using the four answer choices in place of the pronoun. The meaning of the sentence in the context of the passage will not change when you substitute the correct antecedent.

EXERCISE

DIRECTIONS: First, find the pronoun in the following passage. Next, start reading several sentences before the sentence in which the pronoun is found, and continue reading several sentences after it. Then, substitute the words or phrases in the answer choices. Which one does not change the meaning of the sentence? Check your answer using the key on pages 383–384.

The National Road, also known as the Cumberland Road, was constructed in the early 1800s to provide transportation between the established commercial areas of the East and Northwest Territory. By 1818, the road had reached Wheeling, West Virginia, 130 miles from its point of origin in Cumberland, Maryland. The cost was a monumental thirteen thousand dollars per mile.

Upon reaching the Ohio River, the National Road became one of the major trade routes to the western states and territories, providing Baltimore with a trade advantage over neighboring cities. In order to compete, New York state authorized the construction of the Erie Canal, and Philadelphia initiated a transportation plan to link it with Pittsburgh. Towns along the rivers, canals, and the new National Road became important trade centers.

1. The word its refers to
   (A) the Northwest Territory
   (B) 1818
   (C) the road
   (D) Wheeling, West Virginia

2. The word it refers to
   (A) plan
   (B) construction
   (C) canal
   (D) transportation

8 Referring to the Passage

After reading the passage on the TOEFL, you will be asked to find certain information in the passage, and identify it by line number or paragraph.

First, read the question. Then refer to the line numbers and paragraph numbers in the answer choices to scan for the information in the question.

EXERCISE

DIRECTIONS: First, read the following passage. Then, refer back to the passage. Can you find the correct reference? Check your answer using the key on page 384.

In September of 1929, traders experienced a lack of confidence in the stock market's ability to continue its phenomenal rise. Prices fell. For many inexperienced investors, the drop produced a panic. They had all their money tied up in the market, and they were pressed to sell before the prices fell even lower. Sell orders were coming in so fast that the ticker tape at the New York Stock Exchange could not accommodate all the transactions.

To try to reestablish confidence in the market, a powerful group of New York bankers agreed to pool their funds and purchase stock above current market values. Although the buy orders were minimal, they were counting on their reputations to restore confidence on the part of the smaller investors, thereby affecting the number of sell orders. On Thursday, October 24, Richard Whitney, the Vice President of the New York Stock Exchange and a broker for the J.P. Morgan Company, made the effort on their behalf. Initially, it appeared to have been successful, then, on the following Tuesday, the crash began again and accelerated. By 1932, stocks were worth only twenty percent of their value at the 1929 high. The results of the crash had extended into every aspect of the economy, causing a long and painful depression, referred to in American history as the Great Depression.

1. Where in the passage does the author refer to the reason for the stock market crash?

2. Where in the passage does the author suggest that there was a temporary recovery in the stock market?

9 Reading Faster

Read the following passage, using the skills you have learned. Preview, read for main ideas, and use contexts for vocabulary. To read faster, read phrases instead of words. Try to see an entire line of text when you focus your eyes on the passage. Scan for details and evidence. Make inferences.

The computer-based version of this reading passage is best viewed on the CD-ROM that supplements the larger version of this book. Scroll through the passage, using the skills that you have learned. Check your answers on the screen. If you do not have a computer, then use the print version shown below and the following computer-assisted questions (on page 228).

Jazz is an improvisational form of music that originated in the southern United States after the Civil War. Although its origins and history are somewhat vague, we know that it began as the musical expression of black people who had formerly been slaves, combining hymns, spirituals, and traditional work songs into something quite new. The style was a blend of the rhythms brought to America by the Africans
Line who were imported as slave labor and the popular music of the
(9)   era that featured the ragtime piano. The term jazz itself is of obscure and possible nonmusical origin, but it was first used to describe this particular kind of musical expression in about 1915.

A jazz band commonly includes four to twelve musicians with a relatively large proportion of the group in the rhythm section. Customarily, there are a drummer, a bass player, and a pianist. Often there is also a banjo player or guitarist. In traditional jazz, the clarinet, trumpet, and trombone carry the melody.
In more modern jazz, the saxophone, violin, and flute may also be included in the melody section. Some jazz bands employ a blues singer. Most jazz is premised on the principle that an almost infinite number of variations can accommodate themselves to a progression of chords that can be repeated indefinitely to feature an improvisation by solo instruments or vocalists. For example, while the trumpet plays the melody, the clarinet might embellish and invent compatible melodies around the original theme. Such improvisation is a test of the jazz musician's skill and is referred to as tone color.

Jazz first became popular outside the United States in the 1920s when jazz bands began to record, distribute, and even export their recordings to Europe. Since jazz is improvisational, it does not exist in the form of printed scores, and recorded performances were and still are the best way of preserving the music. A very basic library of recorded jazz would include work by such classic artists as Jelly Roll Morton, Louis Armstrong, Duke Ellington, Count Basie, and Billie Holiday. Theirs is probably America's most unique and most important contribution to the musical world, although a few contemporary artists are keeping the tradition alive.

TYPES OF QUESTIONS

Multiple-Choice Questions

Paper-Based TOEFL

1. Which of the following is the main topic of the passage?
   - Ⓐ A definition of jazz
   - Ⓑ Jazz musicians
   - Ⓒ Improvisation in jazz
   - Ⓓ Jazz bands

2. The new music of jazz was first heard
   - Ⓐ in Europe
   - Ⓑ in Africa
   - Ⓒ in South America
   - Ⓓ in North America

3. The word "blend" in the passage is closest in meaning to
   - Ⓐ mixture
   - Ⓑ rejection
   - Ⓒ imitation
   - Ⓓ variety

Computer-Based TOEFL

Which of the following is the main topic of the passage?
   - ● A definition of jazz
   - ○ Jazz musicians
   - ○ Improvisation in jazz
   - ○ Jazz bands

The new music of jazz was first heard
   - ○ in Europe
   - ○ in Africa
   - ○ in South America
   - ● in North America

The word 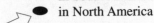 blend in the passage is closest in meaning to
   - ● mixture
   - ○ rejection
   - ○ imitation
   - ○ variety

4. The author mentions all of the
    following as characteristics of
    jazz EXCEPT
    Ⓐ a large number of percussion
        instruments
    Ⓑ a printed score for the music
    Ⓒ a melody played by the
        trumpet
    Ⓓ a ragtime piano

The author mentions all of the
following as characteristics of
jazz EXCEPT
○ a large number of percussion
   instruments
● a printed score for the music
○ a melody played by the
   trumpet
○ a ragtime piano

Answer Sheet

1. ● Ⓑ Ⓒ Ⓓ
2. Ⓐ Ⓑ Ⓒ ●
3. ● Ⓑ Ⓒ Ⓓ
4. Ⓐ ● Ⓒ Ⓓ

Computer-Assisted Questions

Location Questions

On some of the computer-assisted questions, you will be asked to locate information in the passage. These questions are like the multiple-choice questions on the Paper-Based TOEFL where you must locate information by identifying the line numbers in the passage. On the computer-assisted questions, you must click on the sentence or paragraph in the passage.

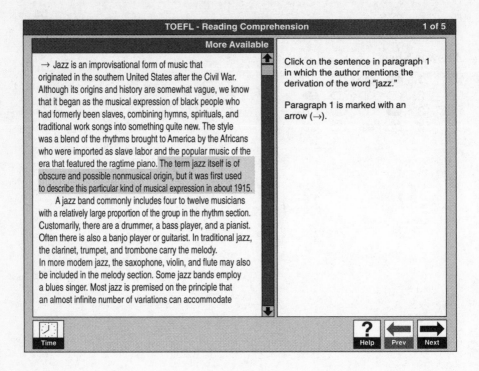

Synonyms

On some of the computer-assisted questions, you will be asked to locate synonyms in the reading passage. You must click on the word or phrase in the passage.

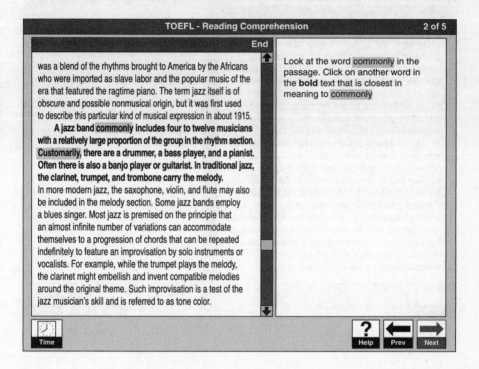

Paraphrased Sentences

On some of the computer-assisted questions, you will be asked to identify paraphrases of sentences in the passage.

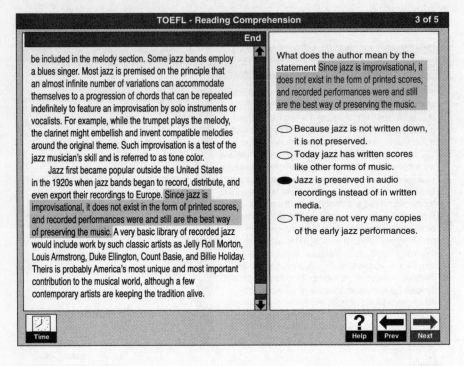

TOEFL - Reading Comprehension — 3 of 5

End

be included in the melody section. Some jazz bands employ
a blues singer. Most jazz is premised on the principle that
an almost infinite number of variations can accommodate
themselves to a progression of chords that can be repeated
indefinitely to feature an improvisation by solo instruments or
vocalists. For example, while the trumpet plays the melody,
the clarinet might embellish and invent compatible melodies
around the original theme. Such improvisation is a test of the
jazz musician's skill and is referred to as tone color.

Jazz first became popular outside the United States
in the 1920s when jazz bands began to record, distribute, and
even export their recordings to Europe. Since jazz is
improvisational, it does not exist in the form of printed scores,
and recorded performances were and still are the best way
of preserving the music. A very basic library of recorded jazz
would include work by such classic artists as Jelly Roll Morton,
Louis Armstrong, Duke Ellington, Count Basie, and Billie Holiday.
Theirs is probably America's most unique and most important
contribution to the musical world, although a few
contemporary artists are keeping the tradition alive.

What does the author mean by the
statement Since jazz is improvisational, it
does not exist in the form of printed scores,
and recorded performances were and still
are the best way of preserving the music.

○ Because jazz is not written down,
it is not preserved.

○ Today jazz has written scores
like other forms of music.

● Jazz is preserved in audio
recordings instead of in written
media.

○ There are not very many copies
of the early jazz performances.

Time

? Help ← Prev → Next

Reference Questions

On some of the computer-assisted questions, you will be asked to locate the nouns to which pronouns refer. These questions are like the multiple-choice questions on the Paper-Based TOEFL where you must choose the noun from four answer choices. On the computer-assisted questions, you must find the noun and click on it in the passage.

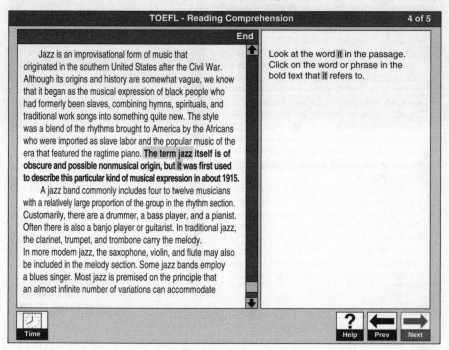

Sentence Insertion Questions

On some of the computer-assisted questions, you will be asked to locate the most logical place in the passage where a sentence could be inserted. You will have several options marked with a square (■) in the passage.

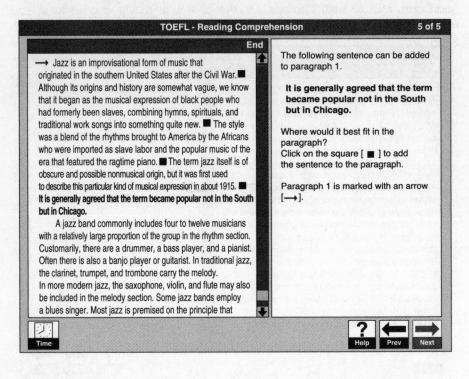

Computer Tutorial for the Reading Section

Testing Tools: Vocabulary, Icons, and Keys

Specific Vocabulary for Reading

Scroll   To move through reading passages on a screen. If the reading passage is long, new sentences will appear at the top and sentences that you have already read will disappear at the bottom.

Specific Icons for Reading

Scroll Bar   An *icon* used to move the reading passages on the screen so that you can see a long passage. First move the *arrow* to the top of the **scroll bar**; then hold the *mouse button* down to move the **scroll bar** from the beginning of the reading passage to the end. Remember, you can see the words *beginning*, *more available*, and *end* at the top of the **scroll bar**. These words show you the place in the passage that is displayed on the screen.

Proceed   An *icon* at the bottom of the screen with the reading passage. *Click* on **Proceed** after you have read the passage in order to see the first question. Remember, you cannot use **Proceed** until you have scrolled down to the end of the passage.

Previous   An *icon* at the bottom of the screen with the questions. *Click* on **Previous** to see the previous question.

Computer Screens for Reading

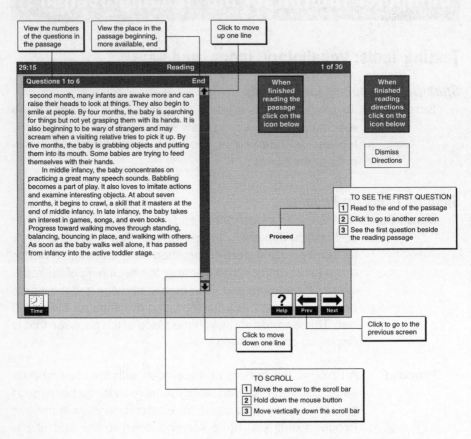

View the numbers of the questions in the passage

View the place in the passage beginning, more available, end

Click to move up one line

29:15 — Reading — 1 of 30

Questions 1 to 6 — End

 second month, many infants are awake more and can raise their heads to look at things. They also begin to smile at people. By four months, the baby is searching for things but not yet grasping them with its hands. It is also beginning to be wary of strangers and may scream when a visiting relative tries to pick it up. By five months, the baby is grabbing objects and putting them into its mouth. Some babies are trying to feed themselves with their hands.
    In middle infancy, the baby concentrates on practicing a great many speech sounds. Babbling becomes a part of play. It also loves to imitate actions and examine interesting objects. At about seven months, it begins to crawl, a skill that it masters at the end of middle infancy. In late infancy, the baby takes an interest in games, songs, and even books. Progress toward walking moves through standing, balancing, bouncing in place, and walking with others. As soon as the baby walks well alone, it has passed from infancy into the active toddler stage.

When finished reading the passage click on the icon below

When finished reading directions click on the icon below

Dismiss Directions

TO SEE THE FIRST QUESTION
1 Read to the end of the passage
2 Click to go to another screen
3 See the first question beside the reading passage

Proceed

Time

? Help ← Prev → Next

Click to move down one line

Click to go to the previous screen

TO SCROLL
1 Move the arrow to the scroll bar
2 Hold down the mouse button
3 Move vertically down the scroll bar

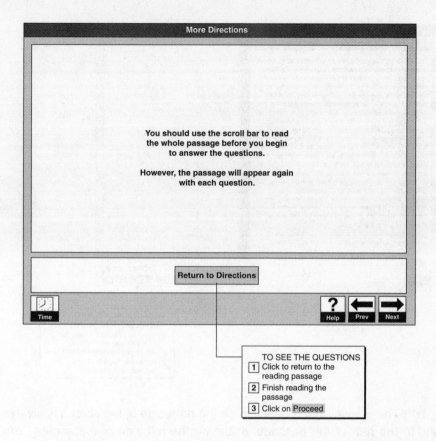

TIP: When you do not scroll to the end of the reading passage the first time you see it, this screen appears. You can spend a lot of time returning to the passage. Until you scroll to the bottom of the passage, you cannot see the questions.

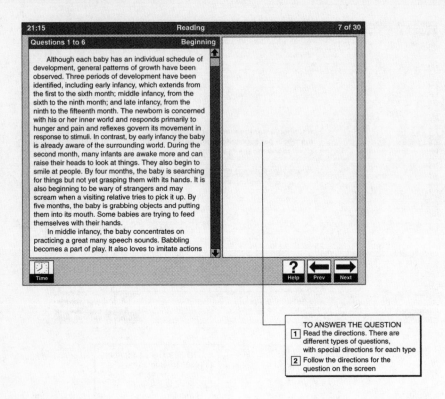

| 21:15 | Reading | 7 of 30 |

Questions 1 to 6   Beginning

Although each baby has an individual schedule of development, general patterns of growth have been observed. Three periods of development have been identified, including early infancy, which extends from the first to the sixth month; middle infancy, from the sixth to the ninth month; and late infancy, from the ninth to the fifteenth month. The newborn is concerned with his or her inner world and responds primarily to hunger and pain and reflexes govern its movement in response to stimuli. In contrast, by early infancy the baby is already aware of the surrounding world. During the second month, many infants are awake more and can raise their heads to look at things. They also begin to smile at people. By four months, the baby is searching for things but not yet grasping them with its hands. It is also beginning to be wary of strangers and may scream when a visiting relative tries to pick it up. By five months, the baby is grabbing objects and putting them into its mouth. Some babies are trying to feed themselves with their hands.

In middle infancy, the baby concentrates on practicing a great many speech sounds. Babbling becomes a part of play. It also loves to imitate actions

Time   Help   Prev   Next

TO ANSWER THE QUESTION
1 Read the directions. There are different types of questions, with special directions for each type
2 Follow the directions for the question on the screen

TIP: The answer to the question on the right side of the screen is always found in the part of the passage visible on the left side of the screen. You usually do not have to scroll through the passage to find the answer.

Simulations for Reading

In order to prepare for the experience that you will have on the Computer-Based TOEFL, you can use the CD-ROM that supplements the larger version of this book, *Barron's How to Prepare for the TOEFL*. Locate the Reading Section on the Model Tests. The computer will simulate the Reading Section on the Computer-Based TOEFL. These model tests are computer-assisted. The Reading Section of the Computer-Based TOEFL is not computer-adaptive.

As part of your study plan, be sure to review all of the questions in all of the Model Tests. Use the Explanatory Answers on the CD-ROM or on pages 385–390.

If you choose not to purchase the larger version of this book, or if you do not have a computer, you can still simulate some of the features of the Computer-Based TOEFL. Section 3 of the Computer-Based Model Tests in Chapter 8 of this book is printed in two columns to give you the same kind of visual impression that you will have when you read from a computer screen.

The on-screen directions for computer-assisted questions are also printed in the book.

Preview of Reading on the Next Generation TOEFL

The Next Generation TOEFL will include authentic textbook passages about twice as long as those that are presented on the current Computer-Based TOEFL.

The next edition of this book will include a new, revised Reading Chapter to introduce you to academic reading strategies for these longer texts.

Watch for *Barron's How to Prepare for the TOEFL, 12th Edition* to be published when the Next Generation TOEFL is introduced.

Advice for the Reading Section

Practice reading on a computer screen. Reading on a computer screen is different from reading on a page. First, there is generally less text visible; second, you must scroll instead of turning pages; and finally, there may be quite a few icons or other distracting visuals surrounding the passage.

To become comfortable with reading on a computer screen, you should take advantage of every opportunity you have to practice. If you have a computer, spend time reading on the screen. Everything you read will help you improve this new skill.

Practice reading the kinds of topics you will find in the Reading section. An inexpensive encyclopedia on CD-ROM would be a good investment. The kinds of passages found on the Computer-Based TOEFL are very similar to those found in a basic English encyclopedia.

If you do not have a computer, you may be able to locate software for an English encyclopedia at a local library where a computer is available for public use.

Become familiar with the directions for each of the question types. The different types of questions will appear at random. Directions will appear with each question, but if you already recognize the type of question presented, and you are familiar with the directions, you will save time. The less time you have to spend reading directions, the more time you will have to read the passages.

Advice for Success

Why are you preparing for the TOEFL? What goal is motivating you to study and improve your score? Do you want to attend a university in the United States, Britain, Australia, or Canada? Do you want to try for a scholarship from a sponsor in your country or region? Is the TOEFL required for graduation from your high school? Do you plan to apply for an assistantship at a graduate school? Do you need the score for a professional license in the United States?

Goals can be experienced as mental images. You can close your eyes and imagine everything, just like a movie. See yourself achieving your goal. Watch yourself as you attend school or practice your profession in your ideal environment. See other people congratulating you. Enjoy the success.

Understand that you cannot control reality with visualization. However, it does change your attitude, it helps you to focus, provides motivation, and reduces stress. Visualization is an excellent way to take a short break from studying.

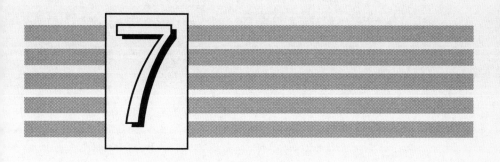

REVIEW OF WRITING

Overview of the Writing Section

QUICK COMPARISON—WRITING
PAPER-BASED TOEFL,
COMPUTER-BASED TOEFL, AND NEXT GENERATION TOEFL

Paper-Based TOEFL	*Computer-Based TOEFL*	*Next Generation TOEFL*
The essay, also called the Test of Written English (TWE), is offered five times each year. You must select a TOEFL test date when the TWE is scheduled if you need an essay score.	The essay is required as part of every TOEFL. You must write the essay as the last part of your TOEFL examination.	The Writing Section is required. It includes two essays.
When you register for the TOEFL on one of the dates when the TWE is offered, you are registered for the TWE at no additional cost.	When you register for the TOEFL, you are registered for the Writing Section at no additional cost.	When you register for the TOEFL, you are registered for the Writing Section at no additional cost.
There is only one topic for each essay.	There is only one topic for each essay.	There is only one topic for the independent writing task. A second topic is based on both a lecture and a reading passage.
Everyone taking the TOEFL writes an essay about the same topic.	The computer selects a topic for you. It may not be the same topic that is selected for someone else taking the TOEFL that day.	Everyone taking the same form of the TOEFL will write about the same topics.
You do not know any of the topics for the essay before the test administration.	All of the topics for the essay are published in the *TOEFL Information Bulletin* for Computer-Based Testing free of charge from ETS. They are also listed on the ETS web site at *www.toefl.org.*	At this point, no writing topics have been published; however, the essay topics for the Computer-Based TOEFL on the ETS web site are good practice for the general-topic essay. Visit *www.toefl.org.*
Most of the topics ask you to agree or disagree with a statement or to express an opinion.	Most of the topics ask you to agree or disagree with a statement or to express an opinion.	The topic for the independent writing task asks you to agree or disagree with a statement or to express an opinion. The integrated task refers to topics from a lecture and a reading passage.

Paper-Based TOEFL	Computer-Based TOEFL	Next Generation TOEFL
The topics are very general and do not require any specialized knowledge of the subject to answer them.	The topics are very general and do not require any specialized knowledge of the subject to answer them.	The independent topics are very general and do not require any specialized knowledge of the subject to answer them. Technical words are explained in the text or in a glossary for the integrated topics.
You have 30 minutes to complete the essay.	You have 30 minutes to complete the essay.	You have 30 minutes to complete the independent writing task. You have 20 minutes to complete the writing sample that refers to a lecture and a reading.
You handwrite your essay on paper provided in the test materials.	You can choose to handwrite your essay on paper or type it on the computer.	You should type your writing samples on the computer. If this is not possible, you can ask for special accommodations.
You have one page to organize your essay. This page is not graded.	You have one page to organize your essay. This page is not graded.	You have paper to take notes and organize your writing. Your notes and outlines are not graded.
Your essay will not be scored for neatness, but the readers must be able to understand what you have written.	Your essay will not be scored for neatness, but the readers must be able to understand what you have written.	Your writing will not be scored for neatness, but the readers must be able to understand what you have written.
You should write about 300 words, or three to five short paragraphs.	You should write about 300 words, or three to five short paragraphs.	You should write 300–350 words for the independent writing task, 200–250 words for the integrated writing sample.
A scale from 1 to 6 is used to grade the essay. The scale is explained on page 247.	A scale from 1 to 6 is used to grade the essay. The scale is explained on page 247.	A scale from 1 to 5 is planned to grade writing samples. Use the checklists on page 391.
The score is reported separately from the TOEFL score. It is not included in the computation of the total TOEFL score and does not affect your score on the multiple-choice TOEFL.	The score is combined with the score on the Structure Section. It is factored in the section score at 50 percent.	The score is reported as a separate Writing Section score.

Review of Strategies and Topics for the Writing Section

This Review can be used to prepare for both the Paper-Based TOEFL and the Computer-Based TOEFL. For the most part, the same types of topics are tested on both the Paper-Based TOEFL and the Computer-Based TOEFL. The essays on both the Paper-Based TOEFL and the Computer-Based TOEFL are scored using the same scale.

Three Steps for Writing Short Essays

There are three steps that most good writers follow in organizing their writing. You should use these steps when you write a short essay. First, tell your reader what you are going to write. Second, write it. Third, tell your reader what you wrote.

To look at these steps another way, your essay should have three parts:
1. A good beginning
2. Several good comments
3. A good ending

In this review of writing, we will discuss and give examples of the three parts of a short essay, using the types of topics that you will find on the TOEFL.

A Good Beginning

This is where you tell the reader what you are going to write. A good beginning has certain requirements.

A good beginning is short. Two or three sentences is enough to tell your reader how you plan to approach the topic.

A good beginning is direct. In the case of a comparison, state both sides of the argument in your first sentence. In a short composition, you don't have enough time for indirect approaches.

A good beginning is an outline. The second sentence usually outlines the organization. It gives the reader a general idea of your plan.

Good Comments

This is where you write.

Good comments include several points. A short essay may have between two and five points. Usually, the writer selects three. In the case of a comparison, three reasons is a standard argument.

Good comments are all related. All of the comments should relate to the general statement in the first sentence.

Good comments are logical. The points should be based on evidence. In the case of a comparison, the evidence should come from sources that can be cited, such as a television program that you have seen, an article that you have read in a magazine, a book that you have read, or a lecture that you have heard.

Good comments are not judgments. Opinions should be identified by phrases such as, "in my view," "in my opinion," or "it seems to me that." Furthermore, opinions should be based on evidence. Opinions that are not based on evidence are judgments. Judgments usually use words like "good" or "bad," "right" or "wrong." Judgments are not good comments.

A Good Ending

This is where you tell the reader what you wrote.

A good ending is a summary. The last sentence is similar to the first sentence. In a short essay, a good ending does not add new information. It does not introduce a new idea.

A good ending is not an apology. A good ending does not apologize for not having said enough, for not having had enough time, or for not using good English.

Scoring Scale for the Essay

The essay is scored on a scale of 1 to 6. A score between two points on the scale—5.5, 4.5, 3.5, 2.5, 1.5—can also be reported. The following guidelines are used by evaluators:

6 shows consistent proficiency	• Is well organized • Addresses the topic • Includes examples and details • Has few errors in grammar and vocabulary
5 shows inconsistent proficiency	• Is well organized • Addresses the topic • Includes fewer examples and details • Has more errors in grammar and vocabulary
4 shows minimal proficiency	• Is adequately organized • Addresses most of the topic • Includes some examples and details • Has errors in grammar and vocabulary that occasionally confuse meaning
3 shows developing proficiency	• Is inadequately organized • Addresses part of the topic • Includes few examples and details • Has many errors in grammar and vocabulary that confuse meaning
2 shows little proficiency	• Is disorganized • Does not address the topic • Does not include examples and details • Has many errors in grammar and vocabulary that consistently confuse meaning
1 shows no proficiency	• Is disorganized • Does not address the topic • Does not include examples and details • Has so many errors in grammar and vocabulary that meaning is not communicated
0 shows no comprehension	• Does not write an essay • Writes an essay on a different topic

Example Essay

The following example essay would receive a score of 6. It is well organized, it addresses the topic, it includes examples and details, and it has some but not many errors in grammar and vocabulary.

Read and study this example essay before you complete the Model Tests.

Question:

Some students like to take distance-learning courses by computer. Other students prefer to study in traditional classroom settings with a teacher. Consider the advantages of both options, and make an argument for the way that students should organize their schedules.

Outline

Advantages distance-learning courses

- *Attend class at your convenience*
- *Complete assignments at own pace*
- *Repeat lectures*

Advantages traditional courses

- *Structured environment*
- *More personal relationship*
- *Immediate response to questions*
- *Study groups and friendships*

Example Essay

Both distance-learning classes and traditional classes provide important but different experiences for college students. On the one hand, there are

Line   many advantages to distance-learning courses. One
(5)   of the most important benefits is the opportunity to attend class on your convenience. This is very important for students who hold full-time jobs since they can choose to take their classes on a schedule that allows them to continue working.

(10)   Another advantage is the chance to complete assignments at your own pace. For students who can work more quick than their classmates, it is possible to earn more credits during the semester. A huge advantage to international students is the

(15)   option of listen to lectures more than once.

On the other hand, there are advantages to attending a traditional class. The structured environment is beneficial, especially for students who are not as highly motivating. In addition, it is

(20)   more likely that you will develop a personal relationship with the teacher, an advantage not only for the course but also after the course when you need a recommendation. By seeing you and talking with you face-to-face, the teacher will remember

(25)   you better. It is also easier to get an immediate response to questions because you only have to raise your hand instead sending e-mail and waiting for an answer. Last, the opportunity for study groups

and friendships is different and more personal
(30) *when you sit in the same room.*

Given all the advantages of both types of
courses, I think that students would be wise to regis-
ter for distance-learning courses and traditional
classroom courses during their college experiences.
(35) *By participating in distance-learning courses,*
they can work independently in classes that may
be more difficult for them, repeating the lectures on
computer at convenient times. By attending tradi-
tional classes, they can get to know the teachers
(40) *personally and will have good references when they*
need them. They will also make friends in the class.
By sharing information with other students, they
can organize their schedules for the following
semester, chosing the best classes and including both
(45) *distance-learning and traditional courses.*

Evaluator's Comments

This writing sample is well-organized with a good topic sentence and good support statements. It addresses the question, and does not digress from the topic. There is a logical progression of ideas and excellent language proficiency, as evidenced by a variety of grammatical structures and appropriate vocabulary. There are only a few grammatical errors that have been corrected below:

Line 6	at your convenience
Line 12	more quickly
Lines 14–15	the option of listening
Line 19	motivated
Line 27	instead of
Line 44	choosing

SCORE: 6

Computer Tutorial for the Writing Section

Testing Tools: Vocabulary, Icons, and Keys

Specific Vocabulary for the Essay

Text
All printed material on the screen. **Text** can refer to a word, a sentence, a paragraph, several paragraphs, or an essay.

Cursor
The line that shows you where you can begin typing. When you move the *mouse*, the **cursor** appears. You can move the **cursor** on your essay by moving the *mouse* on your *mouse pad*.

Blinking
Flashing on and off. The *cursor* is usually **blinking** to help you see it.

Highlight
To select *text* in your essay that you want to edit. To **high-light**, move the *cursor* to the beginning of the place in your essay that you want to change. Hold down the mouse button and move to the end of the place in your essay that you want to change. Release the mouse button. The **highlighted** *text* should be shaded.

Keys
The individual buttons on the keyboard used for typing and editing your essay.

Keys for the Essay

Arrow Keys
Keys that let you move around in your essay. There is an **up arrow**, **down arrow**, **left arrow**, and **right arrow**. They are found between the letters and the numbers on the keyboard. Use the **arrow keys** to move up, down, left, or right.

Page Up, Page Down
Keys that let you see your essay if it is longer than the screen. The **Page Up** and **Page Down** keys are above the *arrow keys* on the keyboard. Use **Page Up** to scroll to the beginning of your essay. Use **Page Down** to scroll to the end of your essay.

Backspace   A key that moves you back one space at a time. Use the **Backspace** key to erase *text* from right to left.

Space Bar   The long key at the bottom of the keyboard. Use the **Space Bar** two or three times to indent a paragraph. Remember, the *Tab* key does not function on your keyboard.

Icons for the Essay

Cut   An example of an *icon*. After you *highlight* the text you want to delete or move, click on **Cut**. The text will disappear. Use the **Cut** icon to delete text or as the first step in moving text.

Paste   An example of an *icon*. After you *cut* text, you can move the *cursor* to the place in the essay where you want to insert the text, and click on **Paste**. The text you *highlighted* will appear. Use the **Paste** icon as the second step in moving text.

Undo   An example of an *icon*. It lets you change your mind. For example, if you move a sentence, and then you want to move it back to the original place in your essay, click on **Undo**. **Undo** will return whatever you did last back to the way it looked before you made the change. Remember, **Undo** will only return your last change, not several changes.

Keyboard for the Essay

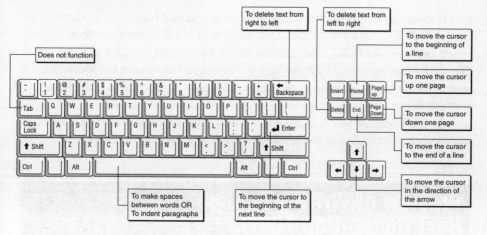

TIP: If you click the mouse, you can delete text. You may even delete your essay! If this happens, click on **Undo** immediately.

Computer Screen for the Essay

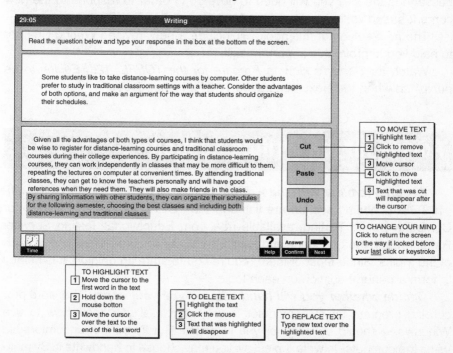

TIP: Be sure that you have completed the essay to your satisfaction before you click on **Answer Confirm**. After you click on **Answer Confirm**, you cannot continue writing or editing your essay.

Simulations for the Essay

In order to simulate the experience that you will have on the Computer-Based TOEFL, type the Model Test essays using the word processing program on the CD-ROM that supplements the larger version of this book, *Barron's How to Prepare for the TOEFL*. If you do not have a computer, handwrite the Model Test essays on paper. Be sure to complete your essay in thirty minutes.

As part of your study plan, it is a good idea to have an English teacher score your essays using the guidelines on page 247 of this book.

Preview of Writing on the Next Generation TOEFL

The Next Generation TOEFL will include content essays as well as personal opinion topics like those on the Computer-Based TOEFL and the Test of Written English (TWE). Summarizing an academic lecture or a textbook passage is the skill you will need to develop in order to respond to the new content-based writing tasks on the Next Generation TOEFL.

The next edition of this book will include a new, revised Writing Chapter to help you improve this important skill.

Watch for *Barron's How to Prepare for the TOEFL, 12th Edition* to be published when the Next Generation TOEFL is introduced.

Advice for the Writing Section

Become familiar with the writing topics. All of the topics from the official TOEFL Writing section are listed in the *TOEFL Information Bulletin* for Computer-Based Testing, available free from Educational Testing Service. Read through the questions and think about how you would respond to each of the topics. Since most of them require you to state an opinion, it is helpful to form a general opinion on each topic.

Decide whether you will handwrite or type your essay. The word processing program for the computer is very simple. If you know how to use Windows, it should be easy for you to adjust. But if you feel uncomfortable using the computer to write the essay, you may choose to handwrite it. By making your decision before you take the TOEFL, you will not waste time thinking about the way you will complete your test. You can use every minute to organize and write the essay.

Write on the topic you are assigned. If you write on a topic other than the one you have been assigned, your test will not be scored.

Get help from the test administrator. If you are having a problem with the word processing program, notify one of the test administrators immediately. There should be several in the room. They cannot help you with the answers on the TOEFL, but they can help you use the computer. That is why they are there. Tell the administrator, "Excuse me. I am trying to _____. What should I do?"

Advice for Success

Supportive people in our lives help us to do our best and be our best. Negative people steal our energy and bring us down with them. If negative people like that are in your life, you may not be able to avoid them completely, but you should consider spending less time with them, at least until you achieve your goal. You can spend the additional time with positive, supportive people who encourage you and energize you.

If you have even one negative person in your study group, he or she will affect the progress of the entire group. If you continue to associate with negative people, they will make it more difficult for you to act on the advice for success in this book. Associate with positive people. This decision will increase your confidence, motivation, and energy. Stay on track with the support of positive family members, teachers, and friends.

TOEFL MODEL TESTS

There are two types of Model Tests to help you prepare for the TOEFL. The questions on Model Tests 1–3 are like those that frequently appear on the Paper-Based and the Computer-Based TOEFL. The questions on Model Test 4 are like those that frequently appear on the Next Generation TOEFL.

Both types of Model Tests are found on the CD-ROM that supplements the larger version of this book, *Barron's How to Prepare for the TOEFL, 11th Edition.*

Model Tests 1–3 in this book appear as Model Tests 1–3 on the CD-ROM. Model Test 4 in this book appears as Model Test 9 on the CD-ROM.

How to Answer Questions for Model Tests 1–4

If you use the CD-ROM to take the Model Tests, you will not need to write in your book. If you do not have access to a computer, mark your responses directly on the tests in the book.

For multiple-choice questions that require you to choose one answer, fill in the oval of the letter that corresponds to the answer you have chosen.

The Palo Verde tree _____ in spring.

● has beautiful yellow blossoms
Ⓑ beautiful yellow blossoms
Ⓒ having beautiful yellow blossoms
Ⓓ with beautiful yellow blossoms

For questions that require you to choose two answers, mark an X in the squares that correspond to the answers you have chosen.

According to the professor, what was the Hemingway style?

Click on two answers.

☒ Powerful descriptions
Ⓑ Imaginative details
☒ Short sentences
Ⓓ Difficult symbolism

For questions that require you to click on sentences to move them into categories on charts, write letters on the charts that correspond to the sentences you have chosen.

How did Hemingway use his experience in different novels?

Click on the sentence.

Then click on the space where

it belongs. Use each sentence

only once.

A He was fishing in the Gulf of Mexico.
B He was driving an ambulance in Italy.
C He was working as a newspaper reporter in Paris.

The Sun Also Rises	C
A Farewell to Arms	B
The Old Man and the Sea	A

For questions that require you to put events in order, write letters in the numbered boxes that correspond to the sequence you have chosen.

The professor briefly describes Hemingway's life as an author. Summarize the biographical data by putting the events in order.

Click on the sentence.

Then click on the space where

it belongs. Use each sentence

only once.

A Hemingway wrote about his experiences as an ambulance driver during the war.

B Hemingway received the Nobel Prize for literature.

C Hemingway published *The Old Man and the Sea.*

D Hemingway was a newspaper reporter in Paris.

1 | D
2 | A
3 | C
4 | B

For questions that require you to click on a word or phrase, circle the word or phrase in the passage.

Look at the word one in the passage.
Click on the word or phrase in the bold
text that one refers to.

> Solar astronomers do know that the sun is
> divided into five general layers or zones. Starting at
> the outside and going down into the sun, the zones are
> the corona, chromosphere, photosphere, convection
> zone, and finally the core. The first three zones are
> regarded as the sun's atmosphere. But since the
> sun has no solid surface, it is hard to tell where the
> atmosphere ends and the main body of the sun
> begins.
> **The sun's outermost layer begins about
> 10,000 miles above the visible surface and
> goes outward for millions of miles. This is the
> only part of the sun that can be seen during an
> (eclipse) such as the one in February 1979.** At
> any other time, the corona can be seen only when
> special instruments are used on cameras and
> telescopes to block the light from the photosphere.
> The corona is a brilliant, pearly white, filmy light,
> about as bright as the full moon. Its beautiful rays
> are a sensational sight during an eclipse. The
> corona's rays flash out in a brilliant fan that has wispy
> spikelike rays near the sun's north and south poles.
> The corona is generally thickest at the sun's equator.
> The corona is made up of gases streaming

For questions that require you to click on a sentence, circle the sentence in the passage.

Click on the sentence in paragraph 4 or 5
in which the author compares the light of
the sun's outermost layer to that of another
astronomical body.

Paragraphs 4 and 5 are marked with arrows
[→]

> cameras and telescopes to block the light from the
> photosphere.
> → The corona is a brilliant, pearly white, filmy light,
> about as bright as the full moon. Its beautiful rays
> are a sensational sight during an eclipse. The
> corona's rays flash out in a brilliant fan that has wispy
> spikelike rays near the sun's north and south poles.
> The corona is generally thickest at the sun's equator.
> → The corona is made up of gases streaming
> outward at tremendous speeds that reach a
> temperature of more than 2 million degrees
> Fahrenheit. The gas thins out as it reaches the
> space around the planets. By the time the gas of
> the corona reaches the Earth it has a relatively low
> density.

For questions that require you to add a sentence, circle the square [■] where the sentence is to be inserted.

The following sentence can be added to paragraph 1.

At the center of the Earth's solar system lies the sun.

Where would it best fit in paragraph 1? Click on the square [■] to add the sentence to the paragraph.

Paragraph 1 is marked with an arrow [→].

→(■)The temperature of the sun is over 10,000 degrees Fahrenheit at the surface, but it rises to perhaps more than 27,000,000° at the center. ■The sun is so much hotter than the Earth that matter can exist only as a gas, except perhaps at the core. In the core of the sun, the pressures are so great that, despite the high temperature, there may be a small solid core. ■However, no one really knows, since the center of the sun can never be directly observed. ■

Solar astronomers do know that the sun is divided into five general layers or zones. Starting at the outside and going down into the sun, the zones are the corona, chromosphere, photosphere, convection zone, and finally the core. The first three zones are regarded as the sun's atmosphere. But since the sun has no solid surface, it is hard to tell where the atmosphere ends and the main body of the sun begins.

The sun's outermost layer begins about 10,000 miles above the visible surface and goes outward for millions of miles. This is the only part of the sun that can be seen during an eclipse such as the one in

Model Test 1
Computer-Assisted TOEFL

Section 1:
Listening

The Listening Section of the test measures the ability to understand conversations and talks in English. You will use headphones to listen to the conversations and talks. While you are listening, pictures of the speakers or other information will be presented on your computer screen. There are two parts to the Listening Section, with special directions for each part.

On the day of the test, the amount of time you will have to answer all of the questions will appear on the computer screen. The time you spend listening to the test material will not be counted. The listening material and questions about it will be presented only one time. You will not be allowed to take notes or have any paper at your computer. You will both see and hear the questions before the answer choices appear. You can take as much time as you need to select an answer; however, it will be to your advantage to answer the questions as quickly as possible. You may change your answer as many times as you want before you confirm it. After you have confirmed an answer, you will not be able to return to the question.

Before you begin working on the Listening Section, you will have an opportunity to adjust the volume of the sound. You may not be able to change the volume after you have started the test.

QUESTION DIRECTIONS—Part A

In Part A of the Listening Section, you will hear short conversations between two people. In some of the conversations, each person speaks only once. In other conversations, one or both of the people speak more than once. Each conversation is followed by one question about it.

Each question in this part has four answer choices. You should click on the best answer to each question. Answer the questions on the basis of what is stated or implied by the speakers.

1. What is the man's problem?

   Ⓐ He doesn't mind the traffic.
   Ⓑ He takes the bus to school.
   Ⓒ He has to stand on the bus if he takes it to school.
   Ⓓ He wants to ride to school with the woman.

2. What does the man mean?

   Ⓐ The woman should not consider her advisor in the decision.
   Ⓑ The woman should not take Dr. Sullivan's section.
   Ⓒ The woman's advisor will not be offended.
   Ⓓ The woman should not take a physics course.

3. What does the woman imply?

   Ⓐ She is not interested in the man.
   Ⓑ She does not like lectures.
   Ⓒ She would go out with the man on another occasion.
   Ⓓ She would rather stay at home.

4. What does the woman mean?

   Ⓐ The bike is in good condition.
   Ⓑ The man needs to replace the bike.
   Ⓒ The bike is missing.
   Ⓓ It is a new bike.

5. What does the man want to drink?

   Ⓐ Something cold.
   Ⓑ Coffee.
   Ⓒ Tea.
   Ⓓ Both coffee and tea.

6. What does the man suggest the woman do?

   Ⓐ Ask directions.
   Ⓑ Walk to the shopping center.
   Ⓒ Take a taxi.
   Ⓓ Wait for the bus.

7. What can be inferred about the woman?

   Ⓐ She does not plan to study.
   Ⓑ She has a very busy schedule.
   Ⓒ She is lost.
   Ⓓ She has not registered yet.

8. What does the man mean?

   Ⓐ He does not want to listen to the radio.
   Ⓑ He has changed his opinion about turning on the radio.
   Ⓒ The radio will not bother him.
   Ⓓ The radio is not working very well.

9. What does the woman suggest Anna do?

   Ⓐ Stop worrying.
   Ⓑ Go out more.
   Ⓒ Talk to a friend.
   Ⓓ Get counseling.

10. What does the man mean?

   Ⓐ He prefers to talk another time.
   Ⓑ He wants the woman to go away.
   Ⓒ He would like the woman to continue.
   Ⓓ He doesn't know what to think.

11. What will the man probably do?

   Ⓐ Accept the woman's apology.
   Ⓑ Allow the woman to go ahead of him.
   Ⓒ Apologize to the woman.
   Ⓓ Go to the front of the line.

12. What does the woman imply?

   Ⓐ The neighbors have parties often.
   Ⓑ She does not like her neighbors.
   Ⓒ The neighbors' party is disturbing her.
   Ⓓ She will not be invited to the neighbors' party.

13. What had the man assumed?

    Ⓐ Dr. Franklin is not very
       understanding.
    Ⓑ The extension was a very bad
       idea.
    Ⓒ He is surprised that the woman
       was denied her request.
    Ⓓ The professor does not have a
       policy.

14. What problem do the man and
    woman have?

    Ⓐ They do not have a telephone.
    Ⓑ They are late.
    Ⓒ They have been left.
    Ⓓ They got lost.

15. What is the woman probably going to
    do?

    Ⓐ Pay the rent for half a month.
    Ⓑ Help the man move.
    Ⓒ Stay where she is living until
       the 15th.
    Ⓓ Move out of the apartment.

16. What had the man assumed about
    MaryAnne?

    Ⓐ She had already taken the test.
    Ⓑ She did not want to take classes.
    Ⓒ She had not taken the placement
       test.
    Ⓓ She would take the math classes
       later.

17. What does the man mean?

    Ⓐ The plan is to remain in the
       class.
    Ⓑ It is not comfortable in the
       classroom.
    Ⓒ He has been absent because he
       was sick.
    Ⓓ The weather has been very bad.

QUESTION DIRECTIONS—Part B

In Part B of the Listening Section, you will hear several longer conversations and talks. Each conversation or talk is followed by several questions. The conversations, talks, and questions will not be repeated.

The conversations and talks are about a variety of topics. You do not need special knowledge of the topics to answer the questions correctly. Rather, you should answer each question on the basis of what is stated or implied by the speakers in the conversations or talks.

For most of the questions, you will need to click on the best of four possible answers. Some questions will have special directions. The special directions will appear in a box on the computer screen.

18. What is Mike's problem?

    Ⓐ He was late arriving at
       registration.
    Ⓑ He needs an advisor's signature
       on a course request form.
    Ⓒ He is not doing well in the class
       because it is so large.
    Ⓓ He must have the permission of
       the instructor to enroll in a class.

19. What does Mike want Professor Day
    to do?

    Ⓐ Help him with the class.
    Ⓑ Explain some technical
       vocabulary.
    Ⓒ Give him special permission to
       take the class.
    Ⓓ Take a form to the registration
       area.

20. What does Mike say about graduation?

   (A) He has planned to graduate in the fall.
   (B) He has to take Professor Day's class in order to graduate.
   (C) He needs the professor to sign his application for graduation.
   (D) He does not have enough credits for graduation.

21. What does Professor Day decide to do?

   (A) Enroll Mike in the class next year.
   (B) Allow Mike to take the class this term.
   (C) Give Mike permission to graduate without the class.
   (D) Register Mike for another class.

22. What is MUZAK?

   (A) A slow, soft song.
   (B) Music in restaurants.
   (C) Background music.
   (D) A pleasant addition to the environment.

23. What is the average increase in productivity when MUZAK is introduced?

   (A) Thirteen percent.
   (B) Five to ten percent.
   (C) One hundred percent.
   (D) Thirty percent.

24. What is stimulus progression?

   (A) Background music that is low in stimulus value.
   (B) Upbeat music that stimulates sales.
   (C) Music engineered to reduce stress.
   (D) Music that starts slow and gets faster at times of the day when people get tired.

25. How does MUZAK influence sales in supermarkets?

   (A) It can cause shoppers to go through the line faster.
   (B) It can cause shoppers to buy thirty percent more or less.
   (C) It can cause shoppers to walk slower and buy more.
   (D) It does not influence sales.

26. What is this announcement mainly about?

   (A) The "Sun-Up Semester" program.
   (B) The Community College campus.
   (C) Video telecourses.
   (D) Technology for distance learning.

27. Why does the speaker mention the "Sun-Up Semester"?

   (A) To clarify how to register.
   (B) To advertise the college.
   (C) To provide a listing of courses.
   (D) To give students an alternative to video tapes.

28. How can students register for a course?

   (A) They should come to campus.
   (B) They can call the Community College.
   (C) They must contact the instructor.
   (D) They can use computers.

29. How can students contact the instructor?

   (A) By using e-mail.
   (B) By calling KCC-TV.
   (C) By writing letters.
   (D) By making video tapes.

30. What is the main topic of this conversation?

   (A) The woman's health.
   (B) The woman's grades.
   (C) The man's joke.
   (D) The man's stress.

31. What was the woman's problem?

    (A) She was taking too many classes.
    (B) She was very tired because she studied too late.
    (C) She had been ill last semester.
    (D) She may have to withdraw from school this semester.

32. Why is mono called the "college disease"?

    (A) Many students get mono while they are in college.
    (B) If one student gets mono, the whole college becomes infected.
    (C) It is a joke about college students that the woman tells.
    (D) The disease was first identified on a college campus.

33. What advice does the woman give the man?

    (A) Drop out of school for a semester and return later.
    (B) Study harder to learn all the lessons this semester.
    (C) Take fewer hours each semester and add one semester to the program.
    (D) Add extra classes to the program even if it requires another semester.

34. What central theme does the lecture examine?

    (A) The relationship between language and culture.
    (B) The culture of Hopi society.
    (C) Native American cultures.
    (D) The life of Benjamin Lee Whorf.

35. Which languages did Whorf use in his research?

    (A) European languages.
    (B) South American languages.
    (C) Native American languages.
    (D) Computer languages.

36. According to the lecturer, what is linguistic relativity?

    (A) All languages are related.
    (B) All Native American languages are related.
    (C) Language influences the manner in which an individual understands reality.
    (D) Language and culture are not related.

37. What is another name for linguistic relativity?

    (A) The Sapir Hypothesis.
    (B) The Sapir-Whorf Hypothesis.
    (C) The Sapir-Whorf-Boas Hypothesis.
    (D) The American Indian Model of the Universe.

38. What is the topic of this discussion?

    (A) Air pollution.
    (B) Acid rain.
    (C) Fossil fuels.
    (D) The Great Lakes.

39. What is acid rain?

    (A) Precipitation that is polluted by sulfuric acid and nitric acid.
    (B) Rain that falls after a long period of severe drought.
    (C) Large concentrations of acid in the soil around the Great Lakes.
    (D) Water vapor that is mixed with a high concentration of sulfur.

40. In which two ways has the environment been damaged along the Great Lakes?

    Click on 2 answers.

    [A] The air now contains dangerous levels of carbon monoxide.
    [B] Weather patterns have been disturbed.
    [C] Water resources have been polluted.
    [D] The soil has been depleted of nutrients.

41. What are the conditions of the Air Quality Accord?

   Ⓐ Companies in the United States must control pollution that could affect Canadian resources.
   Ⓑ There are limits placed on the quantity of acidic deposits that can cross the border.
   Ⓒ Governments and agencies will regulate automobile emissions.
   Ⓓ Fuels cannot contain any sulfur near the border.

42. What is the topic of this lecture?

   Ⓐ Three major types of bacteria.
   Ⓑ How microscopic organisms are measured.
   Ⓒ How bacteria is used for research in genetics.
   Ⓓ Diseases caused by bacteria.

43. Which two characteristics are common in bacteria?

   Click on 2 answers.

   Ⓐ They have one cell.
   Ⓑ They are harmful to humans.
   Ⓒ They reproduce quickly.
   Ⓓ They die when exposed to air.

44. Which of the following slides contain cocci bacteria?

  A   B   C

45. Why are bacteria being used in the research study at the University?

   Ⓐ Bacteria have unusual cell formations.
   Ⓑ Bacteria live harmlessly on the skin, mouth, and intestines.
   Ⓒ Bacteria are similar to other life forms.
   Ⓓ Bacteria cause many diseases in humans.

46. What is the purpose of this conversation?

   Ⓐ The man needs help changing his schedule.
   Ⓑ The man is looking for a job in the morning.
   Ⓒ The man is trying to get a student loan.
   Ⓓ The man is changing his major to sociology.

47. Why does the man need to take at least twelve hours?

   Ⓐ He wants to graduate as soon as possible.
   Ⓑ He must be a full-time student to qualify for his loan.
   Ⓒ His advisor insists that he study full time.
   Ⓓ All the courses are required.

48. Why does the man prefer Sociology 560?

   Ⓐ It is a required course.
   Ⓑ It is offered in the afternoon.
   Ⓒ It is taught by Dr. Brown.
   Ⓓ It is a sociology class.

49. What will Dr. Kelly do?

   Ⓐ Help the man withdraw from school.
   Ⓑ Change the man's class schedule.
   Ⓒ Give the man a student loan.
   Ⓓ Change the man's major.

50. What will the man probably do after the conversation?

   Ⓐ Go to Dr. Brown's office.
   Ⓑ See Dr. Brown in class.
   Ⓒ Call Dr. Brown.
   Ⓓ Send the form to Dr. Brown.

Section 2: Structure

This section measures the ability to recognize language that is appropriate for standard written English. There are two types of questions in this section.

In the first type of question, there are incomplete sentences. Beneath each sentence, there are four words or phrases. You will choose the one word or phrase that best completes the sentence. Clicking on a choice darkens the oval. After you click on **Next** and **Confirm Answer**, the next question will be presented.

The second type of question has four underlined words or phrases. You will choose the one underlined word or phrase that must be changed for the sentence to be correct. Clicking on an underlined word or phrase will darken it. After you click on **Next** and **Confirm Answer**, the next question will be presented.

1. Justice Sandra Day O'Connor was _____ to serve on the U.S. Supreme Court.

    (A) the woman who first
    (B) the first woman
    (C) who the first woman
    (D) the first and a woman

2. North Carolina is well known not only for the Great Smoky Mountains National Park _____ for the Cherokee settlements.

    (A) also
    (B) and
    (C) but also
    (D) because of

3. If biennials were planted this year, they will be likely to bloom
          (A)   (B)   (C)
   next year.
     (D)

4. The value of the dollar declines
           (A)   (B)
   as the rate of inflation raises.
   (C)   (D)

5. General Grant had General Lee _____ him at Appomattox to sign the official surrender of the Confederate forces.

    (A) to meet
    (B) met
    (C) meet
    (D) meeting

6. Anthropologists assert that many of the early Native Americans who lived on the Plains did not engage in planting crops but to hunt, living
              (A)   (B)   (C)
   primarily on buffalo meat.
     (D)

7. The differential attractions of the sun and the moon have a direct effect
                (A)
   in the rising and falling of the tides.
   (B) (C)   (D)

8. _____ both men and women have often achieved their career ambitions by midlife, many people are afflicted by at least a temporary period of dissatisfaction and depression.

    (A) Because
    (B) So
    (C) A
    (D) Who

9. With special enzymes that are
    <u>call</u> restriction enzymes, it is possible
    Ⓐ
    <u>to split off</u> segments of DNA <u>from</u>
       Ⓑ   Ⓒ
    the <u>donor</u> organism.
       Ⓓ

10. <u>Because of</u> the movement of a
       Ⓐ
    glacier, <u>the form of</u> the Great Lakes
            Ⓑ   Ⓒ
    was very <u>slow</u>.
           Ⓓ

11. _____ small specimen of the
    embryonic fluid is removed from a
    fetus, it will be possible to determine
    whether the baby will be born with
    birth defects.

    Ⓐ A
    Ⓑ That a
    Ⓒ If a
    Ⓓ When it is a

12. To generate income, magazine
    publishers must decide whether to
    increase the subscription price or
    _____ .

    Ⓐ to sell advertising
    Ⓑ if they should sell advertising
    Ⓒ selling advertising
    Ⓓ sold advertising

13. <u>If</u> it receives <u>enough</u> rain at the
    Ⓐ   Ⓑ
    proper time, hay <u>will grow</u> quickly,
                Ⓒ
    <u>as</u> grass.
    Ⓓ

14. *Psychology Today* <u>is</u> <u>interesting</u>,
                Ⓐ   Ⓑ
    informative, and <u>it is</u> easy <u>to read</u>.
               Ⓒ   Ⓓ

15. <u>Before</u> she died, Andrew Jackson's
      Ⓐ
    daughter, <u>who</u> <u>lives</u> in the family
            Ⓑ   Ⓒ
    mansion, <u>used to take</u> tourists
            Ⓓ
    through her home.

16. If it _____ more humid in the
    desert of the Southwest, the hot
    temperatures would be unbearable.

    Ⓐ be
    Ⓑ is
    Ⓒ was
    Ⓓ were

17. _____ Java Man, who lived before
    the first Ice Age, is the first manlike
    animal.

    Ⓐ It is generally believed that
    Ⓑ Generally believed it is
    Ⓒ Believed generally is
    Ⓓ That is generally believed

18. It is essential that the temperature <u>is</u>
    <u>not</u> elevated <u>to a point</u> where the
    Ⓐ   Ⓑ
    substance formed <u>may become</u>
                   Ⓒ
    unstable and decompose into <u>its</u>
                       Ⓓ
    constituent elements.

19. John Philip Sousa, <u>who</u> <u>many</u> people
             Ⓐ   Ⓑ
    consider the <u>greatest</u> composer of
              Ⓒ
    marches, wrote his music during the
    era <u>known as</u> the Gay 90s.
        Ⓓ

20. For the investor who _____
    money, silver or bonds are good
    options.

    Ⓐ has so little a
    Ⓑ has very little
    Ⓒ has so few
    Ⓓ has very few

21. Although it can be derived from
    (A)   (B)
    oil, coal, and tar, kerosene is usually
    produced by refine it from petroleum.
    (C)   (D)

22. Aeronomy is the study of the earth's
             (A)   (B)   (C)
    upper atmosphere, which includes
    their composition, temperature,
    (D)
    density, and chemical reactions.

23. The purpose of the United Nations,
                 (A)
    broad speaking, is to maintain peace
        (B)   (C)
    and security and to encourage respect
                     (D)
    for human rights.

24. Of all the cereals, rice is the one
    _____ food for more people than
    any of the other grain crops.

    (A) it provides
    (B) that providing
    (C) provides
    (D) that provides

25. Although Congressional
    representatives and senators
    may serve an unlimited number of
    term, the president is limited to
    (A)   (B)
    two, for a total of eight years.
        (C)   (D)

Section 3:
Reading

This section measures the ability to read and understand short passages similar in topic and style to those that students are likely to encounter in North American universities and colleges. This section contains reading passages and questions about the passages. There are several different types of questions in this section.

In the Reading Section, you will first have the opportunity to read the passage. You will use the scroll bar to view the rest of the passage.

When you have finished reading the passage, you will use the mouse to click on **Proceed**. Then the questions about the passage will be presented. You are to choose the one best answer to each question. Answer all questions about the information in a passage on the basis of what is stated or implied in that passage.

Most of the questions will be multiple-choice questions. To answer these questions you will click on a choice below the question.

To answer some questions, you will click on a word or phrase. To answer some questions, you will click on a sentence in the passage. To answer some questions, you will click on a square to add a sentence to the passage.

The computer screens for selected questions in the Reading section have been printed in this book to provide you with orientation to the format of the Computer-Based TOEFL. Use the screen to find the place in the original reading passage that corresponds to the question you are answering.

It has long been known that when the green parts of plants are exposed to light under suitable conditions of temperature and moisture, carbon dioxide is absorbed by the plant from the atmospheric CO_2, and oxygen is released into the air. This exchange of gases in plants is the opposite of the process that occurs in respiration. In this plant process, which is called photosynthesis, carbohydrates are synthesized in the presence of light from carbon dioxide and water by specialized structures in the cytoplasm of plant cells called chloroplasts. These chloroplasts contain not only two types of light-trapping green chlorophyll but also a vast array of protein substances called enzymes. In most plants, the water required by the photosynthesis process is absorbed from the soil by the roots and translocated through the xylem of the root and stem to the chlorophyll-laden leaves. Except for the usually small percentage used in respiration, the oxygen released in the process diffuses out of the leaf into the atmosphere through stomates. In simple terms, carbon dioxide is the fuel, and oxygen is the product of the chemical reaction. For each molecule of carbon dioxide used, one molecule of oxygen is released. Here is a summary chemical equation for photosynthesis:

$$6CO_2 + 6H_2O \rightarrow C_6H_{12}O_6 + 6O_2$$

As a result of this process, radiant energy from the sun is stored as chemical energy. In turn, the chemical energy is used to decompose carbon dioxide and water. The products of their decomposition are recombined into a new compound, which successively builds up into the more and more complex substances that comprise the plant. These organic substances, that is, the sugars, starches, and cellulose, all belong to the class of organic molecules. In other words, the process of photosynthesis can be understood as an enzyme-induced chemical change from carbon dioxide and water into the simple sugar glucose. This carbohydrate, in turn, is utilized by the plant to generate other forms of energy, such as the long chains of plant cells or polymers that comprise the cellular structures of starches or cellulose. Many intermediate steps are involved in the production of a simple sugar or starch. At the same time, a balance of gases is preserved in the atmosphere by the process of photosynthesis.

1. Which title best expresses the ideas in this passage?

   (A) A Chemical Equation
   (B) The Process of Photosynthesis
   (C) The Parts of Vascular Plants
   (D) The Production of Sugar

2. The combination of carbon dioxide and water to form sugar results in an excess of

   (A) water
   (B) oxygen
   (C) carbon
   (D) chlorophyll

3. Which process is the opposite of photosynthesis?

   (A) Decomposition
   (B) Synthesization
   (C) Diffusion
   (D) Respiration

4. In photosynthesis, energy from the sun is

   (A) changed to chemical energy
   (B) conducted from the xylem to the leaves of green plants
   (C) not necessary to the process
   (D) released one to one for each molecule of carbon dioxide used

5. Click on the sentence in paragraph 1 that describes how oxygen is released into the atmosphere.

   Paragraph 1 is marked with an arrow (→).

   Beginning

   → It has long been known that when the green parts of plants are exposed to light under suitable conditions of temperature and moisture, carbon dioxide is absorbed by the plant from the atmospheric CO_2, and oxygen is released into the air. This exchange of gases in plants is the opposite of the process that occurs in respiration. In this plant process, which is called photosynthesis, carbohydrates are synthesized in the presence of light from carbon dioxide and water by specialized structures in the cytoplasm of plant cells called chloroplasts. These chloroplasts contain not only two types of light-trapping green chlorophyll but also a vast array of protein substances called enzymes. In most plants, the water required for the photosynthesis process is absorbed from the soil by the roots and translocated through the xylem of the root and stem to the chlorophyll-laden leaves. Except for the usually small percentage used in respiration, the oxygen released in the process diffuses out of the leaf into the atmosphere through stomates. In simple terms, carbon dioxide is the fuel, and oxygen is the product of the chemical reaction. For each molecule of carbon dioxide

6. The word stored in paragraph 2 is closest in meaning to

Ⓐ retained
Ⓑ converted
Ⓒ discovered
Ⓓ specified

More Available

leaves. Except for the usually small percentage used in respiration, the oxygen released in the process diffuses out of the leaf into the atmosphere through stomates. In simple terms, carbon dioxide is the fuel, and oxygen is the product of the chemical reaction. For each molecule of carbon dioxide used, one molecule of oxygen is released. Here is a summary chemical equation for photosynthesis:

$$6CO_2 + 6H_2O \rightarrow C_6H_{12}O_6 + 6O_2$$

As a result of this process, radiant energy from the sun is stored as chemical energy. In turn, the chemical energy is used to decompose carbon dioxide and water. The products of their decomposition are recombined into a new compound, which successively builds up into the more and more complex substances that comprise the plant. These organic substances, that is, the sugars, starches, and cellulose, all belong to the class of organic molecules. In other words, the process of photosynthesis can be understood as an enzyme-induced chemical change from carbon dioxide and water into the simple sugar glucose. This carbohydrate, in turn, is utilized by the plant to generate other forms of

7. The word their in paragraph 2 refers to

Ⓐ radiant energy and chemical energy
Ⓑ carbon dioxide and water
Ⓒ products
Ⓓ complex substances

End

As a result of this process, radiant energy from the sun is stored as chemical energy. In turn, the chemical energy is used to decompose carbon dioxide and water. The products of their decomposition are recombined into a new compound, which successively builds up into the more and more complex substances that comprise the plant. These organic substances, that is, the sugars, starches, and cellulose, all belong to the class of organic molecules. In other words, the process of photosynthesis can be understood as an enzyme-induced chemical change from carbon dioxide and water into the simple sugar glucose. This carbohydrate, in turn, is utilized by the plant to generate other forms of energy, such as the long chains of plant cells or polymers that comprise the cellular structures of starches or cellulose. Many intermediate steps are involved in the production of a simple sugar or starch. At the same time, a balance of gases is preserved in the atmosphere by the process of photosynthesis.

8. The word successively in paragraph 2 is closest in meaning to

Ⓐ with effort
Ⓑ in a sequence
Ⓒ slowly
Ⓓ carefully

End

carbon dioxide and water. The products of their decomposition are recombined into a new compound, which successively builds up into the more and more complex substances that comprise the plant. These organic substances, that is, the sugars, starches, and cellulose, all belong to the class of organic molecules. In other words, the process of photosynthesis can be understood as an enzyme-induced chemical change from carbon dioxide and water into the simple sugar glucose. This carbohydrate, in turn, is utilized by the plant to generate other forms of energy, such as the long chains of plant cells or polymers that comprise the cellular structures of starches or cellulose. Many intermediate steps are involved in the production of a simple sugar or starch. At the same time, a balance of gases is preserved in the atmosphere by the process of photosynthesis.

9. Besides the manufacture of food for plants, what is another benefit of photosynthesis?

Ⓐ It produces solar energy.
Ⓑ It diffuses additional carbon dioxide into the air.
Ⓒ It maintains a balance of gases in the atmosphere.
Ⓓ It removes harmful gases from the air.

10. Which of the following is NOT true of the oxygen used in photosynthesis?

Ⓐ Oxygen is absorbed by the roots.
Ⓑ Oxygen is the product of photosynthesis.
Ⓒ Oxygen is used in respiration.
Ⓓ Oxygen is released into the atmosphere through the leaves.

Alfred Bernhard Nobel, a Swedish inventor and philanthropist, bequeathed most of his vast fortune to a trust that he designated as a fund from which annual prizes could be awarded to the individuals and organizations that had achieved through invention or discovery that which would have the greatest benefit to humanity in a particular year. According to the legend, Nobel's death had been erroneously reported in a newspaper, and the focus of the obituary was the fact that Nobel had invented dynamite. He rewrote his will in 1895, thereby establishing, with the original amount of nine million dollars, the Nobel Foundation as the legal owner and administering agent of the funds, and instituting the prizes that are named after him. Statutes to govern the awarding of the prizes were written, along with guidelines for operating procedures. Five years after Nobel's death, the first five prizes, worth about forty thousand dollars each, were to be awarded.

Originally the five classifications for outstanding contributions designated in Nobel's will included chemistry, physics, physiology or medicine, literature, and international peace. These prizes have been administered continually by the Nobel Foundation in Stockholm since they were first awarded in 1901. In 1969, a sixth prize, for accomplishments in the field of economics and endowed by the Central Bank of Sweden, was added. Candidates for the prizes must be nominated in writing by February 1 of each year by a qualified and recognized authority in each of the fields of competition. Recipients in physics, chemistry, and economics are selected by the Royal Swedish Academy, whereas recipients in peace are chosen by the Norwegian Nobel Committee appointed by Norway's parliament. With the King of Sweden officiating, the prizes are usually presented in Stockholm on December 10, the anniversary of Nobel's death. The value, fame, and prestige of the Nobel Prizes have continued to grow. Today the prize includes a medal, a diploma, and a cash award of about one million dollars.

11. What does this passage mainly discuss?

   Ⓐ Alfred Bernhard Nobel
   Ⓑ The Nobel Prizes
   Ⓒ Great contributions to mankind
   Ⓓ Swedish philanthropy

12. Why were the prizes named for Alfred Bernhard Nobel?

   Ⓐ He left money in his will to establish a fund for the prizes.
   Ⓑ He won the first Nobel Prize for his work in philanthropy.
   Ⓒ He is now living in Sweden.
   Ⓓ He serves as chairman of the committee to choose the recipients of the prizes.

13. The word will in paragraph 1 refers to

   Ⓐ Nobel's wishes
   Ⓑ a legal document
   Ⓒ a future intention
   Ⓓ a free choice

14. How often are the Nobel Prizes awarded?

   Ⓐ Five times a year
   Ⓑ Once a year
   Ⓒ Twice a year
   Ⓓ Once every two years

15. The following sentence can be added to the passage.

> **When he read this objective summary of his life, the great chemist, it is said, decided that he wanted his name to be remembered for something more positive and humanitarian than inventing an explosive that was a potential weapon.**

Where would it best fit in the passage?

Click on the square (■) to add the sentence to the passage.

Scroll the passage to see all of the choices.

More Available

particular year. According to the legend, Nobel's death had been erroneously reported in a newspaper, and the focus of the obituary was the fact that Nobel had invented dynamite. He rewrote his will in 1895, thereby establishing, with the original amount of nine million dollars, the Nobel Foundation as the legal owner and administering agent of the funds, and instituting the prizes that are named after him. Statutes to govern the awarding of the prizes were written, along with guidelines for operating procedures. Five years after Nobel's death, the first five prizes, worth about forty thousand dollars each, were to be awarded.

Originally the five classifications for outstanding contributions designated in Nobel's will included chemistry, physics, physiology or medicine, literature, and international peace. These prizes have been administered continually by the Nobel Foundation in Stockholm since they were first awarded in 1901. In 1969, a sixth prize, for accomplishments in the field of economics and endowed by the Central Bank of Sweden, was added. Candidates for the prizes must be

---

More Available

particular year. According to the legend, Nobel's death had been erroneously reported in a newspaper, and the focus of the obituary was the fact that Nobel had invented dynamite. ■ He rewrote his will in 1895, thereby establishing, with the original amount of nine million dollars, the Nobel Foundation as the legal owner and administering agent of the funds, and instituting the prizes that are named after him. ■ Statutes to govern the awarding of the prizes were written, along with guidelines for operating procedures. ■ Five years after Nobel's death, the first five prizes, worth about forty thousand dollars each, were to be awarded. ■

Originally the five classifications for outstanding contributions designated in Nobel's will included chemistry, physics, physiology or medicine, literature, and international peace. These prizes have been administered continually by the Nobel Foundation in Stockholm since they were first awarded in 1901. In 1969, a sixth prize, for accomplishments in the field of economics and endowed by the Central Bank of Sweden, was added. Candidates for the prizes must be

16. The word outstanding in paragraph 2 could best be replaced by

   Ⓐ recent
   Ⓑ unusual
   Ⓒ established
   Ⓓ exceptional

More Available

awarding of the prizes were written, along with guidelines for operating procedures. Five years after Nobel's death, the first five prizes, worth about forty thousand dollars each, were to be awarded.

Originally the five classifications for outstanding contributions designated in Nobel's will included chemistry, physics, physiology or medicine, literature, and international peace. These prizes have been administered continually by the Nobel Foundation in Stockholm since they were first awarded in 1901. In 1969, a sixth prize, for accomplishments in the field of economics and endowed by the Central Bank of Sweden, was added. Candidates for the prizes must be nominated in writing by February 1 of each year by a qualified and recognized authority in each of the fields of competition. Recipients in physics, chemistry, and economics are selected by the Royal Swedish Academy, whereas recipients in peace are chosen by the Norwegian Nobel Committee appointed by Norway's parliament. With the King of Sweden officiating, the prizes are usually presented in Stockholm on December 10,

---

17. A Nobel Prize would NOT be given to

   Ⓐ an author who wrote a novel
   Ⓑ a doctor who discovered a vaccine
   Ⓒ a composer who wrote a symphony
   Ⓓ a diplomat who negotiated a peace settlement

18. What does the author mean by the statement These prizes have been administered continually by the Nobel Foundation in Stockholm since they were first awarded in 1901 ?

   Ⓐ The Nobel Foundation oversees the management of the money and the distribution of the prizes.
   Ⓑ The Nobel Foundation selects the recipients of the prizes.
   Ⓒ The Nobel Foundation solicits applications and recommendations for the prizes.
   Ⓓ The Nobel Foundation recommends new prize classifications.

End

Originally the five classifications for outstanding contributions designated in Nobel's will included chemistry, physics, physiology or medicine, literature, and international peace. These prizes have been administered continually by the Nobel Foundation in Stockholm since they were first awarded in 1901. In 1969, a sixth prize, for accomplishments in the field of economics and endowed by the Central Bank of Sweden, was added. Candidates for the prizes must be nominated in writing by February 1 of each year by a qualified and recognized authority in each of the fields of competition. Recipients in physics, chemistry, and economics are selected by the Royal Swedish Academy, whereas recipients in peace are chosen by the Norwegian Nobel Committee appointed by Norway's parliament. With the King of Sweden officiating, the prizes are usually presented in Stockholm on December 10, the anniversary of Nobel's death. The value, fame, and prestige of the Nobel Prizes have continued to grow. Today the prize includes a medal, a diploma, and a cash award of about one million dollars.

19. Why are the awards presented on December 10?

    Ⓐ It is a tribute to the King of Sweden.

    Ⓑ Alfred Bernhard Nobel died on that day.

    Ⓒ That date was established in Alfred Nobel's will.

    Ⓓ The Central Bank of Sweden administers the trust.

20. Look at the word prize in the passage. Click on the word or phrase in the **bold** text that is closest in meaning to prize.

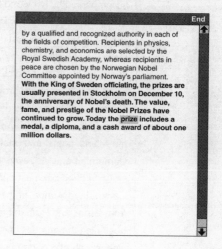

End

by a qualified and recognized authority in each of the fields of competition. Recipients in physics, chemistry, and economics are selected by the Royal Swedish Academy, whereas recipients in peace are chosen by the Norwegian Nobel Committee appointed by Norway's parliament. **With the King of Sweden officiating, the prizes are usually presented in Stockholm on December 10, the anniversary of Nobel's death. The value, fame, and prestige of the Nobel Prizes have continued to grow. Today the prize includes a medal, a diploma, and a cash award of about one million dollars.**

Although stage plays have been set to music since the era of the ancient Greeks, when the dramas of Sophocles and Aeschylus were accompanied by lyres and flutes, the usually accepted date for the beginning of opera as we know it is 1600. As a part of the celebration of the marriage of King Henry IV of France to the Italian aristocrat Maria de Medici, the Florentine composer Jacopo Perí produced his famous *Euridice*, generally considered to be the first opera. Following his example, a group of Italian musicians, poets, and noblemen called the Camerata began to revive the style of musical story that had been used in Greek tragedy. The Camerata took most of the plots for their operas from Greek and Roman history and mythology, beginning the process of creating an opera by writing a libretto or drama that could be used to establish the framework for the music. They called their compositions *opera in musica* or musical works. It is from this phrase that the word "opera" was borrowed and abbreviated.

For several years, the center of opera was Florence in northern Italy, but gradually, during the baroque period, it spread throughout Italy. By the late 1600s, operas were being written and performed in many places throughout Europe, especially in England, France, and Germany. However, for many years, the Italian opera was considered the ideal, and many non-Italian composers continued to use Italian librettos. The European form deemphasized the dramatic aspect of the Italian model. New orchestral effects and even ballet were introduced under the guise of opera. Composers gave in to the demands of singers, writing many operas that were little more than a succession of brilliant tricks for the voice, designed to showcase the splendid voices of the singers who had requested them. It was thus that complicated arias, recitatives, and duets evolved. The aria, which is a long solo, may be compared to a song in which the characters express their thoughts and feelings. The recitative, which is also a solo of sorts, is a recitation set to music, the purpose of which is to continue the story line. The duet is a musical piece written for two voices, a musical device that may serve the function of either an aria or a recitative within the opera.

21. This passage is a summary of

    Ⓐ opera in Italy
    Ⓑ the Camerata
    Ⓒ the development of opera
    Ⓓ *Euridice*

22. Look at the word usually in the passage. Click on the word or phrase in the **bold** text that is closest in meaning to usually.

> **Beginning**
>
> **Although stage plays have been set to music since the era of the ancient Greeks, when the dramas of Sophocles and Aeschylus were accompanied by lyres and flutes, the usually accepted date for the beginning of opera as we know it is 1600. As a part of the celebration of the marriage of King Henry IV of France to the Italian aristocrat Maria de Medici, the Florentine composer Jacopo Perí produced his famous *Euridice*, generally considered to be the first opera.** Following his example, a group of Italian musicians, poets, and noblemen called the Camerata began to revive the style of musical story that had been used in Greek tragedy. The Camerata took most of the plots for their operas from Greek and Roman history and mythology, beginning the process of creating an opera by writing a libretto or drama that could be used to establish the framework for the music. They called their compositions *opera in musica* or musical works. It is from this phrase that the word "opera" was borrowed and abbreviated.
>
>   For several years, the center of opera was Florence in northern Italy, but gradually, during the

23. According to this passage, when did modern opera begin?

    Ⓐ In the time of the ancient Greeks
    Ⓑ In the fifteenth century
    Ⓒ At the beginning of the sixteenth century
    Ⓓ At the beginning of the seventeenth century

24. The word it in paragraph 1 refers to

    Ⓐ opera
    Ⓑ date
    Ⓒ era
    Ⓓ music

> **Beginning**
>
>   Although stage plays have been set to music since the era of the ancient Greeks, when the dramas of Sophocles and Aeschylus were accompanied by lyres and flutes, the usually accepted date for the beginning of opera as we know it is 1600. As a part of the celebration of the marriage of King Henry IV of France to the Italian aristocrat Maria de Medici, the Florentine composer Jacopo Perí produced his famous *Euridice*, generally considered to be the first opera. Following his example, a group of Italian musicians, poets, and noblemen called the Camerata began to revive the style of musical story that had been used in Greek tragedy. The Camerata took most of the plots for their operas from Greek and Roman history and mythology, beginning the process of creating an opera by writing a libretto or drama that could be used to establish the framework for the music. They called their compositions *opera in musica* or musical works. It is from this phrase that the word "opera" was borrowed and abbreviated.
>
>   For several years, the center of opera was Florence in northern Italy, but gradually, during the

25. According to the author, what did Jacopo Perí write?

    Ⓐ Greek tragedy
    Ⓑ The first opera
    Ⓒ The ópera *Maria de Medici*
    Ⓓ The opera *The Camerata*

26. The author suggests that *Euridice* was produced

    Ⓐ in France
    Ⓑ originally by Sophocles and Aeschylus
    Ⓒ without much success
    Ⓓ for the wedding of King Henry IV

27. What was the Camerata?

    Ⓐ A group of Greek musicians
    Ⓑ Musicians who developed a new musical drama based upon Greek drama
    Ⓒ A style of music not known in Italy
    Ⓓ The name given to the court of King Henry IV

28. The word revive in paragraph 1 could best be replaced by

    Ⓐ appreciate
    Ⓑ resume
    Ⓒ modify
    Ⓓ investigate

29. The word plots in paragraph 1 is closest in meaning to

    Ⓐ locations
    Ⓑ instruments
    Ⓒ stories
    Ⓓ inspiration

More Available

know it is 1600. As a part of the celebration of the marriage of King Henry IV of France to the Italian aristocrat Maria de Medici, the Florentine composer Jacopo Perí produced his famous *Euridice*, generally considered to be the first opera. Following his example, a group of Italian musicians, poets, and noblemen called the Camerata began to revive the style of musical story that had been used in Greek tragedy. The Camerata took most of the plots for their operas from Greek and Roman history and mythology, beginning the process of creating an opera by writing a libretto or drama that could be used to establish the framework for the music. They called their compositions *opera in musica* or musical works. It is from this phrase that the word "opera" was borrowed and abbreviated.

For several years, the center of opera was Florence in northern Italy, but gradually, during the baroque period, it spread throughout Italy. By the late 1600s, operas were being written and performed in many places throughout Europe, especially in England, France, and Germany. However, for many years, the Italian opera was

30. From what did the term "opera" derive?

    Ⓐ Greek and Roman history and mythology
    Ⓑ Non-Italian composers
    Ⓒ The Italian phrase that means "musical works"
    Ⓓ The ideas of composer Jacopo Perí

Beginning

Although stage plays have been set to music since the era of the ancient Greeks, when the dramas of Sophocles and Aeschylus were accompanied by lyres and flutes, the usually accepted date for the beginning of opera as we know it is 1600. As a part of the celebration of the marriage of King Henry IV of France to the Italian aristocrat Maria de Medici, the Florentine composer Jacopo Perí produced his famous *Euridice*, generally considered to be the first opera. Following his example, a group of Italian musicians, poets, and noblemen called the Camerata began to revive the style of musical story that had been used in Greek tragedy. The Camerata took most of the plots for their operas from Greek and Roman history and mythology, beginning the process of creating an opera by writing a libretto or drama that could be used to establish the framework for the music. They called their compositions *opera in musica* or musical works. It is from this phrase that the word "opera" was borrowed and abbreviated.

For several years, the center of opera was Florence in northern Italy, but gradually, during the

31. Look at the word them in the passage. Click on the word or phrase in the **bold** text that them refers to.

End

However, for many years, the Italian opera was considered the ideal, and many non-Italian composers continued to use Italian librettos. The European form deemphasized the dramatic aspect of the Italian model. **New orchestral effects and even ballet were introduced under the guise of opera. Composers gave in to the demands of singers, writing many operas that were little more than a succession of brilliant tricks for the voice, designed to showcase the splendid voices of the singers who had requested them. It was thus that complicated arias, recitatives, and duets evolved.** The aria, which is a long solo, may be compared to a song in which the characters express their thoughts and feelings. The recitative, which is also a solo of sorts, is a recitation set to music, the purpose of which is to continue the story line. The duet is a musical piece written for two voices, a musical device that may serve the function of either an aria or a recitative within the opera.

32. Look at the word function in the passage. Click on the word or phrase in the **bold** text that is closest in meaning to function.

End

aspect of the Italian model. New orchestral effects and even ballet were introduced under the guise of opera. Composers gave in to the demands of singers, writing many operas that were little more than a succession of brilliant tricks for the voice, designed to showcase the splendid voices of the singers who had requested them. **It was thus that complicated arias, recitatives, and duets evolved. The aria, which is a long solo, may be compared to a song in which the characters express their thoughts and feelings. The recitative, which is also a solo of sorts, is a recitation set to music, the purpose of which is to continue the story line. The duet is a musical piece written for two voices, a musical device that may serve the function of either an aria or a recitative within the opera.**

According to the controversial sunspot theory, great storms or eruptions on the surface of the sun hurl streams of solar particles into space and eventually into the atmosphere of our planet, causing shifts in the weather on the Earth and interference with radio and television communications.

A typical sunspot consists of a dark central umbra, a word derived from the Latin word for shadow, which is surrounded by a lighter penumbra of light and dark threads extending out from the center like the spokes of a wheel. Actually, the sunspots are cooler than the rest of the photosphere, which may account for their apparently darker color. Typically, the temperature in a sunspot umbra is about 4000 K, whereas the temperature in a penumbra registers 5500 K, and the granules outside the spot are 6000 K.

Sunspots range in size from tiny granules to complex structures with areas stretching for billions of square miles. About 5 percent of all sunspots are large enough so that they can be seen from Earth without instruments; consequently, observations of sunspots have been recorded for thousands of years.

Sunspots have been observed in arrangements of one to more than one hundred spots, but they tend to occur in pairs. There is also a marked tendency for the two spots of a pair to have opposite magnetic polarities. Furthermore, the strength of the magnetic field associated with any given sunspot is closely related to the spot's size. Sunspots have also been observed to occur in cycles, over a period of eleven years. At the beginning of a cycle, the storms occur between 20 and 40 degrees north and south of the equator on the sun. As the cycle continues, some of the storms move closer to the equator. As the cycle diminishes, the number of sunspots decreases to a minimum and they cluster between 5 and 15 degrees north and south latitude.

Although there is no theory that completely explains the nature and function of sunspots, several models show scientists' attempts to relate the phenomenon to magnetic field lines along the lines of longitude from the north and south poles of the sun.

33. What is the author's main purpose in the passage?

   Ⓐ To propose a theory to explain sunspots
   Ⓑ To describe the nature of sunspots
   Ⓒ To compare the umbra and the penumbra in sunspots
   Ⓓ To argue for the existence of magnetic fields in sunspots

34. The word controversial in paragraph 1 is closest in meaning to

   Ⓐ widely accepted
   Ⓑ open to debate
   Ⓒ just introduced
   Ⓓ very complicated

35. Solar particles are hurled into space by

   Ⓐ undetermined causes
   Ⓑ disturbances of wind
   Ⓒ small rivers on the surface of the sun
   Ⓓ changes in the Earth's atmosphere

36. The word particles in paragraph 1 refers to

   Ⓐ gas explosions in the atmosphere
   Ⓑ light rays from the sun
   Ⓒ liquid streams on the sun
   Ⓓ small pieces of matter from the sun

Beginning

According to the controversial sunspot theory, great storms or eruptions on the surface of the sun hurl streams of solar particles into space and eventually into the atmosphere of our planet, causing shifts in the weather on the Earth and interference with radio and television communications.

A typical sunspot consists of a dark central umbra, a word derived from the Latin word for shadow, which is surrounded by a lighter penumbra of light and dark threads extending out from the center like the spokes of a wheel. Actually, the sunspots are cooler than the rest of the photosphere, which may account for their apparently darker color. Typically, the temperature in a sunspot umbra is about 4000 K, whereas the temperature in a penumbra registers 5500 K, and the granules outside the spot are 6000 K.

Sunspots range in size from tiny granules to complex structures with areas stretching for billions of square miles. About 5 percent of all sunspots are large enough so that they can be seen from Earth without instruments; consequently, observations of sunspots have been recorded for thousands of years.

Beginning

According to the controversial sunspot theory, great storms or eruptions on the surface of the sun hurl streams of solar particles into space and eventually into the atmosphere of our planet, causing shifts in the weather on the Earth and interference with radio and television communications.

A typical sunspot consists of a dark central umbra, a word derived from the Latin word for shadow, which is surrounded by a lighter penumbra of light and dark threads extending out from the center like the spokes of a wheel. Actually, the sunspots are cooler than the rest of the photosphere, which may account for their apparently darker color. Typically, the temperature in a sunspot umbra is about 4000 K, whereas the temperature in a penumbra registers 5500 K, and the granules outside the spot are 6000 K.

Sunspots range in size from tiny granules to complex structures with areas stretching for billions of square miles. About 5 percent of all sunspots are large enough so that they can be seen from Earth without instruments; consequently, observations of sunspots have been recorded for thousands of years.

37. How can we describe matter from the sun that enters the Earth's atmosphere?

Ⓐ Very small
Ⓑ Very hot
Ⓒ Very bright
Ⓓ Very hard

38. What does the author mean by the statement Actually, the sunspots are cooler than the rest of the photosphere, which may account for their apparently darker color?

Ⓐ Neither sunspots nor the photosphere is hot.
Ⓑ Sunspots in the photosphere do not have any color.
Ⓒ The color of sunspots could be affected by their temperature.
Ⓓ The size of a sunspot affects its temperature.

More Available

of light and dark threads extending out from the center like the spokes of a wheel. Actually, the sunspots are cooler than the rest of the photosphere, which may account for their apparently darker color. Typically, the temperature in a sunspot umbra is about 4000 K, whereas the temperature in a penumbra registers 5500 K, and the granules outside the spot are 6000 K.
    Sunspots range in size from tiny granules to complex structures with areas stretching for billions of square miles. About 5 percent of all sunspots are large enough so that they can be seen from Earth without instruments; consequently, observations of sunspots have been recorded for thousands of years.
    Sunspots have been observed in arrangements of one to more than one hundred spots, but they tend to occur in pairs. There is also a marked tendency for the two spots of a pair to have opposite magnetic polarities. Furthermore, the strength of the magnetic field associated with any given sunspot is closely related to the spot's size. Sunspots have also been observed to occur in cycles, over a period of eleven years. At the

39. Look at the word tiny in the passage. Click on the word or phrase in the **bold** text that is opposite in meaning to tiny.

More Available

color. Typically, the temperature in a sunspot umbra is about 4000 K, whereas the temperature in a penumbra registers 5500 K, and the granules outside the spot are 6000 K.
    Sunspots range in size from tiny granules to complex structures with areas stretching for billions of square miles. About 5 percent of all sunspots are large enough so that they can be seen from Earth without instruments; consequently, observations of sunspots have been recorded for thousands of years.
    Sunspots have been observed in arrangements of one to more than one hundred spots, but they tend to occur in pairs. There is also a marked tendency for the two spots of a pair to have opposite magnetic polarities. Furthermore, the strength of the magnetic field associated with any given sunspot is closely related to the spot's size. Sunspots have also been observed to occur in cycles, over a period of eleven years. At the beginning of a cycle, the storms occur between 20 and 40 degrees north and south of the equator on the sun. As the cycle continues, some of the storms move closer to the equator. As the cycle

40. The word they in paragraph 2 refers to

Ⓐ structures
Ⓑ spots
Ⓒ miles
Ⓓ granules

More Available

color. Typically, the temperature in a sunspot umbra is about 4000 K, whereas the temperature in a penumbra registers 5500 K, and the granules outside the spot are 6000 K.
    Sunspots range in size from tiny granules to complex structures with areas stretching for billions of square miles. About 5 percent of all sunspots are large enough so that they can be seen from Earth without instruments; consequently, observations of sunspots have been recorded for thousands of years.
    Sunspots have been observed in arrangements of one to more than one hundred spots, but they tend to occur in pairs. There is also a marked tendency for the two spots of a pair to have opposite magnetic polarities. Furthermore, the strength of the magnetic field associated with any given sunspot is closely related to the spot's size. Sunspots have also been observed to occur in cycles, over a period of eleven years. At the beginning of a cycle, the storms occur between 20 and 40 degrees north and south of the equator on the sun. As the cycle continues, some of the storms move closer to the equator. As the cycle

41. The word consequently in paragraph 2 could best be replaced by

    (A) as a result
    (B) nevertheless
    (C) without doubt
    (D) in this way

More Available

color. Typically, the temperature in a sunspot umbra is about 4000 K, whereas the temperature in a penumbra registers 5500 K, and the granules outside the spot are 6000 K.

Sunspots range in size from tiny granules to complex structures with areas stretching for billions of square miles. About 5 percent of all sunspots are large enough so that they can be seen from Earth without instruments; consequently, observations of sunspots have been recorded for thousands of years.

Sunspots have been observed in arrangements of one to more than one hundred spots, but they tend to occur in pairs. There is also a marked tendency for the two spots of a pair to have opposite magnetic polarities. Furthermore, the strength of the magnetic field associated with any given sunspot is closely related to the spot's size. Sunspots have also been observed to occur in cycles, over a period of eleven years. At the beginning of a cycle, the storms occur between 20 and 40 degrees north and south of the equator on the sun. As the cycle continues, some of the storms move closer to the equator. As the cycle

---

42. In which configuration do sunspots usually occur?

    (A) In one spot of varying size
    (B) In a configuration of two spots
    (C) In arrangements of one hundred or more spots
    (D) In groups of several thousand spots

43. How are sunspots explained?

    (A) Sunspots appear to be related to magnetic fields on the Earth.
    (B) Sunspots may be related to magnetic fields that follow longitudinal lines on the sun.
    (C) Sunspots are explained by storms that occur on the Earth.
    (D) Sunspots have no theory or model to explain them.

44. Click on the paragraph that discusses the visibility of sunspots.

    Scroll the passage to see all of the paragraphs.

45. The sunspot theory is

    (A) not considered very important
    (B) widely accepted
    (C) subject to disagreement
    (D) relatively new

To check your answers for Model Test 1, refer to the Answer Key on page 385. For an explanation of the answers, refer to the Explanatory Answers for Model Test 1 on pages 395–417.

Writing Section Model Test 1

When you take a Model Test, you should use one sheet of paper, both sides. Time each Model Test carefully. After you have read the topic, you should spend 30 minutes writing. For results that would be closest to the actual testing situation, it is recommended that an English teacher score your test, using the guidelines on page 247 of this book.

> Many people enjoy participating in sports for recreation; others enjoy participating in the arts. Give the benefits of each, take a position, and defend it.

Notes

To check your essay, refer to the Checklist on page 386. For an Example Essay, refer to the Explanatory Answers for Model Test 1 on page 417.

Model Test 2
Computer-Assisted TOEFL

Section 1:
Listening

The Listening Section of the test measures the ability to understand conversations and talks in English. You will use headphones to listen to the conversations and talks. While you are listening, pictures of the speakers or other information will be presented on your computer screen. There are two parts to the Listening Section, with special directions for each part.

On the day of the test, the amount of time you will have to answer all of the questions will appear on the computer screen. The time you spend listening to the test material will not be counted. The listening material and questions about it will be presented only one time. You will not be allowed to take notes or have any paper at your computer. You will both see and hear the questions before the answer choices appear. You can take as much time as you need to select an answer; however, it will be to your advantage to answer the questions as quickly as possible. You may change your answer as many times as you want before you confirm it. After you have confirmed an answer, you will not be able to return to the question.

Before you begin working on the Listening Section, you will have an opportunity to adjust the volume of the sound. You may not be able to change the volume after you have started the test.

QUESTION DIRECTIONS—Part A

In Part A of the Listening Section, you will hear short conversations between two people. In some of the conversations, each person speaks only once. In other conversations, one or both of the people speak more than once. Each conversation is followed by one question about it.

Each question in this part has four answer choices. You should click on the best answer to each question. Answer the questions on the basis of what is stated or implied by the speakers.

1. What had the man assumed?

    Ⓐ The woman was not truthful.
    Ⓑ Fewer students would attend.
    Ⓒ There would be a large group.
    Ⓓ Only foreign students would come.

2. What does the woman imply that the man should do?

    Ⓐ Knock on the door.
    Ⓑ Come back later.
    Ⓒ See Dr. Smith.
    Ⓓ Look at the sign.

3. What is the woman probably going to do?

   (A) Take a class from Professor Wilson.
   (B) Help the man with his class.
   (C) Take an extra class.
   (D) Do a project for her class.

4. What does the woman say about Paul?

   (A) That he wants something to eat.
   (B) That he will tell them if there is a problem.
   (C) That he is not hungry.
   (D) That he is angry.

5. What does the woman mean?

   (A) Good grades are not that important to her.
   (B) She did not get an A on the exam either.
   (C) Two students got higher grades than she did.
   (D) Besides hers, there were several other A grades.

6. What problem does the woman have?

   (A) There is no time to finish.
   (B) She cannot do it quickly.
   (C) She has to study.
   (D) She doesn't know what time it is.

7. What does the woman mean?

   (A) She does not agree with the man.
   (B) She thinks that it is better to wait.
   (C) She thinks that it is better to drive at night.
   (D) She does not think that the man made a wise decision.

8. What is the man going to do?

   (A) Go to class.
   (B) See a movie.
   (C) Study at the library.
   (D) Make an appointment.

9. What does the man mean?

   (A) The message was not clear.
   (B) There was no message on the machine.
   (C) It was his intention to return the woman's call.
   (D) He did not hear the woman's message.

10. What does the woman mean?

    (A) They do not have as many people working as usual.
    (B) The machine is broken.
    (C) The man is next to be served.
    (D) There is usually a long line.

11. What does the woman suggest that the man do?

    (A) Get directions to the Math Department.
    (B) Speak with the secretary.
    (C) Go into Dr. Davis's office.
    (D) Take the elevator to the fourth floor.

12. What can be inferred about Tom?

    (A) He has finished the class.
    (B) He has been sick.
    (C) He does not have to take the final exam.
    (D) He is not very responsible.

13. What does the man mean?

    (A) He cannot find the woman's house.
    (B) He has to change their plans.
    (C) He will be happy to see the woman.
    (D) He wants to know whether they have a date.

14. What will the woman probably do?

    (A) Register for Dr. Collin's class.
    (B) Graduate at a later date.
    (C) Enroll in the section marked "staff."
    (D) Find out who is teaching the other section of the class.

15. What does the woman think that the man should do?

    Ⓐ Wait for the results to be mailed.
    Ⓑ Call about the score.
    Ⓒ Take the test.
    Ⓓ Show more concern.

16. What does the woman mean?

    Ⓐ They have more time to travel.
    Ⓑ They are taking advantage of travel opportunities.
    Ⓒ They travel more than the man does.
    Ⓓ They spend most of their time traveling.

17. What does the man mean?

    Ⓐ The tickets are lost.
    Ⓑ Judy was responsible for getting the tickets.
    Ⓒ There were no tickets available.
    Ⓓ He does not have the tickets yet.

QUESTION DIRECTIONS—Part B

In Part B of the Listening Section, you will hear several longer conversations and talks. Each conversation or talk is followed by several questions. The conversations, talks, and questions will not be repeated.

The conversations and talks are about a variety of topics. You do not need special knowledge of the topics to answer the questions correctly. Rather, you should answer each question on the basis of what is stated or implied by the speakers in the conversations or talks.

For most of the questions, you will need to click on the best of four possible answers. Some questions will have special directions. The special directions will appear in a box on the computer screen.

18. What are the man and woman talking about?

    Ⓐ A chapter in their textbook.
    Ⓑ An experiment referred to in a group presentation.
    Ⓒ A lecture in class.
    Ⓓ A program on television.

19. Why is the moon an ideal environment for the experiment?

    Ⓐ There is no air resistance on the moon.
    Ⓑ There is no gravitational acceleration on the moon.
    Ⓒ The gravity on the moon affects vertical motion.
    Ⓓ There is no horizontal resistance for motions like pushing.

20. Why was it easier to lift the hammer on the moon?

    Ⓐ The moon's gravitational acceleration was lower.
    Ⓑ The hammer fell when it was released.
    Ⓒ The surface of the moon encouraged motion.
    Ⓓ The hammer was created for that environment.

21. How did the woman feel about the presentation?

    Ⓐ She was surprised by it.
    Ⓑ She was not interested in it.
    Ⓒ She was impressed by it.
    Ⓓ She was confused about it.

22. What was the video about?

    Ⓐ The national health.
    Ⓑ Stress.
    Ⓒ Heart attacks.
    Ⓓ Health care for women.

23. What did the students learn about women?

    Ⓐ They are under more stress than men.
    Ⓑ They have more heart attacks than men.
    Ⓒ They do not get the same level of care as men.
    Ⓓ They have less serious heart attacks than men.

24. How did the man feel about the video?

    Ⓐ He did not see it.
    Ⓑ He thought it was interesting.
    Ⓒ He would not recommend it.
    Ⓓ He was not surprised by it.

25. What will the woman probably do?

    Ⓐ Discuss the video with the man.
    Ⓑ Go to the library to see the video.
    Ⓒ Check the video out of the library.
    Ⓓ Get ready for class.

26. What is the main topic of this lecture?

    Ⓐ Poet laureates.
    Ⓑ The Victorian period.
    Ⓒ Love poems in the English language.
    Ⓓ Elizabeth Barrett Browning.

27. According to the lecturer, what was one reason that Elizabeth Barrett was considered for the title of Poet Laureate?

    Ⓐ Because her husband was a famous poet.
    Ⓑ Because of her publication, *Sonnets from the Portuguese.*
    Ⓒ Because the monarch was a woman.
    Ⓓ Because of her friendship with William Wordsworth.

28. Where did Elizabeth and Robert Browning live after their elopement?

    Ⓐ In Spain.
    Ⓑ In Italy.
    Ⓒ In Portugal.
    Ⓓ In England.

29. When did Elizabeth Barrett Browning die?

    Ⓐ In 1843.
    Ⓑ In 1849.
    Ⓒ In 1856.
    Ⓓ In 1861.

30. What is the main topic of this lecture?

    Ⓐ The history of medicine in Greece.
    Ⓑ The contributions of biology to medicine.
    Ⓒ The scientific method.
    Ⓓ Medical advances in the twentieth century.

31. What was Hippocrates' greatest contribution to medicine?

    Ⓐ The classification of plants on the basis of body structure.
    Ⓑ The sterilization of surgical instruments.
    Ⓒ The scientific recording of symptoms and treatments.
    Ⓓ The theory that disease was caused by the gods.

32. Who is known as the father of biology?

    Ⓐ Hippocrates.
    Ⓑ Aristotle.
    Ⓒ Dioscorides.
    Ⓓ Edward Jenner.

33. What was the contribution made to medicine by William Harvey?

    Ⓐ The theory of germs and bacteria.
    Ⓑ The discovery of a vaccine against smallpox.
    Ⓒ The discovery of a mechanism for the circulation of the blood.
    Ⓓ The *Materia Medica.*

34. What was surprising about Thrasher's study?

   (A) The size of the study, which included 1300 gangs.
   (B) The excellent summary by the student who located the research.
   (C) The changes that were reported in the history of gangs in the United States.
   (D) The fact that gang activity has been prevalent for many years.

35. According to the study by Moore, what causes gang activity?

   (A) Cliques that form in high school.
   (B) Normal feelings of insecurity that teenagers experience.
   (C) Dangerous neighborhoods and schools.
   (D) Loyalty to friends and family.

36. In which two ways are gang members identified by law enforcement authorities?

   Click on 2 answers.

   [A] By their tattoos.
   [B] By their clothing.
   [C] By maps of their territories.
   [D] By research studies.

37. What is the role of women in gangs?

   (A) Women are full members of the gangs.
   (B) Women are protected by the gangs.
   (C) Women are a support system for the gangs.
   (D) Women do not have any contact with the gangs.

38. What is Mary's problem?

   (A) She does not want to work for Dr. Brown.
   (B) She has a schedule conflict.
   (C) She has been late to work too often.
   (D) She needs to obtain a work-study position.

39. When is Mary's class next semester?

   (A) Every day in the afternoon.
   (B) Three hours a day, three times a week.
   (C) Ten-thirty on Monday.
   (D) Nine o'clock, three times a week.

40. How does Dr. Brown resolve the problem?

   (A) He changes her work hours.
   (B) He assigns her fewer hours.
   (C) He finds a different job for her.
   (D) He gives her permission to arrive late.

41. What is a work-study employee?

   (A) A person who works on campus.
   (B) A new employee who is being trained.
   (C) A student who can study at work after the job is complete.
   (D) A part-time student with a full-time job.

42. What is the topic of this lecture?

   (A) Reinforced concrete in buildings.
   (B) Shear walls in earthquakes.
   (C) Earthquake-resistant buildings.
   (D) Understanding construction sites.

43. Which technique is used to reinforce walls?

   (A) Cross-bracing.
   (B) Shear cores.
   (C) Bolts.
   (D) Base isolators.

44. Which two materials are used in base isolators?

   Click on 2 answers.

   [A] Rubber.
   [B] Steel.
   [C] Concrete.
   [D] Soil.

45. What happens to fill dirt during an earthquake?

    Ⓐ It allows the building to sway.
    Ⓑ It reduces earthquake damage.
    Ⓒ It collapses.
    Ⓓ It creates shock waves.

46. Which two types represent the most common vein patterns in leaves?

    Click on 2 answers.

    Ⓐ Needle leaves.
    Ⓑ Parallel leaves.
    Ⓒ Palmate leaves.
    Ⓓ Pinnate leaves.

47. According to the lecturer, what is a midrib?

    Ⓐ One of the major classifications of veins in plants.
    Ⓑ The large vein that extends down the middle of a pinnate leaf.
    Ⓒ The central vein in a parallel leaf.
    Ⓓ The stem of a plant.

48. How does the lab assistant help students remember the palmate classification?

    Ⓐ She shows them a visual.
    Ⓑ She explains it carefully.
    Ⓒ She compares it to her hand.
    Ⓓ She refers them to their lab manual.

49. Match the leaves with their vein patterns.

    Click on the leaf. Then click on the empty box in the correct row. Use each leaf only once.

    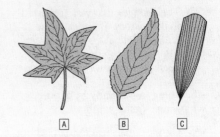

	Pinnate
	Palmate
	Parallel

50. What will the students probably do after the short lecture?

    Ⓐ Classify leaves.
    Ⓑ Take a lab quiz.
    Ⓒ Read fifty-two pages in their manuals.
    Ⓓ Discuss the lecture.

Section 2:
Structure

This section measures the ability to recognize language that is appropriate for standard written English. There are two types of questions in this section.

In the first type of question, there are incomplete sentences. Beneath each sentence, there are four words or phrases. You will choose the one word or phrase that best completes the sentence. Clicking on a choice darkens the oval. After you click on **Next** and **Confirm Answer**, the next question will be presented.

The second type of question has four underlined words or phrases. You will choose the one underlined word or phrase that must be changed for the sentence to be correct. Clicking on an underlined word or phrase will darken it. After you click on **Next** and **Confirm Answer**, the next question will be presented.

1. One of the most effective vegetable protein substitutes is the soybean _____ used to manufacture imitation meat products.

    Ⓐ which can be
    Ⓑ it can be
    Ⓒ who can be
    Ⓓ can be

2. _____ 1000 species of finch have been identified.

    Ⓐ As many as
    Ⓑ As many
    Ⓒ As much as
    Ⓓ Much as

3. The first electric lamp had two
    Ⓐ
    carbon rods from which vapor
    　　　　　　　　　　Ⓑ
    serves to conduct the current
    Ⓒ　　　Ⓓ
    across the gap.

4. A thunderhead, dense clouds that
    Ⓐ
    rise high into the sky in huge
    Ⓑ　Ⓒ
    columns, produce hail, rain, or
    　　　　　　Ⓓ
    snow.

5. According to the economic laws, the greater the demand, _____ the price.

    Ⓐ higher
    Ⓑ high
    Ⓒ the higher
    Ⓓ the high

6. Although no country has exactly
    　　　　　　Ⓐ
    the same folk music like that of
    　　　　　　　　Ⓑ　Ⓒ
    any other, it is significant that similar
    songs exist among widely separated
    　　　　　　　　Ⓓ
    people.

7. Despite of the Taft-Hartley Act
    Ⓐ
    which forbids unfair union
    　　Ⓑ
    practices, some unions such as
    　　　　　　　　　　Ⓒ
    the air traffic controllers have voted
    to strike even though this action
    Ⓓ
    might endanger the national security.

8. The Continental United States is
_____ that there are four time
zones.

    Ⓐ much big
    Ⓑ too big
    Ⓒ so big
    Ⓓ very big

9. Benjamin West contributed a great
deal to American art: _____ .

    Ⓐ painting, teaching, and lecturing
    Ⓑ painting, as a teacher and
lecturer
    Ⓒ painting, teaching, and as a
lecturer
    Ⓓ painting, a teacher, and a
lecturer

10. Operant conditioning involves
rewarding or punishing certain
<u>behave</u> to <u>reinforce</u> or <u>extinguish</u>
    Ⓐ   Ⓑ   Ⓒ
<u>its occurrence.</u>
   Ⓓ

11. <u>There is</u> an unresolved
   Ⓐ
controversy as to <u>whom</u> <u>is</u> the
             Ⓑ Ⓒ
real author of the Elizabethan
plays <u>commonly</u> credited to
        Ⓓ
William Shakespeare.

12. A catalytic agent <u>such</u> platinum
               Ⓐ
may be used <u>so</u> that the chemical
         Ⓑ
reaction <u>advances</u> more <u>rapidly.</u>
     Ⓒ   Ⓓ

13. Upon hatching, _____ .

    Ⓐ young ducks know how to swim
    Ⓑ swimming is known by young
ducks
    Ⓒ the knowledge of swimming is
in young ducks
    Ⓓ how to swim is known in young
ducks

14. The observation deck at the World
Trade Center _____ in New
York.

    Ⓐ was highest than any other one
    Ⓑ was higher than any other one
    Ⓒ was highest that any other one
    Ⓓ was higher that any other one

15. When a patient's blood pressure is
<u>much</u> higher <u>than</u> it <u>should be,</u>
  Ⓐ   Ⓑ   Ⓒ
a doctor usually insists that he
<u>will not</u> smoke.
  Ⓓ

16. <u>It</u> <u>was</u> <u>the invent</u> of the hand-
  Ⓐ Ⓑ   Ⓒ
held electronic calculator that
provided the original technology
for <u>the present</u> generation of
      Ⓓ
small but powerful computers.

17. _____ is necessary for the
development of strong bones and
teeth.

    Ⓐ It is calcium
    Ⓑ That calcium
    Ⓒ Calcium
    Ⓓ Although calcium

18. Located <u>in</u> the cranial cavity in
       Ⓐ
the skull, <u>the brain</u> is the <u>larger</u>
        Ⓑ   Ⓒ
mass of nerve tissue in the
<u>human body.</u>
  Ⓓ

19. <u>Alike</u> other forms of energy,
  Ⓐ
natural gas <u>may be used</u> <u>to heat</u>
        Ⓑ   Ⓒ
homes, cook food, and even <u>run</u>
               Ⓓ
automobiles.

20. An organ <u>is</u> a group <u>of tissues</u>
    Ⓐ   Ⓑ
    capable <u>to perform</u> some special
            Ⓒ
    function, as, <u>for example</u>, the
                  Ⓓ
    heart, the liver, or the lungs.

21. _____ withstands testing, we
    may not conclude that it is true, but
    we may retain it.

    Ⓐ If a hypothesis
    Ⓑ That a hypothesis
    Ⓒ A hypothesis
    Ⓓ Hypothesis

22. <u>Insulin, it is</u> used <u>to treat</u> diabetes
    Ⓐ   Ⓑ
    and <u>is</u> secured <u>chiefly</u> from the
        Ⓒ   Ⓓ
    pancreas of cattle and hogs.

23. Not until a monkey is several years
    old _____ to exhibit signs of
    independence from its mother.

    Ⓐ it begins
    Ⓑ does it begin
    Ⓒ and begin
    Ⓓ beginning

24. Since Elizabeth Barrett Browning's
    father never approved of _____
    Robert Browning, the couple eloped
    to Italy, where they lived and wrote.

    Ⓐ her to marry
    Ⓑ her marrying
    Ⓒ she marrying
    Ⓓ she to marry

25. <u>In autumn</u>, brilliant yellow, orange,
    Ⓐ
    and red leaves are <u>commonly</u> <u>to</u> both
                        Ⓑ   Ⓒ
    the Sweet Gum tree <u>and</u> the Maple.
                        Ⓓ

Section 3:
Reading

This section measures the ability to read and understand short passages similar in topic and style to those that students are likely to encounter in North American universities and colleges. This section contains reading passages and questions about the passages. There are several different types of questions in this section.

In the Reading Section, you will first have the opportunity to read the passage. You will use the scroll bar to view the rest of the passage.

When you have finished reading the passage, you will use the mouse to click on **Proceed**. Then the questions about the passage will be presented. You are to choose the one best answer to each question. Answer all questions about the information in a passage on the basis of what is stated or implied in that passage.

Most of the questions will be multiple-choice questions. To answer these questions you will click on a choice below the question.

To answer some questions, you will click on a word or phrase. To answer some questions, you will click on a sentence in the passage. To answer some questions, you will click on a square to add a sentence to the passage.

The computer screens for selected questions in the Reading section have been printed in this book to provide you with orientation to the format of the Computer-Based TOEFL. Use the screen to find the place in the original reading passage that corresponds to the question you are answering.

Recent technological advances in manned and unmanned undersea vehicles, along with breakthroughs in satellite technology and computer equipment, have overcome some of the limitations of divers and diving equipment for scientists doing research on the great oceans of the world. Without a vehicle, divers often became sluggish, and their mental concentration was severely limited. Because undersea pressure affects their speech organs, communication among divers has always been difficult or impossible. But today, most oceanographers avoid the use of vulnerable human divers, preferring to reduce the risk to human life and make direct observations by means of instruments that are lowered into the ocean, from samples taken from the water, or from photographs made by orbiting satellites. Direct observations of the ocean floor can be made not only by divers but also by deep-diving submarines in the water and even by the technology of sophisticated aerial photography from vantage points above the surface of the water. Some submarines can dive to depths of more than seven miles and cruise at depths of fifteen thousand feet. In addition, radio-equipped buoys can be operated by remote control in order to transmit information back to land-based laboratories via satellite. Particularly important for ocean study are data about water temperature, currents, and weather. Satellite photographs can show the distribution of sea ice, oil slicks, and cloud formations over the ocean. Maps created from satellite pictures can represent the temperature and the color of the ocean's surface, enabling researchers to study the ocean currents from laboratories on dry land. Furthermore, computers help oceanographers to collect, organize, and analyze data from submarines and satellites. By creating a model of the ocean's movement and characteristics, scientists can predict the patterns and possible effects of the ocean on the environment.

Recently, many oceanographers have been relying more on satellites and computers than on research ships or even submarine vehicles because they can supply a greater range of information more quickly and more effectively. Some of humankind's most serious problems, especially those concerning energy and food, may be solved with the help of observations made possible by this new technology.

1. With what topic is the passage primarily concerned?

   (A) Technological advances in oceanography
   (B) Communication among divers
   (C) Direct observation of the ocean floor
   (D) Undersea vehicles

2. The word sluggish in paragraph 1 is closest in meaning to

   (A) nervous
   (B) confused
   (C) slow moving
   (D) very weak

Beginning

Recent technological advances in manned and unmanned undersea vehicles, along with breakthroughs in satellite technology and computer equipment, have overcome some of the limitations of divers and diving equipment for scientists doing research on the great oceans of the world. Without a vehicle, divers often became sluggish, and their mental concentration was severely limited. Because undersea pressure affects their speech organs, communication among divers has always been difficult or impossible. But today, most oceanographers avoid the use of vulnerable human divers, preferring to reduce the risk to human life and make direct observations by means of instruments that are lowered into the ocean, from samples taken from the water, or from photographs made by orbiting satellites. Direct observations of the ocean floor can be made not only by divers but also by deep-diving submarines in the water and even by the technology of sophisticated aerial photography from vantage points above the surface of the water. Some submarines can dive to depths of more than seven miles and cruise at

3. Divers have had problems in communicating underwater because

   (A) the pressure affected their speech organs
   (B) the vehicles they used have not been perfected
   (C) they did not pronounce clearly
   (D) the water destroyed their speech organs

4. This passage suggests that the successful exploration of the ocean depends upon

   (A) vehicles as well as divers
   (B) radios that divers use to communicate
   (C) controlling currents and the weather
   (D) the limitations of diving equipment

5. Undersea vehicles

   (A) are too small for a man to fit inside
   (B) are very slow to respond
   (C) have the same limitations that divers have
   (D) make direct observations of the ocean floor

6. The word █cruise█ in paragraph 1 could best be replaced by

   (A) travel at a constant speed
   (B) function without problems
   (C) stay in communication
   (D) remain still

   > More Available
   >
   > affects their speech organs, communication
   > among divers has always been difficult or
   > impossible. But today, most oceanographers
   > avoid the use of vulnerable human divers,
   > preferring to reduce the risk to human life and
   > make direct observations by means of instruments
   > that are lowered into the ocean, from samples
   > taken from the water, or from photographs made
   > by orbiting satellites. Direct observations of the
   > ocean floor can be made not only by divers but
   > also by deep-diving submarines in the water and
   > even by the technology of sophisticated aerial
   > photography from vantage points above the
   > surface of the water. Some submarines can dive
   > to depths of more than seven miles and █cruise█ at
   > depths of fifteen thousand feet. In addition, radio-
   > equipped buoys can be operated by remote
   > control in order to transmit information back to
   > land-based laboratories via satellite. Particularly
   > important for ocean study are data about water
   > temperature, currents, and weather. Satellite
   > photographs can show the distribution of sea ice,
   > oil slicks, and cloud formations over the ocean.
   > Maps created from satellite pictures can represent

7. How is a radio-equipped buoy operated?

   (A) By operators inside the vehicle in the part underwater
   (B) By operators outside the vehicle on a ship
   (C) By operators outside the vehicle on a diving platform
   (D) By operators outside the vehicle in a laboratory on shore

8. Look at the word █information█ in the passage. Click on the word or phrase in the **bold** text that is closest in meaning to █information█.

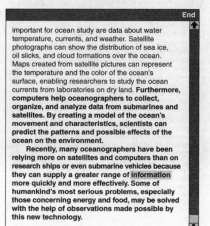

> End
>
> important for ocean study are data about water
> temperature, currents, and weather. Satellite
> photographs can show the distribution of sea ice,
> oil slicks, and cloud formations over the ocean.
> Maps created from satellite pictures can represent
> the temperature and the color of the ocean's
> surface, enabling researchers to study the ocean
> currents from laboratories on dry land. **Furthermore,
> computers help oceanographers to collect,
> organize, and analyze data from submarines and
> satellites. By creating a model of the ocean's
> movement and characteristics, scientists can
> predict the patterns and possible effects of the
> ocean on the environment.**
> **Recently, many oceanographers have been
> relying more on satellites and computers than on
> research ships or even submarine vehicles because
> they can supply a greater range of █information█
> more quickly and more effectively. Some of
> humankind's most serious problems, especially
> those concerning energy and food, may be solved
> with the help of observations made possible by
> this new technology.**

9. Which of the following are NOT shown in satellite photographs?

   (A) The temperature of the ocean's surface
   (B) Cloud formations over the ocean
   (C) A model of the ocean's movements
   (D) The location of sea ice

10. Look at the word those in the passage. Click on the word or phrase in the **bold** text that those refers to.

End

important for ocean study are data about water temperature, currents, and weather. Satellite photographs can show the distribution of sea ice, oil slicks, and cloud formations over the ocean. Maps created from satellite pictures can represent the temperature and the color of the ocean's surface, enabling researchers to study the ocean currents from laboratories on dry land. Furthermore, computers help oceanographers to collect, organize, and analyze data from submarines and satellites. By creating a model of the ocean's movement and characteristics, scientists can predict the patterns and possible effects of the ocean on the environment.

Recently, many oceanographers have been relying more on satellites and computers than on research ships or even submarine vehicles because they can supply a greater range of information more quickly and more effectively. Some of humankind's most serious problems, especially those concerning energy and food, may be solved with the help of observations made possible by this new technology.

11. Click on the paragraph in the passage that discusses problems that new technology might help eliminate.

Scroll the passage to see all of the paragraphs.

Although speech is generally accepted as the most advanced form of communication, there are many ways of communicating without using words. In every known culture, signals, signs, symbols, and gestures are commonly utilized as instruments of communication. There is a great deal of agreement among communication scientists as to what each of these methods is and how each differs from the others. For instance, the basic function of any signal is to impinge upon the environment in such a way that it attracts attention, as, for example, the dots and dashes that can be applied in a telegraph circuit. Coded to refer to speech, the potential for communication through these dots and dashes—short and long intervals as the circuit is broken—is very great. Less adaptable to the codification of words, signs also contain agreed upon meaning; that is, they convey information in and of themselves. Two examples are the hexagonal red sign that conveys the meaning of *stop*, and the red and white swirled pole outside a shop that communicates the meaning of *barber*.

Symbols are more difficult to describe than either signals or signs because of their intricate relationship with the receiver's cultural perceptions. In some cultures, applauding in a theater provides performers with an auditory symbol of approval. In other cultures, if done in unison, applauding can be a symbol of the audience's discontent with the performance. Gestures such as waving and handshaking also communicate certain cultural messages.

Although signals, signs, symbols, and gestures are very useful, they also have a major disadvantage in communication. They usually do not allow ideas to be shared without the sender being directly adjacent to the receiver. Without an exchange of ideas, interaction comes to a halt. As a result, means of communication intended to be used across long distances and extended periods must be based upon speech. To radio, television, and the telephone, one must add fax, paging systems, electronic mail, and the Internet, and no one doubts but that there are more means of communication on the horizon.

12. Which of the following would be the best title for the passage?

    Ⓐ Signs and Signals
    Ⓑ Gestures
    Ⓒ Communication
    Ⓓ Speech

13. What does the author say about speech?

    Ⓐ It is the only true form of communication.
    Ⓑ It is dependent upon the advances made by inventors.
    Ⓒ It is necessary for communication to occur.
    Ⓓ It is the most advanced form of communication.

14. Click on the sentence in paragraph 1 that defines the function of a signal.

Paragraph 1 is marked with an arrow (→).

15. The phrase impinge upon in paragraph 1 is closest in meaning to

    Ⓐ intrude
    Ⓑ improve
    Ⓒ vary
    Ⓓ prohibit

Beginning

Although speech is generally accepted as the most advanced form of communication, there are many ways of communicating without using words. In every known culture, signals, signs, symbols, and gestures are commonly utilized as instruments of communication. There is a great deal of agreement among communication scientists as to what each of these methods is and how each differs from the others. For instance, the basic function of any signal is to impinge upon the environment in such a way that it attracts attention, as, for example, the dots and dashes that can be applied in a telegraph circuit. Coded to refer to speech, the potential for communication through these dots and dashes—short and long intervals as the circuit is broken—is very great. Less adaptable to the codification of words, signs also contain agreed upon meaning; that is, they convey information in and of themselves. Two examples are the hexagonal red sign that conveys the meaning of *stop*, and the red and white swirled pole outside a shop that communicates the meaning of *barber*.
Symbols are more difficult to describe than

Beginning

→ Although speech is generally accepted as the most advanced form of communication, there are many ways of communicating without using words. In every known culture, signals, signs, symbols, and gestures are commonly utilized as instruments of communication. There is a great deal of agreement among communication scientists as to what each of these methods is and how each differs from the others. For instance, the basic function of any signal is to impinge upon the environment in such a way that it attracts attention, as, for example, the dots and dashes that can be applied in a telegraph circuit. Coded to refer to speech, the potential for communication through these dots and dashes—short and long intervals as the circuit is broken—is very great. Less adaptable to the codification of words, signs also contain agreed upon meaning; that is, they convey information in and of themselves. Two examples are the hexagonal red sign that conveys the meaning of *stop*, and the red and white swirled pole outside a shop that communicates the meaning of *barber*.
Symbols are more difficult to describe than

16. The word it in paragraph 1 refers to

    (A) function
    (B) signal
    (C) environment
    (D) way

Beginning

Although speech is generally accepted as the most advanced form of communication, there are many ways of communicating without using words. In every known culture, signals, signs, symbols, and gestures are commonly utilized as instruments of communication. There is a great deal of agreement among communication scientists as to what each of these methods is and how each differs from the others. For instance, the basic function of any signal is to impinge upon the environment in such a way that it attracts attention, as, for example, the dots and dashes that can be applied in a telegraph circuit. Coded to refer to speech, the potential for communication through these dots and dashes—short and long intervals as the circuit is broken—is very great. Less adaptable to the codification of words, signs also contain agreed upon meaning; that is, they convey information in and of themselves. Two examples are the hexagonal red sign that conveys the meaning of *stop*, and the red and white swirled pole outside a shop that communicates the meaning of *barber*.

Symbols are more difficult to describe than

---

17. The word potential in paragraph 1 could best be replaced by

    (A) range
    (B) advantage
    (C) organization
    (D) possibility

Beginning

Although speech is generally accepted as the most advanced form of communication, there are many ways of communicating without using words. In every known culture, signals, signs, symbols, and gestures are commonly utilized as instruments of communication. There is a great deal of agreement among communication scientists as to what each of these methods is and how each differs from the others. For instance, the basic function of any signal is to impinge upon the environment in such a way that it attracts attention, as, for example, the dots and dashes that can be applied in a telegraph circuit. Coded to refer to speech, the potential for communication through these dots and dashes—short and long intervals as the circuit is broken—is very great. Less adaptable to the codification of words, signs also contain agreed upon meaning; that is, they convey information in and of themselves. Two examples are the hexagonal red sign that conveys the meaning of *stop*, and the red and white swirled pole outside a shop that communicates the meaning of *barber*.

Symbols are more difficult to describe than

---

18. Look at the word themselves in the passage. Click on the word or phrase in the **bold** text that themselves refers to.

More Available

scientists as to what each of these methods is and how each differs from the others. For instance, the basic function of any signal is to impinge upon the environment in such a way that it attracts attention, as, for example, the dots and dashes that can be applied in a telegraph circuit. **Coded to refer to speech, the potential for communication through these dots and dashes—short and long intervals as the circuit is broken—is very great. Less adaptable to the codification of words, signs also contain agreed upon meaning; that is, they convey information in and of themselves. Two examples are the hexagonal red sign that conveys the meaning of *stop*, and the red and white swirled pole outside a shop that communicates the meaning of *barber*.**

Symbols are more difficult to describe than either signals or signs because of their intricate relationship with the receiver's cultural perceptions. In some cultures, applauding in a theater provides performers with an auditory symbol of approval. In other cultures, if done in unison, applauding can be a symbol of the audience's discontent with the performance. Gestures such as waving and

---

19. The word intricate in paragraph 2 could best be replaced by which of the following?

    (A) inefficient
    (B) complicated
    (C) historical
    (D) uncertain

More Available

also contain agreed upon meaning; that is, they convey information in and of themselves. Two examples are the hexagonal red sign that conveys the meaning of *stop*, and the red and white swirled pole outside a shop that communicates the meaning of *barber*.

Symbols are more difficult to describe than either signals or signs because of their intricate relationship with the receiver's cultural perceptions. In some cultures, applauding in a theater provides performers with an auditory symbol of approval. In other cultures, if done in unison, applauding can be a symbol of the audience's discontent with the performance. Gestures such as waving and handshaking also communicate certain cultural messages.

Although signals, signs, symbols, and gestures are very useful, they also have a major disadvantage in communication. They usually do not allow ideas to be shared without the sender being directly adjacent to the receiver. Without an exchange of ideas, interaction comes to a halt. As a result, means of communication intended to be used across long distances and extended periods

20. Applauding was cited as an example of

    (A) a signal
    (B) a sign
    (C) a symbol
    (D) a gesture

21. The following sentence can be added to the passage.

    A loud smacking of the lips after a meal can be either a kinesthetic and auditory symbol of approval and appreciation, or simply a rude noise.

    Where would it best fit in the passage?

    Click on the square (■) to add the sentence to the passage.

    Scroll the passage to see all of the choices.

    > More Available
    >
    > also contain agreed upon meaning; that is, they convey information in and of themselves. ■ Two examples are the hexagonal red sign that conveys the meaning of *stop*, and the red and white swirled pole outside a shop that communicates the meaning of *barber*.
    >   ■ Symbols are more difficult to describe than either signals or signs because of their intricate relationship with the receiver's cultural perceptions. In some cultures, applauding in a theater provides performers with an auditory symbol of approval. In other cultures, if done in unison, applauding can be a symbol of the audience's discontent with the performance. ■ Gestures such as waving and handshaking also communicate certain cultural messages.
    >   Although signals, signs, symbols, and gestures are very useful, they also have a major disadvantage in communication. ■ They usually do not allow ideas to be shared without the sender being directly adjacent to the receiver. Without an exchange of ideas, interaction comes to a halt. As a result, means of communication intended to be used across long distances and extended periods

22. Why were the telephone, radio, and TV invented?

    (A) People were unable to understand signs, symbols, and signals.
    (B) People wanted to communicate across long distances.
    (C) People believed that signs, signals, and symbols were obsolete.
    (D) People wanted new forms of entertainment.

23. Look at the word communication in the passage. Click on the word or phrase in the **bold** text that is closest in meaning to communication.

    > End
    >
    > In some cultures, applauding in a theater provides performers with an auditory symbol of approval. In other cultures, if done in unison, applauding can be a symbol of the audience's discontent with the performance. Gestures such as waving and handshaking also communicate certain cultural messages.
    >   **Although signals, signs, symbols, and gestures are very useful, they also have a major disadvantage in communication. They usually do not allow ideas to be shared without the sender being directly adjacent to the receiver. Without an exchange of ideas, interaction comes to a halt. As a result, means of communication intended to be used across long distances and extended periods must be based upon speech.** To radio, television, and the telephone, one must add fax, paging systems, electronic mail, and the Internet, and no one doubts but that there are more means of communication on the horizon.

Fertilizer is any substance that can be added to the soil to provide chemical elements essential for plant nutrition so that the yield can be increased. Natural substances such as animal droppings, ashes from wood fires, and straw have been used as fertilizers in fields for thousands of years, and lime has been used since the Romans introduced it during the Empire. It was not until the nineteenth century, however, that chemical fertilizers became widely accepted as normal agricultural practice. Today, both natural and synthetic fertilizers are available in a variety of forms.

A complete fertilizer is usually marked with a formula consisting of three numbers, such as 4-8-2 or 6-6-4, which designate the percentage of content of nitrogen, phosphoric acid, and potash in the order stated. Synthetic fertilizers, produced by factories, are available in either solid or liquid form. Solids, in the shape of chemical granules, are in demand because they are not only easy to store but also easy to apply. Recently, liquids have shown an increase in popularity, accounting for about 20 percent of the nitrogen fertilizer used throughout the world. Formerly, powders were also used, but they were found to be less convenient than either solids or liquids.

Fertilizers have no harmful effects on the soil, the crop, or the consumer as long as they are used according to recommendations based on the results of local research. Occasionally, however, farmers may use more fertilizer than necessary, in which case the plants do not need, and therefore do not absorb, the total amount of fertilizer applied to the soil. The surplus of fertilizer thus can damage not only the crop but also the animals or human beings that eat the crop. Furthermore, fertilizer that is not used in the production of a healthy plant is leached into the water table. Accumulations of chemical fertilizer in the water supply accelerate the growth of algae and,

consequently, may disturb the natural cycle of
life, contributing to the death of fish. Too much
fertilizer on grass can cause digestive disorders
in cattle and in infants who drink cow's milk.
Fertilizer must be used with great attention to
responsible use or it can harm the environment.

24. With which of the following topics is the passage primarily concerned?

Ⓐ Local research and harmful effects of fertilizer
Ⓑ Advantages and disadvantages of liquid fertilizer
Ⓒ A formula for the production of fertilizer
Ⓓ Content, form, and effects of fertilizer

25. The word essential in paragraph 1 could best be replaced by which of the following?

Ⓐ limited
Ⓑ preferred
Ⓒ anticipated
Ⓓ required

26. Which of the following has the smallest percentage content in the formula 4-8-2?

Ⓐ Nitrogen
Ⓑ Phosphorus
Ⓒ Acid
Ⓓ Potash

27. What is the percentage of nitrogen in a 5-8-7 formula fertilizer?

Ⓐ 3 percent
Ⓑ 5 percent
Ⓒ 7 percent
Ⓓ 8 percent

28. The word designate in paragraph 2 could be replaced by

Ⓐ modify
Ⓑ specify
Ⓒ limit
Ⓓ increase

Beginning

Fertilizer is any substance that can be added to the soil to provide chemical elements essential for plant nutrition so that the yield can be increased. Natural substances such as animal droppings, ashes from wood fires, and straw have been used as fertilizers in fields for thousands of years, and lime has been used since the Romans introduced it during the Empire. It was not until the nineteenth century, however, that chemical fertilizers became widely accepted as normal agricultural practice. Today, both natural and synthetic fertilizers are available in a variety of forms.

A complete fertilizer is usually marked with a formula consisting of three numbers, such as 4-8-2 or 6-6-4, which designate the percentage of content of nitrogen, phosphoric acid, and potash in the order stated. Synthetic fertilizers, produced by factories, are available in either solid or liquid form. Solids, in the shape of chemical granules, are in demand because they are not only easy to store but also easy to apply. Recently, liquids have shown an increase in popularity, accounting for about 20 percent of the nitrogen fertilizer used throughout the world. Formerly, powders were

Beginning

Fertilizer is any substance that can be added to the soil to provide chemical elements essential for plant nutrition so that the yield can be increased. Natural substances such as animal droppings, ashes from wood fires, and straw have been used as fertilizers in fields for thousands of years, and lime has been used since the Romans introduced it during the Empire. It was not until the nineteenth century, however, that chemical fertilizers became widely accepted as normal agricultural practice. Today, both natural and synthetic fertilizers are available in a variety of forms.

A complete fertilizer is usually marked with a formula consisting of three numbers, such as 4-8-2 or 6-6-4, which designate the percentage of content of nitrogen, phosphoric acid, and potash in the order stated. Synthetic fertilizers, produced by factories, are available in either solid or liquid form. Solids, in the shape of chemical granules, are in demand because they are not only easy to store but also easy to apply. Recently, liquids have shown an increase in popularity, accounting for about 20 percent of the nitrogen fertilizer used throughout the world. Formerly, powders were

29. Which of the following statements about fertilizer is true?

   Ⓐ Powders are more popular than ever.

   Ⓑ Solids are difficult to store.

   Ⓒ Liquids are increasing in popularity.

   Ⓓ Chemical granules are difficult to apply.

30. The word they in paragraph 2 refers to

   Ⓐ powders

   Ⓑ solids

   Ⓒ liquids

   Ⓓ fertilizer

More Available

content of nitrogen, phosphoric acid, and potash in the order stated. Synthetic fertilizers, produced by factories, are available in either solid or liquid form. Solids, in the shape of chemical granules, are in demand because they are not only easy to store but also easy to apply. Recently, liquids have shown an increase in popularity, accounting for about 20 percent of the nitrogen fertilizer used throughout the world. Formerly, powders were also used, but they were found to be less convenient than either solids or liquids.

Fertilizers have no harmful effects on the soil, the crop, or the consumer as long as they are used according to recommendations based on the results of local research. Occasionally, however, farmers may use more fertilizer than necessary, in which case the plants do not need, and therefore do not absorb, the total amount of fertilizer applied to the soil. The surplus of fertilizer thus can damage not only the crop but also the animals or human beings that eat the crop. Furthermore, fertilizer that is not used in the production of a healthy plant is leached into the water table. Accumulations of chemical fertilizer in the water

31. The word convenient in paragraph 2 is closest in meaning to

   Ⓐ effective

   Ⓑ plentiful

   Ⓒ easy to use

   Ⓓ cheap to produce

More Available

content of nitrogen, phosphoric acid, and potash in the order stated. Synthetic fertilizers, produced by factories, are available in either solid or liquid form. Solids, in the shape of chemical granules, are in demand because they are not only easy to store but also easy to apply. Recently, liquids have shown an increase in popularity, accounting for about 20 percent of the nitrogen fertilizer used throughout the world. Formerly, powders were also used, but they were found to be less convenient than either solids or liquids.

Fertilizers have no harmful effects on the soil, the crop, or the consumer as long as they are used according to recommendations based on the results of local research. Occasionally, however, farmers may use more fertilizer than necessary, in which case the plants do not need, and therefore do not absorb, the total amount of fertilizer applied to the soil. The surplus of fertilizer thus can damage not only the crop but also the animals or human beings that eat the crop. Furthermore, fertilizer that is not used in the production of a healthy plant is leached into the water table. Accumulations of chemical fertilizer in the water

32. Click on the sentence in paragraph 3 that describes the effect of an accumulation of fertilizer in the water supply.

Paragraph 3 is marked with an arrow (→).

End

→ Fertilizers have no harmful effects on the soil, the crop, or the consumer as long as they are used according to recommendations based on the results of local research. Occasionally, however, farmers may use more fertilizer than necessary, in which case the plants do not need, and therefore do not absorb, the total amount of fertilizer applied to the soil. The surplus of fertilizer thus can damage not only the crop but also the animals or human beings that eat the crop. Furthermore, fertilizer that is not used in the production of a healthy plant is leached into the water table. Accumulations of chemical fertilizer in the water supply accelerate the growth of algae and, consequently, may disturb the natural cycle of life, contributing to the death of fish. Too much fertilizer on grass can cause digestive disorders in cattle and in infants who drink cow's milk. Fertilizer must be used with great attention to responsible use or it can harm the environment.

33. Look at the word harm in the passage. Click on the word or phrase in the **bold** text that is closest in meaning to harm.

> End
>
> Fertilizers have no harmful effects on the soil, the crop, or the consumer as long as they are used according to recommendations based on the results of local research. Occasionally, however, farmers may use more fertilizer than necessary, in which case the plants do not need, and therefore do not absorb, the total amount of fertilizer applied to the soil. **The surplus of fertilizer thus can damage not only the crop but also the animals or human beings that eat the crop. Furthermore, fertilizer that is not used in the production of a healthy plant is leached into the water table. Accumulations of chemical fertilizer in the water supply accelerate the growth of algae and, consequently, may disturb the natural cycle of life, contributing to the death of fish. Too much fertilizer on grass can cause digestive disorders in cattle and in infants who drink cow's milk. Fertilizer must be used with great attention to responsible use or it can harm the environment.**

34. The following sentence can be added to the passage.

    One objection to powders was their propensity to become solid chunks if the bags got damp.

    Where would it best fit in the passage?

    Click on the square (■) to add the sentence to the passage.

    Scroll the passage to see all of the choices.

> More Available
>
> content of nitrogen, phosphoric acid, and potash in the order stated. Synthetic fertilizers, produced by factories, are available in either solid or liquid form. Solids, in the shape of chemical granules, are in demand because they are not only easy to store but also easy to apply. ■ Recently, liquids have shown an increase in popularity, accounting for about 20 percent of the nitrogen fertilizer used throughout the world. ■ Formerly, powders were also used, but they were found to be less convenient than either solids or liquids. ■
>
> Fertilizers have no harmful effects on the soil, the crop, or the consumer as long as they are used according to recommendations based on the results of local research. ■ Occasionally, however, farmers may use more fertilizer than necessary, in which case the plants do not need, and therefore do not absorb, the total amount of fertilizer applied to the soil. The surplus of fertilizer thus can damage not only the crop but also the animals or human beings that eat the crop. Furthermore, fertilizer that is not used in the production of a healthy plant is leached into the water table. Accumulations of chemical fertilizer in the water

The development of the horse has been recorded from the beginning through all of its evolutionary stages to the modern form. It is, in fact, one of the most complete and well-documented chapters of paleontological history. Fossil finds provide us not only with detailed information about the horse itself but also with valuable insights into the migration of herds, and even evidence for speculation about the climatic conditions that could have instigated such migratory behavior.

Geologists believe that the first horses appeared on Earth about sixty million years ago as compared with two million years ago for the appearance of human beings. There is evidence of early horses on both the American and European continents, but it has been documented that, almost twelve million years ago at the beginning of the Pliocene Age, a horse about midway through its evolutionary development crossed a land bridge where the Bering Strait is now located, from Alaska into the grasslands of Asia, and traveled all the way to Europe. This early horse was a hipparion, about the size of a modern-day pony with three toes and specialized cheek teeth for grazing. In Europe, the hipparion encountered another less advanced horse called the anchitheres, which had previously invaded Europe by the same route, probably during the Miocene Period. Less developed and smaller than the hipparion, the anchitheres was eventually completely replaced by it.

By the end of the Pleistocene Age both the anchitheres and the hipparion had become extinct in North America, where they had originated, as fossil evidence clearly indicates. In Europe, they evolved into the larger and stronger animal that is very similar to the horse as we know it today. For many years, the horse was probably hunted for food by early tribes of human beings. Then the qualities of the horse that would have made it a good servant were noted—mainly its strength and speed. It was time for the horse to be tamed, used as a draft animal at the dawning of agriculture, and then ridden as the need for transportation increased. It was the descendant of this domesticated horse that was brought back to the Americas by European colonists.

35. What is this passage mainly about?
   Ⓐ The evolution of the horse
   Ⓑ The migration of horses
   Ⓒ The modern-day pony
   Ⓓ The replacement of the anchitheres by the hipparion

36. According to the author, fossils are considered valuable for all of the following reasons EXCEPT
   Ⓐ they suggest how the climate may have been
   Ⓑ they provide information about migration
   Ⓒ they document the evolution of the horse
   Ⓓ they maintain a record of life prior to the Miocene Age

37. The word instigated in paragraph 1 could best be replaced by
   Ⓐ explained
   Ⓑ caused
   Ⓒ improved
   Ⓓ influenced

Beginning

The development of the horse has been recorded from the beginning through all of its evolutionary stages to the modern form. It is, in fact, one of the most complete and well-documented chapters of paleontological history. Fossil finds provide us not only with detailed information about the horse itself but also with valuable insights into the migration of herds, and even evidence for speculation about the climatic conditions that could have instigated such migratory behavior.

Geologists believe that the first horses appeared on Earth about sixty million years ago as compared with two million years ago for the appearance of human beings. There is evidence of early horses on both the American and European continents, but it has been documented that, almost twelve million years ago at the beginning of the Pliocene Age, a horse about midway through its evolutionary development crossed a land bridge where the Bering Strait is now located, from Alaska into the grasslands of Asia, and traveled all the way to Europe. This early horse was a hipparion, about the size of a modern-day pony with three toes and specialized

38. What does the author mean by the statement Geologists believe

that the first horses appeared on

Earth about sixty million years

ago as compared with two

million years ago for the

appearance of human beings?

Ⓐ Horses appeared long before human beings according to the theories of geologists.
Ⓑ Both horses and human beings appeared several million years ago, if we believe geologists.
Ⓒ The geological records for the appearance of horses and human beings are not very accurate.
Ⓓ Horses and human beings cannot be compared by geologists because they appeared too long ago.

39. Which of the following conclusions may be made on the basis of information in the passage?

Ⓐ The hipparions migrated to Europe to feed in developing grasslands.
Ⓑ There are no fossil remains of either the anchitheres or the hipparion.
Ⓒ There were horses in North America when the first European colonists arrived.
Ⓓ Very little is known about the evolution of the horse.

40. According to this passage, the hipparions were

Ⓐ five-toed animals
Ⓑ not as highly developed as the anchitheres
Ⓒ larger than the anchitheres
Ⓓ about the size of a small dog

41. The word it in paragraph 2 refers to

Ⓐ anchitheres
Ⓑ hipparion
Ⓒ Miocene Period
Ⓓ route

Beginning

The development of the horse has been recorded from the beginning through all of its evolutionary stages to the modern form. It is, in fact, one of the most complete and well-documented chapters of paleontological history. Fossil finds provide us not only with detailed information about the horse itself but also with valuable insights into the migration of herds, and even evidence for speculation about the climatic conditions that could have instigated such migratory behavior.
    Geologists believe that the first horses appeared on Earth about sixty million years ago as compared with two million years ago for the appearance of human beings. There is evidence of early horses on both the American and European continents, but it has been documented that, almost twelve million years ago at the beginning of the Pliocene Age, a horse about midway through its evolutionary development crossed a land bridge where the Bering Strait is now located, from Alaska into the grasslands of Asia, and traveled all the way to Europe. This early horse was a hipparion, about the size of a modern-day pony with three toes and specialized

More Available

appearance of human beings. There is evidence of early horses on both the American and European continents, but it has been documented that, almost twelve million years ago at the beginning of the Pliocene Age, a horse about midway through its evolutionary development crossed a land bridge where the Bering Strait is now located, from Alaska into the grasslands of Asia, and traveled all the way to Europe. This early horse was a hipparion, about the size of a modern-day pony with three toes and specialized cheek teeth for grazing. In Europe, the hipparion encountered another less advanced horse called the anchitheres, which had previously invaded Europe by the same route, probably during the Miocene Period. Less developed and smaller than the hipparion, the anchitheres was eventually completely replaced by it.
    By the end of the Pleistocene Age both the anchitheres and the hipparion had become extinct in North America, where they had originated, as fossil evidence clearly indicates. In Europe, they evolved into the larger and stronger animal that is very similar to the horse as we know it today. For

42. The word extinct in paragraph 3 is closest in meaning to

    Ⓐ familiar
    Ⓑ widespread
    Ⓒ nonexistent
    Ⓓ tame

> End
>
> cheek teeth for grazing. In Europe, the hipparion encountered another less advanced horse called the anchitheres, which had previously invaded Europe by the same route, probably during the Miocene Period. Less developed and smaller than the hipparion, the anchitheres was eventually completely replaced by it.
>
> By the end of the Pleistocene Age both the anchitheres and the hipparion had become extinct in North America, where they had originated, as fossil evidence clearly indicates. In Europe, they evolved into the larger and stronger animal that is very similar to the horse as we know it today. For many years, the horse was probably hunted for food by early tribes of human beings. Then the qualities of the horse that would have made it a good servant were noted—mainly its strength and speed. It was time for the horse to be tamed, used as a draft animal at the dawning of agriculture, and then ridden as the need for transportation increased. It was the descendant of this domesticated horse that was brought back to the Americas by European colonists.

43. Click on the paragraph that refers to the potential for conclusions from the evidence supplied by fossil remains.

    Scroll the passage to see all of the paragraphs.

44. Look at the word domesticated in the passage. Click on the word or phrase in the **bold** text that is closest in meaning to domesticated.

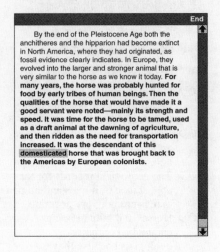

> End
>
> By the end of the Pleistocene Age both the anchitheres and the hipparion had become extinct in North America, where they had originated, as fossil evidence clearly indicates. In Europe, they evolved into the larger and stronger animal that is very similar to the horse as we know it today. **For many years, the horse was probably hunted for food by early tribes of human beings. Then the qualities of the horse that would have made it a good servant were noted—mainly its strength and speed. It was time for the horse to be tamed, used as a draft animal at the dawning of agriculture, and then ridden as the need for transportation increased. It was the descendant of this domesticated horse that was brought back to the Americas by European colonists.**

45. It can be concluded from this passage that the

    Ⓐ Miocene Period was prior to the Pliocene
    Ⓑ Pleistocene Period was prior to the Miocene
    Ⓒ Pleistocene Period was prior to the Pliocene
    Ⓓ Pliocene Period was prior to the Miocene

To check your answers for Model Test 2, refer to the Answer Key on pages 386–387. For an explanation of the answers, refer to the Explanatory Answers for Model Test 2 on pages 417–438.

Writing Section Model Test 2

When you take a Model Test, you should use one sheet of paper, both sides. Time each Model Test carefully. After you have read the topic, you should spend 30 minutes writing. For results that would be closest to the actual testing situation, it is recommended that an English teacher score your test, using the guidelines on page 247 of this book.

Read and think about the following statement:

Pets should be treated like family members.

Do you agree or disagree with the statement? Give reasons to support your opinion.

Notes

To check your essay, refer to the Checklist on page 387. For an Example Essay, refer to the Explanatory Answers for Model Test 2 on page 439.

Model Test 3
Computer-Assisted TOEFL

Section 1:
Listening

The Listening Section of the test measures the ability to understand conversations and talks in English. You will use headphones to listen to the conversations and talks. While you are listening, pictures of the speakers or other information will be presented on your computer screen. There are two parts to the Listening Section, with special directions for each part.

On the day of the test, the amount of time you will have to answer all of the questions will appear on the computer screen. The time you spend listening to the test material will not be counted. The listening material and questions about it will be presented only one time. You will not be allowed to take notes or have any paper at your computer. You will both see and hear the questions before the answer choices appear. You can take as much time as you need to select an answer; however, it will be to your advantage to answer the questions as quickly as possible. You may change your answer as many times as you want before you confirm it. After you have confirmed an answer, you will not be able to return to the question.

Before you begin working on the Listening Section, you will have an opportunity to adjust the volume of the sound. You may not be able to change the volume after you have started the test.

QUESTION DIRECTIONS—Part A

In Part A of the Listening Section, you will hear short conversations between two people. In some of the conversations, each person speaks only once. In other conversations, one or both of the people speak more than once. Each conversation is followed by one question about it.

Each question in this part has four answer choices. You should click on the best answer to each question. Answer the questions on the basis of what is stated or implied by the speakers.

1. What does the woman mean?

    (A) She will not go home for spring vacation.
    (B) She has not taken a vacation for a long time.
    (C) She does not plan to graduate.
    (D) She does not want to go home after graduation in May.

2. What are the speakers talking about?

    (A) The class.
    (B) The weekend.
    (C) Homework.
    (D) Books.

3. What does the man mean?

Ⓐ He should have prepared more.
Ⓑ He is very worried.
Ⓒ He has been studying a lot.
Ⓓ He needs a few more days.

4. What will the man probably do?

Ⓐ Buy a textbook.
Ⓑ Come back later.
Ⓒ Go to the bookstore.
Ⓓ Drop his English class.

5. What does the woman mean?

Ⓐ She does not like the class.
Ⓑ Her classmates are really great.
Ⓒ The professor is not very nice.
Ⓓ The class is interesting.

6. What will the woman probably do?

Ⓐ Make an appointment with Dr. Peterson's T.A.
Ⓑ Cancel her appointment with the T.A.
Ⓒ Postpone her appointment with Dr. Peterson's T.A.
Ⓓ See the T.A. more often.

7. What does the man mean?

Ⓐ He would rather have American food.
Ⓑ He has always liked American food.
Ⓒ He is accustomed to eating American food.
Ⓓ He ate American food more in the past.

8. What does the man mean?

Ⓐ He should go to bed.
Ⓑ He did not know the time.
Ⓒ He is trying to bring his work up to date.
Ⓓ He is not sleepy yet.

9. What is the woman going to do?

Ⓐ Spend some time with the man.
Ⓑ Make a list of the names.
Ⓒ Pass out the names.
Ⓓ Let someone else call the names.

10. What does the man mean?

Ⓐ The woman has missed the deadline.
Ⓑ He will investigate the situation.
Ⓒ The deadline has been canceled.
Ⓓ An exception might be possible.

11. What does the man mean?

Ⓐ The book is confusing.
Ⓑ He is doing well in the class.
Ⓒ The teacher is not very clear.
Ⓓ The lectures are from the book.

12. What does the woman mean?

Ⓐ She wants to submit her paper early.
Ⓑ The answers on the paper are all correct.
Ⓒ The deadline has passed for the paper.
Ⓓ The paper is not quite finished.

13. What does the woman say about the class?

Ⓐ She does not like the class.
Ⓑ It is not a required class.
Ⓒ She has already taken the class.
Ⓓ The man will have to take the class.

14. What did the T.A. suggest the students do?

Ⓐ Study together.
Ⓑ Prepare for an oral final.
Ⓒ Review the quizzes.
Ⓓ Take the professor's advice.

15. What is the woman going to do?

    Ⓐ Make an appointment.
    Ⓑ Give the man a pen.
    Ⓒ Sign the form for the man.
    Ⓓ Wait for the man.

16. What is the woman going to do?

    Ⓐ Revise her work.
    Ⓑ Close the window.
    Ⓒ Copy from the man.
    Ⓓ Hand in the work.

17. What had the man assumed about the loan payment?

    Ⓐ The computer made an error.
    Ⓑ The payment is due on the fifth of every month.
    Ⓒ The loan must be paid by the first of the month.
    Ⓓ The loan had already been paid in full.

QUESTION DIRECTIONS—Part B

In Part B of the Listening Section, you will hear several longer conversations and talks. Each conversation or talk is followed by several questions. The conversations, talks, and questions will not be repeated.

The conversations and talks are about a variety of topics. You do not need special knowledge of the topics to answer the questions correctly. Rather, you should answer each question on the basis of what is stated or implied by the speakers in the conversations or talks.

For most of the questions, you will need to click on the best of four possible answers. Some questions will have special directions. The special directions will appear in a box on the computer screen.

18. Why did Betty see Professor Hayes?

    Ⓐ To enroll in a class.
    Ⓑ To ask his opinion about a university.
    Ⓒ To find out who is chair of the selection committee.
    Ⓓ To get a letter for graduate school.

19. What does Professor Hayes think about Betty?

    Ⓐ She might need to take his seminar.
    Ⓑ She should do well in graduate school.
    Ⓒ She had better go to another university.
    Ⓓ She needs to apply before the end of April.

20. Who will decide whether Betty is accepted to the program?

    Ⓐ The chair of the selection committee.
    Ⓑ The entire selection committee.
    Ⓒ Professor Hayes.
    Ⓓ Dr. Warren.

21. When does Betty need to submit all her materials?

    Ⓐ On May 1.
    Ⓑ In three days.
    Ⓒ Before the April 30th deadline.
    Ⓓ Today.

22. Who is the speaker?

    Ⓐ A professor of religion.
    Ⓑ A professor of history.
    Ⓒ A guest lecturer in a drama class.
    Ⓓ A guest lecturer in a writing class.

23. According to the speaker, how did England control trade in the eighteenth century?

    A By threatening to go to war.
    B By competing with farmers.
    C By keeping manufacturing processes secret.
    D By stealing plans from the colonies.

24. What did Samuel Slater do?

    A He kept designs for English machinery from being used in the colonies.
    B He prevented Moses Brown from opening a mill.
    C He committed designs for English machinery to memory.
    D He smuggled drawings for English machines into the United States.

25. What happened as a result of the Slater-Brown partnership?

    A A change from agriculture to industry began to occur in the United States.
    B A rise in prices for English goods was evidenced.
    C Many small farmers began to send their products to England.
    D Americans had to keep their manufacturing processes secret.

26. What is the purpose of this conversation?

    A The man wants to reserve textbooks for the following semester.
    B The man is complaining about not having his books this semester.
    C The woman needs to order enough books for the class.
    D The woman is helping the man register for his courses.

27. What was the man's problem last semester?

    A The bookstore was closed for three weeks.
    B His books did not arrive before the semester began.
    C He did not have any books this semester.
    D He did not understand how to order his books.

28. How can the man order books?

    A The teacher will order books for the class.
    B He could fill out a form and pay for the books now.
    C He must wait until the semester begins.
    D He has to register for the classes, and the books will be ordered for him.

29. How will the man know that the books have arrived?

    A He will receive a form in the mail.
    B He will get a phone call.
    C He will stop by the bookstore at the beginning of the semester.
    D He will receive the books from his teacher in class.

30. What is the instructor defining?

    A The term "essay."
    B Prose writing.
    C Personal viewpoint.
    D Brainstorming.

31. What is the main point of the talk?

    A The work of Alexander Pope.
    B The difference between prose and poetry.
    C The general characteristics of essays.
    D The reason that the phrase "personal essay" is redundant.

32. According to the talk, which of the characteristics are NOT true of an essay?

    Ⓐ It is usually short.
    Ⓑ It can be either prose or poetry.
    Ⓒ It expresses a personal point of view.
    Ⓓ It discusses one topic.

33. What will the students probably do as an assignment?

    Ⓐ They will prepare for a quiz.
    Ⓑ They will write their first essay.
    Ⓒ They will read works by Pope.
    Ⓓ They will review their notes.

34. What is the main purpose of this talk?

    Ⓐ To provide an overview of U.S. history from 1743 to 1826.
    Ⓑ To discuss Jefferson's contribution to the American Revolution.
    Ⓒ To analyze Jefferson's presidency.
    Ⓓ To summarize Jefferson's life.

35. Jefferson was a member of which political group?

    Ⓐ Monarchist.
    Ⓑ Federalist.
    Ⓒ Republican.
    Ⓓ Democrat.

36. How did Jefferson become president?

    Ⓐ He received the most votes.
    Ⓑ Congress approved him.
    Ⓒ Aaron Burr withdrew from the race.
    Ⓓ As vice president, he automatically became president.

37. According to the lecturer, what was it that Jefferson was NOT?

    Ⓐ An effective public speaker.
    Ⓑ An architect.
    Ⓒ A literary draftsman.
    Ⓓ A diplomat.

38. What are the two most common places where fossils may be found?

    Click on 2 answers.

    A   Ice.
    B   Mud.
    C   Sand.
    D   Water.

39. The professor briefly explains a process. Summarize the process by putting the events in order.

    Click on a sentence. Then click on the space where it belongs. Use each sentence only once.

    A   A mold of the organism preserves the shape of the organism.
    B   Water soaks into the organism.
    C   Organisms are buried in mud or sand.
    D   Minerals in the water dissolve the original organism.

    1 [   ]

    2 [   ]

    3 [   ]

    4 [   ]

40. What is lost in the process of replacement?

    (A) The fine shapes of fragile structures.
    (B) The internal features of the plant or animal.
    (C) The minerals in the deposit.
    (D) The original fossil mold.

41. Why are the layers of sedimentary rock important to the fossil record?

    (A) The ages of the fossils may be determined by their location in the layers of rock.
    (B) The shapes of the fossils may be preserved in the layers of rock.
    (C) The rock protects the fossils from the mineral water that dissolves them.
    (D) Plants and animals that are formed at the same time are buried in different layers of rock.

42. Why didn't the man apply for graduation?

    (A) He wasn't sure that he had completed the requirements.
    (B) He did not have enough credit hours.
    (C) He did not have a program of study.
    (D) He did not understand that it was necessary.

43. How did the man select his courses?

    (A) By reading the catalog.
    (B) By consulting with the woman.
    (C) By referring to his signed program of study.
    (D) By making an appointment with his advisor.

44. What does the woman suggest?

    (A) The man should take the required courses for graduation.
    (B) The man should see an academic advisor to help him.
    (C) The man should read the requirements in the college catalog.
    (D) The man should bring her a copy of his transcript.

45. What is the man's problem?

    (A) He may not have enough credit hours to graduate.
    (B) He may not have taken the correct classes to graduate.
    (C) He may not be able to see an academic advisor before graduation.
    (D) He may not have time to take the rest of the required courses.

46. In which class would this discussion probably take place?

    (A) Sociology.
    (B) Education.
    (C) Linguistics.
    (D) Geography.

47. According to the discussion, what is the definition of a standard dialect?

    (A) The dialect that is selected by the government.
    (B) The dialect that is of a higher value than the others.
    (C) The dialect that is able to express everything necessary.
    (D) The dialect that is the model taught in schools.

48. What is the linguistic perspective put forward in the articles that were assigned?

    Ⓐ Some accents are not permitted in schools.
    Ⓑ There is only one standard accent in the United States.
    Ⓒ There is one major dialect in the United States.
    Ⓓ All dialects are of equal value.

49. Which two linguistic components are included in a dialect?

    Click on 2 answers.

    [A] Grammar.
    [B] Pronunciation.
    [C] Vocabulary.
    [D] Spelling.

50. What do sociologists tell us about accents?

    Ⓐ Some accents are more prestigious because they are spoken by the upper classes.
    Ⓑ Because they are more comprehensible, some accents are inherently better than others.
    Ⓒ One of the purposes of schools is to teach the accents that are considered most important.
    Ⓓ In general, accents are not as important as dialects because there is no standard for them.

Section 2: Structure

This section measures the ability to recognize language that is appropriate for standard written English. There are two types of questions in this section.

In the first type of question, there are incomplete sentences. Beneath each sentence, there are four words or phrases. You will choose the one word or phrase that best completes the sentence. Clicking on a choice darkens the oval. After you click on **Next** and **Confirm Answer**, the next question will be presented.

The second type of question has four underlined words or phrases. You will choose the one underlined word or phrase that must be changed for the sentence to be correct. Clicking on an underlined word or phrase will darken it. After you click on **Next** and **Confirm Answer**, the next question will be presented.

1. In simple animals, _____ reflex movement or involuntary response to stimuli.

    (A) behavior mostly
    (B) most is behavior
    (C) most behavior is
    (D) the most behavior

2. Although the weather in Martha's Vineyard isn't _____ to have a year-round tourist season, it has become a favorite summer resort.

    (A) goodly enough
    (B) good enough
    (C) good as enough
    (D) enough good

3. A swarm of locusts <u>is responsible</u> the
                              (A)
   consumption of <u>enough plant material</u>
                              (B)
   <u>to feed</u> a million <u>and a half</u> people.
     (C)   (D)

4. Oyster <u>farming</u> has been <u>practice</u>
                (A)   (B)
   in <u>most</u> parts of the world <u>for</u>
        (C)   (D)
   many years.

5. <u>It</u> was Shirley Temple Black
    (A)
   <u>which</u> <u>represented</u> her country in
    (B)   (C)
   the United Nations and <u>later</u>
                              (D)
   became an ambassador.

6. According to the wave theory, _____ population of the Americas may have been the result of a number of separate migrations.

    (A) the
    (B) their
    (C) that
    (D) whose

7. It is presumed that rules governing the sharing of food influenced _____ that the earliest cultures evolved.

    (A) that the way
    (B) is the way
    (C) the way
    (D) which way

8. The prices <u>at</u> chain stores <u>are</u> as
                 (A)   (B)
   reasonable, <u>if not more</u> reasonable,
                  (C)
   <u>as</u> those at discount stores.
    (D)

9. Historically there has been only
   (A)   (B)   (C)   (D)
   two major factions in the Republican
   Party—the liberals and the
   conservatives.

10. Whitman wrote *Leaves of Grass* as a
    tribute to the Civil War soldiers who
    had laid on the battlefields and
      (A)
    whom he had seen while serving as
     (B)   (C)   (D)
    an army nurse.

11. Calculus, _____ elegant and
    economical symbolic system, can
    reduce complex problems to simple
    terms.

    (A) it is an
    (B) that an
    (C) an
    (D) is an

12. Canada does not require that U.S.
    citizens obtain passports to enter the
    country, and _____ .

    (A) Mexico does neither
    (B) Mexico doesn't either
    (C) neither Mexico does
    (D) either does Mexico

13. The Chinese were the first and
      (A)
    large ethnic group to work on
     (B)   (C)
    the construction of the transcontinental
                     (D)
    railroad system.

14. The range of plant life on a
    mountainside is a results of
                   (A) (B)
    differences in temperature and
      (C)
    precipitation at varying altitudes.
                       (D)

15. The poet _____ just beginning
    to be recognized as an important
    influence at the time of his death.

    (A) being Walt Whitman
    (B) who was Walt Whitman
    (C) Walt Whitman
    (D) Walt Whitman was

16. _____ the formation of the sun,
    the planets, and other stars began
    with the condensation of an
    interstellar cloud.

    (A) It accepted that
    (B) Accepted that
    (C) It is accepted that
    (D) That is accepted

17. The more the relative humidity
    reading rises, the worst the heat
               (A)   (B)
    affects us.
      (C) (D)

18. Because correlations are not
    causes, statistical data which are
      (A)   (B)
    extremely easy to misuse.
        (C)   (D)

19. As a general rule, the standard of
    living _____ by the average
    output of each person in society.

    (A) is fixed
    (B) fixed
    (C) has fixed
    (D) fixes

20. Despite of many attempts
      (A)   (B)
    to introduce a universal
      (C)
    language, notably Esperanto and
    Idiom Neutral, the effort has met
    with very little success.
              (D)

21. The *Consumer Price Index* lists
_____ .

    Ⓐ how much costs every car
    Ⓑ how much does every car cost
    Ⓒ how much every car costs
    Ⓓ how much are every car cost

22. As every other nation, the United
    Ⓐ   Ⓑ
    States used to define its unit of
    Ⓒ   Ⓓ
    currency, the dollar, in terms of the
    gold standard.

23. The Ford Theater where Lincoln was
    shot _____ .

    Ⓐ must restore
    Ⓑ must be restoring
    Ⓒ must have been restored
    Ⓓ must restored

24. John Dewey thought that children
    will learn better through participating
    Ⓐ   Ⓑ
    in experiences rather than through
    Ⓒ
    listening to lectures.
    Ⓓ

25. Some methods to prevent soil
    Ⓐ   Ⓑ
    erosion are plowing parallel with
    Ⓒ
    the slopes of hills, to plant trees
    Ⓓ
    on unproductive land, and rotating
    crops.

Section 3: Reading

This section measures the ability to read and understand short passages similar in topic and style to those that students are likely to encounter in North American universities and colleges. This section contains reading passages and questions about the passages. There are several different types of questions in this section.

In the Reading Section, you will first have the opportunity to read the passage. You will use the scroll bar to view the rest of the passage.

When you have finished reading the passage, you will use the mouse to click on **Proceed**. Then the questions about the passage will be presented. You are to choose the one best answer to each question. Answer all questions about the information in a passage on the basis of what is stated or implied in that passage.

Most of the questions will be multiple-choice questions. To answer these questions you will click on a choice below the question.

To answer some questions, you will click on a word or phrase. To answer some questions, you will click on a sentence in the passage. To answer some questions, you will click on a square to add a sentence to the passage.

The computer screens for selected questions in the Reading Section have been printed in this book to provide you with orientation to the format of the Computer-Based TOEFL. Use the screen to find the place in the original reading passage that corresponds to the question you are answering.

Few men have influenced the development of American English to the extent that Noah Webster did. Born in West Hartford, Connecticut, in 1758, Webster graduated from Yale in 1778. He was admitted to the bar in 1781 and thereafter began to practice law in Hartford. Later, when he turned to teaching, he discovered how inadequate the available schoolbooks were for the children of a new and independent nation. In response to the need for truly American textbooks, Webster published *A Grammatical Institute of the English Language*, a three-volume work that consisted of a speller, a grammar, and a reader. The first volume, which was generally known as *The American Spelling Book*, was so popular that eventually it sold more than 80 million copies and provided him with a considerable income for the rest of his life. While teaching, Webster began work on the *Compendious Dictionary of the English Language*, which was published in 1806, and was also very successful.

In 1807, Noah Webster began his greatest work, *An American Dictionary of the English Language*. In preparing the manuscript, he devoted ten years to the study of English and its relationship to other languages, and seven more years to the writing itself. Published in two volumes in 1828, *An American Dictionary of the English Language* has become the recognized authority for usage in the United States. Webster's purpose in writing it was to demonstrate that the American language was developing distinct meanings, pronunciations, and spellings from those of British English. He is responsible for advancing simplified spelling forms: *develop* instead of *develope*; *plow* instead of *plough*; *jail* instead of *gaol*; *theater* and *center* instead of *theatre* and *centre*; *color* and *honor* instead of *colour* and *honour*.

Webster was the first author to gain copyright protection in the United States by being awarded a copyright for his *American Speller*. He continued, for the next fifty years, to lobby for improvements in the protection of intellectual properties, that is, authors' rights. In 1840 Webster brought out a second edition of his dictionary, which included 70,000 entries instead of the original 38,000. The name Webster has become synonymous with American dictionaries. This edition served as the basis for the many revisions that have been produced by others, ironically, under the uncopyrighted Webster name.

1. Which of the following would be the best title for the passage?

    Ⓐ Webster's Work
    Ⓑ Webster's Dictionaries
    Ⓒ Webster's School
    Ⓓ Webster's Life

2. The word inadequate in paragraph 1 could best be replaced by

    Ⓐ unavailable
    Ⓑ expensive
    Ⓒ difficult
    Ⓓ unsatisfactory

3. Why did Webster write *A Grammatical Institute of the English Language*?

    Ⓐ He wanted to supplement his income.
    Ⓑ There were no books available after the Revolutionary War.
    Ⓒ He felt that British books were not appropriate for American children.
    Ⓓ The children did not know how to spell.

4. From which publication did Webster earn a lifetime income?

    Ⓐ *Compendious Dictionary of the English Language*
    Ⓑ *An American Dictionary of the English Language*
    Ⓒ *An American Dictionary of the English Language: Second Edition*
    Ⓓ *The American Spelling Book*

Beginning

Few men have influenced the development of American English to the extent that Noah Webster did. Born in West Hartford, Connecticut, in 1758, Webster graduated from Yale in 1778. He was admitted to the bar in 1781 and thereafter began to practice law in Hartford. Later, when he turned to teaching, he discovered how inadequate the available schoolbooks were for the children of a new and independent nation. In response to the need for truly American textbooks, Webster published *A Grammatical Institute of the English Language*, a three-volume work that consisted of a speller, a grammar, and a reader. The first volume, which was generally know as *The American Spelling Book*, was so popular that eventually it sold more than 80 million copies and provided him with a considerable income for the rest of his life. While teaching, Webster began work on the *Compendious Dictionary of the English Language*, which was published in 1806, and was also very successful.

In 1807, Noah Webster began his greatest work, *An American Dictionary of the English Language*. In preparing the manuscript, he devoted

5. Look at the word popular in the passage. Click on the word or phrase in the **bold** text that is closest in meaning to popular.

Beginning

Few men have influenced the development of American English to the extent that Noah Webster did. Born in West Hartford, Connecticut, in 1758, Webster graduated from Yale in 1778. He was admitted to the bar in 1781 and thereafter began to practice law in Hartford. Later, when he turned to teaching, he discovered how inadequate the available schoolbooks were for the children of a new and independent nation. **In response to the need for truly American textbooks, Webster published *A Grammatical Institute of the English Language,* a three-volume work that consisted of a speller, a grammar, and a reader. The first volume, which was generally know as *The American Spelling Book,* was so popular that eventually it sold more than 80 million copies and provided him with a considerable income for the rest of his life. While teaching, Webster began work on the *Compendious Dictionary of the English Language,* which was published in 1806, and was also very successful.**

In 1807, Noah Webster began his greatest work, *An American Dictionary of the English Language.* In preparing the manuscript, he devoted

6. The word considerable in paragraph 1 most nearly means

A large
B prestigious
C steady
D unexpected

Beginning

Few men have influenced the development of American English to the extent that Noah Webster did. Born in West Hartford, Connecticut, in 1758, Webster graduated from Yale in 1778. He was admitted to the bar in 1781 and thereafter began to practice law in Hartford. Later, when he turned to teaching, he discovered how inadequate the available schoolbooks were for the children of a new and independent nation. In response to the need for truly American textbooks, Webster published *A Grammatical Institute of the English Language,* a three-volume work that consisted of a speller, a grammar, and a reader. The first volume, which was generally know as *The American Spelling Book,* was so popular that eventually it sold more than 80 million copies and provided him with a considerable income for the rest of his life. While teaching, Webster began work on the *Compendious Dictionary of the English Language,* which was published in 1806, and was also very successful.

In 1807, Noah Webster began his greatest work, *An American Dictionary of the English Language.* In preparing the manuscript, he devoted

7. When was *An American Dictionary of the English Language* published?

A 1817
B 1807
C 1828
D 1824

8. The word it in paragraph 2 refers to

A language
B usage
C authority
D dictionary

More Available

American Spelling Book, was so popular that eventually it sold more than 80 million copies and provided him with a considerable income for the rest of his life. While teaching, Webster began work on the *Compendious Dictionary of the English Language,* which was published in 1806, and was also very successful.

In 1807, Noah Webster began his greatest work, *An American Dictionary of the English Language.* In preparing the manuscript, he devoted ten years to the study of English and its relationship to other languages, and seven more years to the writing itself. Published in two volumes in 1828, *An American Dictionary of the English Language* has become the recognized authority for usage in the United States. Webster's purpose in writing it was to demonstrate that the American language was developing distinct meanings, pronunciations, and spellings from those of British English. He is responsible for advancing simplified spelling forms: *develop* instead of *develope; plow* instead of *plough; jail* instead of *gaol; theater* and *center* instead of *theatre* and *centre; color* and *honor* instead of *colour* and *honour.*

9. Click on the sentence in paragraph 2 that explains Webster's purpose for writing an American dictionary.

Paragraph 2 is marked with an arrow (→).

> More Available
>
> *American Spelling Book,* was so popular that eventually it sold more than 80 million copies and provided him with a considerable income for the rest of his life. While teaching, Webster began work on the *Compendious Dictionary of the English Language,* which was published in 1806, and was also very successful.
> → In 1807, Noah Webster began his greatest work, *An American Dictionary of the English Language.* In preparing the manuscript, he devoted ten years to the study of English and its relationship to other languages, and seven more years to the writing itself. Published in two volumes in 1828, *An American Dictionary of the English Language* has become the recognized authority for usage in the United States. Webster's purpose in writing it was to demonstrate that the American language was developing distinct meanings, pronunciations, and spellings from those of British English. He is responsible for advancing simplified spelling forms: *develop* instead of *develope; plow* instead of *plough; jail* instead of *gaol; theater* and *center* instead of *theatre* and *centre; color* and *honor* instead of *colour* and *honour.*

10. The word **distinct** in paragraph 2 is closest in meaning to

- Ⓐ new
- Ⓑ simple
- Ⓒ different
- Ⓓ exact

> More Available
>
> *American Spelling Book,* was so popular that eventually it sold more than 80 million copies and provided him with a considerable income for the rest of his life. While teaching, Webster began work on the *Compendious Dictionary of the English Language,* which was published in 1806, and was also very successful.
> In 1807, Noah Webster began his greatest work, *An American Dictionary of the English Language.* In preparing the manuscript, he devoted ten years to the study of English and its relationship to other languages, and seven more years to the writing itself. Published in two volumes in 1828, *An American Dictionary of the English Language* has become the recognized authority for usage in the United States. Webster's purpose in writing it was to demonstrate that the American language was developing distinct meanings, pronunciations, and spellings from those of British English. He is responsible for advancing simplified spelling forms: *develop* instead of *develope; plow* instead of *plough; jail* instead of *gaol; theater* and *center* instead of *theatre* and *centre; color* and *honor* instead of *colour* and *honour.*

11. According to this passage, which one of the following spellings would Webster have approved in his dictionaries?

- Ⓐ *Develope*
- Ⓑ *Theatre*
- Ⓒ *Color*
- Ⓓ *Honour*

The San Andreas Fault line is a fracture at the congruence of two major plates of the Earth's crust, one of which supports most of the North American continent, and the other of which underlies the coast of California and part of the ocean floor of the Pacific Ocean. The fault originates about six hundred miles south of the Gulf of California, runs north in an irregular line along the western coast to San Francisco, and continues north for about two hundred more miles before angling off into the ocean. In places, the trace of the fault is marked by a trench, or, in geological terms, a rift, and small ponds called sag ponds dot the landscape. Its western side always moves north in relation to its eastern side. The total net slip along the San Andreas Fault and the length of time it has been active are matters of conjecture, but it has been estimated that, during the past fifteen million years, coastal California along the San Andreas Fault has moved about 190 miles in a northwesterly direction with respect to the North American plate. Although the movement along the fault averages only a few inches a year, it is intermittent and variable. Some segments of the fault do not move at all for long periods of time, building up tremendous pressure that must be released. For this reason, tremors are not unusual along the San Andreas Fault, some of which are classified as major earthquakes. Also for this reason, small tremors are interpreted as safe, since they are understood to be pressure that releases without causing much damage.

It is worth noting that the San Andreas Fault passes uncomfortably close to several major metropolitan areas, including Los Angeles and San Francisco. In addition, the San Andreas Fault has created smaller fault systems, many of which underlie the smaller towns and cities along the California coast. For this reason, Californians have long anticipated the recurrence of what they refer to as the "Big One," a chain reaction of destructive earthquakes that would measure near 8 on the Richter scale, similar in intensity to those that occurred in 1857 and 1906. Such a quake would wreak devastating effects on the life and property in the region. Unfortunately, as pressure continues to build along the fault, the likelihood of such an earthquake increases substantially.

12. What is the author's main purpose in the passage?

   (A) To describe the San Andreas Fault
   (B) To give a definition of a fault
   (C) To explain the reason for tremors and earthquakes
   (D) To classify different kinds of faults

13. How does the author define the San Andreas Fault?

   (A) A plate that underlies the North American continent
   (B) A crack in the Earth's crust between two plates
   (C) Occasional tremors and earthquakes
   (D) Intense pressure that builds up

14. The word originates in paragraph 1 could best be replaced by

   (A) gets wider
   (B) changes direction
   (C) begins
   (D) disappears

Beginning

The San Andreas Fault line is a fracture at the congruence of two major plates of the Earth's crust, one of which supports most of the North American continent, and the other of which underlies the coast of California and part of the ocean floor of the Pacific Ocean. The fault originates about six hundred miles south of the Gulf of California, runs north in an irregular line along the western coast to San Francisco, and continues north for about two hundred more miles before angling off into the ocean. In places, the trace of the fault is marked by a trench, or, in geological terms, a rift, and small ponds called sag ponds dot the landscape. Its western side always moves north in relation to its eastern side. The total net slip along the San Andreas Fault and the length of time it has been active are matters of conjecture, but it has been estimated that, during the past fifteen million years, coastal California along the San Andreas Fault has moved about 190 miles in a northwesterly direction with respect to the North American plate. Although the movement along the fault averages only a few inches a year, it is intermittent and variable. Some

15. In which direction does the western side of the fault move?

   (A) West
   (B) East
   (C) North
   (D) South

16. The word it in paragraph 1 refers to

(A) San Francisco
(B) ocean
(C) coast
(D) fault

Beginning

The San Andreas Fault line is a fracture at the congruence of two major plates of the Earth's crust, one of which supports most of the North American continent, and the other of which underlies the coast of California and part of the ocean floor of the Pacific Ocean. The fault originates about six hundred miles south of the Gulf of California, runs north in an irregular line along the western coast to San Francisco, and continues north for about two hundred more miles before angling off into the ocean. In places, the trace of the fault is marked by a trench, or, in geological terms, a rift, and small ponds called sag ponds dot the landscape. Its western side always moves north in relation to its eastern side. The total net slip along the San Andreas Fault and the length of time it has been active are matters of conjecture, but it has been estimated that, during the past fifteen million years, coastal California along the San Andreas Fault has moved about 190 miles in a northwesterly direction with respect to the North American plate. Although the movement along the fault averages only a few inches a year, it is intermittent and variable. Some

17. The word intermittent in paragraph 1 could best be replaced by which of the following?

(A) dangerous
(B) predictable
(C) uncommon
(D) occasional

Beginning

The San Andreas Fault line is a fracture at the congruence of two major plates of the Earth's crust, one of which supports most of the North American continent, and the other of which underlies the coast of California and part of the ocean floor of the Pacific Ocean. The fault originates about six hundred miles south of the Gulf of California, runs north in an irregular line along the western coast to San Francisco, and continues north for about two hundred more miles before angling off into the ocean. In places, the trace of the fault is marked by a trench, or, in geological terms, a rift, and small ponds called sag ponds dot the landscape. Its western side always moves north in relation to its eastern side. The total net slip along the San Andreas Fault and the length of time it has been active are matters of conjecture, but it has been estimated that, during the past fifteen million years, coastal California along the San Andreas Fault has moved about 190 miles in a northwesterly direction with respect to the North American plate. Although the movement along the fault averages only a few inches a year, it is intermittent and variable. Some

18. Along the San Andreas Fault, tremors are

(A) small and insignificant
(B) rare, but disastrous
(C) frequent events
(D) very unpredictable

19. The phrase "the Big One" refers to which of the following?

(A) A serious earthquake
(B) The San Andreas Fault
(C) The Richter scale
(D) California

20. Look at the word destructive in the passage. Click on the word or phrase in the **bold** text that is closest in meaning to destructive.

End

It is worth noting that the San Andreas Fault passes uncomfortably close to several major metropolitan areas, including Los Angeles and San Francisco. In addition, the San Andreas Fault has created smaller fault systems, many of which underlie the smaller towns and cities along the California coast. **For this reason, Californians have long anticipated the recurrence of what they refer to as the "Big One," a chain reaction of destructive earthquakes that would measure near 8 on the Richter scale, similar in intensity to those that occurred in 1857 and 1906. Such a quake would wreak devastating effects on the life and property in the region. Unfortunately, as pressure continues to build along the fault, the likelihood of such an earthquake increases substantially.**

21. Look at the word those in the passage. Click on the word or phrase in the **bold** text that those refers to.

It is worth noting that the San Andreas Fault passes uncomfortably close to several major metropolitan areas, including Los Angeles and San Francisco. In addition, the San Andreas Fault has created smaller fault systems, many of which underlie the smaller towns and cities along the California coast. For this reason, Californians have long anticipated the recurrence of what they refer to as the "Big One," a chain reaction of destructive earthquakes that would measure near 8 on the Richter scale, similar in intensity to those that occurred in 1857 and 1906. Such a quake would wreak devastating effects on the life and property in the region. Unfortunately, as pressure continues to build along the fault, the likelihood of such an earthquake increases substantially.

22. Which of the following words best describes the San Andreas Fault?

- Ⓐ Straight
- Ⓑ Deep
- Ⓒ Wide
- Ⓓ Rough

The body of an adult insect is subdivided into three sections, including a head, a three-segment thorax, and segmented abdomen. Ordinarily, the thorax bears three pairs of legs and a single or double pair of wings. The vision of most adult insects is specialized through two large compound eyes and multiple simple eyes.

Features of an insect's mouth parts are used in classifying insects into types. Biting mouth parts, called mandibles, such as the mouth parts found in grasshoppers and beetles, are common among insects. Behind the mandibles are located the maxillae, or lower jaw parts, which serve to direct food into the mouth between the jaws. A labrum above and one below are similar to another animal's upper and lower lips. In an insect with a sucking mouth function, the mandibles, maxillae, labrum, and labium are modified in such a way that they constitute a tube through which liquid such as water, blood, or flower nectar can be drawn. In a butterfly or moth, this coiled drinking tube is called the proboscis because of its resemblance, in miniature, to the trunk of an elephant or a very large nose. Composed chiefly of modified maxillae fitted together, the insect's proboscis can be flexed and extended to reach nectar deep in a flower. In mosquitoes or aphids, mandibles and maxillae are modified to sharp stylets with which the insect can drill through surfaces like human or vegetable skin membranes to reach juice. In a housefly, the expanding labium forms a spongelike mouth pad that it can use to stamp over the surface of food, sopping up food particles and juices.

Insects, the most numerous creatures on our planet, are also the most adaptable. They require little food because they are small. They easily find shelter and protection in small crevices in trees and surface geological formations. Species of insects can evolve quickly because of their rapid reproduction cycle; they live in every climate, some making their homes in the frozen Arctic regions and many others choosing the humid, warm, and nutrient-rich rain forest environment. An active part of the natural food cycle, insects provide nutrition for animals and devour waste products of other life forms.

23. What is the best title for this passage?

    Ⓐ An Insect's Environment
    Ⓑ The Structure of an Insect
    Ⓒ Grasshoppers and Beetles
    Ⓓ The Stages of Life of an Insect

24. Look at the word subdivided in the passage. Click on the word or phrase in the **bold** text that is closest in meaning to subdivided.

> Beginning
>
> **The body of an adult insect is subdivided into three sections, including a head, a three-segment thorax, and segmented abdomen. Ordinarily, the thorax bears three pairs of legs and a single or double pair of wings. The vision of most adult insects is specialized through two large compound eyes and multiple simple eyes.**
>
> **Features of an insect's mouth parts are used in classifying insects into types.** Biting mouth parts, called mandibles, such as the mouth parts found in grasshoppers and beetles, are common among insects. Behind the mandibles are located the maxillae, or lower jaw parts, which serve to direct food into the mouth between the jaws. A labrum above and one below are similar to another animal's upper and lower lips. In an insect with a sucking mouth function, the mandibles, maxillae, labrum, and labium are modified in such a way that they constitute a tube through which liquid such as water, blood, or flower nectar can be drawn. In a butterfly or moth, this coiled drinking tube is called the proboscis because of its resemblance, in miniature, to the trunk of an elephant or a very large nose. Composed chiefly

25. How are insects classified?

    Ⓐ By the environment in which they live
    Ⓑ By the food they eat
    Ⓒ By the structure of the mouth
    Ⓓ By the number and type of wings

26. The word common in paragraph 2 is closest in meaning to

    Ⓐ normal
    Ⓑ rare
    Ⓒ important
    Ⓓ necessary

> Beginning
>
> The body of an adult insect is subdivided into three sections, including a head, a three-segment thorax, and segmented abdomen. Ordinarily, the thorax bears three pairs of legs and a single or double pair of wings. The vision of most adult insects is specialized through two large compound eyes and multiple simple eyes.
>
> Features of an insect's mouth parts are used in classifying insects into types. Biting mouth parts, called mandibles, such as the mouth parts found in grasshoppers and beetles, are common among insects. Behind the mandibles are located the maxillae, or lower jaw parts, which serve to direct food into the mouth between the jaws. A labrum above and one below are similar to another animal's upper and lower lips. In an insect with a sucking mouth function, the mandibles, maxillae, labrum, and labium are modified in such a way that they constitute a tube through which liquid such as water, blood, or flower nectar can be drawn. In a butterfly or moth, this coiled drinking tube is called the proboscis because of its resemblance, in miniature, to the trunk of an elephant or a very large nose. Composed chiefly

27. The author compares labrum and labium to

    Ⓐ an upper and lower lip
    Ⓑ mandibles
    Ⓒ maxillae
    Ⓓ jaws

28. What is the proboscis?

    Ⓐ Nectar
    Ⓑ A tube constructed of modified maxillae
    Ⓒ A kind of butterfly
    Ⓓ A kind of flower

29. Which of the following have mandibles and maxillae that have been modified to sharp stylets?

    Ⓐ Grasshoppers
    Ⓑ Butterflies
    Ⓒ Mosquitoes
    Ⓓ Houseflies

30. The phrase drill through in paragraph 2 could best be replaced by

    Ⓐ penetrate
    Ⓑ saturate
    Ⓒ explore
    Ⓓ distinguish

More Available

the maxillae, or lower jaw parts, which serve to direct food into the mouth between the jaws. A labrum above and one below are similar to another animal's upper and lower lips. In an insect with a sucking mouth function, the mandibles, maxillae, labrum, and labium are modified in such a way that they constitute a tube through which liquid such as water, blood, or flower nectar can be drawn. In a butterfly or moth, this coiled drinking tube is called the proboscis because of its resemblance, in miniature, to the trunk of an elephant or a very large nose. Composed chiefly of modified maxillae fitted together, the insect's proboscis can be flexed and extended to reach nectar deep in a flower. In mosquitoes or aphids, mandibles and maxillae are modified to sharp stylets with which the insect can drill through surfaces like human or vegetable skin membranes to reach juice. In a housefly, the expanding labium forms a spongelike mouth pad that it can use to stamp over the surface of food, sopping up food particles and juices.

Insects, the most numerous creatures on our planet, are also the most adaptable. They require

31. The word it in paragraph 2 refers to

    Ⓐ pad
    Ⓑ food
    Ⓒ housefly
    Ⓓ mouth

More Available

the maxillae, or lower jaw parts, which serve to direct food into the mouth between the jaws. A labrum above and one below are similar to another animal's upper and lower lips. In an insect with a sucking mouth function, the mandibles, maxillae, labrum, and labium are modified in such a way that they constitute a tube through which liquid such as water, blood, or flower nectar can be drawn. In a butterfly or moth, this coiled drinking tube is called the proboscis because of its resemblance, in miniature, to the trunk of an elephant or a very large nose. Composed chiefly of modified maxillae fitted together, the insect's proboscis can be flexed and extended to reach nectar deep in a flower. In mosquitoes or aphids, mandibles and maxillae are modified to sharp stylets with which the insect can drill through surfaces like human or vegetable skin membranes to reach juice. In a housefly, the expanding labium forms a spongelike mouth pad that it can use to stamp over the surface of food, sopping up food particles and juices.

Insects, the most numerous creatures on our planet, are also the most adaptable. They require

32. The following sentence can be added to the passage.

> **Although some insects, like the cockroach, have remained essentially unchanged for eons, most insects adapt readily to changing environmental conditions.**

Where would it best fit in the passage?

Click on the square (■) to add the sentence to the passage.

Scroll the passage to see all of the choices.

End

proboscis can be flexed and extended to reach nectar deep in a flower. In mosquitoes or aphids, mandibles and maxillae are modified to sharp stylets with which the insect can drill through surfaces like human or vegetable skin membranes to reach juice. In a housefly, the expanding labium forms a spongelike mouth pad that it can use to stamp over the surface of food, sopping up food particles and juices.

■ Insects, the most numerous creatures on our planet, are also the most adaptable. They require little food because they are small. ■ They easily find shelter and protection in small crevices in trees and surface geological formations. ■ Species of insects can evolve quickly because of their rapid reproduction cycle; they live in every climate, some making their homes in the frozen Arctic regions and many others choosing the humid, warm, and nutrient-rich rain forest environment. An active part of the natural food cycle, insects provide nutrition for animals and devour waste products of other life forms. ■

---

33. What is the purpose of this passage?

Ⓐ To complain
Ⓑ To persuade
Ⓒ To entertain
Ⓓ To inform

The protozoans, minute aquatic creatures, each of which consists of a single cell of protoplasm, constitute a classification of the most primitive forms of animal life. The very name *protozoan* indicates the scientific understanding of the animals. *Proto-* means first or primitive, and *zoa* refers to animal. They are fantastically diverse, but three major groups may be identified on the basis of their motility. The Mastigophora have one or more long tails that they use to propel themselves forward. The Ciliata, which use the same basic means for locomotion as the Mastigophora, have a larger number of short tails. The Sarcodina, which include amoebae, float or row themselves about on their crusted bodies.

In addition to their form of movement, several other features discriminate among the three groups of protozoans. For example, at least two nuclei per cell have been identified in the Ciliata, usually a large nucleus that regulates growth but decomposes during reproduction, and a smaller one that contains the genetic code necessary to generate the large nucleus.

Chlorophyll, which is the green substance encountered in plants, is found in the bodies of some protozoans, enabling them to make some of their own food from water and carbon dioxide. Protozoans are not considered plants but animals, because unlike pigmented plants to which some protozoans are otherwise almost identical, they do not live on simple organic compounds. Their cell demonstrates all of the major characteristics of the cells of higher animals, such as eating, breathing, and reproducing.

Many species of protozoans collect into colonies, physically connected to one another and responding uniformly to outside stimulae. Current research into this phenomenon along with investigations carried out with advanced microscopes may necessitate a redefinition of what constitutes protozoans, even calling into question the basic premise that they have only one cell. Nevertheless, with the current data available, almost 40,000 species of protozoans have been identified. No doubt, as technology improves methods of observation, better models of classification of these simple single cells will be proposed.

34. With what topic is the passage primarily concerned?

   Ⓐ Colonies of protozoans
   Ⓑ Mastigophora
   Ⓒ Motility in protozoans
   Ⓓ Characteristics of protozoans

35. The word minute in paragraph 1 could best be replaced by

   Ⓐ very common
   Ⓑ very fast
   Ⓒ very old
   Ⓓ very small

36. What is protoplasm?

   Ⓐ A class of protozoan
   Ⓑ The substance that forms the cell of a protozoan
   Ⓒ A primitive animal similar to a protozoan
   Ⓓ An animal that developed from a protozoan

37. Look at the word motility in the passage. Click on the word or phrase in the **bold** text that is closest in meaning to motility.

Beginning

   The protozoans, minute aquatic creatures, each of which consists of a single cell of protoplasm, constitute a classification of the most primitive forms of animal life. The very name *protozoan* indicates the scientific understanding of the animals. *Proto-* means first or primitive, and *zoa* refers to animal. They are fantastically diverse, but three major groups may be identified on the basis of their motility. The Mastigophora have one or more long tails that they use to propel themselves forward. The Ciliata, which use the same basic means for locomotion as the Mastigophora, have a larger number of short tails. The Sarcodina, which include amoebae, float or row themselves about on their crusted bodies.

   In addition to their form of movement, several other features discriminate among the three groups of protozoans. For example, at least two nuclei per cell have been identified in the Ciliata, usually a large nucleus that regulates growth but decomposes during reproduction, and a smaller one that contains the genetic code necessary to generate the large nucleus.

   Chlorophyll, which is the green substance

Beginning

   The protozoans, minute aquatic creatures, each of which consists of a single cell of protoplasm, constitute a classification of the most primitive forms of animal life. The very name *protozoan* indicates the scientific understanding of the animals. *Proto-* means first or primitive, and *zoa* refers to animal. **They are fantastically diverse, but three major groups may be identified on the basis of their motility. The Ciliata, which use the same basic means for locomotion as the Mastigophora, have a larger number of short tails. The Sarcodina, which include amoebae, float or row themselves about on their crusted bodies.**

   In addition to their form of movement, several other features discriminate among the three groups of protozoans. For example, at least two nuclei per cell have been identified in the Ciliata, usually a large nucleus that regulates growth but decomposes during reproduction, and a smaller one that contains the genetic code necessary to generate the large nucleus.

   Chlorophyll, which is the green substance

38. What does the author mean by the statement They are fantastically diverse, but three major groups may be identified on the basis of their motility?

Ⓐ The three major groups are unique in that they all move in the same manner.
Ⓑ Everything we know about the protozoans is tied into their manner of movement.
Ⓒ The manner of movement is critical when classifying the three major groups of protozoans.
Ⓓ Mobility in the protozoans is insignificant.

Beginning

The protozoans, minute aquatic creatures, each of which consists of a single cell of protoplasm, constitute a classification of the most primitive forms of animal life. The very name *protozoan* indicates the scientific understanding of the animals. *Proto-* means first or primitive, and *zoa* refers to animal. They are fantastically diverse, but three major groups may be identified on the basis of their motility. The Mastigophora have one or more long tails that they use to propel themselves forward. The Ciliata, which use the same basic means for locomotion as the Mastigophora, have a larger number of short tails. The Sarcodina, which include amoebae, float or row themselves about on their crusted bodies.

In addition to their form of movement, several other features discriminate among the three groups of protozoans. For example, at least two nuclei per cell have been identified in the Ciliata, usually a large nucleus that regulates growth but decomposes during reproduction, and a smaller one that contains the genetic code necessary to generate the large nucleus.

Chlorophyll, which is the green substance

---

39. To which class of protozoans do the amoebae belong?

Ⓐ Mastigophora
Ⓑ Ciliata
Ⓒ Sarcodina
Ⓓ Motility

40. What is the purpose of the large nucleus in the Ciliata?

Ⓐ It generates the other nucleus.
Ⓑ It contains the genetic code for the small nucleus.
Ⓒ It regulates growth.
Ⓓ It reproduces itself.

41. Why are protozoans classified as animals?

Ⓐ They do not live on simple organic compounds.
Ⓑ They collect in colonies.
Ⓒ They respond uniformly to outside stimulae.
Ⓓ They may have more than one cell.

42. The word they in paragraph 3 refers to

Ⓐ protozoans
Ⓑ microscopes
Ⓒ investigations
Ⓓ colonies

More Available

In addition to their form of movement, several other features discriminate among the three groups of protozoans. For example, at least two nuclei per cell have been identified in the Ciliata, usually a large nucleus that regulates growth but decomposes during reproduction, and a smaller one that contains the genetic code necessary to generate the large nucleus.

Chlorophyll, which is the green substance encountered in plants, is found in the bodies of some protozoans, enabling them to make some of their own food from water and carbon dioxide. Protozoans are not considered plants but animals, because unlike pigmented plants to which some protozoans are otherwise almost identical, they do not live on simple organic compounds. Their cell demonstrates all of the major characteristics of the cells of higher animals, such as eating, breathing, and reproducing.

Many species of protozoans collect into colonies, physically connected to one another and responding uniformly to outside stimulae. Current research into this phenomenon along with investigations carried out with advanced

43. Click on the sentence in paragraph 4 that brings into question the current belief that protozoans are single celled.

    Paragraph 4 is marked with an arrow (→).

    > End
    > some protozoans, enabling them to make some of their own food from water and carbon dioxide. Protozoans are not considered plants but animals, because unlike pigmented plants to which some protozoans are otherwise almost identical, they do not live on simple organic compounds. Their cell demonstrates all of the major characteristics of the cells of higher animals, such as eating, breathing, and reproducing.
    > → Many species of protozoans collect into colonies, physically connected to one another and responding uniformly to outside stimulae. Current research into this phenomenon along with investigations carried out with advanced microscopes may necessitate a redefinition of what constitutes protozoans, even calling into question the basic premise that they have only one cell. Nevertheless, with the current data available, almost 40,000 species of protozoans have been identified. No doubt, as technology improves methods of observation, better models of classification of these simple single cells will be proposed.

44. The word uniformly in paragraph 4 is closest in meaning to

    Ⓐ in the same way
    Ⓑ once in a while
    Ⓒ all of a sudden
    Ⓓ in the long run

    > End
    > some protozoans, enabling them to make some of their own food from water and carbon dioxide. Protozoans are not considered plants but animals, because unlike pigmented plants to which some protozoans are otherwise almost identical, they do not live on simple organic compounds. Their cell demonstrates all of the major characteristics of the cells of higher animals, such as eating, breathing, and reproducing.
    > Many species of protozoans collect into colonies, physically connected to one another and responding uniformly to outside stimulae. Current research into this phenomenon along with investigations carried out with advanced microscopes may necessitate a redefinition of what constitutes protozoans, even calling into question the basic premise that they have only one cell. Nevertheless, with the current data available, almost 40,000 species of protozoans have been identified. No doubt, as technology improves methods of observation, better models of classification of these simple single cells will be proposed.

45. Which of the following statements is NOT true of protozoans?

    Ⓐ There are approximately 40,000 species.
    Ⓑ They are the most primitive forms of animal life.
    Ⓒ They have a large cell and a smaller cell.
    Ⓓ They are difficult to observe.

To check your answers for Model Test 3, refer to the Answer Key on page 388. For an explanation of the answers, refer to the Explanatory Answers for Model Test 3 on pages 440–460.

Writing Section Model Test 3

When you take a Model Test, you should use one sheet of paper, both sides. Time each Model Test carefully. After you have read the topic, you should spend 30 minutes writing. For results that would be closest to the actual testing situation, it is recommended that an English teacher score your test, using the guidelines on page 247 of this book.

> Many people have learned a foreign language in their own country; others have learned a foreign language in the country in which it is spoken. Which is better? Give the advantages of each and support your viewpoint.

Notes

To check your essay, refer to the Checklist on page 389. For an Example Essay, refer to the Explanatory Answers for Model Test 3 on pages 460–461.

Model Test 4
Next Generation TOEFL

Note: Model Test 4 appears as Model Test 9 in the larger version of this book, *Barron's How to Prepare for the TOEFL, 11th Edition.*

Listening Section

This is the Listening Section of the Next Generation TOEFL Model Test. This section tests your ability to understand campus conversations and academic lectures. During the test, you will respond to two conversations and four lectures. You will hear each conversation and lecture one time. You may take notes while you listen. You may use your notes to answer the questions. After each conversation or lecture, you will have five or six questions to answer. Choose the best answer for multiple-choice questions. Follow the directions on the page or on the screen for computer-assisted questions. Click on **OK** and **Next** to go to the next question. You cannot return to previous questions. You have 25 minutes to answer all of the questions. A clock on the screen will show you how much time you have to complete your answers for the section. The clock does not count the time you are listening to the conversations and lectures.

Independent Listening 1: "Career Counseling"

Directions:
Choose the best answer for multiple-choice questions. Follow the directions on the page for computer-assisted questions.

1. What are the students mainly discussing?

   Ⓐ Group sessions in the Office of Career Development.
   Ⓑ The advantages of career counseling for the man.
   Ⓒ The woman's internship in the Office of Career Development.
   Ⓓ How to find employment in the field of career counseling.

2. What is the man's problem?

   Ⓐ He does not have time to see an advisor.
   Ⓑ He does not have an internship yet.
   Ⓒ He does not know which career to choose.
   Ⓓ He does not have a job offer after graduation.

3. Why does the woman tell the man about her experience?

   Ⓐ To demonstrate the benefits of going to the Office of Career Development.
   Ⓑ To encourage the man to talk with an advisor about an internship.
   Ⓒ To suggest that he change his major from math to library science.
   Ⓓ To give the man her opinion about his career decision.

4. What is the woman's attitude toward her internship?

   Ⓐ She would rather go to graduate school.
   Ⓑ She is looking forward to interning.
   Ⓒ She thinks that it is a very positive experience.
   Ⓓ She will be happy when she completes it.

5. What will the man probably do?

   Ⓐ He will make an appointment with his academic advisor.
   Ⓑ He will go to the Office of Career Development.
   Ⓒ He will apply for a job at the library.
   Ⓓ He will ask the woman to help him with his tests.

Independent Listening 2: "Admission"

Directions:
Choose the best answer for multiple-choice questions. Follow the directions on the page for computer-assisted questions.

6. Why does the student go to the admissions office?

   Ⓐ He is applying for financial aid.
   Ⓑ He is requesting an official transcript.
   Ⓒ He is transferring to another college.
   Ⓓ He is trying to enroll in classes.

7. What is missing from the student's file?

   Ⓐ A financial aid application.
   Ⓑ A transcript from County Community College.
   Ⓒ Grades from Regional College.
   Ⓓ An official copy of the application.

8. Listen again to part of the conversation. Then answer the question.

   "Oh, and you haven't been able to register for your courses here at State University because the computer shows that you are missing some of your application materials. Is that it?"

   Why does the woman say this:

   "Is that it?"

   Ⓐ She is asking the man to finish explaining the situation.
   Ⓑ She is confirming that she understands the problem.
   Ⓒ She is expressing impatience with the man's explanation.
   Ⓓ She is trying to comprehend a difficult question.

9. What does the woman suggest that the man do?

    Ⓐ Make a copy of his transcripts for his personal file.
    Ⓑ Complete all of the admissions forms as soon as possible.
    Ⓒ Change his provisional status to regular status before registering.
    Ⓓ Continue to request an official transcript from County Community College.

10. What will the student most probably do now?

    Ⓐ Return later in the day to see the woman in the Admissions Office.
    Ⓑ Go to the Office for Transfer Students to be assigned an advisor.
    Ⓒ Enter information in the computer to complete the application process.
    Ⓓ See the woman's superior to get a provisional admission to State University.

Independent Listening 3: "Groups"

Directions:
Choose the best answer for multiple-choice questions. Follow the directions on the page for computer-assisted questions.

11. What is the main topic of the talk?

    Ⓐ The problems inherent in group decisions.
    Ⓑ Ways that individuals become popular in groups.
    Ⓒ The influence of groups on individual behavior.
    Ⓓ The differences in social influence across cultures.

12. According to the professor, what two results were reported in the Asch and Abrams studies?

    Click on 2 answers.

    Ⓐ A larger group exerts significantly more pressure than a smaller group.
    Ⓑ Subjects conformed to group opinion in more than one-third of the trials.
    Ⓒ When the subject knows the group socially, there is greater pressure to conform.
    Ⓓ A majority opinion has as much influence as a unanimous opinion.

13. Listen again to part of the lecture. Then answer the question.

    "Later Asch manipulated the size of the control group . . . I'm sorry . . . the experimental group . . . to see whether group size would affect pressure, and it did, but probably less than you might expect."

    Why does the professor say this:

    "I'm sorry. The experimental group . . ."

    Ⓐ She regretted the result of the experiment.
    Ⓑ She knew that the students would not like the information.
    Ⓒ She needed to correct what she had said in a previous statement.
    Ⓓ She neglected to mention important facts.

14. What generally happens after a group makes a decision?

    Ⓐ Some group members regret their decision.
    Ⓑ At least one group member presents a new idea.
    Ⓒ As a whole, the group is even more united in its judgment.
    Ⓓ The popular group members compete for leadership.

15. Based on information in the lecture, indicate whether the statements describe the Asch study.

    For each sentence, click in the YES or NO column.

	YES	NO
A Only one subject is being tested.		
B The cards can be interpreted several ways.		
C Some of the group collaborate with the experimenter.		

Independent Listening 4: "Photography"

Directions:
Choose the best answer for multiple-choice questions. Follow the directions on the page for computer-assisted questions.

16. What is the main topic of this lecture?

    Ⓐ The process of fixing a photograph.
    Ⓑ The problem of exposure time.
    Ⓒ The experiments by Louis Daguerre.
    Ⓓ The history of early photography.

17. According to the professor, what two limitations were noted in Daguerre's process for developing and fixing latent images?

    Click on 2 answers.

    Ⓐ The photograph disappeared after a few minutes.
    Ⓑ The images were very delicate and easily fell apart.
    Ⓒ Multiple images could not be made from the plate.
    Ⓓ The exposure time was still several hours long.

18. Listen again to part of the lecture. Then answer the question.

"At first, he couldn't figure out why, but eventually, he concluded that this must have occurred as a result of mercury vapor from a broken thermometer that was also...enclosed in the cupboard. Supposedly, from this fortunate accident, he was able to invent a process for developing latent images on . . . exposed plates."

Why does the professor say this:

"Supposedly, from this fortunate accident, he was able to invent a process for developing latent images on . . . exposed plates."

   Ⓐ She is trying to generate interest in the topic.
   Ⓑ She makes reference to a story in the textbook.
   Ⓒ She is not certain that the account is true.
   Ⓓ She wants the students to use their imaginations.

19. What substance was first used to fix the images?

   Ⓐ Copper powder.
   Ⓑ Table salt.
   Ⓒ Mercury vapor.
   Ⓓ Hot water.

20. What can we assume about photographers in the 1800s?

   Ⓐ Most of them had originally been painters before they became interested in photography.
   Ⓑ Portrait photographers were in the highest demand since people wanted images of their families.
   Ⓒ There were only a few photographers who were willing to work in such a new profession.
   Ⓓ Some of them must have experienced health problems as a result of their laboratory work.

Independent Listening 5: "Authority"

Directions:
Choose the best answer for multiple-choice questions. Follow the directions on the page for computer-assisted questions.

21. What is the main purpose of this lecture?

    Ⓐ To discuss three types of authority.
    Ⓑ To distinguish between power and authority.
    Ⓒ To examine alternatives to Weber's model.
    Ⓓ To argue in favor of a legal rational system.

22. According to the professor, what two factors are associated with charismatic authority?

    Click on 2 answers.

    Ⓐ Sacred customs.
    Ⓑ An attractive leader.
    Ⓒ A social cause.
    Ⓓ Legal elections.

23. Listen again to part of the lecture. Then answer the question.

    "But what about power that is accepted by members of society as right and just, that is, legitimate power? Now we're talking about authority. And that is what I want to focus on today."

    Why does the professor say this:

    "But what about power that is accepted by members of society as right and just, that is, legitimate power?"

    Ⓐ He is asking the students to answer a question.
    Ⓑ He is introducing the topic of the lecture.
    Ⓒ He is expressing an opinion about the subject.
    Ⓓ He is reminding students of a previous point.

24. In an evolutionary model, how is rational legal authority viewed?

    Ⓐ The most modern form of authority.
    Ⓑ A common type of authority in the industrial age.
    Ⓒ Authority used by traditional leaders.
    Ⓓ A replacement for the three ideal types of authority.

25. What does the professor imply about the three types of authority?

    Ⓐ There is only one legitimate type of authority in modern societies.
    Ⓑ Sociologists do not agree about the development of the types of authority.
    Ⓒ Societies tend to select and retain one type of authority indefinitely.
    Ⓓ Weber's model explains why the social structure rejects power over time.

Independent Listening 6: "Mineral Exploitation"

Directions:
Choose the best answer for multiple-choice questions. Follow the directions on the
page for computer-assisted questions.

26. What is the main topic of this lecture?

    Ⓐ How to exploit nonrenewable mineral resources.
    Ⓑ The exploitation of minerals in protected environments.
    Ⓒ Pollution as a by-product of mineral exploitation.
    Ⓓ The economic and environmental costs of exploiting minerals.

27. According to the professor, what are two problems that can be anticipated when
    roads are cut into an area for mining?

    Click on 2 answers.

    Ⓐ The labor is difficult to retain.
    Ⓑ The natural landscape is damaged.
    Ⓒ The roadbeds create waste piles.
    Ⓓ The ecosystem is disturbed.

28. Listen again to part of the lecture. Then answer the question.

    "And I was just thinking that in addition to the economic costs of the transporta-
    tion for trucks and fuel and labor and everything, there could be, there might be
    some construction too, if there aren't any roads in and out of the area." "And that
    would mean . . ."

    Why does the professor say this:

    "And that would mean . . ."

    Ⓐ As encouragement for the student to give a more complete answer.
    Ⓑ Because he doesn't understand the student's answer.
    Ⓒ To give another student an opportunity to speak.
    Ⓓ For positive reinforcement of a correct answer.

29. What option is proposed as an alternative when all of the mineral resources in eas-
    ily accessible locations have been depleted?

    Ⓐ Converting to nonrenewable resources.
    Ⓑ Concentrating on conservation of the resources.
    Ⓒ Developing synthetic resources to replace minerals.
    Ⓓ Using new technology to search the area again.

30. What does the professor imply about the environmental costs of mineral exploitation?

    Ⓐ He thinks that the environmental costs are less than the economic costs.
    Ⓑ He regrets that the environment is damaged during mineral exploitation.
    Ⓒ He opposes mineral exploitation when it is done close to urban areas.
    Ⓓ He believes in exploiting the reserves in national parks and historic reserves.

To check your answers for the Listening Section of Model Test 4, refer to the Answer Key on page 389. For an explanation of the answers, refer to the Explanatory Answers for Model Test 4 on pages 462–478.

Speaking Section

This is the Speaking Section of the Next Generation TOEFL Model Test. This section tests your ability to communicate in English in an academic context. During the test, you will respond to six speaking questions. You may take notes as you listen. You may use your notes to answer the questions. The reading passages and the questions are printed in the book, but most of the directions will be spoken. Your speaking will be evaluated on both the fluency of the language and the accuracy of the content. A clock on the screen will show you how much time you have to prepare your answer and how much time you have to record it.

Independent Speaking Question 1: "A Book"

Question:
Think about a book that you have enjoyed reading. Why did you like it? What was especially interesting about the book? Use specific details and examples to support your response.

Preparation Time: 15 seconds
Recording Time: 45 seconds

Independent Speaking Question 2: "Foreign Travel"

Question:
Some people think that it is better to travel as part of a tour group when they are visiting a foreign country. Other people prefer to make their own travel plans so that they can travel independently. Which approach do you think is better and why? Use specific reasons and examples to support your opinion.

Preparation Time: 15 seconds
Recording Time: 45 seconds

Integrated Speaking Question 3: "Old Main"

Reading Time: 45 seconds

Notice Concerning Old Main

The college will be celebrating the one-hundredth anniversary of the founding of the school by renovating Old Main, the original building. Two alternative plans are being considered. One plan would leave the outer structure intact and concentrate on electrical and plumbing upgrades as well as minor structural support. The other plan would demolish all of the building except the clock tower, which would form the centerpiece of a new structure. An open meeting is scheduled for Friday afternoon at three o'clock in the Old Main auditorium.

Question:
The professor expresses her opinion of the plan for the renovation of Old Main. Report her opinion and explain the reasons that she gives for having that opinion.

Preparation Time: 30 seconds
Recording Time: 60 seconds

Integrated Speaking Question 4: "Communication with Primates"

Reading Time: 45 seconds

Communication with Primates

Early experiments to teach primates to communicate with their voices failed because of the differences in their vocal organs, not their intellectual capacity. Dramatic progress was observed when researchers began to communicate by using American Sign Language. Some chimpanzees were able to learn several hundred signs that they put together to express a number of relationships similar to the initial language acquisition of children. In addition, success was achieved by using plastic symbols on a magnetic board, each of which represented a word. For example, a small blue triangle represented an apple. Chimpanzees were able to respond correctly to basic sequences and even to form some higher-level concepts by using the representative system.

Question:
Explain the importance of the Kanzi experiment in the context of research on primate communication.

Preparation Time: 30 seconds
Recording Time: 60 seconds

Integrated Speaking Question 5: "Headaches"

Question:
Describe the woman's problem and the two suggestions that her friend makes about how to handle it. What do you think the woman should do, and why?

Preparation Time: 20 seconds
Recording Time: 60 seconds

Integrated Speaking Question 6: "Fax Machines"

Question:
Using the main points and examples from the lecture, describe the three parts of a fax machine and then explain how the fax process works.

Preparation Time: 20 seconds
Recording Time: 60 seconds

To check your answers for the Speaking Section of Model Test 4, refer to the Checklists on pages 389–390. For Example Answers, refer to the Explanatory Answers for Model Test 4 on pages 478–485.

Reading Section

This is the Reading Section of the Next Generation TOEFL Model Test. This section tests your ability to understand reading passages like those in college textbooks. There are three passages. After each passage, you will answer twelve or thirteen questions about it. Most questions are worth one point, but one question in each passage is worth more than one point. You will have 25 minutes to read each passage and answer the comprehension questions. You may take notes while you read. You may use your notes to answer the questions. Choose the best answer for multiple-choice questions. Follow the directions on the page or on the screen for computer-assisted questions. Click on **Next** to go to the next question. Click on **Back** to return to the previous question. You may return to previous questions in the same reading passage, but after you go to the next passage, you may not return to a previous passage. A clock on the screen will show you how much time you have to complete each passage.

Independent Reading 1: "Symbiotic Relationships"

Directions:
Choose the best answer for multiple-choice questions. Follow the directions on the page for computer-assisted questions.

Symbiosis is a close, long-lasting, physical relationship between two different species. In other words, the two species are usually in physical contact and at least one of them derives some sort of benefit from this contact. There are three different categories of symbiotic relationships: parasitism, commensalism, and mutualism.

Parasitism is a relationship in which one organism, known as the parasite, lives in or on another organism, known as the host, from which it derives nourishment. Generally, the parasite is much smaller than the host. Although the host is harmed by the interaction, it is generally not killed immediately by the parasite, and some host individuals may live a long time and be relatively little affected by their parasites. Some parasites are much more destructive than others, however. Newly established parasite/host relationships are likely to be more destructive than those that have a long evolutionary history. With a long-standing interaction between the parasite and the host, the two species generally evolve in such a way that they can accommodate one another. It is not in the parasite's best interest to kill its host. If it does, it must find another. Likewise, the host evolves defenses against the parasite, often reducing the harm done by the parasite to a level the host can tolerate.

Parasites that live on the surface of their hosts are known as **ectoparasites**. Fleas, lice, and some molds and mildews are examples of ectoparasites. Many other parasites, like tapeworms, malaria parasites, many kinds of bacteria, and some fungi are called **endoparasites** because they live inside the bodies of their hosts. A tapeworm lives in the intestines of its host where it is able to resist being digested and makes use of the nutrients in the intestine.

Even plants can be parasites. Mistletoe is a flowering plant that is parasitic on trees. It establishes itself on the surface of a tree when a bird transfers the seed to the tree. It then grows down into the water-conducting tissues of the tree and uses the water and minerals it obtains from these tissues to support its own growth.

If the relationship between organisms is one in which one organism benefits while the other is not affected, it is called **commensalism**. It is possible to visualize a parasitic relationship evolving into a commensal one. Since parasites generally evolve to do as little harm to their host as possible and the host is combating the negative effects of the parasite, they might eventually evolve to the point where the host is not harmed at all. There are many examples of commensal relationships. Many orchids use trees as a surface upon which to grow. The tree is not harmed or helped, but the orchid needs a surface upon which to establish itself and also benefits by being close to the top of the tree, where it can get more sunlight and rain. Some mosses, ferns, and many vines also make use of the surfaces of trees in this way.

In the ocean, many sharks have a smaller fish known as a remora attached to them. Remoras have a sucker on the top of their heads that they can use to attach to the shark. In this way, they can hitchhike a ride as the shark swims along. When the shark feeds, the remora frees itself and obtains small bits of food that the shark misses. Then, the remora reattaches. The shark does not appear to be positively or negatively affected by remoras.

Mutualism is another kind of symbiotic relationship and is actually beneficial to both species involved. In many mutualistic relationships, the relationship is obligatory; the species cannot live without each other. In others, the species can exist separately but are more successful when they are involved in a mutualistic relationship. Some species of *Acacia*, a thorny tree, provide food in the form of sugar solutions in little structures on their stems. Certain species of ants feed on the solutions and live in the tree, which they will protect from other animals by attacking any animal that begins to feed on the tree. Both organisms benefit; the ants receive food and a place to live, and the tree is protected from animals that would use it as food.

One soil nutrient that is usually a limiting factor for plant growth is nitrogen. Many kinds of plants, such as beans, clover, and alder trees, have bacteria that live in their roots in little nodules. The roots form these nodules when they are infected with certain kinds of bacteria. The bacteria do not cause disease but provide the plants with nitrogen-containing molecules that the plants can use for growth. The nitrogen-fixing bacteria benefit from the living site and nutrients that the plants provide, and the plants benefit from the nitrogen they receive.

Glossary:
sucker: an adaptation for sucking nourishment or sticking to a surface
nodules: growths in the form of knots

Question References: "Symbiotic Relationships"

Symbiosis is a close, long-lasting, physical relationship between two different species. In other words, the two species are usually in physical contact and at least one of them derives some sort of benefit from this contact. There are three different categories of symbiotic relationships: parasitism, commensalism, and mutualism.

Parasitism is a relationship in which one organism, known as the parasite, lives in or on another organism, known as the host, from which it derives nourishment. Generally, the parasite is much smaller than the host. Although the host is harmed by the interaction, it is generally not killed immediately by the parasite, and some host individuals may live a long time and be relatively little affected by their parasites. Some parasites are much more destructive than others, however. Newly established parasite/host relationships are likely to be more destructive than those that have a long evolutionary history. With a long-standing interaction between the parasite and the host, the two species generally evolve in such a way that they can accommodate one another. It is not in the parasite's best interest to kill its host. If it does, it must find another. Likewise, the host evolves defenses against the parasite, often reducing the harm done by the parasite to a level the host can tolerate.

Parasites that live on the surface of their hosts are known as **ectoparasites**. Fleas, lice, and some molds and mildews are examples of ectoparasites. [A] Many other parasites, like tapeworms, malaria parasites, many kinds of bacteria, and some fungi are called **endoparasites** because they live inside the bodies of their hosts. [B] A tapeworm lives in the intestines of its host where it is able to resist being digested and makes use of the nutrients in the intestine. [C]

Even plants can be parasites. Mistletoe is a flowering plant that is parasitic on trees. It establishes itself on the surface of a tree when a bird transfers the seed to the tree. It then grows down into the water-conducting tissues of the tree and uses the water and minerals it obtains from these tissues to support its own growth. [D]

If the relationship between organisms is one in which one organism benefits while the other is not affected, it is called **commensalism**. It is possible to visualize a parasitic relationship evolving into a commensal one. Since parasites generally evolve to do as little harm to their host as possible and the host is combating the negative effects of the parasite, they might eventually evolve to the point where the host is not harmed at all. There are many examples of commensal relationships. Many orchids use trees as a surface upon which to grow. The tree is not harmed or helped, but the orchid needs a surface upon which to establish itself and also benefits by being close to the top of the tree, where it can get more sunlight and rain. Some mosses, ferns, and many vines also make use of the surfaces of trees in this way.

In the ocean, many sharks have a smaller fish known as a remora attached to them. Remoras have a sucker on the top of their heads that they can use to attach to the shark. In this way, they can hitchhike a ride as the shark swims along. When the shark feeds, the remora frees itself and obtains small bits of food that the shark misses. Then, the remora reattaches. The shark does not appear to be positively or negatively affected by remoras.

Mutualism is another kind of symbiotic relationship and is actually beneficial to both species involved. In many mutualistic relationships, the relationship is obligatory; the species cannot live without each other. In others, the species can exist separately but are more successful when they are involved in a mutualistic relationship. Some species of *Acacia*, a thorny tree, provide food in the form of sugar solutions in little structures on their stems. Certain species of ants feed on the solutions and live in the tree, which they will protect from other animals by attacking any animal that begins to feed on the tree. Both organisms benefit; the ants receive food and a place to live, and the tree is protected from animals that would use it as food.

One soil nutrient that is usually a limiting factor for plant growth is nitrogen. Many kinds of plants, such as beans, clover, and alder trees, have bacteria that live in their roots in little nodules. The roots form these nodules when they are infected with certain kinds of bacteria. The bacteria do not cause disease but provide the plants with nitrogen-containing molecules that the plants can use for growth. The nitrogen-fixing bacteria benefit from the living site and nutrients that the plants provide, and the plants benefit from the nitrogen they receive.

Glossary:
sucker: an adaptation for sucking nourishment or sticking to a surface
nodules: growths in the form of knots

1. The word derives in the passage is closest in meaning to

   Ⓐ requests
   Ⓑ pursues
   Ⓒ obtains
   Ⓓ rejects

2. The word it in the passage refers to

   Ⓐ host
   Ⓑ organism
   Ⓒ parasite
   Ⓓ relationship

3. The word relatively in the passage is closest in meaning to

   Ⓐ comparatively
   Ⓑ routinely
   Ⓒ adversely
   Ⓓ frequently

4. Which of the sentences below best expresses the information in the highlighted statement in the passage? The other choices change the meaning or leave out important information.

   Ⓐ A parasite is less likely to destroy the host when it attaches itself at first.
   Ⓑ Parasites that have lived on a host for a long time have probably done a lot of damage.
   Ⓒ The most destructive phase for a host is when the parasite first invades it.
   Ⓓ The relationship between a parasite and a host will evolve over time.

5. The word tolerate in the passage is closest in meaning to

   Ⓐ permit
   Ⓑ oppose
   Ⓒ profit
   Ⓓ avoid

6. According to paragraph 3, how do ectoparasites survive?
   Ⓐ They live in mold and mildew on their hosts.
   Ⓑ They digest food in the intestines of their hosts.
   Ⓒ They live on the nutrients in their bacterial hosts.
   Ⓓ They inhabit the outside parts of their hosts.

7. Which of the following is mentioned as an example of a commensal relationship?

   Ⓐ Orchids
   Ⓑ Mistletoe
   Ⓒ Ants
   Ⓓ Fungus

8. The word actually in the passage is closest in meaning to

   Ⓐ frequently
   Ⓑ initially
   Ⓒ really
   Ⓓ usually

9. In paragraph 7, why does the author use the example of the *Acacia* tree?

   Ⓐ To demonstrate how ants survive by living in trees
   Ⓑ To explain how two species can benefit from contact
   Ⓒ To show the relationship between plants and animals
   Ⓓ To present a problem that occurs often in nature

10. How does bacteria affect beans and clover?

   Ⓐ It causes many of the plants to die.
   Ⓑ It limits the growth of young plants.
   Ⓒ It supplies nitrogen to the crops.
   Ⓓ It infects the roots with harmful nodules.

11. Four squares (☐) indicate where the following sentence can be added to the passage.

    They live on the feathers of birds or the fur of animals.

    Where would the sentence best fit into the passage?

12. In which of the following chapters would this passage most probably appear?

    Ⓐ Environment and Organisms
    Ⓑ Pollution and Policies
    Ⓒ Human Influences on Ecosystems
    Ⓓ Energy Resources

13. Complete a summary of the passage by choosing THREE answer choices that express the most important ideas. The other three sentences do not belong in the summary because they express ideas that are not in the passage or they are minor points that are not as important as the three major points. ***This question is worth 2 points.***

    What are the categories of relationships between species?

    Ⓐ In commensalism, one species benefits, and the other is not affected.
    Ⓑ Mistletoe is a flowering plant that establishes a parasitic relationship on trees.
    Ⓒ A mutualistic relationship allows both species to benefit from their contact.
    Ⓓ Bacteria provides plants with nitrogen while deriving nutrients from the plants.
    Ⓔ Parasites live and feed in or on another organism referred to as a host.
    Ⓕ Sharks and remora enjoy a commensal relationship in which the shark is not harmed.

Independent Reading 2: "Civilization"

Directions:
Choose the best answer for multiple-choice questions. Follow the directions on the page for computer-assisted questions.

Between 4000 and 3000 B.C., significant technical developments began to transform the Neolithic towns. The invention of writing enabled records to be kept, and the use of metals marked a new level of human control over the environment and its resources. Already before 4000 B.C., craftspeople had discovered that metal-bearing rocks could be heated to liquefy metals, which could then be cast in molds to produce tools and weapons that were more useful than stone instruments. Although copper was the first metal to be utilized in producing tools, after 4000 B.C., craftspeople in western Asia discovered that a combination of copper and tin produced bronze, a much harder and more durable metal than copper. Its widespread use has led historians to speak of a Bronze Age from around 3000 to 1200 B.C., when bronze was increasingly replaced by iron.

At first, Neolithic settlements were hardly more than villages. But as their inhabitants mastered the art of farming, they gradually began to give birth to more complex human societies. As wealth increased, such societies began to develop armies and to build walled cities. By the beginning of the Bronze Age, the concentration of larger numbers of people in the river valleys of Mesopotamia and Egypt was leading to a whole new pattern for human life.

As we have seen, early human beings formed small groups that developed a simple culture that enabled them to survive. As human societies grew and developed greater complexity, a new form of human existence—called civilization—came into being. A civilization is a complex culture in which large numbers of human beings share a number of common elements. Historians have identified a number of basic characteristics of civilizations, most of which are evident in the Mesopotamian and Egyptian civilizations. These include (1) an urban revolution: cities became the focal points for political, economic, social, cultural, and religious development; (2) a distinct religious structure: the gods were deemed crucial to the community's success, and professional priestly classes, as stewards of the gods' property, regulated relations with the gods; (3) new political and military structures: an organized government bureaucracy arose to meet the administrative demands of the growing population while armies were organized to gain land and power; (4) a new social structure based on economic power: while kings and an upper class of priests, political leaders, and warriors dominated, there also existed a large group of free people (farmers, artisans, craftspeople) and at the very bottom, socially, a class of slaves; (5) the development of writing: kings, priests, merchants, and artisans used writing to keep records; and (6) new forms of significant artistic and intellectual activity, such as monumental architectural structures, usually religious, occupied a prominent place in urban environments.

Why early civilizations developed remains difficult to explain. Since civilizations developed independently in India, China, Mesopotamia, and Egypt, can general causes be identified that would explain why all of these civilizations emerged? A number of possible explanations of the beginning of civilization have been suggested. A theory of challenge and response maintains that challenges forced human beings to make efforts that resulted in the rise of civilization. Some scholars have adhered to a material explanation. Material forces, such as the growth of food surpluses, made possible the specialization of labor and development of large communities with bureaucratic organization. But the area of the Fertile Crescent, in which Mesopotamian civilization emerged, was not naturally conducive to agriculture. Abundant food could only be produced with a massive human effort to carefully manage the water, an effort that created the need for organization and bureaucratic control and led to civilized cities. Some historians have argued that nonmaterial forces, primarily religious, provided the sense of unity and purpose that made such organized activities possible. Finally, some scholars doubt that we are capable of ever discovering the actual causes of early civilization.

Question References: "Civilization"

Between 4000 and 3000 B.C., significant technical developments began to transform the Neolithic towns. The invention of writing enabled records to be kept, and the use of metals marked a new level of human control over the environment and its resources. Already before 4000 B.C., craftspeople had discovered that metal-bearing rocks could be heated to liquefy metals, which could then be cast in molds to produce tools and weapons that were more useful than stone instruments. Although copper was the first metal to be utilized in producing tools, after 4000 B.C., craftspeople in western Asia discovered that a combination of copper and tin produced bronze, a much harder and more durable metal than copper. Its widespread use has led historians to speak of a Bronze Age from around 3000 to 1200 B.C., when bronze was increasingly replaced by iron.

At first, Neolithic settlements were hardly more than villages. But as their inhabitants mastered the art of farming, they gradually began to give birth to more complex human societies. As wealth increased, such societies began to develop armies and to build walled cities. By the beginning of the Bronze Age, the concentration of larger numbers of people in the river valleys of Mesopotamia and Egypt was leading to a whole new pattern for human life.

As we have seen, early human beings formed small groups that developed a simple culture that enabled them to survive. As human societies grew and developed greater complexity, a new form of human existence—called civilization—came into being. A civilization is a complex culture in which large numbers of human beings share a number of common elements. Historians have identified a number of basic characteristics of civilizations, most of which are evident in the Mesopotamian and Egyptian civilizations. These include (1) an urban revolution: cities became the focal points for political, economic, social, cultural, and religious development; (2) a distinct religious structure: the gods were deemed crucial to the community's success, and professional priestly classes, as stewards of the gods' property, regulated relations with the gods; (3) new political and military structures: an organized government bureaucracy arose to meet the administrative demands of the growing population while armies were organized to gain land and power; (4) a new social structure based on economic power: while kings and an upper class of priests, political leaders, and warriors dominated, there also existed a large group of free people (farmers, artisans, craftspeople) and at the very bottom, socially, a class of slaves; (5) the development of writing: kings, priests, merchants, and artisans used writing to keep records; and (6) new forms of significant artistic and intellectual activity, such as monumental architectural structures, usually religious, occupied a prominent place in urban environments.

Why early civilizations developed remains difficult to explain. [A] Since civilizations developed independently in India, China, Mesopotamia, and Egypt, can general causes be identified that would explain why all of these civilizations emerged? [B] A number of possible explanations of the beginning of civilization have been suggested. [C] A theory of challenge and response maintains that challenges forced human beings to make efforts that resulted in the rise of civilization. Some scholars have adhered to a material explanation. [D] Material forces, such as the growth of food surpluses, made possible the specialization of labor and development of large communities with bureaucratic organization. But the area of the Fertile Crescent, in which Mesopotamian civilization emerged, was not naturally conducive to agriculture. Abundant food could only be produced with a massive human effort to carefully manage the water, an effort that created the need for organization and bureaucratic control and led to civilized cities. Some historians have argued that nonmaterial forces, primarily religious, provided the sense of unity and purpose that made such organized activities possible. Finally, some scholars doubt that we are capable of ever discovering the actual causes of early civilization.

1. Which of the following is the best definition of a civilization?

   Ⓐ Neolithic towns and cities
   Ⓑ Types of complex cultures
   Ⓒ An agricultural community
   Ⓓ Large population centers

2. The word its in the passage refers to

   Ⓐ copper
   Ⓑ bronze
   Ⓒ metal
   Ⓓ iron

3. According to paragraph 2, what happens as societies become more prosperous?

   Ⓐ More goods are produced.
   Ⓑ Walled cities are built.
   Ⓒ Laws are instituted.
   Ⓓ The size of families is increased.

4. The word hardly in the passage is closest in meaning to

   Ⓐ frequently
   Ⓑ likely
   Ⓒ barely
   Ⓓ obviously

5. Why does the author mention Neolithic towns?

   Ⓐ To give an example of a civilization
   Ⓑ To explain the invention of writing systems
   Ⓒ To argue that they should be classified as villages
   Ⓓ To contrast them with the civilizations that evolved

6. According to paragraph 3, how was the class system structured?

   Ⓐ There was an upper class and a lower class.
   Ⓑ There were slaves, free people, and a ruling class.
   Ⓒ There was a king, an army, and slaves.
   Ⓓ There were intellectuals and uneducated farmers and workers.

7. Which of the sentences below best expresses the information in the highlighted statement in the passage? The other choices change the meaning or leave out important information.

   Ⓐ Mesopotamian and Egyptian civilizations exhibit the majority of the characteristics identified by historians.
   Ⓑ The characteristics that historians have identified are not found in the Egyptian and Mesopotamian cultures.
   Ⓒ Civilizations in Mesopotamia and Egypt were identified by historians who were studying the characteristics of early cultures.
   Ⓓ The identification of most historical civilizations includes either Egypt or Mesopotamia on the list.

8. The word crucial in the passage is closest in meaning to

   Ⓐ fundamental
   Ⓑ arbitrary
   Ⓒ disruptive
   Ⓓ suitable

9. The word prominent in the passage is closest in meaning to

   Ⓐ weak
   Ⓑ important
   Ⓒ small
   Ⓓ new

10. According to paragraph 4, how can the independent development of civilization in different geographic regions be explained?

    Ⓐ Scholars agree that food surpluses encouraged populations to be concentrated in certain areas.
    Ⓑ There are several theories that explain the rise of civilization in the ancient world.
    Ⓒ The model of civilization was probably carried from one region to another along trade routes.
    Ⓓ Historians attribute the emergence of early cities at about the same time as a coincidence.

11. All of the following are cited as reasons why civilizations developed EXCEPT

    Ⓐ Religious practices unified the population.
    Ⓑ The management of water required organization.
    Ⓒ A major climate change made living in groups necessary.
    Ⓓ Extra food resulted in the expansion of population centers.

12. Four squares (☐) indicate where the following sentence can be added to the passage.

Some historians believe they can be established.

Where would the sentence best fit into the passage?

13. Complete a summary of the passage by choosing THREE answer choices that express the most important ideas. The other three sentences do not belong in the summary because they express ideas that are not in the passage or they are minor points that are not as important as the three major points. *This question is worth 2 points.*

What are some of the qualities that define a civilization?

Ⓐ Free citizens who work in professions for pay
Ⓑ Bureaucracies for the government and armies
Ⓒ Libraries to house art and written records
Ⓓ A strategic location near rivers or the sea
Ⓔ Organized religion, writing, and art
Ⓕ A densely populated group with a class structure

Independent Reading 3: "The Scientific Method"

Directions:
Choose the best answer for multiple-choice questions. Follow the directions on the page for computer-assisted questions.

In brief, the modern **scientific method** is an organized approach to explaining observed facts, with a model of nature, subject to the constraint that any proposed model must be testable and the provision that the model must be modified or discarded if it fails these tests.

In its most idealized form, the scientific method begins with a set of observed facts. A fact is supposed to be a statement that is objectively true. For example, we consider it a fact that the Sun rises each morning, that the planet Mars appeared in a particular place in our sky last night, and that the Earth rotates. Facts are not always obvious, as illustrated by the case of the Earth's rotation. For most of human history, the Earth was assumed to be stationary at the center of the universe. In addition, our interpretations of facts often are based on beliefs about the world that others might not share. For example, when we say that the Sun rises each morning, we assume that it is the same Sun day after day—an idea that might not have been accepted by ancient Egyptians, whose mythology held that the Sun died with every sunset and was reborn with every sunrise. Nevertheless, facts are the raw material that scientific models seek to explain, so it is important that scientists agree on the facts. In the context of science, a fact must therefore be something that anyone can verify for himself or herself, at least in principle.

Once the facts have been collected, a model can be proposed to explain them. A useful model must also make predictions that can be tested through further observations or experiments. Ptolemy's model of the universe was useful because it predicted future locations of the Sun, Moon, and planets in the sky. However, although the Ptolemaic model remained in use for nearly 1,500 years, eventually it became clear that its predictions didn't quite match actual observations—a key reason why the Earth-centered model of the universe finally was discarded.

In summary, the idealized scientific method proceeds as follows:

- *Observation*: The scientific method begins with the collection of a set of observed facts.
- *Hypothesis*: A model is proposed to explain the observed facts and to make new predictions. A proposed model is often called a **hypothesis**, which essentially means an *educated guess*.
- *Further observations/experiments*: The model's predictions are tested through further observations or experiments. When a prediction is verified, we gain confidence that the model truly represents nature. When a prediction fails, we recognize that the model is flawed, and we therefore must refine or discard the model.
- *Theory*: A model must be continually challenged with new observations or experiments by many different scientists. A model achieves the status of a scientific theory only after a broad range of its predictions has been repeatedly verified. Note that, while we can have great confidence that a scientific theory truly represents nature, we can never prove a theory to be true *beyond all doubt*. Therefore, even well-established theories must be subject to continuing challenges through further observations and experiments.

In reality, scientific discoveries rarely are made by a process as mechanical as the idealized scientific method described here. For example, Johannes Kepler, who discovered the laws of planetary motion in the early 1600s, tested his model against observations that had been made previously, rather than verifying new predictions based on his model. Moreover, like most scientific work, Kepler's work involved intuition, collaboration with others, moments of insight, and luck. Nevertheless, with hindsight we can look back at Kepler's theory and see that other scientists eventually made plenty of observations to verify the planetary positions predicted by his model. In that sense, the scientific method represents an ideal prescription for judging objectively whether a proposed model of nature is close to the truth.

Question References: "The Scientific Method"

In brief, the modern **scientific method** is an organized approach to explaining observed facts, with a model of nature, subject to the constraint that any proposed model must be testable and the provision that the model must be modified or discarded if it fails these tests.

In its most idealized form, the scientific method begins with a set of observed facts. $\boxed{\text{A}}$ A fact is supposed to be a statement that is objectively true. For example, we consider it a fact that the Sun rises each morning, that the planet Mars appeared in a particular place in our sky last night, and that the Earth rotates. Facts are not always obvious, as illustrated by the case of the Earth's rotation. For most of human history, the Earth was assumed to be stationary at the center of the universe. $\boxed{\text{B}}$ In addition, our interpretations of facts often are based on beliefs about the world that others might not share. For example, when we say that the Sun rises each morning, we assume that it is the same Sun day after day—an idea that might not have been accepted by ancient Egyptians, whose mythology held that the Sun died with every sunset and was reborn with every sunrise. $\boxed{\text{C}}$ Nevertheless, facts are the raw material that scientific models seek to explain, so it is important that scientists agree on the facts. $\boxed{\text{D}}$ In the context of science, a fact must therefore be something that anyone can verify for himself or herself, at least in principle.

Once the facts have been collected, a model can be proposed to explain them. A useful model must also make predictions that can be tested through further observations or experiments. Ptolemy's model of the universe was useful because it predicted future locations of the Sun, Moon, and planets in the sky. However, although the Ptolemaic model remained in use for nearly 1,500 years, eventually it became clear that its predictions didn't quite match actual observations—a key reason why the Earth-centered model of the universe finally was discarded.

In summary, the idealized scientific method proceeds as follows:

* *Observation*: The scientific method begins with the collection of a set of observed facts.
* *Hypothesis*: A model is proposed to explain the observed facts and to make new predictions. A proposed model is often called a **hypothesis**, which essentially means an *educated guess*.
* *Further observations/experiments*: The model's predictions are tested through further observations or experiments. When a prediction is verified, we gain confidence that the model truly represents nature. When a prediction fails, we recognize that the model is flawed, and we therefore must refine or discard the model.
* *Theory*: A model must be continually challenged with new observations or experiments by many different scientists. A model achieves the status of a scientific theory only after a broad range of its predictions has been repeatedly verified. Note that, while we can have great confidence that a scientific theory truly represents nature, we can never prove a theory to be true *beyond all doubt*. Therefore, even well-established theories must be subject to continuing challenges through further observations and experiments.

In reality, scientific discoveries rarely are made by a process as mechanical as the idealized scientific method described here. For example, Johannes Kepler, who discovered the laws of planetary motion in the early 1600s, tested his model against observations that had been made previously, rather than verifying new predictions based on his model. Moreover, like most scientific work, Kepler's work involved intuition, collaboration with others, moments of insight, and luck. Nevertheless, with hindsight we can look back at Kepler's theory and see that other scientists eventually made plenty of observations to verify the planetary positions predicted by his model. In that sense, the scientific method represents an ideal prescription for judging objectively whether a proposed model of nature is close to the truth.

1. The word obvious in the passage is closest in meaning to

   Ⓐ interesting
   Ⓑ clear
   Ⓒ simple
   Ⓓ correct

2. Why did the author give the example of the ancient Egyptians in paragraph 2?

   Ⓐ To explain the rotation of the Earth and the Sun
   Ⓑ To prove that facts may be interpreted differently across cultures
   Ⓒ To present a fact that can be verified by the reader
   Ⓓ To discard a model that was widely accepted

3. The word essentially in the passage is closest in meaning to

   Ⓐ obviously
   Ⓑ occasionally
   Ⓒ basically
   Ⓓ oddly

4. The word flawed in the passage is closest in meaning to

   Ⓐ not perfect
   Ⓑ not modern
   Ⓒ not routine
   Ⓓ not accepted

5. Which of the sentences below best expresses the information in the highlighted statement in the passage? The other choices change the meaning or leave out important information.

   Ⓐ An ideal form of the scientific method is explained in this passage.
   Ⓑ Making a discovery by using an ideal form of the scientific method is unusual.
   Ⓒ The description of the scientific method is a mechanical process.
   Ⓓ Here is an idealized description of the scientific process for scientific discovery.

6. According to paragraph 3, why was the Ptolemaic model replaced?

    Ⓐ The model was not useful in forecasting the movement of the Sun.
    Ⓑ The predictions did not conform to observations of the universe.
    Ⓒ The Ptolemaic model had been in use for about 1,500 years.
    Ⓓ Most scientists believed that the Earth was the center of the universe.

7. According to paragraph 4, theories that are generally accepted

    Ⓐ must still be verified
    Ⓑ have several models
    Ⓒ can be unscientific
    Ⓓ are very simple

8. According to paragraph 5, what did Kepler do to verify his theory of planetary motion?

    Ⓐ He made predictions based on the model.
    Ⓑ He asked other scientists to make predictions.
    Ⓒ He used prior observations to test the model.
    Ⓓ He relied on insight to verify the theory.

9. The word plenty in the passage is closest in meaning to

    Ⓐ broad
    Ⓑ reliable
    Ⓒ detailed
    Ⓓ numerous

10. All of the following statements are part of a definition of the term *fact* EXCEPT

    Ⓐ A fact is objectively true.
    Ⓑ A fact can be verified.
    Ⓒ A fact may be interpreted.
    Ⓓ A fact must be comprehensible.

11. It may be concluded from information in this passage that a model

    Ⓐ does not always reflect observations
    Ⓑ is not subject to change like theories are
    Ⓒ is considered true without doubt
    Ⓓ does not require further experimentation

12. Four squares (☐) indicate where the following sentence can be added to the passage.

    Clearly, cultural orientation will influence the way that scientists will explain their observations.

Where would the sentence best fit into the passage?

13. Complete a summary of the passage by choosing THREE answer choices that express the most important ideas. The other three sentences do not belong in the summary because they express ideas that are not in the passage or they are minor points that are not as important as the three major points. *This question is worth 2 points.*

What are the three basic steps in the scientific method?

Ⓐ   Observational data collection
Ⓑ   Proof without question
Ⓒ   The testing of a hypothesis
Ⓓ   Intuitive discoveries
Ⓔ   A model that supports predictions
Ⓕ   The general approval of a paradigm

To check your answers for the Reading Section of Model Test 4, refer to the Answer Key on page 390. For an explanation of the answers, refer to the Explanatory Answers for Model Test 4 on pages 485–488.

Writing Section

This is the Writing Section of the Next Generation TOEFL Model Test. This section tests your ability to write essays in English. During the test, you will write two essays. The independent essay usually asks for your opinion about a familiar topic. The integrated essay asks for your response to an academic reading passage, a lecture, or both. You may take notes as you read and listen. You may use your notes to write the essays. If a lecture is included, it will be spoken, but the directions and the questions will be written. A clock on the screen will show you how much time you have to complete each essay.

Independent Writing: "Study in the United States"

Directions:
You have 30 minutes to plan, write, and revise your essay. Typically, a good response will require that you write a minimum of 300 words.

Question:
You are planning to study in the United States. What do you think you will like and dislike about this experience? Why? Use specific reasons and details to support your answer.

Notes

Use this space for essay notes only. Work done on this work sheet will *not* be scored.

Essay

Integrated Writing: "Problem Solving"

Directions:
You have 20 minutes to plan, write and revise your response to a reading passage and a lecture on the same topic. First, read the passage below and take notes. Then, listen to the lecture and take notes. Finally, write your response to the writing question. Typically, a good response will require that you write 200–250 words.

Solving a problem can be broken down into several steps. First, the problem must be identified correctly. Psychologists refer to this step as *problem representation*. For many problems, figuring out which information is relevant and which is extraneous can be difficult and can interfere with arriving at a good solution. Clearly, before a problem can be solved, it must be obvious what the problem is, however, this is not as easy as it might seem. One obstacle to efficient problem representation is *functional fixedness*, that is, allowing preconceived notions and even prejudices to color the facts. Most people tend to see objects and events in certain fixed ways, and by being inflexible in viewing the problem, they may be unable to notice the tools for the solution. Once the problem is identified accurately, however, the second step consists of considering the alternatives for a solution. A common way to evaluate alternatives is to write them down and then make a list of advantages and disadvantages for each solution. Here again, people may be limited by prior experiences. Often people adopt *mental sets* that lead them to the same problem-solving strategies that were successful for problems in the past. Although that can be helpful most of the time, sometimes a new situation requires a different strategy. In that case, the mental set must be abandoned, and new alternatives must be explored. This can be a difficult adjustment for some people.

After the alternatives have been compared, a strategy must be selected from among them. One way to avoid becoming mired in the options is to try the best option with a view to abandoning it for another if the results are unfavorable. This attitude allows many people to move on expeditiously to the next step—action. The strategy selected must be implemented and tested. If it solves the problem, no further action is necessary, but if not, then an unsuccessful solution may actually lead to a more successful option. If the solution is still not apparent, then the cycle begins again, starting with problem identification. By continuing to review the problem and repeat the problem-solving steps, the solution can be improved upon and refined.

Question:
Summarize the main points in the lecture, referring to the way that they relate to the reading passage.

Notes

Use this space for essay notes only. Work done on this work sheet will *not* be scored.

To check your answers for the Writing Section of Model Test 4, refer to the Checklists on page 391. For an explanation of the answers, refer to the Explanatory Answers for Model Test 4 on pages 488–490.

Essay

ANSWER KEYS

ANSWER KEY—EXERCISES FOR STRUCTURE

Patterns

Problem		Part A	Part B	
Problem	1	(A)	(A)	have
Problem	2	(C)	(A)	to evolve
Problem	3	(D)	(B)	smoking
Problem	4	(D)	(B)	permitting
Problem	5	(C)	(A)	saw
Problem	6	(A)	(B)	turns *or* will turn
Problem	7	(A)	(C)	will have to pay *or* may have to pay
Problem	8	(A)	(C)	unless they complete
Problem	9	(D)	(B)	be used
Problem	10	(B)	(A)	be
Problem	11	(B)	(B)	for making *or* to make
Problem	12	(C)	(C)	measured
Problem	13	(A)	(A)	It is believed
Problem	14	(D)	(C)	will have succeeded
Problem	15	(B)	(B)	is losing
Problem	16	(B)	(D)	should be discontinued
Problem	17	(A)	(D)	for them
Problem	18	(A)	(A)	which
Problem	19	(C)	(C)	eight or ten computers
Problem	20	(C)	(A)	Religion
Problem	21	(B)	(A)	Space
Problem	22	(C)	(A)	Progress
Problem	23	(B)	(C)	pieces of equipment
Problem	24	(C)	(A)	Spelling *or* To spell
Problem	25	(B)	(A)	~~It is~~
Problem	26	(A)	(A)	The philosophy
Problem	27	(D)	(B)	no
Problem	28	(C)	(A)	Most of *or* Almost all of
Problem	29	(C)	(A)	Sex education
Problem	30	(A)	(B)	four-stage
Problem	31	(A)	(B)	so expensive
Problem	32	(B)	(B)	the same
Problem	33	(C)	(D)	like

Problem		Part A	Part B	
Problem	34	(A)	(B)	differ from *or* are different from
Problem	35	(C)	(A)	as much as
Problem	36	(A)	(A)	more than
Problem	37	(C)	(C)	as many as
Problem	38	(C)	(B)	most
Problem	39	(C)	(B)	worse
Problem	40	(C)	(A)	the more intense
Problem	41	(A)	(B)	like that of England
Problem	42	(B)	(B)	besides
Problem	43	(C)	(C)	because
Problem	44	(D)	(D)	also easy to install
Problem	45	(B)	(D)	complete
Problem	46	(D)	(C)	the plane is
Problem	47	(B)	(B)	does the same major league baseball team win
Problem	48	(C)	(A)	since 1930
Problem	49	(C)	(B)	as a whole
Problem	50	(B)	(B)	~~That~~

Style

Problem		Part A	Part B	
Problem	1	(C)	(C)	were
Problem	2	(C)	(B)	gave
Problem	3	(B)	(B)	enables
Problem	4	(C)	(A)	is
Problem	5	(B)	(A)	There are
Problem	6	(D)	(D)	its
Problem	7	(B)	(C)	their
Problem	8	(B)	(A)	Having designed
Problem	9	(D)	(C)	find
Problem	10	(C)	(B)	to develop
Problem	11	(B)	(D)	to use as currency
Problem	12	(B)	(B)	rapidly
Problem	13	(B)	(A)	an old one *or* an ancient one
Problem	14	(C)	(A)	~~is~~
Problem	15	(B)	(A)	raised
Problem	16	(C)	(A)	lies
Problem	17	(B)	(B)	sits
Problem	18	(B)	(C)	do
Problem	19	(A)	(B)	depends on
Problem	20	(B)	(B)	differ

ANSWER KEY—EXERCISES FOR READING

Problem 1.   Previewing

<u>A black hole is a region of space created by the total gravitational collapse of matter</u>. It is so intense that nothing, not even light or radiation, can escape. In other words, it is a one-way surface through which matter can fall inward but cannot emerge.

<u>Some astronomers believe that a black hole may be formed when a large star collapses inward from its own weight</u>. So long as they are emitting heat and light into space, stars support themselves against their own gravitational pull with the outward thermal pressure generated by heat from nuclear reactions deep in their interiors. But if a star eventually exhausts its nuclear fuel, then its unbalanced gravitational attraction could cause it to contract and collapse. <u>Furthermore, it could begin to pull in surrounding matter, including nearby comets and planets, creating a black hole.</u>

The topic is black holes.

Problem 2.   Reading for Main Ideas

<u>For more than a century, despite attacks by a few opposing scientists, Charles Darwin's theory of evolution by natural selection has stood firm. Now, however, some respected biologists are beginning to question whether the theory accounts for major developments such as the shift from water to land habitation.</u> Clearly, evolution has not proceeded steadily but has progressed by radical advances. Recent research in molecular biology, particularly in the study of DNA, provides us with a new possibility. Not only environmental changes but also genetic codes in the underlying structure of DNA could govern evolution.

The main idea is that biologists are beginning to question Darwin's theory.
A good title would be "Questions about Darwin's Theory."

Problem 3.   Using Contexts for Vocabulary

1. *To auction* means to sell.
2. *Proprietor* means an owner.
3. *Formerly* means in the past.
4. *To sample* means to try or to taste.
5. *Royalty* means payment.

Problem 4. Scanning for Details

To prepare for a career in engineering, a student must begin planning in high school. Mathematics and science should form the core curriculum. For example, in a school where sixteen credit hours are required for high school graduation, four should be in mathematics, one each in chemistry, biology, and physics. The remaining credits should include four in English and at least three in the humanities and social sciences. The average entering freshman in engineering should have achieved at least a 2.5 grade point average on a 4.0 scale in his or her high school. Although deficiencies can be corrected during the first year, the student who needs additional work should expect to spend five instead of four years to complete a degree.

1. What is the average grade point for an entering freshman in engineering?
   2.5

2. When should a student begin planning for a career in engineering?
   in high school

3. How can a student correct deficiencies in preparation?
   by spending five years

4. How many credits should a student have in English?
   four

5. How many credits are required for a high school diploma?
   sixteen

Problem 5. Making Inferences

When an acid is dissolved in water, the acid molecule divides into two parts, a hydrogen ion and another ion. An ion is an atom or a group of atoms which has an electrical charge. The charge can be either positive or negative. If hydrochloric acid is mixed with water, for example, it divides into hydrogen ions and chlorine ions.

A strong acid ionizes to a great extent, but a weak acid does not ionize so much. The strength of an acid, therefore, depends on how much it ionizes, not on how many hydrogen ions are produced. It is interesting that nitric acid and sulfuric acid become greatly ionized whereas boric acid and carbonic acid do not.

1. What kind of acid is sulfuric acid?

   A strong acid ionizes to a great extent, and sulfuric acid becomes greatly ionized.
   Conclusion: Sulfuric acid is a strong acid.

2. What kind of acid is boric acid?

   A weak acid does not ionize so much and boric acid does not ionize greatly.
   Conclusion: Boric acid is a weak acid.

Problem 6. Identifying Exceptions

All music consists of two elements—expression and design. Expression is inexact and subjective, and may be enjoyed in a personal or instinctive way. Design, on the other hand is exact and must be analyzed objectively in order to be understood and appreciated. The folk song, for example, has a definite musical <u>design which relies on simple repetition</u> with a <u>definite beginning and ending</u>. A folk song generally consists of one stanza of music repeated for each stanza of verse.

Because of their communal, and usually <u>uncertain origin</u>, folk songs are often popular verse set to music. They are not always recorded, and tend to be passed on in a kind of musical version of oral history. Each singer revises and perfects the song. In part as a consequence of this continuous revisionprocess, most folk songs are almost perfect in their construction and design. A particular singer's interpretation of the folk song may provide an interesting expression, but the simple design that underlies the song itself is stable and enduring.

1. All of the following are true of a folk song EXCEPT
   ✓ There is a clear start and finish.
   ✓ The origin is often not known.
   The design may change in the interpretation.
   ✓ Simple repetition is characteristic of its design.

Problem 7. Locating References

Line
(5)

The National Road, also known as the Cumberland Road, was constructed in the early 1800s to provide transportation between the established commercial areas of the East and Northwest Territory. By 1818, <u>the road</u> had reached Wheeling, West Virginia, 130 miles from (its) point of origin in Cumberland, Maryland. The cost was a monumental thirteen thousand dollars per mile.

Upon reaching the Ohio River, the National Road became one of the major trade routes to the western states and territo-
(10) ries, providing Baltimore with a trade advantage over neigh-boring cities. In order to compete, New York state authorized the construction of <u>the Erie Canal</u>, and Philadelphia initiated a transportation plan to link (it) with Pittsburgh. Towns along the rivers, canals, and the new National Road became important trade centers.

1. The word "its" in line 5 refers to *the road.*

2. The word "it" in line 13 refers to *the canal.*

Problem 8. Referring to the Passage

In September of 1929, traders experienced <u>a lack of confidence in the stock market's ability to continue its phe-nomenal rise. Prices fell. For many inexperienced investors,</u>
Line <u>the drop produced a panic.</u> They had all their money tied up in
(5) the market, and they were pressed to sell before the prices fell even lower. Sell orders were coming in so fast that the ticker tape at the New York Stock Exchange could not accommodate all the transactions.

To try to reestablish confidence in the market, a power-
(10) ful group of New York bankers agreed to pool their funds and purchase stock above current market values. Although the buy orders were minimal, they were counting on their reputations to restore confidence on the part of the smaller investors, there-by affecting the number of sell orders. On Thursday, October
(15) 24, Richard Whitney, the Vice President of the New York Stock Exchange and a broker for the J.P. Morgan Company, made the effort on their behalf. <u>Initially, it appeared to have been suc-cessful,</u> then, on the following Tuesday, the crash began again and accelerated. By 1932, stocks were worth only twenty per-
(20) cent of their value at the 1929 high. The results of the crash had extended into every aspect of the economy, causing a long and painful depression, referred to in American history as the Great Depression.

1. Where in the passage does the author refer to the reason for the stock market crash? *Lines 1-4.*

2. Where in the passage does the author suggest that there was a temporary recovery in the stock market? *Lines 17-18.*

ANSWER KEY—MODEL TESTS

Model Test 1—Computer-Assisted TOEFL

Section 1: Listening

1. **(C)**	10. **(C)**	19. **(C)**	28. **(B)**	37. **(B)**	46. **(A)**
2. **(A)**	11. **(B)**	20. **(B)**	29. **(A)**	38. **(B)**	47. **(B)**
3. **(C)**	12. **(A)**	21. **(B)**	30. **(A)**	39. **(A)**	48. **(C)**
4. **(A)**	13. **(C)**	22. **(C)**	31. **(C)**	40. **(C)(D)**	49. **(B)**
5. **(A)**	14. **(B)**	23. **(B)**	32. **(A)**	41. **(B)**	50. **(B)**
6. **(B)**	15. **(C)**	24. **(D)**	33. **(C)**	42. **(A)**	
7. **(D)**	16. **(C)**	25. **(C)**	34. **(A)**	43. **(A)(C)**	
8. **(C)**	17. **(C)**	26. **(C)**	35. **(C)**	44. **(B)**	
9. **(D)**	18. **(D)**	27. **(D)**	36. **(C)**	45. **(C)**	

Section 2: Structure

1. **(B)**	6. **(B)**	10. **(B)**	14. **(C)**	18. **(A)**	22. **(D)**
2. **(C)**	7. **(B)**	11. **(C)**	15. **(C)**	19. **(A)**	23. **(B)**
3. **(A)**	8. **(A)**	12. **(A)**	16. **(D)**	20. **(B)**	24. **(D)**
4. **(D)**	9. **(A)**	13. **(D)**	17. **(A)**	21. **(D)**	25. **(A)**
5. **(C)**					

Section 3: Reading

1. **(B)**
2. **(B)**
3. **(D)**
4. **(A)**
5. **sentence 6, paragraph 1**
6. **(A)**
7. **(B)**
8. **(B)**
9. **(C)**
10. **(A)**
11. **(B)**
12. **(A)**
13. **(B)**
14. **(B)**
15. **". . . invented dynamite. When he read . . ."**
16. **(D)**
17. **(C)**
18. **(A)**
19. **(B)**
20. **award**
21. **(C)**
22. **generally**
23. **(D)**
24. **(A)**
25. **(B)**
26. **(D)**
27. **(B)**
28. **(B)**
29. **(C)**
30. **(C)**
31. **brilliant tricks**
32. **purpose**
33. **(B)**
34. **(B)**
35. **(B)**
36. **(D)**
37. **(A)**
38. **(C)**
39. **large**
40. **(B)**
41. **(A)**
42. **(B)**
43. **(B)**
44. **sentence 2, paragraph 3**
45. **(C)**

Writing: Checklist for Essay

❑ The essay answers the topic question.
❑ The point of view or position is clear.
❑ The essay is direct and well-organized.
❑ The sentences are logically connected to each other.
❑ Details and examples support the main idea.
❑ The writer expresses complete thoughts.
❑ The meaning is easy for the reader to understand.
❑ A wide range of vocabulary is used.
❑ Various types of sentences are included.
❑ There are only minor errors in grammar and idioms.
❑ The general topic essay is within a range of 300–350 words.

Model Test 2—Computer-Assisted TOEFL

Section 1: Listening

1. **(B)**	14. **(C)**	27. **(C)**	40. **(A)**
2. **(D)**	15. **(A)**	28. **(B)**	41. **(C)**
3. **(D)**	16. **(B)**	29. **(D)**	42. **(C)**
4. **(B)**	17. **(B)**	30. **(B)**	43. **(A)**
5. **(D)**	18. **(B)**	31. **(C)**	44. **(A)(B)**
6. **(A)**	19. **(A)**	32. **(B)**	45. **(C)**
7. **(B)**	20. **(A)**	33. **(C)**	46. **(C)(D)**
8. **(A)**	21. **(C)**	34. **(D)**	47. **(B)**
9. **(C)**	22. **(B)**	35. **(B)**	48. **(C)**
10. **(A)**	23. **(C)**	36. **(A)(B)**	49. **(B)(A)(C)**
11. **(B)**	24. **(B)**	37. **(C)**	50. **(A)**
12. **(D)**	25. **(B)**	38. **(B)**	
13. **(D)**	26. **(D)**	39. **(D)**	

Section 2: Structure

1. **(A)**	6. **(B)**	11. **(B)**	16. **(C)**	21. **(A)**
2. **(A)**	7. **(A)**	12. **(A)**	17. **(C)**	22. **(A)**
3. **(C)**	8. **(C)**	13. **(A)**	18. **(C)**	23. **(B)**
4. **(D)**	9. **(A)**	14. **(B)**	19. **(A)**	24. **(B)**
5. **(C)**	10. **(A)**	15. **(D)**	20. **(C)**	25. **(B)**

Section 3: Reading

1. (A)	17. (D)	32. sentence 5,
2. (C)	18. signs	paragraph 3
3. (A)	19. (B)	33. damage
4. (A)	20. (C)	34. ". . . solids
5. (D)	21. ". . . a rude	or liquids.
6. (A)	noise. Gestures	One objection . . ."
7. (D)	such as . . ."	35. (A)
8. data	22. (B)	36. (D)
9. (C)	23. interaction	37. (B)
10. problems	24. (D)	38. (A)
11. sentence 2,	25. (D)	39. (A)
paragraph 2	26. (D)	40. (C)
12. (C)	27. (B)	41. (B)
13. (D)	28. (B)	42. (C)
14. sentence 4,	29. (C)	43. sentence 3,
paragraph 1	30. (A)	paragraph 1
15. (A)	31. (C)	44. tamed
16. (B)		45. (A)

Writing: Checklist for Essay

- ❏ The essay answers the topic question.
- ❏ The point of view or position is clear.
- ❏ The essay is direct and well-organized.
- ❏ The sentences are logically connected to each other.
- ❏ Details and examples support the main idea.
- ❏ The writer expresses complete thoughts.
- ❏ The meaning is easy for the reader to understand.
- ❏ A wide range of vocabulary is used.
- ❏ Various types of sentences are included.
- ❏ There are only minor errors in grammar and idioms.
- ❏ The general topic essay is within a range of 300–350 words.

Model Test 3—Computer-Assisted TOEFL

Section 1: Listening

1. (A)	14. (A)	27. (B)	40. (B)
2. (C)	15. (C)	28. (B)	41. (A)
3. (C)	16. (A)	29. (B)	42. (D)
4. (A)	17. (B)	30. (A)	43. (A)
5. (A)	18. (D)	31. (C)	44. (B)
6. (A)	19. (B)	32. (B)	45. (B)
7. (C)	20. (B)	33. (B)	46. (C)
8. (C)	21. (C)	34. (D)	47. (D)
9. (D)	22. (B)	35. (C)	48. (D)
10. (B)	23. (C)	36. (B)	49. (A)(C)
11. (A)	24. (C)	37. (A)	50. (A)
12. (A)	25. (A)	38. (B)(C)	
13. (D)	26. (A)	39. (C)(B)(D)(A)	

Section 2: Structure

1. (C)	6. (A)	11. (C)	16. (C)	21. (C)
2. (B)	7. (C)	12. (B)	17. (B)	22. (A)
3. (A)	8. (D)	13. (B)	18. (B)	23. (C)
4. (B)	9. (C)	14. (B)	19. (A)	24. (A)
5. (B)	10. (A)	15. (D)	20. (A)	25. (D)

Section 3: Reading

1. (A)	18. (C)	33. (D)
2. (D)	19. (A)	34. (D)
3. (C)	20. devastating	35. (D)
4. (D)	21. earthquakes	36. (B)
5. very successful	22. (D)	37. locomotion
6. (A)	23. (B)	38. (C)
7. (C)	24. segmented	39. (C)
8. (D)	25. (C)	40. (C)
9. sentence 4, paragraph 2	26. (A)	41. (A)
10. (C)	27. (A)	42. (A)
11. (C)	28. (B)	43. sentence 2, paragraph 4
12. (A)	29. (C)	44. (A)
13. (B)	30. (A)	45. (C)
14. (C)	31. (C)	
15. (C)	32. ". . . other life forms. Although some insects . . ."	
16. (D)		
17. (D)		

Writing: Checklist for Essay

☐ The essay answers the topic question.
☐ The point of view or position is clear.
☐ The essay is direct and well-organized.
☐ The sentences are logically connected to each other.
☐ Details and examples support the main idea.
☐ The writer expresses complete thoughts.
☐ The meaning is easy for the reader to understand.
☐ A wide range of vocabulary is used.
☐ Various types of sentences are included.
☐ There are only minor errors in grammar and idioms.
☐ The general topic essay is within a range of 300–350 words.

Model Test 4—Next Generation TOEFL

Listening: Independent Listening 1–6

1. **(B)**	11. **(C)**	19. **(B)**	29. **(C)**
2. **(C)**	12. **(B) (C)**	20. **(D)**	30. **(B)**
3. **(A)**	13. **(C)**	21. **(A)**	
4. **(C)**	14. **(C)**	22. **(B) (C)**	
5. **(B)**	15. **(A) YES**	23. **(B)**	
6. **(D)**	**(B) NO**	24. **(A)**	
7. **(B)**	**(C) YES**	25. **(B)**	
8. **(B)**	16. **(D)**	26. **(D)**	
9. **(D)**	17. **(B) (C)**	27. **(B) (D)**	
10. **(B)**	18. **(C)**	28. **(A)**	

Speaking: Checklist for Questions 1 and 2

☐ The talk answers the topic question.
☐ The point of view or position is clear.
☐ The talk is direct and well-organized.
☐ The sentences are logically connected to each other.
☐ Details and examples support the main idea.
☐ The speaker expresses complete thoughts.
☐ The meaning is easy for the listener to comprehend.
☐ A wide range of vocabulary is used.
☐ There are only minor errors in grammar and idioms.
☐ The talk is within a range of 125–150 words.

Speaking: Checklist for Questions 3, 4, 5, 6

☐ The talk answers the topic question.
☐ There are only minor inaccuracies in the content.
☐ The talk is direct and well-organized.
☐ The sentences are logically connected to each other.
☐ Details and examples support the main idea.
☐ The speaker expresses complete thoughts.
☐ The meaning is easy for the listener to comprehend.
☐ A wide range of vocabulary is used.
☐ The speaker paraphrases, using his or her own words.
☐ The speaker credits the lecturer with wording when necessary.
☐ There are only minor errors in grammar and idioms.
☐ The talk is within a range of 125–150 words.

Reading: Independent Reading 1

1. **(C)**	6. **(D)**	11. **(B)**
2. **(C)**	7. **(A)**	12. **(A)**
3. **(A)**	8. **(C)**	13. **(A) (C) (E)**
4. **(A)**	9. **(B)**	
5. **(A)**	10. **(C)**	

Reading: Independent Reading 2

1. **(B)**	6. **(B)**	11. **(C)**
2. **(B)**	7. **(A)**	12. **(B)**
3. **(B)**	8. **(A)**	13. **(B) (E) (F)**
4. **(C)**	9. **(B)**	
5. **(D)**	10. **(B)**	

Reading: Independent Reading 3

1. **(B)**	6. **(B)**	11. **(A)**
2. **(B)**	7. **(A)**	12. **(C)**
3. **(C)**	8. **(C)**	13. **(A) (C) (E)**
4. **(A)**	9. **(D)**	
5. **(B)**	10. **(D)**	

Writing: Checklist for Independent Writing

❑ The essay answers the topic question.
❑ The point of view or position is clear.
❑ The essay is direct and well-organized.
❑ The sentences are logically connected to each other.
❑ Details and examples support the main idea.
❑ The writer expresses complete thoughts.
❑ The meaning is easy for the reader to understand.
❑ A wide range of vocabulary is used.
❑ Various types of sentences are included.
❑ There are only minor errors in grammar and idioms.
❑ The general topic essay is within a range of 300–350 words.

Writing: Checklist for Integrated Writing

❑ The essay answers the topic question.
❑ There are only minor inaccuracies in the content.
❑ The essay is direct and well-organized for the topic.
❑ The sentences are logically connected to each other.
❑ Details and examples support the main idea.
❑ The writer expresses complete thoughts.
❑ The meaning is easy for the reader to comprehend.
❑ A wide range of vocabulary is used.
❑ The writer paraphrases, using his or her own words.
❑ The writer credits the author with wording when necessary.
❑ There are only minor errors in grammar and idioms.
❑ The academic topic essay is within a range of 200–250 words.

EXPLANATORY ANSWERS
AND AUDIO SCRIPTS

NOTE

The Explanatory Answers include the transcript for the Listening Sections of the TOEFL Model Tests included in this book. Note that the Listening Sections always appear as Section 1 of the examinations.

When you take the Model Tests in this book as a preliminary step in your preparation for the actual examination, you should use the compact disks that supplement this book. If you use compact disks, you will hear the audio, but you will not see the visuals. If you use the CD-ROM that supplements the larger version of this book, you will see visuals on your computer screen.

If you have someone read the TOEFL transcript to you, be sure that he or she understands the timing sequences. The reader should work with a stopwatch or with a regular watch with a second hand in order to keep careful track of the timed pauses between questions. The time for the pauses between questions is about 10 seconds. Be sure that the reader speaks clearly and at a moderately paced rate. For results that would be closest to the actual testing situation, it is recommended that three persons be asked to read, since some of the Listening Sections include dialogues.

Model Test 1—Computer-Assisted TOEFL

Section 1: Listening

The Listening Section of the test measures the ability to understand conversations and talks in English. You will use headphones to listen to the conversations and talks. While you are listening, pictures of the speakers or other information will be presented on your computer screen. There are two parts to the Listening Section, with special directions for each part.

On the day of the test, the amount of time you will have to answer all of the questions will appear on the computer screen. The time you spend listening to the test material will not be counted. The listening material and questions about it will be presented only one time. You will not be allowed to take notes or have any paper at your computer. You will both see and hear the questions before the answer choices appear. You can take as much time as you need to select an answer; however, it will be to your advantage to answer the questions as quickly as possible. You may change your answer as many times as you want before you confirm it. After you have confirmed an answer, you will not be able to return to the question.

Before you begin working on the Listening Section, you will have an opportunity to adjust the volume of the sound. You may not be able to change the volume after you have started the test.

QUESTION DIRECTIONS—Part A

In Part A of the Listening Section, you will hear short conversations between two people. In some of the conversations, each person speaks only once. In other conversations, one or both of the people speak more than once. Each conversation is followed by one question about it.

Each question in this part has four answer choices. You should click on the best answer to each question. Answer the questions on the basis of what is stated or implied by the speakers.

Audio

1. Woman: If I were you I'd take the bus to school. Driving in that rush-hour traffic is terrible.
   Man: But by the time the bus gets to my stop, there aren't any seats left.
   Narrator: What is the man's problem?

Answer

(C) Since the man says that there aren't any seats left, it must be concluded that he has to stand when he takes the bus to school. Choice (B) refers to the woman's suggestion, not to the man's response. Choices (A) and (D) are not mentioned and may not be concluded from information in the conversation.

Audio

2. Woman: I'd like to take Dr. Sullivan's section of Physics 100, but my advisor is teaching it too, and I don't want her to be offended.
   Man: Who cares?
   Woman: Well, I don't want to get on her bad side.
   Man: I wouldn't worry about it.
   Narrator: What does the man mean?

Answer

(A) *Who cares* means that it "isn't important" [that her advisor might be offended]. Choice (C) refers to the woman's concern, not to the man's response. Choices (B) and (D) are not mentioned and may not be concluded from information in the conversation.

Audio

3. Man: Let's go to the dance at the Student Center on Friday.
   Woman: Sounds great, but I'm going to a lecture. Thanks for asking me though.
   Narrator: What does the woman imply?

Answer

(C) Because the woman says that the invitation sounds "great" and she thanks the man for asking her, it must be concluded that she would go out with the man on another occasion. Choice (A) is not correct because she responds so positively while refusing the invitation. Choices (B) and (D) are not correct because she has plans to attend a lecture.

Audio

4. Man: That's a nice bike.
   Woman: I got it almost five years ago.
   Man: You did? It looks new.
   Woman :   Yes, it's still in really good shape.
   Narrator: What does the woman mean?

Answer

(A) *In good shape* is an idiomatic expression that means the item is "in good condition." Choice (B) is not correct because the man thinks the bike is new, and the woman says it is in good shape. Choice (C) is not correct because the speakers are talking about a bike that is able to be seen. Choice (D) is not correct because the woman got the bike almost five years ago.

Audio

5. Woman: Would you like some hot coffee or tea?
   Man: I like them both, but I'd rather have something cold.
   Narrator: What does the man want to drink?

Answer

(A) The man says that he would rather have something cold. Choices (B), (C), and (D) refer to what the man likes, not to what he wants.

Audio

6. Woman: How can I get to the shopping center from here? Not the one on campus. The one downtown.
   Man: You can take a bus or a taxi, but it isn't too far to walk.
   Narrator: What does the man suggest the woman do?

Answer

(B) ". . . it isn't too far to walk [to the shopping center]." Choice (A) is not correct because he is already giving the woman information about the shopping center. Choices (C) and (D) are alternative possibilities that the man mentions before making his suggestion.

Audio

7. Man: Have you found a class yet?
   Woman: I'm just checking the schedule now.
   Narrator: What can be inferred about the woman?

Answer

(D) Since the woman says that she is just checking the schedule now, it must be concluded that she has not registered yet. Choice (A) is not correct because she is checking the schedule for a class. Choices (B) and (C) are not mentioned and may not be concluded from information in the conversation.

Audio

8. Woman: Do you mind if I turn on the radio for a while?
   Man: No, I don't mind.
   Narrator: What does the man mean?

Answer

(C) To *not mind* is an idiomatic expression that means the speaker will "not be bothered" by an activity or situation. Choices (A), (B), and (D) are not paraphrases of the expression.

Audio

9. Man: I'm worried about Anna. She's really been depressed lately. All she does is stay in her room all day.

    Woman: That sounds serious. She'd better see someone at the Counseling Center.

    Narrator: What does the woman suggest Anna do?

Answer

(D) "She'd better see someone at the Counseling Center." Choices (A), (B), and (C) are not mentioned and may not be concluded from information in the conversation.

Audio

10. Woman: If you have a few minutes, I'd like to talk with you about my project.

    Man: Please go on.

    Narrator: What does the man mean?

Answer

(C) *Please go on* is an idiomatic expression that means the speaker wants the other person to "continue." Choices (A), (B), and (D) are not paraphrases of the expression.

Audio

11. Woman: Excuse me. I was in line here first.

    Man: Oh, I'm sorry. I didn't realize that you were waiting.

    Narrator: What will the man probably do?

Answer

(B) Since the man apologizes for going ahead of the woman in line, he will most probably allow her to go ahead of him. Choice (A) is not correct because it is the man, not the woman, who apologizes. Choice (C) is not correct because he has already apologized. Choice (D) is not mentioned and may not be concluded from information in the conversation.

Audio

12. Man: The neighbors are going to have another party.

    Woman: Not again!

    Narrator: What does the woman imply?

Answer

(A) *Not again* is an idiomatic expression that means the speaker is impatient with some kind of repeated behavior or activity. Choice (C) is not correct because she does not know about the party until the man informs her. Choices (B) and (D) are not mentioned and may not be concluded from information in the conversation.

Audio

13. Man: You mean Dr. Franklin said you couldn't have an extension?
    Woman: He said it was not his policy.
    Man: Really?
    Woman: Yes, so now I have to work over the holiday weekend.
    Narrator: What had the man assumed?

Answer

(C) Since the man says "Really?" it must be concluded that he is surprised by the professor's response to the woman's request. Choice (D) is not correct because the professor says it was not his policy. Choices (A) and (B) are not mentioned and may not be concluded from information in the conversation.

Audio

14. Man: We really should have left already.
    Woman: Maybe we ought to call and let them know.
    Narrator: What problem do the man and woman have?

Answer

(B) Since the man says that they should have left already, it must be concluded that they are late. Choice (A) is not likely because of the woman's suggestion that they make a call. Choices (C) and (D) are not mentioned and may not be concluded from information in the conversation.

Audio

15. Man: Have you moved out of your apartment yet?
    Woman: No. I'm paid up until the 15th.
    Narrator: What is the woman probably going to do?

Answer

(C) Since the woman says that she has her rent paid until the 15th, she will probably stay where she is living until the 15th. The reference to half a month in Choice (A) refers to the fact that the woman already has her rent paid until the 15th, not to what she will do. Choice (B) is not correct because the woman, not the man, is planning to move. Choice (D) is not correct because the woman mentions having her rent paid.

Audio

16. Woman: Mary Anne took the math placement test.
    Man: So, she *finally* did it!
    Narrator: What had the man assumed about Mary Anne?

Answer

(C) Since the man expresses surprise, it must be concluded that he thought she had not taken the placement test. Choice (A) is not correct because the man was surprised. Choices (B) and (D) are not mentioned and may not be concluded from information in the conversation.

Audio

17. Woman: Where have you been? I haven't seen you in class all week.
    Man: I caught cold, so I stayed in.
    Narrator: What does the man mean?

Answer

(**C**) To *catch cold* is an idiomatic expression that means to "get sick." Choices (A), (B), and (D) are not paraphrases of the expression and may not be concluded from information in the conversation.

QUESTION DIRECTIONS—Part B

In Part B of the Listening Section, you will hear several longer conversations and talks. Each conversation or talk is followed by several questions. The conversations, talks, and questions will not be repeated.

The conversations and talks are about a variety of topics. You do not need special knowledge of the topics to answer the questions correctly. Rather, you should answer each question on the basis of what is stated or implied by the speakers in the conversations or talks.

For most of the questions, you will need to click on the best of four possible answers. Some questions will have special directions. The special directions will appear in a box on the computer screen.

Audio Conversation

Narrator: Listen to a conversation with a professor.

Man: Professor Day, may I see you for a minute?
Woman: Sure. Come on in, Mike. What's the matter?
Man: I've got a problem.
Woman: Okay.
Man: I need your technical writing class. And, I knew I had to have it so I went early to registration, but by the time I got to the front of the line, it was closed. See, my advisor signed my course request and everything. I was just too far back in the line.
Woman: That's a big class already, Mike. If it's closed, that means I have fifty students in it.
Man: I'm not surprised. It's supposed to be a really good class.
Woman: Can't you take it next year? We offer it every fall.
Man: Well, that's the problem. I'm supposed to be graduating this spring. But, of course, I can't graduate without your class.
Woman: I see. In that case, I'll sign an override for you. It looks like there will be fifty-one. Take this form back to the registration area and they'll get you in.
Man: Thanks, Professor Day. I really appreciate this!

Now get ready to answer the questions

Audio
18. What is Mike's problem?

Answer
(D) "I need your technical writing class. . . . In that case, I'll sign an override for you." Choice (A) is not correct because he went early to registration. Choice (B) is not correct because his advisor signed his course request. Choice (C) is not correct because the course will not be taught until fall semester.

Audio
19. What does Mike want Professor Day to do?

Answer
(C) "...I'll sign an override. . . . Take this form back to the registration area and they'll get you in." Choice (D) refers to something that the professor tells Mike to do, not to something that Mike wants the professor to do. Choices (A) and (B) are not mentioned and may not be concluded from information in the conversation.

Audio
20. What does Mike say about graduation?

Answer
(B) "...I can't graduate without your class." Choice (A) is not correct because he plans to graduate in the spring. Choices (C) and (D) are not mentioned and may not be concluded from information in the conversation.

Audio
21. What does Professor Day decide to do?

Answer
(B) ". . . I'll sign an override for you." Choice (A) refers to the suggestion that the professor makes at the beginning of the conversation, not to what she actually decides to do. Choices (C) and (D) are not mentioned and may not be concluded from information in the conversation.

Audio Talk
Narrator: Listen to a talk by a business instructor.

Today's lecture is about the effects of background music on employee performance and retail sales. As you know, every day millions of people in offices and factories around the world do their work to the accompaniment of background music, more commonly known as MUZAK. But did you know that MUZAK is more than a pleasant addition to the environment? Studies show that this seemingly innocent background music can be engineered to control behavior. In fact, MUZAK can improve employee performance by reducing stress, boredom, and fatigue. In one survey, overall productivity increased by thirty percent, although five to ten percent is the average.

The key to MUZAK's success is something called stimulus progression, which means quite simply that the background music starts with a slow, soft song that is low in stimulus value and builds up gradually to an upbeat song that is high in stimulus value. The fastest, loudest sounds are programmed for about ten-thirty in the morning and two-thirty in the afternoon when people are generally starting to tire.

Besides employee performance, MUZAK can increase sales. In supermarkets, slow music can influence shoppers to walk slower and buy more. In restaurants, fast music can cause customers to eat quickly so that the same number of tables may be used to serve more people during peak times such as the lunch hour.

> Now get ready to answer the questions

Audio
22. What is MUZAK?

Answer
(C) ". . . background music, more commonly known as MUZAK." Choice (A) is one kind of MUZAK, but it is not correct because MUZAK can be upbeat songs, too. Choice (B) is one place where MUZAK is played, but it is not correct because MUZAK can be played in the workplace and the supermarket, too. Choice (D) is not correct because MUZAK is more than a pleasant addition to the environment.

Audio
23. What is the average increase in productivity when MUZAK is introduced?

Answer
(B) "In one survey, overall productivity increased by thirty percent, although five to ten percent is the average." Choice (D) refers to one survey, not to the average. Choices (A) and (C) are not mentioned and may not be concluded from information in the talk.

Audio
24. What is stimulus progression?

Answer
(D) ". . . stimulus progression . . . starts with a slow, soft song . . . and builds up . . . to an upbeat song . . . programmed . . . when people are generally starting to tire." Choice (A) refers to the first stage of stimulus progression, not to the total progression. Choices (B) and (C) refer to varieties of MUZAK, not to stimulus progression.

Audio
25. How does MUZAK influence sales in supermarkets?

Answer
(C) "In supermarkets, slow music can influence shoppers to walk slower and buy more." Choice (D) is not correct because it can influence shoppers to buy more. Choices (A) and (B) are not mentioned and may not be concluded from information in the talk.

Audio Announcement
Narrator: Listen to a public service announcement.

Community College understands that everyone who wants to attend college will not be able to come to campus. So, as part of the Distance Learning Program, Community College offers a series of video telecourses to meet the needs of students who prefer to complete coursework in their homes, at their convenience.

These telecourses are regular college credit classes taught on videocassette tapes by a Community College professor. To use the materials for the course, you will need your own VHS-type VCR player. Some telecourses will also be broadcast on KCC7-TV's "Sun-Up Semester." This program airs from six o'clock in the morning to seven-thirty, Monday through Friday, and a complete listing of courses is printed in your regular television guide.

To register for a telecourse, phone the Community College Distance Learning Program at 782-6394. The course syllabus, books, and videotapes will be available at the Community College bookstore. During the first week of classes, your instructor will contact you to discuss the course and answer any questions you might have about the course requirements. Then, throughout the rest of the semester, you can use either an 800 telephone number or an e-mail address to contact your instructor.

> Now get ready to answer the questions

Audio
26. What is this announcement mainly about?

Answer
(C) " . . . Community College offers a series of video telecourses to meet the needs of students who prefer to complete coursework in their homes." Choices (A) and (B) are secondary themes used to develop the main theme of the talk. Choice (D) is not mentioned and may not be concluded from information in the conversation.

Audio
27. Why does the speaker mention the "Sun-Up Semester"?

Answer
(D) "Some telecourses will also be broadcast on KCC7-TV's 'Sun-Up Semester.' " Choice (A) is not correct because students should call the Community College Distance Learning Program to register. Choice (C) is not correct because a listing of courses is printed in the television guide. Choice (B) is not mentioned and may not be concluded from information in the conversation.

Audio
28. How can students register for a course?

Answer
(B) "To register for a telecourse, phone the Community College . . . ." Choice (A) is not correct because the program is designed to meet the needs of students who are not able to come to campus. Choices (C) and (D) are not mentioned and may not be concluded from information in the conversation.

Audio

29. How can students contact the instructor?

Answer

(A) ". . . you can use either an 800 telephone number or an e-mail address to contact your instructor." Choices (B), (C), and (D) are not mentioned and may not be concluded from information in the conversation.

Audio Conversation

Narrator:	Listen to part of a conversation between two friends on campus.
Donna:	Hi, Bill.
Bill:	Hi, Donna. Where have you been? I haven't seen you for weeks.
Donna:	I know. I had to drop out last semester. I thought I had a cold, but it was mono.
Bill:	I'm sorry to hear that. What is mono anyway?
Donna:	It's a virus, actually, that attacks your immune system. You really become susceptible to it when you stay up late, stress out, and get run down. It was my own fault. I just kept going, studying late. I didn't get enough rest. You know the story.
Bill:	Wow! All too well. I'm surprised that we all don't have it.
Donna:	A lot of college students do get it. In fact, it is jokingly called the "college disease." I can tell you though, it's no joke.
Bill:	So how are you now?
Donna:	I'm still tired. But I learned my lesson though. This semester I'm taking twelve hours, and I'm not pushing myself so hard.
Bill:	Good for you. I'm taking twenty-one hours. Sometimes I just don't know why I put so much pressure on myself. If I took one more semester to finish my program, then I wouldn't be so overloaded.
Donna:	Listen, if you get sick like I did, you'll have to drop out and you'll end up with an extra semester anyway. So you might as well slow down.
Bill:	True. Well, it's something to think about. Take care of yourself, Donna.
Donna:	I will. You, too.

> Now get ready to answer the questions

Audio

30. What is the main topic of this conversation?

Answer

(A) "I thought I had a cold, but it was mono. . . . It's a virus. . . ." The work *joke* in Choice (C) refers to the phrase *no joke,* which means something that "isn't funny." Choice (D) is mentioned but is not the main topic of the conversation. Choice (B) is not mentioned and may not be concluded from information in the conversation.

Audio

31. What was the woman's problem?

Answer
(C) "I had to drop out last semester." Choices (A) and (B) are probably true, but they caused her problem; they were not the problem. Choice (D) is not correct because she had to withdraw last semester, not this semester.

Audio
32. Why is mono called the "college disease"?

Answer
(A) "A lot of college students get it [mono]." The work *joke* in Choice (C) refers to the phrase *no joke* which means something that "isn't funny." Choices (B) and (D) are not mentioned and may not be concluded from information in the conversation.

Audio
33. What advice does the woman give the man?

Answer
(C) ". . . if you get sick . . . you'll end up with an extra semester. . . . .So you might as well slow down." The woman warns the man that he will have to drop out of school if he gets sick, but she does not advise him to drop out as in Choice (A). Choices (B) and (D) are not correct because the woman suggests that the man slow down.

Audio Talk
Narrator: Listen to a talk by a college professor.

Now I would like to outline the development of the Sapir-Whorf Hypothesis concerning the relationship between language and culture.

When Edward Sapir was teaching at Yale, Benjamin Lee Whorf enrolled in his class. Whorf was recognized for his investigations of the Hopi language, including his authorship of a grammar book and a dictionary. Even in his early publications, it is clear that he was developing the theory that the very different grammar of Hopi might indicate a different manner of conceiving and perceiving the world on the part of the native speaker of Hopi.

In 1936, he wrote "An American Indian Model of the Universe," which explored the implications of the Hopi verb system with regard to the Hopi conception of space and time.

Whorf is probably best known for his article "The Relation of Habitual Thought and Behavior to Language" and for the three articles that appeared in 1941 in the *Technology Review.*

In these articles, he proposed what he called the principle of "linguistic relativity," which states, at least as a hypothesis, that the grammar of a language influences the manner in which the speaker understands reality and behaves with respect to it.

Since the theory did not emerge until after Whorf had begun to study with Sapir, and since Sapir had most certainly shared in the development of the idea, it came to be called the Sapir-Whorf Hypothesis.

Now get ready to answer the questions

Audio
34. What central theme does the lecture examine?

Answer
(A) "Now I would like to outline the development of the Sapir-Whorf Hypothesis concerning the relationship between language and culture." Choices (B), (C), and (D) are secondary themes that are used to develop the main theme of the lecture.

Audio
35. Which languages did Whorf use in his research?

Answer
(C) "In 1936, he [Whorf] wrote 'An American Indian Model of the Universe,' which explored the implications of the Hopi verb system. . . ." Choice (A) refers to historical linguistics, not to the languages that Whorf used in his research. Choices (B) and (D) are not mentioned and may not be concluded from information in the talk.

Audio
36. According to the lecturer, what is linguistic relativity?

Answer
(C) ". . . 'linguistic relativity,' which states, at least as a hypothesis, that the grammar of a language influences the manner in which the speaker understands reality and behaves with respect to it." Choice (D) is not correct because grammar influences cultural behavior. Choices (A) and (B) are not mentioned and may not be concluded from information in the talk.

Audio
37. What is another name for linguistic relativity?

Answer
(B) ". . . it [linguistic relativity] came to be called the Sapir-Whorf Hypothesis." Choice (A) is incomplete because it does not include the name of Whorf. Choice (C) includes the name of Boas, who contributed to the hypothesis but was not named in it. Choice (D) refers to a paper written by Whorf regarding the Hopi verb system, not to linguistic relativity.

Audio Discussion

Narrator:	Listen to part of a class discussion in an environmental science class.
Dr. Green:	Let's begin our discussion today by defining acid rain. Joanne?
Joanne:	Acid rain is, uh, pollution that results when sulfur dioxide and nitrogen oxide mix with the water vapor in the atmosphere.
Dr. Green:	Good. But why do we call it acid rain, then?
Joanne:	Oh, well, sulfur dioxide and nitrogen oxide combine with water vapor and form sulfuric acid and nitric acid.
Dr. Green:	And the acid corrodes the environment?
Joanne:	It does. According to the book, acid reaches the Earth as rain, sleet, snow, fog, or even mist, but we call all of these various forms of pollution acid rain.

Dr. Green:	Exactly right. Now, who can explain how the sulfur dioxide and nitrogen oxide are introduced into the atmosphere in the first place? Ted?
Ted:	Fossil fuels, mostly. Right?
Dr. Green:	Right. Could you elaborate on that a little?
Ted:	Sure. The fossil fuels can be the result of natural events such as volcanic eruptions or forest fires, but most of the time, they are introduced into the atmosphere by industrial processes like the smelting of metals or the burning of oil, coal, and gas.
Dr. Green:	Anything else we should add to that? Yes, Joanne?
Joanne:	Dr. Green, I think it's important to mention the extent of the damage to areas like the Great Lakes.
Dr. Green:	Good point, Joanne. Acidity in the water and on the shorelines has all but eliminated some of the fish populations once found in the Great Lakes region along the United States-Canadian border. Any other damaging effects?
Ted:	I'm an agriculture major, Dr. Green, so I am more familiar with the large concentrations of acids that have been deposited in the soil around the Great Lakes.
Dr. Green:	And what has happened to the vegetation in that region?
Ted:	Well, the rain has caused a chemical change in the soil, which is absorbed by the roots of plants. The plants don't get the nutrients they need, and as a consequence, they die, and uh…
Dr. Green:	Yes?
Ted:	And it just occurred to me that acid rain is having an adverse effect not only on the environment but also on the economy, especially forestry and agriculture.
Dr. Green:	Excellent deduction. Now, let me give you the good news. In the Great Lakes region that was mentioned in our book, an Air Quality Accord was signed by Canada and the United States about ten years ago to establish limits for the amount of acidic deposits that may flow across international boundaries. Since then, many companies on both sides of the border have installed equipment that limits sulfur dioxide emissions, and some have even changed to fuels that are lower in sulfur content.
Ted:	Excuse me. Isn't it automobile emission that accounts for a high percentage of the nitrogen oxide?
Dr. Green:	Yes, it is, Ted. And that problem presents a somewhat larger challenge to the governments and their agencies.

> Now get ready to answer the questions

Audio

38. What is the topic of this discussion?

Answer

(B) "Let's begin our discussion today by defining acid rain." Choices (A), (C), and (D) are all secondary points of discussion that are used to develop the main topic of the discussion.

Audio
39. What is acid rain?

Answer
(A) "... Acid rain is ... sulfur dioxide and nitrogen oxide [that] combine with water vapor and form sulfuric acid and nitric acid." Choice (C) refers to the result of acid rain, not to a definition of it. Choice (D) is not correct because sulfur dioxide and nitrogen oxide, not just sulfur, combine with water vapor. Choice (B) is not mentioned and may not be concluded from information in the discussion.

Audio
40. In which two ways has the environment been damaged along the Great Lakes?

Answer
(C) (D) "Acidity...has all but eliminated ... fish populations ... in the Great Lakes ... [and] rain has caused a chemical change in the soil. ... Plants don't get the nutrients they need...." Choices (A) and (B) are not mentioned and may not be concluded from information in the discussion.

Audio
41. What are the conditions of the Air Quality Accord?

Answer
(B) "... Air Quality Accord ... to establish limits for the amount of acidic deposits that may flow across international boundaries." Choice (A) refers to the result of the legislation, not to the conditions of it. Choice (C) is not correct because the problem of automobile emissions is a larger challenge to governments and their agencies. Choice (D) is not correct because the fuels are lower in sulfur, but some sulfur still remains in the fuels.

Audio Lecture
Narrator: Listen to part of a lecture in a microbiology class.

Bacteria is the common name for a very large group of one-celled microscopic organisms that, we believe, may be the smallest, simplest, and perhaps even the very first form of cellular life that evolved on Earth. Because they are so small, bacteria must be measured in microns, with one micron measuring about 0.00004 inches long. Most bacteria range from about 0.1 microns to 4 microns wide and 0.2 microns to 50 microns long. So you can understand that they are observable only under a microscope.

There are three main types of bacteria, which are classified according to their shape. The slides that I am going to show you are photographic enlargements of bacteria that I observed under the microscope in the lab earlier today. This slide is an example of bacilli.

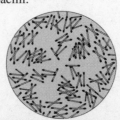

The bacilli are a group of bacteria that occur in the soil and air. As you can see, they are shaped like rods, and if you were to see them in motion, they would be rolling or tumbling under the microscope. These bacilli are largely responsible for food spoilage.

The next slide is a very different shape of bacteria.

It is referred to as the cocci group, and it tends to grow in chains. This example is of the common streptococci that causes strep throat.

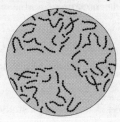

Finally, let's look at the spiral-shaped bacteria called the spirilla. They look a little like corkscrews, and they are responsible for a number of diseases in humans.

Some species of bacteria do cause diseases, but for the most part, bacteria live harmlessly on the skin, in the mouth, and in the intestines. In fact, bacteria are very helpful to researchers. Bacterial cells resemble the cells of other life forms in many ways, and may be studied to give us insights. For example, we have a major research project in genetics in progress here at the University. Since bacteria reproduce very rapidly, we are using them to determine how certain characteristics are inherited.

> Now get ready to answer the questions

Audio
42. What is the topic of this lecture?

Answer
(A) "There are three main types of bacteria. . . . " Choices (B), (C), and (D) are all secondary points of discussion that are used to develop the main topic of discussion.

Audio
43. Which two characteristics are common in bacteria?

Answer

(A) (C) "Bacteria is the common name for a very large group of one-celled microscopic organisms. . . . Bacteria reproduce very rapidly. . . . " Choice (B) is not correct because, for the most part, bacteria live harmlessly on the skin, in the mouth, and in the intestines. Choice (D) is not mentioned and may not be concluded from information in the lecture.

Audio

44. Which of the following slides contain cocci bacteria?

Answer

(B) Visual B is the slide for the cocci bacteria. Visual A is the slide for the bacilli bacteria. Visual C is the slide for the spirilla bacteria.

Audio

45. Why are bacteria being used in the research study at the University?

Answer

(C) "Bacterial cells resemble the cells of other life forms. . . . " Choice (A) is not correct because bacteria cells resemble the cells of other life forms. Choices (B) and (D) are true, but they are not the reasons that bacteria are being used in research studies.

Audio Conversation

Narrator: Listen to part of a conversation between a student and an academic
                advisor on campus.

Man: Dr. Kelly, do you have a minute?
Dr. Kelly: Sure. Come in.
Man: Thanks. I need to talk with you about my sociology class.
Dr. Kelly: Let's see, that would be Sociology 530 with Dr. Brown.
Man: Right. The problem is that when I scheduled that class, it was sup-
                posed to be offered at three o'clock in the afternoon, Tuesdays and
                Thursdays, but for some reason the time has been changed to nine
                in the morning. Since I work mornings, I can't take it at that time.
Dr. Kelly: I see. Well, would you like to drop the class?
Man: Yes, but I also need to pick up another class. I have to be a full-
                time student in order to qualify for my student loan.
Dr. Kelly: So you need at least twelve hours. And you need afternoon classes.
Man: That's right. Or evening classes.
Dr. Kelly: Did you have anything in mind?
Man: Yes. I was considering Sociology 560 or 570. I thought I'd get
                your opinion.
Dr. Kelly: Either one will fit into your program since you are a Soc major,
                and they are both electives. Too bad you can't get a required
                course.
Man: I know, but they all seem to be offered in the morning.
Dr. Kelly: Okay, then. Which one is the most interesting to you?
Man: I'm interested in both of them, but I was thinking since Dr. Brown
                teaches Soc 560, I might prefer that one. I've been trying to take a
                class with her because I hear that she is an excellent professor.

Dr. Kelly: Good. The class is open, and I'll just sign that drop-add form for you to drop 530 and add 560. You can just tell Dr. Brown what happened when you see her in class.

Man: Okay. Thanks a lot, Dr. Kelly. I really appreciate it.

Dr. Kelly: Don't mention it.

> Now get ready to answer the questions

Audio

46. What is the purpose of this conversation?

Answer

(A) "It [the class] was supposed to be offered at three o'clock . . . the time has been changed. . . . " Choice (B) is not correct because the man has a job in the morning that conflicts with his class schedule. Choice (C) is not correct because the man has a student loan. Choice (D) is not correct because the man is already a sociology major.

Audio

47. Why does the man need to take at least twelve hours?

Answer

(B) "I have to be a full-time student in order to qualify for my student loan." Choice (D) is not correct because the courses are electives. Choices (A) and (C) are not mentioned and may not be concluded from information in the lecture.

Audio

48. Why does the man prefer Sociology 560?

Answer

(C) "Dr. Brown teaches Soc 560. . . . I've been trying to take a class with her. . . . " Choice (A) is not correct because it is an elective, not a required course. Choice (B) is not correct because it has been changed to nine in the morning. Choice (D) is not correct because both courses are sociology classes.

Audio

49. What will Dr. Kelly do?

Answer

(B) "...when I scheduled that class, it was supposed to be offered at three o'clock . . . but . . . the time has been changed. . . . " Choice (A) is not correct because the man is trying to register for classes. Choice (C) is not correct because the man already has a student loan. Choice (D) is not correct because the man is a sociology major, and he is trying to add a sociology class.

Audio

50. What will the man probably do after the conversation?

Answer

(B) "... tell Dr. Brown what happened when you see her in class." Choices (A), (C), and (D) are not correct because he will tell Dr. Brown what happened when he goes to her class.

Section 2: Structure

1. **(B)** A cardinal number is used after a noun. *The* is used with an ordinal number before a noun. Choice (A) is incomplete because there is no verb after *who*. Choices (C) and (D) are redundant.

2. **(C)** *But also* is used in correlation with the inclusive *not only*. Choice (B) would be used in correlation with *both*. Choices (A) and (D) are not used in correlation with another inclusive.

3. **(A)** A past form in the condition requires either *would* or *could* and a verb word in the result. Because the past form *planted* is used in the condition, *will* should be *would* in the result.

4. **(D)** In order to refer to an *increase* in the rate of inflation, *rises* should be used. *To raise* means to move to a higher place. *To rise* means to increase.

5. **(C)** A form of *have* with someone such as *General Lee* and a verb word expresses a causative. Choice (A) is an infinitive, not a verb word. Choice (B) is a participle. Choice (D) is an *-ing* form.

6. **(B)** Ideas after exclusives should be expressed by parallel structures. *To hunt* should be *in hunting* to provide for parallelism with the phrase *in planting*.

7. **(B)** *Effect on* is a prepositional idiom. *In* should be *on*.

8. **(A)** *Because* is used before a subject and verb to introduce cause. Choices (B), (C), and (D) are not accepted for statements of cause.

9. **(A)** The word order for a passive sentence is a form of BE followed by a participle. *Call* should be *called*.

10. **(B)** *Form* should be *formation*. Although both are nouns derived from verbs, the *-ation* ending is needed here. *Form* means the structure. *Formation* means the process of forming over time.

11. **(C)** For scientific results, a present form in the condition requires a present or future form in the result. Choices (A), (B), and (D) are not conditional statements.

12. **(A)** Ideas in a series should be expressed by parallel structures. Only *to sell* in Choice (A) provides for parallelism with the infinitive *to increase*. Choices (B), (C), and (D) are not parallel.

13. **(D)** Because it is a prepositional phrase, *as grass* should be *like grass*. *As* functions as a conjunction. *Like* functions as a preposition.

14. **(C)** Ideas in a series should be expressed by parallel structures. *It is* should be deleted to provide for parallelism with the adjectives *interesting*, *informative*, and *easy*.

15. **(C)** Activities of the dead logically establish a point of view in the past. *Lives* should be *lived* in order to maintain the point of view.

16. **(D)** In contrary-to-fact clauses, *were* is the only accepted form of the verb BE. Choices (A), (B), and (C) are forms of the verb BE, but they are not accepted in contrary-to-fact clauses.

17. **(A)** The anticipatory clause *it is generally believed that* introduces a subject and verb, *Java Man...is.* In Choices (B) and (C) the verb *is* is repeated. Choice (D) may be used as a subject clause preceding a main verb, not preceding a subject and verb. "That it is generally believed that Java Man, who lived before the first Ice Age, is the first man-like animal *is* the result of entries in textbooks" would also be correct.

18. **(A)** A verb word must be used in a clause after an impersonal expression. *Is not* should be *not be* after the impersonal expression *it is essential*.

19. **(A)** *Who* should be *whom* because it is the complement of the clause *many people consider*. *Who* functions as a subject. *Whom* functions as a complement.

20. **(B)** Only Choice (B) may be used with a noncount noun such as *money*. Choices (A), (C), and (D) may be used with count nouns.

21. **(D)** *By* expresses means before an *-ing* form. *Refine* should be *refining* after the preposition *by*.

22. **(D)** There must be agreement between pronoun and antecedent. *Their* should be *its* to agree with the singular antecedent *atmosphere*.

23. **(B)** Most adverbs of manner are formed by adding *-ly* to adjectives. *Broad* should be *broadly* to qualify the manner in which the speaking was done.

24. **(D)** An adjective clause modifies a noun in the main clause. *That provides food* modifies *the one*. Choice (A) is a subject and verb without the clause marker *that*. Choice (B) is a clause marker *that* with an *-ing* form, not a verb. Choice (C) is a verb without a clause marker.

25. **(A)** Plural count nouns are used after a number or a reference to a number of items. *Term* should be *terms*.

Section 3: Reading

1. **(B)** "The Process of Photosynthesis" is the best title because it states the main idea of the passage. The other choices are secondary ideas which are used to develop the main idea. Choice (A) describes the process in the form of an equation. In Choice (C), the parts of plants are named because of their roles in the process. Choice (D) is one of the products of the process.

2. **(B)** "…the green parts of plants use carbon dioxide from the atmosphere and release oxygen to it. Oxygen is the product of the reaction." The water referred to in Choice (A) and the carbon referred to in Choice (C) are used in photosynthesis, but neither one is mentioned as occurring in excess as a result of the process. Choice (D) refers to the natural substance in the chloroplasts of plants, not to a chemical combination of carbon dioxide and water.

3. **(D)** "These exchanges are the opposite of those that occur in respiration." Choices (A), (B), and (C) refer to processes which occur in photosynthesis, not to processes which are the opposite.

4. **(A)** "…radiant energy from the sun is stored as chemical energy." In Choice (B), it is water, not energy from the sun, which is conducted from the xylem to the leaves. Choice (C) is not correct because energy from the sun is the source of the chemical energy used in decomposing carbon dioxide and water. Choice (D) is not correct because it is oxygen, not energy, that is released one to one for each molecule of carbon dioxide used.

5. "Except for the usually small percentage used in respiration, the oxygen released in the process diffuses out of the leaf into the atmosphere through stomates." Quotation from sentence 6, paragraph 1.

6. **(A)** In the context of this passage, stored is closest in meaning to retained . Choices (B), (C), and (D) are not accepted definitions of the word.

7. **(B)** "The products of their decomposition [carbon dioxide and water] are recombined into a new compound, which is successively built up into more and more complex substances." Choices (A), (C), and (D) would change the meaning of the sentence.

8. **(B)** In the context of this passage, successively is closest in meaning to in a sequence . Choices (A), (C), and (D) are not accepted definitions of the word.

9. **(C)** "At the same time, a balance of gases is preserved in the atmosphere." Energy from the sun, referred to in Choice (A), and carbon dioxide, referred to in Choice (B), are used in the process of photosynthesis, not produced as a result of it. Choice (D) is not mentioned and may not be concluded from information in the passage.

10. **(A)** Choices (B), (C), and (D) are mentioned in sentences 6 and 7, paragraph 1. Water, not oxygen, is absorbed by the roots.

11. **(B)** The other choices are secondary ideas that are used to develop the main idea, "the Nobel Prizes." Choices (A), (C), and (D) are historically significant to the discussion.

12. **(A)** "The Nobel Prizes…were made available by a fund bequeathed for that purpose…by Alfred Bernhard Nobel." Because of the reference to *bequeath*, it must be concluded that Nobel left money in a will. In Choice (B), Nobel was the founder of the prizes, not a recipient. Choice (C) refers to the place where Nobel was born, not to where he is living now. Since Nobel has bequeathed funds, it must be concluded that he is dead and could not serve as chairman of a committee as in Choice (D).

13. **(B)** In the context of this passage, will refers to a legal document. Choices (A), (C), and (D) are not accepted definitions of the word in this context.

14. **(B)** "The Nobel Prizes, awarded annually…" Because of the reference to *annually*, it must be concluded that the prizes are awarded once a year. Choices (A), (C), and (D) are not mentioned and may not be concluded from information in the passage.

15. "According to the legend, Nobel's death had been erroneously reported in a newspaper, and the focus of the obituary was the fact that Nobel had invented dynamite. When he read this objective summary of his life [the obituary], the great chemist, it is said, decided that he wanted his name to be remembered for something more positive and humanitarian than inventing an explosive that was a potential weapon." The connection between these two sentences is the reference to "the obituary."

16. **(D)** In the context of this passage, outstanding could best be replaced by exceptional. Choices (A), (B), and (C) are not accepted definitions of the word.

17. **(C)** "The Nobel Prizes [are] awarded annually for distinguished work in chemistry, physics, physiology or medicine, literature, and international peace." Since there is no prize for music, a composer, in Choice (C) would not be eligible for an award. Choice (A) could be awarded a prize for literature. Choice (B) would be awarded a prize for medicine. Choice (D) could be awarded a prize for peace.

18. **(A)** Choice (A) is a restatement of the sentence referred to in the passage. To *administer* means to oversee or to manage. Choices (B), (C), and (D) would change the meaning of the original sentence.

19. **(B)** "The prizes are … presented … on December 10 … on the anniversary of his [Alfred Nobel's] death." Choice (A) is not correct because it is a tribute to Nobel, not to the King of Sweden. Choice (D) is not correct because the Nobel Foundation, not the Central Bank of Sweden, administers the trust. Choice (C) is not mentioned and may not be concluded from information in the passage.

20. In the context of this passage, the word award is closest in meaning to prize . No other words or phrases in the **bold** text are close to the meaning of the word prize .

21. **(C)** The other choices are secondary ideas that are used to develop the main idea, "the development of opera." Choices (A), (B), and (D) are historically significant to the discussion.

22. In the context of this passage, the word generally is closest in meaning to usually . No other words or phrases in the **bold** text are close to the meaning of the word usually .

23. **(D)** "The usually accepted date for the beginning of opera as we know it is 1600." Choice (A) refers to Greek tragedy, the inspiration for modern opera. Choices (B) and (C) are not

mentioned and may not be concluded from information in the passage.

24. **(A)** "Although stage plays have been set to music since the era of the ancient Greeks, when the dramas of Sophocles and Aeschylus were accompanied by lyres and flutes, the usually accepted date for the beginning of opera as we know it [the opera] is 1600." Choices (B), (C), and (D) would change the meaning of the sentence.

25. **(B)** "…composer Jacopo Perí produced his famous *Euridice*, generally considered to be the first opera." Choice (A) refers to the form of musical story that inspired Perí, not to the opera that he wrote. Choice (C) refers to the wife of Henry IV for whose marriage the opera was written, not to the title of the opera. Choice (D) refers to the group of musicians who introduced the opera form, not to the title of an opera written by them.

26. **(D)** "As part of the celebration of the marriage of King Henry IV…Jacopo Perí produced his famous *Euridice*." Choice (A) is not correct because *Euridice* was produced in Florence, the native city of King Henry's wife and the place where the wedding was celebrated. Choice (B) refers to Greek tragedy, not to modern opera. Choice (C) is improbable because *Euridice* has become so famous.

27. **(B)** "…a group of Italian musicians called the Camerata began to revive the style of musical story that had been used in Greek tragedy." In Choice (A), musicians in the Camerata were Italian, not Greek. Choice (C) is not correct because the center of the Camerata was Florence, Italy. King Henry IV referred to in Choice (D) was a patron of opera, but the name given to his court was not mentioned and may not be concluded from information in the passage.

28. **(B)** In the context of this passage, revive could best be replaced by

resume . Choices (A), (C), and (D) are not accepted definitions of the word.

29. **(C)** In the context of this passage, plots is closest in meaning to stories . Choices (A), (B), and (D) are not accepted definitions of the word.

30. **(C)** "They called their compositions *opera in musica* or musical works. It is from this phrase that the word 'opera' is borrowed." Choice (A) refers to the origin of the plots for opera, not to the term. Choice (B) is not correct because the Camerata was a group of Italian musicians. Choice (D) refers to the composer of the first opera.

31. "Composers gave in to the demands of singers, writing many operas that were little more than a succession of brilliant tricks for the voice, designed to showcase the splendid voices of the singers who had requested them [brilliant tricks]." Other choices would change the meaning of the sentence.

32. In the context of this passage, the word purpose is closest in meaning to function . No other words or phrases in the **bold** text are close to the meaning of the word function .

33. **(B)** The author's main purpose is to describe the nature of sunspots. Choice (A) is not correct because there is no theory that completely explains sunspots. Choices (C) and (D) are important to the discussion, and provide details that support the main idea.

34. **(B)** In the context of this passage, controversial is closest in meaning to open to debate . Choices (A), (C), and (D) are not accepted definitions of the word.

35. **(B)** "…great storms on the surface of the sun hurl streams of solar particles into the atmosphere." *Storms* refer to disturbances of wind. Choice (A) is not correct because great storms have been identified as the cause of particles being hurled into space. In Choice (C), there are storms, not rivers on the sur-

face of the sun. Choice (D) refers to what happens as a result of the particles being hurled into space.

36. **(D)** In the context of this passage, particles refers to small pieces of matter. Choices (A), (B), and (C) are not accepted definitions of the word.

37. **(A)** "…streams of solar particles [are hurled] into the atmosphere." Because of the reference to *particles*, it must be concluded that the matter is very small. Choices (B), (C), and (D) are not mentioned and may not be concluded from information in the passage.

38. **(C)** Choice (C) is a restatement of the sentence referred to in the passage. The fact that the cooler sunspots may account for their color means that the color could be affected by the cooler temperature.

39. In the context of this passage, the word large is most opposite in meaning to tiny . No other words or phrases in the **bold** text are opposite in meaning to the word tiny .

40. **(B)** "About five percent of the spots are large enough so that they [the spots] can be seen without instruments; consequently, observations of sunspots have been recorded for several thousand years." Choices (A), (C), and (D) would change the meaning of the sentence.

41. **(A)** In the context of this passage, consequently could best be replaced by as a result . Choices (B), (C), and (D) are not accepted definitions of the word.

42. **(B)** "Sunspots…tend to occur in pairs." Choices (A) and (C) refer to possibilities for arrangements, but not to the configuration in which sunspots usually occur. Choice (D) is not mentioned in the range of numbers for sunspots, from one to more than one hundred. The number *one thousand* refers to the number of years sunspots have been recorded, not to the number in a configuration.

43. **(B)** "…several models attempt to relate the phenomenon [of sunspots] to magnetic fields along the lines of longitude from the north and south poles of the sun." Choice (A) is not correct because the magnetic fields are on the sun, not the Earth. Choice (C) is not correct because the storms are on the sun, not on the Earth. Choice (D) is not correct because several models attempt to relate sunspots to magnetic fields.

44. "About 5 percent of all sunspots are large enough so that they can be seen from Earth without instruments; consequently, observations of sunspots have been recorded for thousands of years." Quotation from sentence 2, paragraph 3.

45. **(C)** "…the controversial sunspot theory." Because the theory is controversial, it must be concluded that it is subject to disagreement. Choice (B) is not correct because the theory is controversial. Choices (A) and (D) are not mentioned and may not be concluded from information in the passage.

Writing Section

Question
Many people enjoy participating in sports for recreation; others enjoy participating in the arts. Give the benefits of each, take a position, and defend it.

Outline
Benefits sports
- Group membership—teams
- Good health
- Life lessons—winning and losing

Benefits arts
- Creative outlet
- Cultural lessons—traditions
- Spiritual experience

Divide my time—balance
- Soccer
- Photography

Map

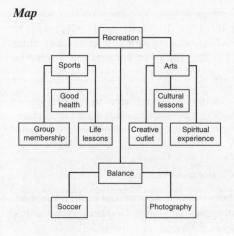

Example Essay

Many people enjoy participating in sports for recreation because it offers an opportunity to be part of a group. As a participant, you can join a team and enjoy all the benefits of membership—shared experiences, travel to other sites to play, and a feeling of belonging. In training for a sport, an exercise routine usually contributes to good health. Probably even more important than group identity and good health are the life lessons that participation in a sport provides. Setting a goal and working toward it, collaborating with others, and putting a plan into action are all good lessons that can be learned on the playing field. How to win graciously and lose gracefully are important not only in playing a game but also in being successful in life.

The arts offer another avenue for recreation. By spending time in artistic endeavors, you can explore your creativity and appreciate or make something beautiful—a picture, a song, or a floral arrangement. Besides the creative outlet, participating in the arts offers an opportunity to learn about the culture and traditions that infuse art with meaning. For some people, participating in or even viewing art can be a spiritual experience. To create and appreciate a beautiful environment is important not only for personal recreation but also because it makes the world a nicer place for everyone.

When I have time for recreational activities, I participate in both sports and the arts. By dividing my time between them, I can take advantage of all the benefits of both types of recreation. I enjoy playing soccer at school, which allows me to be part of a team. The training routine includes both physical and mental exercises. I also enjoy photography, which gives me a creative outlet. I find that alternating these activities provides balance in my life.

Model Test 2—Computer-Assisted TOEFL

Section 1: Listening

The Listening Section of the test measures the ability to understand conversations and talks in English. You will use headphones to listen to the conversations and talks. While you are listening, pictures of the speakers or other information will be presented on your computer screen. There are two parts to the Listening Section, with special directions for each part.

On the day of the test, the amount of time you will have to answer all of the questions will appear on the computer screen. The time you spend listening to the test material will not be counted. The listening material and questions about it will be presented only one time. You will not be allowed to take notes or have any paper at your computer. You will both see and hear the questions before the answer choices appear. You can take as much time as you need to select an answer; however, it will be to your advantage to answer the questions as quickly as possible. You may change your answer as many times as you want before you confirm it. After you have confirmed an answer, you will not be able to return to the question.

Before you begin working on the Listening Section, you will have an opportunity to adjust the volume of the sound. You may not be able to change the volume after you have started the test.

QUESTION DIRECTIONS—Part A

In Part A of the Listening Section, you will hear short conversations between two people. In some of the conversations, each person speaks only once. In other conversations, one or both of the people speak more than once. Each conversation is followed by one question about it.

Each question in this part has four answer choices. You should click on the best answer to each question. Answer the questions on the basis of what is stated or implied by the speakers.

Audio

1. Man: How many did you have for the orientation?
   Woman: Well, let me see. Fifty had registered, but everyone didn't show up. I believe that we had twenty-five from the Middle East and at least fifteen from Latin America.
   Man: You don't mean it!
   Narrator: What had the man assumed?

Answer
(B) *You don't mean it* is an idiomatic expression that means the speaker is surprised. Choice (C) is not correct because the man is surprised by the large turn out. Choices (A) and (D) are not mentioned and may not be concluded from information in the conversation.

Audio

2. Man: Excuse me. Could you tell me when Dr. Smith has office hours?
   Woman: Not really, but there's a sign on the door I think.
   Narrator: What does the woman imply that the man should do?

Answer
(D) Since the woman points out the sign on the door, she implies that the man should look at it. Choices (A), (B), and (C) are not mentioned and may not be concluded from information in the conversation.

Audio

3. Man: I heard that Professor Wilson will let you do a project for extra credit.
   Woman: That's great! I could use some.
   Narrator: What is the woman probably going to do?

Answer

(D) Since the woman expressed interest in and enthusiasm for the opportunity to do a project for extra credit, it must be concluded that she intends to do one. Choice (A) is not correct because the woman is already taking a class from Professor Wilson. Choice (C) is not correct because the reference to "extra" is to extra credit, not to an extra class. Choice (B) is not mentioned and may not be concluded from information in the conversation.

Audio

4. Man: Is Paul angry?
   Woman: If he were, he'd tell us.
   Narrator: What does the woman say about Paul?

Answer

(B) Listen carefully for the distinction between the words *angry* and *hungry*. Because the woman says that Paul would tell them if he were angry, it must be concluded that Paul would tell them if there were a problem. In Choices (A) and (C), the word *angry* is confused with the word *hungry*. Choice (B) refers to what the woman, not the man, thinks about Paul.

Audio

5. Man: I heard you got an A on the final exam. I think you're the only one who did!
   Woman: Not really. There were a couple of other As.
   Narrator: What does the woman mean?

Answer

(D) Since the woman says that there were a couple of As, it must be concluded that several other students received A grades. Choice (B) is not correct because she refers to other As, implying that she received one. Choices (A) and (C) are not mentioned and may not be concluded from information in the conversation.

Audio

6. Woman: Oh, no. It's five o'clock already and I haven't finished studying for the quiz in Dr. Taylor's class.
   Man: Don't worry. That clock is half an hour fast.
   Narrator: What problem does the woman have?

Answer

(C) Since the man says that the clock is fast, it must be concluded that the woman still has time to study. Choice (A) is not correct because a half hour is left. Choice (D) is not correct because the man knows the clock is fast. Choice (B) is not mentioned and may not be concluded from information in the conversation.

Audio

7. Man: It's much better to wait until tomorrow to go. Don't you agree?
   Woman: Yes. I couldn't agree more.
   Narrator: What does the woman mean?

Answer
(B) To *not agree more* means to "agree very much." Choices (A) and (D) misinterpret the phrase *couldn't agree more* as a negative. Choice (C) is not mentioned and may not be concluded from information in the conversation.

Audio
8. Man: I have to go to class because I have a test, but if I could, I'd go with you to the movie.
   Woman: That's too bad. I wish that you could come along.
   Narrator: What is the man going to do?

Answer
(A) The man says that he has to go to class. Choice (B) refers to what the woman, not the man, is going to do. Choices (C) and (D) are not mentioned and may not be concluded from information in the conversation.

Audio
9. Woman: I left a message on your answering machine a couple of days ago.
   Man: Yes. I've been meaning to get back with you.
   Narrator: What does the man mean?

Answer
(C) *Meaning to* is an idiomatic expression that means intention on the part of the speaker. To "get back with" someone means to return a call or otherwise communicate. Choice (B) is not correct because a message was left on the machine. Choice (D) is not correct because the man acknowledges the message. Choice (A) is not mentioned and may not be concluded from information in the conversation.

Audio
10. Man: I think it's my turn.
    Woman: Sorry you had to wait so long. One of the other secretaries is out today.
    Narrator: What does the woman mean?

Answer
(A) To be *out* is an idiomatic expression that means to be "absent." Choices (B), (C), and (D) are not paraphrases of the expression and may not be concluded from information in the conversation.

Audio
11. Man: Could you please tell me what room Dr. Robert Davis is in?
    Woman: Yes, he's in the Math Department on the fourth floor. Check with the secretary before going in, though.
    Narrator: What does the woman suggest that the man do?

Answer
(B) "Check with the secretary before going in . . ." Choice (A) is not correct because the woman has already given him directions to the Math Department. Choice (C) is not correct because the woman tells him to check with the secretary first. Choice (D) is not mentioned and may not be concluded from information in the conversation.

Audio

12. Man: Tom wasn't in class again today!
    Woman: I know. I wonder whether he'll show up for the final exam.
    Narrator: What can be inferred about Tom?

Answer

(D) Since Tom is often absent and there is doubt that he will be present for the final exam, it must be concluded that Tom is not very responsible. Choices (A), (B), and (C) are not mentioned and may not be concluded from information in the conversation.

Audio

13. Man: Hey, Kathy.
    Woman: Hi Ted. How are you doing?
    Man: Fine. Are we still on for tonight?
    Woman: I'm looking forward to it.
    Narrator: What does the man mean?

Answer

(D) *Are we still on* is an idiomatic expression that is used to confirm a date. Choice (C) refers to the woman's feelings, not to the man's feelings. Choices (A) and (B) are not mentioned and may not be concluded from information in the conversation.

Audio

14. Woman: So the course *is* closed. This is terrible! I have to have it to graduate.
    Man: You're okay. Just Dr. Collin's section is closed. There's another section that's still open, but nobody knows who's teaching it. It's marked "staff."
    Narrator: What will the woman probably do?

Answer

(C) Since the woman must have the course to graduate and Dr. Collin's section is closed, she will probably enroll in the section marked "staff." Choice (A) is not correct because Dr. Collin's section is closed. Choice (B) is not correct because the woman is distressed because she is planning to graduate soon. Choice (D) is not correct because she needs the course to graduate and is more interested in the course than in the instructor.

Audio

15. Woman: What's wrong?
    Man: I still haven't received my score on the GMAT test. Maybe I should call to check on it.
    Woman: Don't worry so much. It takes at least six weeks to receive your score.
    Narrator: What does the woman think that the man should do?

Answer

(A) Since the woman says that it takes six weeks to receive the score, she implies that the man should wait for the results to be mailed. Choice (B) refers to the man's plan, not to the woman's suggestion. Choice (C) is not correct because the man has already taken the test and is waiting for the score. Choice (D) is not correct because the woman tells him not to worry.

Audio
16. Man: You've been doing a lot of traveling, haven't you?
    Woman: Yes. We want to make the most of our time here.
    Narrator: What does the woman mean?

Answer
(B) To *make the most of* something is an idiomatic expression that means to "take advantage of" an opportunity. Choices (A), (C), and (D) are not paraphrases of the expression and may not be concluded from information in the conversation.

Audio
17. Woman: Did you get your tickets?
    Man: I talked to Judy about it, and she took care of it for me.
    Narrator: What does the man mean?

Answer
(B) To *take care of something* is an idiomatic expression that means to "be responsible" for it. Choices (A), (C), and (D) are not paraphrases of the expression and may not be concluded from information in the conversation.

QUESTION DIRECTIONS—Part B

In Part B of the Listening Section, you will hear several longer conversations and talks. Each conversation or talk is followed by several questions. The conversations, talks, and questions will not be repeated.

The conversations and talks are about a variety of topics. You do not need special knowledge of the topics to answer the questions correctly. Rather, you should answer each question on the basis of what is stated or implied by the speakers in the conversations or talks.

For most of the questions, you will need to click on the best of four possible answers. Some questions will have special directions. The special directions will appear in a box on the computer screen.

Audio Conversation
    Narrator: Listen to part of a conversation between two classmates on a college campus.

    Man: Did you understand that experiment that Bill mentioned in the group presentation?
    Woman: The one about free fall?
    Man: Right. The one that was conducted on the moon.
    Woman: Sure. The astronaut held a hammer in one hand and a feather in the other. Then he dropped them at the same time...
    Man: ...and both of them hit the ground at the same time.
    Woman: Yes. So that proves Galileo's theory that all objects fall at the same rate in the absence of air resistance.
    Man: Okay. That was the part that was missing for me. The part about air resistance.

Woman:	Oh. Well, since there is no air resistance on the moon, it is the ideal environment for the experiment.
Man:	That makes sense.
Woman:	Actually, the part that surprised me was how much easier it is to lift the hammer on the moon than it is on Earth because of the moon's lower rate of gravitational acceleration.
Man:	But didn't they say that it was just as difficult to push the hammer along the surface when it fell?
Woman:	Right again. Because gravity only governs vertical motion like lifting, but not horizontal motion like pushing.
Man:	Thanks for going over this with me.
Woman:	You're welcome. I really liked the presentation. I think the group did a good job.

> Now get ready to answer the questions

Audio

18. What are the man and woman talking about?

Answer

(B) "Did you understand that experiment that Bill mentioned in the group presentation?" Choices (A), (C), and (D) are not mentioned and may not be concluded from information in the discussion.

Audio

19. Why is the moon an ideal environment for the experiment?

Answer

(A) ". . . since there is no air resistance on the moon, it is the ideal environment for the experiment." Choice (B) refers to the fact that the moon has a lower gravitational acceleration, not that there is no gravitational acceleration. Choices (C) and (D) are true, but they are not the reason the moon is an ideal environment.

Audio

20. Why was it easier to lift the hammer on the moon?

Answer

(A) ". . . much easier . . . to lift the hammer on the moon . . . because of the moon's lower rate of gravitational acceleration." Choice (B) is true, but it is not the reason lifting the hammer on the moon is easier. Choices (C) and (D) are not mentioned and may not be concluded from information in the discussion.

Audio

21. How did the woman feel about the presentation?

Answer

(C) "I really liked the presentation." Choice (A) refers to information about the hammer, not to the entire presentation. Choice (B) is not correct because she liked the presentation. Choice (D) is not mentioned and may not be concluded from information in the discussion.

Audio Conversation

Narrator:	Listen to a conversation between two college students.
Man:	What did you think about the video we were supposed to watch for Professor Stephen's class?
Woman:	I didn't see it. Was it good?
Man:	Really it was. It was about stress.
Woman:	How to relieve stress?
Man:	Not really. More the effects of stress on the national health.
Woman:	Oh.
Man:	But it was interesting, though.
Woman:	Really?
Man:	Yes. I think they said that one out of nine women age forty-five through sixty-five will have a heart attack.
Woman:	I'm surprised at that.
Man:	I was, too. Oh, another thing. They said that women usually don't get the same level of care that men do, so the heart attack is likely to be more serious.
Woman:	Why is that?
Man:	Because many members of the medical profession still think of a heart attack as a male problem, so they don't recognize the symptoms in their women patients.
Woman:	Well, it does sound like an interesting video. I'm going to try to see it before class next time so I'll be ready for the discussion.
Man:	It's on reserve in the library, so you can't check it out, but you can use one of the viewing rooms. It's only an hour long.

> Now get ready to answer the questions

Audio
22. What was the video about?

Answer
(B) "It [the video] was about stress." Choices (A), (C), and (D) are secondary themes used to develop the main theme of the video.

Audio
23. What did the students learn about women?

Answer
(C) "They said that women usually don't get the same level of care that men do. . . ." Choice (D) is not correct because the heart attacks suffered by women are likely to be more serious. Choices (A) and (B) are not mentioned and may not be concluded from information in the conversation.

Audio
24. How did the man feel about the video?

Answer
(B) "Really it was [good]." Choice (A) is not correct because he explains the video to the woman. Choice (C) is not correct because he encourages the woman to view it. Choice (D) is not correct because he was surprised by the report on the number of women who have heart attacks.

Audio
25. What will the woman probably do?

Answer
(B) "It's on reserve in the library. . . ." Choice (A) refers to the fact that the man and woman have already discussed the video, not to what the woman will do. Choice (C) is not correct because tapes on reserve cannot be checked out. Choice (D) refers to what the woman will do after she sees the video.

Audio Lecture
Narrator: Listen to a lecture by an English instructor.

The romance and marriage of Elizabeth Barrett to Robert Browning inspired some of the greatest love poems written in the English language. Elizabeth, without a doubt the greatest woman poet of the Victorian period, was born in Durham County, England, in 1806. Her first important publication was *The Seraphim and Other Poems,* which appeared in 1838.

By 1843, she was so widely recognized that her name was suggested to replace the late Poet Laureate as the official national poet of England. In part because the sovereign was a woman, there was great support for a movement to break with the tradition of a male Poet Laureate. Nevertheless, she lost the competition to William Wordsworth.

A short time later, she married Robert Browning, himself a gifted poet, and they fled to Florence, Italy. A play, *The Barretts of Wimpole Street*, recounts their confrontation with Elizabeth's father and their eventual elopement against his wishes.

While living in Florence, their only son was born. A year later, in 1850, Elizabeth published her collected works, along with a volume of new poems entitled *Sonnets from the Portuguese*, so named because her husband often called her his "Portuguese." *Aurora Leigh*, her longest work, appeared in 1856, only five years before her death in Italy in 1861.

> Now get ready to answer the questions

Audio
26. What is the main topic of this lecture?

Answer
(D) Elizabeth Barrett Browning is the main topic of this lecture. Choices (A), (B), and (C) are secondary topics that are used to develop the main topic of the lecture.

Audio
27. According to the lecturer, what was one reason that Elizabeth Barrett was considered for the title of Poet Laureate?

Answer
(C) "In part because the sovereign was a woman, there was great support for a movement to break with the tradition of a male Poet Laureate." Choice (A) is not correct because Elizabeth Barrett was not married at the time that she was considered for the title of Poet Laureate. Choice (B) is not correct because *Sonnets from the Portuguese* was not published at the time that she was considered for the title. Choice (D) is not mentioned and may not be concluded from information in the talk.

Audio
28. Where did Elizabeth and Robert Browning live after their elopement?

Answer
(B) ". . . she married Robert Browning, himself a gifted poet, and they fled to Florence, Italy." The place in Choice (C) refers to the title of one of Elizabeth's most famous works, *Sonnets from the Portuguese*, not to a place where she lived. The place in Choice (D) refers to the country where she lived before, not after, her marriage. Choice (A) is not mentioned and may not be concluded from information in the talk.

Audio
29. When did Elizabeth Barrett Browning die?

Answer
(D) "*Aurora Leigh*, her longest work, appeared in 1856, only five years before her death in Italy in 1861." Choice (A) refers to the date when Elizabeth Barrett was suggested to replace the Poet Laureate, not to the date of her death. Choice (B) refers to the date when her son was born, one year before she published her collected works in 1850. Choice (C) refers to the date when *Aurora Leigh* was published, five years before her death.

Audio Lecture
Narrator: Listen to a lecture by a biology instructor.

Today's lecture will include the most outstanding achievements in biology as it relates to the medical sciences.

Early in Greek history, Hippocrates began to study the human body and to apply scientific method to the problems of diagnosis and the treatment of diseases. Unlike other physicians of his time, he discarded the theory that disease was caused by the gods. Instead, he kept careful records of symptoms and treatments, indicating the success or failure of the patient's cure. He has been recognized as the father of modern medicine.

About a century later, Aristotle began a scientific study of plants and animals, classifying more than five hundred types on the basis of body structure. Because of his great contribution to the field, Aristotle has been called the father of biology.

By the first century A.D., Dioscorides had collected a vast amount of information on plants, which he recorded in the now famous *Materia Medica,* a book that remained an authoritative reference among physicians for fifteen hundred years.

During the Middle Ages, scientific method was scorned in favor of alchemy. Thus, medicine and biology had advanced very little from the time of the ancients until the seventeenth century when the English physician and anatomist William Harvey discovered a mechanism for the circulation of the blood in the body.

> Now get ready to answer the questions

Audio
30. What is the main topic of this lecture?

Answer
(B) The contributions of biology to medicine are the main topic of this lecture. Choices (A), (C), and (D) are secondary topics that are used to develop the main topic of the lecture.

Audio
31. What was Hippocrates' greatest contribution to medicine?

Answer
(C) "Hippocrates began . . . to apply scientific method to the problems of diagnosis and the treatment of diseases. . . . He kept careful records of symptoms and treatments." Choice (A) refers to the work of Aristotle, not Hippocrates. Choice (D) refers to a theory that Hippocrates discarded in favor of the scientific method, not to his work. Choice (B) is not mentioned and may not be concluded from information in the lecture.

Audio
32. Who is known as the father of biology?

Answer
(B) "Because of his great contribution to the field, Aristotle has been called the father of biology." Choice (A) refers to the father of modern medicine, not to the father of biology. Choice (C) refers to the author of *Materia Medica.* Choice (D) is not mentioned and may not be concluded from information in the lecture.

Audio
33. What was the contribution made to medicine by William Harvey?

Answer
(C) ". . . the English physician and anatomist William Harvey discovered a mechanism for the circulation of the blood in the body." Choice (D) refers to a reference book that was a contribution by Dioscorides. Choices (A) and (B) are not mentioned and may not be concluded from information in the lecture.

Audio Discussion

Narrator:	Listen to part of a class discussion in a sociology class.
Dr. Jackson:	Last class, I asked you to locate some articles about gang activity. Let's just go around the table and share what we found. Tracy, will you begin please?
Tracy:	Okay. Actually, I did a search of sociological studies on gang activity, and I found that gangs have been prevalent for much longer than I had assumed. I was so surprised. For some reason, I thought that gang activity was a fairly recent phenomenon, but actually, one of the largest studies was carried out by Thrasher in 1936.
Dr. Jackson:	Good. Good. I'm pleased that you did that. Thrasher's study is a classic research investigation. Can you summarize the findings?
Tracy:	Sure. First, I should say that the study included more than 1300 gangs with more than 25,000 members. According to Thrasher, a gang is a group that may form spontaneously, but after that, will integrate through conflict and violence. Over time, a spirit of solidarity and an attachment to a local territory form. What is most interesting, besides the long history of gangs in the United States, is the fact that not much has changed over the years. And, oh yes, gang behavior seems pretty similar even across cultures.
Dr. Jackson:	That is interesting.
Bill:	Dr. Jackson, may I go next? I have just a brief comment that seems to fit in here.
Dr. Jackson:	Please.
Bill:	Well, another classic study, much later, about 1987 or 8, I think, by Joan Moore, indicated that gang behavior is probably caused by normal adolescent insecurities—the desire for peer approval, respect, support, acceptance, and, in some cases, protection, if the neighborhood is perceived as dangerous. It seems that gangs take the place of the more childish and acceptable cliques that develop in high schools.
Sandy:	Is it my turn? Well, I looked up the definitions of gang members by police departments and law enforcement agencies. According to the California Youth Gang Task Force, for example, a gang member will be recognizable because of gang-related tattoos, clothing, and paraphernalia like scarves and hats that identify a particular gang, and allow others to confirm that the wearer has a right to be on the gang's turf. And, to follow up on Tracy's comments about the history of gangs, these criteria have been in place for a long time.
Dr. Jackson:	Good job. So far, what I am hearing, though, refers to male gang membership. What about females? Did anyone find any research on their role in gang activity?
Bill:	I did. Although there are a few girl gangs, females are generally not considered members of the male-dominated gang. They are viewed as more of a support system, and an extended social group—friends and girlfriends to party with.
Sandy:	That's what I found, too.

> Now get ready to answer the questions

Audio
34. What was surprising about Thrasher's study?

Answer
(D) ". . . gangs have been prevalent for much longer than I had assumed. I was so surprised." The number in Choice (A) is true, but it was not what surprised the student. Choice (C) is not correct because not much has changed over the years. Choice (B) is not mentioned and may not be concluded from information in the discussion.

Audio
35. According to the study by Moore, what causes gang activity?

Answer
(B) ". . . Joan Moore, indicated that gang behavior is probably caused by normal adolescent insecurities. . . ." Choice (A) refers to a similar form of behavior but not to the cause of gang activity. Choice (C) refers to the neighborhoods where gang activity takes place, but they are not the cause of gang activity. Choice (D) is not mentioned and may not be concluded from information in the discussion.

Audio
36. In which two ways are gang members identified by law enforcement authorities?

Answer
(A) (B) ". . . a gang member will be recognizable because of gang-related tattoos, clothing. . . ." The phrase *research studies* in Choice (D) refers to the research reported in the discussion, not to ways that gang members are identified. Choice (C) is not mentioned and may not be concluded from information in the discussion.

Audio
37. What is the role of women in gangs?

Answer
(C) "They [women] are viewed as more of a support system. . . ." Choice (A) is not correct because women are not considered members of gangs. Choice (D) is not correct because women are part of the extended social group of a gang. Choice (B) is not mentioned and may not be concluded from information in the discussion.

Audio Conversation

Narrator:	Listen to part of a conversation between a student and a professor in the professor's office.
Mary:	Dr. Brown, could I speak with you for a minute?
Dr. Brown:	Sure, Mary. Come in.
Mary:	I'm afraid I have a problem.
Dr. Brown:	Oh?
Mary:	You see, I really like my job here.
Dr. Brown:	That's good. Because we really like having you here.
Mary:	Thank you. But the problem is I won't be able to work here next semester. You see, I have a problem with my schedule at school.
Dr. Brown:	Well, what exactly is the problem?

Mary:	I have a required class at nine o'clock on Monday, Wednesday, and Friday.
Dr. Brown:	Oh. Okay. Remind me what your hours are here.
Mary:	I work from nine to one every day. Which has been great, because I have been able to schedule all my classes in the afternoon, until now.
Dr. Brown:	I see. When does the class end?
Mary:	It's a three-hour class, so it meets for an hour three times a week.
Dr. Brown:	So you're finished at ten.
Mary:	Yes. And it would take me half an hour to get here after class, so you see, I would be an hour and a half late on those days.
Dr. Brown:	Well, we need someone four hours a day. But, how about this— you could come in at ten-thirty on Monday, Wednesday, and Friday, and work until two-thirty on those days. That would give you a fairly late lunch, but if that's not a problem for you, then we can do it.
Mary:	That would be great. So I'd just keep my regular hours on Tuesday and Thursday then.
Dr. Brown:	Right. Listen, Mary. You're a work-study employee, and that means that you have two responsibilities—to work and to study. We know that. As long as you put in the hours to get the job done, we expect to fit your work hours around your school schedule. And don't forget, you can study on the job as long as the work is done first.

> Now get ready to answer the questions

Audio
38. What is Mary's problem?

Answer
(B) "I have a problem with my schedule." Choice (A) is not correct because Mary really likes her job. Choice (D) is not correct because she is a work-study employee. Choice (C) is not mentioned and may not be concluded from information in the conversation.

Audio
39. When is Mary's class next semester?

Answer
(D) "I have a required class at nine o'clock on Monday, Wednesday, and Friday." The phrase *every day* in Choice (A) refers to her work schedule, not to her class schedule. The phrase *ten-thirty on Monday* in Choice (C) refers to the time she will report to work, not to the time for her class. Choice (B) is not mentioned and may not be concluded from information in the conversation.

Audio
40. How does Dr. Brown resolve the problem?

Answer
(A) "...you could come in at ten-thirty . . . and work until two-thirty. . . ." Choice (B) is not correct because she will continue to work four hours a day. Choice (D) is

not correct because he changes her work schedule. Choice (C) is not mentioned and may not be concluded from information in the conversation.

Audio
41. What is a work-study employee?

Answer
(C) "You're a work-study employee, and that means . . . you can study on the job as long as the work is done first." Choice (A) is true, but it is not a complete definition of a work-study employee. Choices (B) and (D) are not mentioned and may not be concluded from information in the conversation.

Audio Lecture
Narrator: Listen to part of a lecture in an engineering class.

In recent years, we have developed several techniques for building more earthquake-resistant structures. For relatively small buildings, all we have to do is bolt the buildings to their foundations and provide some support walls.

These walls are referred to as shear walls in your textbook. They are made of reinforced concrete, and by that I mean concrete with steel rods embedded in it. This not only strengthens the structure but also diminishes the forces that tend to shake a building during a quake. In addition to the shear walls that surround a building, shear walls can be situated in the center of a building around an elevator shaft or a stairwell. This is really an excellent reinforcement. It is commonly known as a shear core, and it, too, contains reinforced concrete.

Walls can also be reinforced, using a technique called cross-bracing. Imagine steel beams that cross diagonally from the ceiling to the floor of each story in a building. Before the walls are finished, you can see a vertical row of steel x's on the structure.

Besides steel reinforcements, engineers have also devised base isolators, which are positioned below the building to absorb the shock of the sideways shaking that can undermine a building and cause it to collapse. Most of the base isolators that are currently being used are made of alternating layers of steel and synthetic rubber. The steel is for strength, but the rubber absorbs shock waves. In higher buildings, a moat of flexible materials allows the building to sway during seismic activity.

The combination of a reinforced structure and flexible materials has been proven to reduce earthquake damage. But even these engineering techniques are insufficient if the building has been constructed on filled ground. Soil used in fill dirt can lose its bearing strength when subjected to the shock waves of an earthquake, and the buildings constructed on it can literally disappear into the Earth.

In areas where earthquakes are known to occur, understanding the terrain and using the techniques we have discussed today can greatly reduce property damage, and can save lives as well.

Now get ready to answer the questions

Audio

42. What is the topic of this lecture?

Answer

(C) ". . . we have developed several techniques for building more earthquake-resist-ant structures." Choices (A), (B), and (D) are all mentioned in the lecture, but they are secondary ideas used to develop the main topic of the lecture.

Audio

43. Which technique is used to reinforce walls?

Answer

(A) "Walls can also be reinforced, using . . . cross-bracing." Choice (B) refers to a structure in the center of a building. Choice (D) refers to a device positioned below the building. Choice (C) is not mentioned and may not be concluded from informa-tion in the lecture.

Audio

44. Which two materials are used in base isolators?

Answer

(A) (B) "Most . . . base isolators . . . are made of . . . layers of steel and synthetic rubber." Choice (C) refers to construction material but not to material used in base isolators. Choice (D) refers to fill dirt.

Audio

45. What happens to fill dirt during an earthquake?

Answer

(C) ". . . fill dirt can lose its bearing strength . . . and the buildings constructed on it can . . . disappear into the Earth." Choice (A) refers to the characteristics of a moat, not to those of fill dirt. Choice (B) refers to the techniques for building earthquake-resistant structures. The phrase *shock waves* in Choice (D) refers to the advantage of rubber, not to a characteristic of fill dirt.

Audio Lecture

Narrator: Listen to part of a lecture in a botany lab. The lab assistant is talk-ing about leaves.

Food and water are carried throughout leaves by their veins. Today we will be looking at some examples of the main types of vein patterns in leaves. The most common are the pinnate and the palmate. This is a pin-nate leaf, which is characteristic of trees like the beech and birch that you see outside this building on campus.

Remember that a pinnate leaf has one large central vein called the midrib, with large veins branching off on each side of it. The midrib extends the full length of the leaf.

Notice how different this leaf is. This is an example of a palmate leaf from a maple tree. A good way to remember this classification is to think of the palm of your hand. In a palmate leaf, there are several main veins of about equal size that originate at the base of the leaf and extend out to the edge of the leaf—like fingers.

A few very narrow leaves are neither pinnate nor palmate. This leaf of grass for example has a parallel pattern.

Several veins extend themselves from the base of the blade to the tip, as you can see here.

Needle leaves are so small that they only have one, or occasionally two, veins in the center of the needle. I don't have a good slide of a needle leaf, but there is a drawing in your lab manual for you to refer to.

Now, I'd like you to turn to chapter three in the manual, and use page fifty-two as a reference for your lab activity. You will find twenty leaves in a plastic bag on your lab table. Please work with your lab partner to classify the veining of each leaf.

Now get ready to answer the questions

Audio
46. Which two types represent the most common vein patterns in leaves?

Answer
(C) (D) "The most common [vein patterns] are the pinnate and the palmate." Choices (A) and (B) refer to vein patterns, but they are not the most common vein patterns.

Audio
47. According to the lecturer, what is a midrib?

Answer
(B) ". . . a pinnate leaf has one large central vein called the midrib . . . [that] extends the full length of the leaf." Choice (A) is not correct because the pinnate leaf, not the midrib, is one of the major classifications. Choice (C) is not correct because the midrib is a central vein in the pinnate, not the parallel, leaf. Choice (D) is not mentioned and may not be concluded from information in the lecture.

Audio

48. How does the lab assistant help students remember the palmate classification?

Answer

(C) "A good way to remember this classification [palmate] is to think of the palm of your hand." Choices (A) and (B) are both true, but she did not use the visual or the explanation as a memory aid. The phrase *lab manual* in Choice (D) refers to a reference for the lab activity, not to a way to remember the classification.

Audio

49. Match the leaves with their vein patterns.

Answer

(B) Pinnate **(A)** Palmate **(C)** Parallel

Audio

50. What will the students probably do after the short lecture?

Answer

(A) ". . . work with your lab partner to classify the veining of each leaf." The word *fifty-two* in Choice (C) refers to the page number in the lab manual, not to the number of pages to read. Choices (B) and (D) are not mentioned and may not be concluded from information in the lecture.

Section 2: Structure

1. **(A)** In some dependent clauses, the clause marker is the subject of the dependent clause. *Which* refers to *the soybeans* and is the subject of the verb *can be used*. Choices (B) and (D) do not have clause markers. Choice (C) is a clause marker that refers to a person, not to *soybeans*.

2. **(A)** Only Choice (A) may be used with a count noun like *species* and a number. Choices (C) and (D) may be used with noncount nouns. Choice (B) may be used with count nouns without a number. "As many species of finch have been identified" would also be correct.

3. **(C)** The verb *had* establishes a point of view in the past. *Serves* should be *served* in order to maintain the point of view.

4. **(D)** There must be agreement between subject and verb. *Produce* should be *produces* to agree with the singular subject *a thunderhead*.

5. **(C)** When the degree of one quality, *the price*, is dependent upon the degree of another quality, *the demand*, two comparatives are required, each of which must be preceded by *the*. Choice (A) is a comparative, but it is not preceded by *the*. Choices (B) and (D) are not accepted comparative forms.

6. **(B)** *The same like* is a combination of *the same as* and *like*. *Like* should be *as* in the phrase with *the same*.

7. **(A)** *Despite of* is a combination of *despite* and *in spite of*. Either *despite* or *in spite of* should be used.

8. **(C)** *So* is used with an adjective to express cause. Choice (A) may be used before a noun, not before an adjective such as *big*. Choices (B) and (D) may not be used to express cause before a clause of result such as *that there are four time zones*. "The United States is very big" would be correct without the clause of result.

9. **(A)** Ideas in a series should be expressed by parallel structures. Only Choice (A) has three parallel *-ing*

forms. Choices (B), (C), and (D) are not parallel.

10. **(A)** *Behave* should be *behavior*. *Behave* is a verb. *Behavior* is a noun.

11. **(B)** *Whom* should be *who* because it is the subject of the verb *is*. *Whom* functions as a complement. *Who* functions as a subject.

12. **(A)** *Such as* is commonly used to introduce an example.

13. **(A)** An introductory verbal phrase should immediately precede the noun that it modifies. Only Choice (A) provides a noun that could be logically modified by the introductory verbal phrase *upon hatching. Swimming, the knowledge,* and *how to swim* could not logically *hatch* as would be implied by Choices (B), (C), and (D).

14. **(B)** Comparative forms are usually followed by *than. Highest* in Choices (A) and (C) may be used to compare more than two decks. Choice (D) correctly compares *this deck* with *any other one*, but *that,* not *than,* follows the comparative.

15. **(D)** A verb word must be used in a clause after the verb *to insist. Will not smoke* should be *not smoke.*

16. **(C)** *Invent* should be *invention. Invent* is a verb. *Invention* is a noun.

17. **(C)** *Calcium* is the subject of the verb *is.* Choice (A) may be used with the word *that.* Choice (B) may be used as a subject clause preceding a main verb. Choice (D) may be used preceding a subject and verb. "It is calcium *that* is necessary for the development of strong bones and teeth." "That calcium is necessary for the development of strong bones and teeth *is* known," and "Although calcium is necessary for strong bones and teeth, *other minerals are* also important" would also be correct.

18. **(C)** *Larger* should be *largest.* Because there are more than two masses of nerve tissue in the human body, a superlative form must be used.

19. **(A)** *Like* is a preposition. *Alike* should be *like.*

20. **(C)** *Capable of* is a prepositional idiom. *To perform* should be *of performing.*

21. **(A)** For scientific results, a present form in the condition requires a present or future form in the result. Only Choice (A) introduces a conditional.

22. **(A)** Repetition of the subject by a subject pronoun is redundant. *It* should be deleted.

23. **(B)** A negative phrase introduces inverted order. *Not until* requires an auxiliary verb, subject, and main verb. In Choice (A) there is no auxiliary. In Choices (C) and (D), there is no subject and no auxiliary.

24. **(B)** The verb phrase *to approve of* requires an *-ing* form in the complement. *-Ing* forms are modified by possessive pronouns. Choices (A) and (D) are infinitives, not *-ing* forms. Choice (C) is an *-ing* form, but it is modified by a subject, not a possessive pronoun.

25. **(B)** *Commonly* should be *common. Commonly* is an adverb. *Common* is an adjective.

Section 3: Reading

1. **(A)** The other choices are secondary ideas that are used to develop the main idea, "Technological Advances in Oceanography." Choices (B), (C), and (D) are important to the discussion, and provide details that support the main idea.

2. **(C)** In the context of this passage, sluggish is closest in meaning to slow moving. Choices (A), (B), and (D) are not accepted definitions of the word.

3. **(A)** "Because of undersea pressure that affected their speech organs, communication among divers was difficult or impossible." Choices (B), (C), and (D) are not mentioned and may not be concluded from information in the passage.

4. **(A)** "Direct observations of the ocean floor are made not only by divers but

also by deep-diving submarines." Choices (B), (C), and (D) are not correct because observations are made by deep-diving submarines as well as by divers.

5. **(D)** "Direct observations of the ocean floor are made ... by deep-diving submarines." Choice (A) is not correct because some of the vehicles are manned. Choice (B) refers to the divers, not to the undersea vehicles. Choice (C) is not correct because undersea vehicles have overcome some of the limitations of divers.

6. **(A)** In the context of this passage, cruise could best be replaced by travel at a constant speed . Choices (B), (C), and (D) are not accepted definitions of the word.

7. **(D)** "Radio-equipped buoys can be operated by remote control in order to transmit information back to the land-based laboratories." Choices (A), (B), and (C) are not mentioned and may not be concluded from information in the passage.

8. In the context of this passage, the word data is closest in meaning to information . No other words or phrases in the **bold** text are close to the meaning of the word information .

9. **(C)** Choices (A), (B) and (D) are mentioned in sentences 8 and 9, paragraph 1. Choice (C) refers to computers, not to satellites.

10. "Some of humankind's most serious problems, especially those [problems] concerning energy and food, may be solved with the help of observations made possible by this new technology." Other choices would change the meaning of the sentence.

11. "Some of humankind's most serious problems, especially those concerning energy and food, may be solved with the help of observations made possible by this new technology." Quotation from sentence 2, paragraph 2.

12. **(C)** "Communication" is the best title because it states the main idea of the

passage. The other choices are all examples of communication that provide details in support of the main idea.

13. **(D)** "Whereas speech is the most advanced form of communication...." Choice (A) is not correct because there are many ways to communicate without speech including signals, signs, symbols, and gestures. Choice (B) is not correct because the advances are dependent upon speech; speech is not dependent upon the advances. Choice (C) is not mentioned and may not be concluded from information in the passage.

14. "For instance, the function of any signal is to impinge upon the environment in such a way that it attracts attention, as for example, the dots and dashes that can be applied in a telegraph circuit." Quotation from sentence 4, paragraph 1.

15. **(A)** In the context of this passage, impinge upon is closest in meaning to intrude . Choices (B), (C), and (D) are not accepted definitions of the word.

16. **(B)** "The basic function of a signal is to impinge upon the environment in such a way that it [the signal] attracts attention, as, for example, the dots and dashes of a telegraph circuit." Choices (A), (C), and (D) would change the meaning of the sentence.

17. **(D)** In the context of this passage, potential could best be replaced by possibility . Choices (A), (B), and (C) are not accepted definitions of the word.

18. "Less adaptable to the codification of words, signs also contain agreed upon meaning; that is, they [signs] convey information in and of themselves [the signs]." Other choices would change the meaning of the sentence.

19. **(B)** In the context of this passage, intricate could best be replaced by complicated . Choices (A), (C), and (D) are not accepted definitions of the word.

20. **(C)** "…applauding in a theater provides performers with an auditory symbol." A telegraph circuit was cited as an example of Choice (A). A stop sign and a barber pole were cited as examples of Choice (B). Waving and handshaking were cited as examples of Choice (D).

21. "A loud smacking of the lips after a meal can be either a kinesthetic and auditory symbol of approval and appreciation, or simply a rude noise. Gestures such as waving and handshaking also communicate certain cultural messages." The connection between the two sentences is the reference to cultural symbols and cultural messages. The second sentence with the word *also* must be mentioned after the first sentence.

22. **(B)** "…means of communication intended to be used for long distances and extended periods are based upon speech. Radio, television, and telephone are only a few." Choices (A), (C), and (D) are not mentioned and may not be concluded from information in the passage.

23. In the context of this passage, the word interaction is closest in meaning to communication. No other words or phrases in the **bold** text are close to the meaning of the word communication.

24. **(D)** Choices (A), (B), and (C) are important to the discussion and provide details that support the primary topic, "the content, form, and effects of fertilizer."

25. **(D)** In the context of this passage, essential could best be replaced by required. Choices (A), (B), and (C) are not accepted definitions of the word.

26. **(D)** Since the last number in the formula represents the percentage content of potash, and since the last number is the smallest, it must be concluded that potash has the smallest percentage content. Choice (A) refers to the number 4 in the formula. Choices (B) and (C) are the substances found in phosphoric acid which refers to the number 8 in the formula.

27. **(B)** Since the content of nitrogen is represented by the first number in the formula, it must be concluded that there is 5 percent nitrogen in the fertilizer. The number in Choice (A) refers to the quantity of numbers in the formula. The percentage in Choice (C) refers to potash. The percentage in Choice (D) refers to phosphoric acid.

28. **(B)** In the context of this passage, designate could best be replaced by specify. Choices (A), (C), and (D) are not accepted definitions of the word.

29. **(C)** "Recently, liquids have shown an increase in popularity…." Choice (A) refers to a form of fertilizers that used to be used, but was found to be less convenient, not to a form that is more popular than ever. Choices (B) and (D) are not correct because solids in the shape of chemical granules are easy to store and apply.

30. **(A)** "Formerly, powders were also used, but these [powders] were found to be less convenient than either solids or liquids." Choices (B), (C), and (D) would change the meaning of the sentence.

31. **(C)** In the context of this passage, convenient is closest in meaning to easy to use. Choices (A), (B), and (D) are not accepted definitions of the word.

32. "Accumulations of chemical fertilizer in the water supply accelerate the growth of algae and, consequently, may disturb the natural cycle of life, contributing to the death of fish." Quotation from sentence 5, paragraph 3.

33. In the context of this passage, the word damage is closest in meaning to harm. No other words or phrases in the **bold** text are close to the meaning of the word harm.

34. "Formerly, powders were also used, but these were found to be less convenient than either solids or liquids. One objection to powders was their propensity to become solid chunks if the bags got damp." The connection between the two sentences is the reference to "powders." The first sentence is a general sentence, and the second sentence is an example.

35. **(A)** The other choices are secondary ideas that are used to develop the main idea, "the evolution of the horse." Choices (B), (C), and (D) are significant steps in the evolution.

36. **(D)** Choices (A), (B), and (C) are mentioned in sentence 3, paragraph 1. The Miocene Age is the earliest historical period mentioned in the passage.

37. **(B)** In the context of this passage, instigated could best be replaced by caused . Choices (A), (C), and (D) are not accepted definitions of the word.

38. **(A)** Choice (A) is a restatement of the sentence referred to in the passage. Since horses appeared 60 million years ago and humans appeared two million years ago, it must be concluded that horses appeared long before human beings.

39. **(A)** "...a horse crossed...from Alaska into the grasslands of Europe." Because of the reference to *grasslands*, it must be concluded that the hipparions migrated to Europe to feed in developing grasslands. Choice (B) is not correct because the European colonists brought horses to North America where the species had become extinct. Choice (D) is not correct because the evolution of the horse has been recorded from its beginnings through all of its evolutionary stages.

40. **(C)** "...smaller than the hipparion, the anchitheres was completely replaced by it." Choice (A) refers to the very early form of the horse, not to the hipparion. Choice (B) is not correct because the hipparion was a more highly evolved form than the anchitheres. Choice (D) is not correct because the hipparion was about the size of a small pony.

41. **(B)** "Less developed and smaller than the hipparion, the anchitheres was completely replaced by it [the hipparion]." Choices (A), (C), and (D) would change the meaning of the sentence.

42. **(C)** In the context of this passage, extinct is closest in meaning to nonexistent . Choices (A), (B), and (D) are not accepted definitions of the word.

43. "Fossil finds provide us not only with detailed information about the horse itself, but also with valuable insights into the migration of herds, and even evidence for speculation about the climatic conditions that could have instigated such migratory behavior." Quotation from sentence 3, paragraph 1.

44. In the context of this passage, tamed is closest in meaning to domesticated . No other words or phrases in the **bold** text are close to the meaning of the word domesticated .

45. **(A)** "At the beginning of the Pliocene Age, a horse...crossed...into the grasslands of Europe. The horse was the hipparion....The hipparion encountered...the anchitheres, which had previously invaded Europe... probably during the Miocene Period." Because the anchitheres invaded Europe during the Miocene and was already there when the hipparion arrived in the Pliocene, it must be concluded that the Miocene Period was prior to the Pliocene Period. By the Pleistocene referred to in Choices (B) and (C), the anchitheres and the hipparion had become extinct. Therefore, the Pleistocene Period must have been after both the Miocene and the Pliocene.

Writing Section

Question:

Read and think about the following statement:

Pets should be treated like family members.

Do you agree or disagree with the statement? Give reasons to support your opinion.

Outline

Agree that pets should be treated like family members
- Children—learn how to care for brother, sister
- Couple—substitute for babies
- Disabled, elderly—help, caring like family members
- Every stage in life

Map

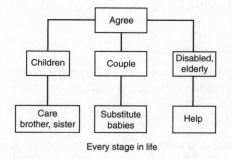

Every stage in life

Example Essay

Although the argument has been made that money spent on pets could better be directed to programs that provide assistance for needy people, I agree that pets should be treated like family members because they live in our homes and interact with us like family members do. Often parents allow children to have pets in order to teach them to be responsible. By feeding, walking, and grooming a dog, children learn to be dependable and kind. Parents expect their children to take care of the pets as if they were members of the family in order to learn these valuable lessons. For many children, a dog or a kitten is also a best friend and a wonderful way to learn how to treat a new brother or sister when the family expands.

Besides the friendship that children enjoy with animals, pets can substitute for the absence of other family members. Sometimes a couple who is unable to have children will adopt pets and treat them like babies. They shower the love on their cats that they might have provided a child and receive affection and companionship in return. Many people who are living alone enjoy the companionship of a pet instead of loved ones who are at a distance or have passed away. The pet becomes a family member for these people and deserves the same kind of treatment that a family member would receive.

Many articles have appeared in the popular press citing the benefits of pets to the disabled and the elderly. In addition to the usual services that pets may provide, such as bringing objects to their owners or helping a vision-impaired owner to walk in unfamiliar surroundings, there is evidence that pets actually extend the life expectancy of their owners. In a real sense, these pets are caring for their owners like family members would, and for this reason, they should be treated like family.

At every stage in life we interact with our pets in the same ways that we interact with family. Children, young married couples, and elderly people have reason to treat their pets like family members.

Model Test 3—Computer-Assisted TOEFL

Section 1: Listening

The Listening Section of the test measures the ability to understand conversations and talks in English. You will use headphones to listen to the conversations and talks. While you are listening, pictures of the speakers or other information will be presented on your computer screen. There are two parts to the Listening Section, with special directions for each part.

On the day of the test, the amount of time you will have to answer all of the questions will appear on the computer screen. The time you spend listening to the test material will not be counted. The listening material and questions about it will be presented only one time. You will not be allowed to take notes or have any paper at your computer. You will both see and hear the questions before the answer choices appear. You can take as much time as you need to select an answer; however, it will be to your advantage to answer the questions as quickly as possible. You may change your answer as many times as you want before you confirm it. After you have confirmed an answer, you will not be able to return to the question.

Before you begin working on the Listening Section, you will have an opportunity to adjust the volume of the sound. You may not be able to change the volume after you have started the test.

QUESTION DIRECTIONS—Part A

In Part A of the Listening Section, you will hear short conversations between two people. In some of the conversations, each person speaks only once. In other conversations, one or both of the people speak more than once. Each conversation is followed by one question about it.

Each question in this part has four answer choices. You should click on the best answer to each question. Answer the questions on the basis of what is stated or implied by the speakers.

Audio
1. Man: It doesn't make any sense for us to go home for spring vacation now.
   Woman: Especially since we'll be graduating in May.
   Narrator: What does the woman mean?

Answer
(A) Since the woman agrees with the man, it must be concluded that she will not go home for spring vacation. Choice (C) is not correct because she will be graduating in May. Choices (B) and (D) are not mentioned and may not be concluded from information in the conversation.

Audio
2. Man: Could you please explain the assignment for Monday, Miss Smith?
   Woman: Certainly. Read the next chapter in your textbook and come to class prepared to discuss what you've read.
   Narrator: What are the speakers talking about?

Answer
(C) From the reference to *the assignment for Monday*, it must be concluded that the speakers are talking about homework. Choices (A), (B), and (D) are all mentioned in the conversation in reference to the assignment.

Audio
3. Woman: Are you ready for this?
   Man: I should be. I've been cramming for the past three days.
   Narrator: What does the man mean?

Answer
(C) *Cramming* is an idiomatic expression that means "studying a lot," especially just before a test. Choices (A), (B), and (D) are not correct because the man is confident about being ready for the test.

Audio
4. Man: I need a book for English two-twenty-one.
   Woman: All of the textbooks are on the shelves in the back of the store.
   Narrator: What will the man probably do?

Answer
(A) Since the man says that he needs a book for an English course, it must be concluded that he will buy the textbook. Choice (C) is not correct because he is already in the bookstore. Choice (D) is not correct because he needs a book for the course. Choice (B) is not mentioned and may not be concluded from information in the conversation.

Audio
5. Man: You're in my economics class, aren't you?
   Woman: Yes. I'm not an economics major, though.
   Man: So, what do you think of Professor Collins?
   Woman: I think he's a great person, but the class just turns me off.
   Narrator: What does the woman mean?

Answer
(A) To *turn someone off* is an idiomatic expression that means the speaker "does not like" something or someone. Choice (D) is not correct because the woman does not like the class. Choice (C) is not correct because the woman thinks Professor Collins is a great person. Choice (B) is not mentioned and may not be concluded from information in the conversation.

Audio
6. Man: Have you made an appointment with Dr. Peterson's T.A. yet?
   Woman: No. And I really can't put it off anymore.
   Narrator: What will the woman probably do?

Answer
(A) To *not put off* is an idiomatic expression that means to "stop postponing." Choices (B) and (C) are not correct because the woman has not made an appointment yet. Choice (D) is not mentioned and may not be concluded from information in the conversation.

Audio
7. Woman: How do you like American food?
   Man: I'm used to it now.
   Narrator: What does the man mean?

Answer
(C) To be *used to something* is an idiomatic expression that means to be "accustomed to" something. Choices (A), (B), and (D) are not paraphrases of the expression and may not be concluded from information in the conversation.

Audio
8. Woman: Are you still studying? It's two o'clock in the morning.
   Man: I know. I just can't seem to get caught up.
   Narrator: What does the man mean?

Answer
(C) To *get caught up* is an idiomatic expression that means to "bring work or assignments up to date." Choice (B) is not correct because the man says he knows what time it is. Choices (A) and (D) are not mentioned and may not be concluded from information in the conversation.

Audio
9. Man: It's your turn to call the names on the list if you want to.
   Woman: I think I'll pass this time.
   Narrator: What is the woman going to do?

Answer
(D) To *pass* is an idiomatic expression that means to "agree to lose a turn." Choices (A), (B), and (C) are not paraphrases of the expression and may not be concluded from information in the conversation.

Audio
10. Woman: I'm pretty sure that the deadline for applications has passed.
    Man: Why don't you let me look into it for you?
    Narrator: What does the man mean?

Answer
(B) To *look into something* is an idiomatic expression that means to "investigate." Choice (A) refers to the woman's conclusion, not to the man's intention. Choices (C) and (D) are not mentioned and may not be concluded from information in the conversation.

Audio
11. Man: This is the first time I've had to get a tutor.
    Woman: What seems to be the problem?
    Man: Well, I understand the lectures but I get mixed up when I try to read the book.
    Narrator: What does the man mean?

Answer
(A) To *get mixed up* is an idiomatic expression that means to "become confused." Choice (C) is not correct because the man understands the lectures. Choices (B) and (D) are not mentioned and may not be concluded from information in the conversation.

Audio

12. Man: The paper isn't due until next week.
    Woman: Yes, I know. But I wanted to turn it in ahead of time if that's all
                    right.
    Narrator: What does the woman mean?

Answer

(A) To *turn in* is an idiomatic expression that means to "submit." *Ahead of time*
means "early." Choice (C) is not correct because she wants to turn in the paper
before it is due. Choice (D) is not correct because she is ready to turn in the paper.
Choice (B) is not mentioned and may not be concluded from information in the conversation.

Audio

13. Man: I can't stand this class!
    Woman: Well, you might as well get used to it. You have to take it in order
                    to graduate.
    Narrator: What does the woman say about the class?

Answer

(D) "You have to take it [the class] in order to graduate." Choice (A) refers to the
man's attitude, not to the woman's opinion. Choice (B) is not correct because the
class is required for graduation. Choice (C) is not mentioned and may not be concluded from information in the conversation.

Audio

14. Woman: How are you going to get ready for an oral final?
    Man: The professor said we should study alone, but the T.A. said to get
                    into a study group and quiz each other.
    Narrator: What did the T.A. suggest the students do?

Answer

(A) ". . . the T.A. said to get into a study group and quiz each other." Choice (B)
refers to the type of exam that they will be given, not to the T.A.'s suggestion.
Choice (C) refers to quizzes, but the T.A. suggests that they "quiz each other," which
means to ask each other questions. Choice (D) is not correct because the professor
recommends studying alone, not in a group.

Audio

15. Man: I need an advisor's signature on my course request form. Could I
                    make an appointment, please?
    Woman: Oh, well, you don't need to make an appointment. Just wait here.
                    I'll get a pen.
    Narrator: What is the woman going to do?

Answer

(C) Since the woman goes to get a pen, it must be concluded that she will sign the
form. Choice (A) is not correct because the woman says he doesn't need an appointment. Choice (B) refers to the pen that the woman, not the man, will use. Choice (D)
is not correct because the man is asked to wait for the woman.

Audio

16. Woman: Thanks for reading my paper.
    Man: Sure. This copy looks good. Why don't you just hand it in?
    Woman: No, I'd better make one more draft.
    Narrator: What is the woman going to do?

Answer

(A) "I'd better make one more draft." A "draft" is a revision of written work. Choice (D) refers to the man's suggestion, not to what the woman is going to do. Choices (B) and (C) are not mentioned and may not be concluded from information in the conversation.

Audio

17. Woman: Your loan payment is due on the first. Oh, sorry, the computer has you scheduled for the fifth.
    Man: That's good. That's what I thought.
    Narrator: What had the man assumed about the loan payment?

Answer

(B) "That's what I thought [that the computer . . . scheduled for the fifth]. Choice (C) refers to the woman's original statement, not to her final conclusion. Choice (D) is not correct because payments are still due. Choice (A) refers to an error made by the woman, not the computer.

QUESTION DIRECTIONS—Part B

In Part B of the Listening Section, you will hear several longer conversations and talks. Each conversation or talk is followed by several questions. The conversations, talks, and questions will not be repeated.

The conversations and talks are about a variety of topics. You do not need special knowledge of the topics to answer the questions correctly. Rather, you should answer each question on the basis of what is stated or implied by the speakers in the conversations or talks.

For most of the questions, you will need to click on the best of four possible answers. Some questions will have special directions. The special directions will appear in a box on the computer screen.

Audio Conversation

Narrator: Listen to a conversation between a student and a professor.

Woman: Hello, Professor Hayes. I'm Betty Peterson. I'm in your senior seminar this semester.
Man: Oh, yes, Betty. How are you?
Woman: Just fine, thanks. I'm here because I'm applying for graduate school, and I need three letters of recommendation. Would you be willing to write me one?
Man: Why yes, Betty. I'd be happy to. I think you are an excellent candidate for graduate school. Are you applying here or to another university?

Woman:	Here. That's why I think your letter is so important. Everyone on the selection committee knows and respects you.
Man:	Let's see, Dr. Warren is the chair of that committee, isn't she?
Woman:	Yes. So, if you would just write the letter to her, that would be great.
Man:	Okay. And when do you need this? I don't recall the deadline for applications.
Woman:	The committee meets on April 30, so all the materials must be submitted before then.
Man:	All right. I'll send it directly to her office.
Woman:	Thank you. I really appreciate it.
Man:	You're welcome. Glad to do it.

> Now get ready to answer the questions

Audio

18. Why did Betty see Professor Hayes?

Answer

(D) ". . . I need three letters of recommendation. Would you be willing to write me one?" Choice (A) is not correct because Betty is already in the professor's seminar class. Choice (C) refers to additional information that the professor gives to Betty, not to the purpose of her visit. Choice (B) is not mentioned and may not be concluded from information in the conversation.

Audio

19. What does Professor Hayes think about Betty?

Answer

(B) "I think you are an excellent candidate for graduate school." Choice (A) is not correct because Betty is already taking the seminar. Choice (D) is not correct because the professor does not recall the deadline for applications. Choice (C) is not mentioned and may not be concluded from information in the conversation.

Audio

20. Who will decide whether Betty is accepted to the program?

Answer

(B) "The committee meets on April 30." Choices (A) and (D) refer to the person who will receive the letter, not to who will make the decision. Choice (C) refers to the person who will make a recommendation.

Audio

21. When does Betty need to submit all her materials?

Answer

(C) "The committee meets on April 30, so all the materials must be submitted before then." Choice (A) is not correct because the materials must be submitted before April 30. Choices (B) and (D) are not mentioned and may not be concluded from information in the conversation.

Audio Lecture

Narrator: Listen to a lecture by a history professor.

I know that this is probably a digression from the topic of today's lecture, but it is worth noting that although England no longer ruled her former colonies after the eighteenth century, she controlled trade with them by selling products so cheaply that it was not possible for the new countries to manufacture and compete with English prices. To maintain this favorable balance of trade, England went to fantastic lengths to keep secret the advanced manufacturing processes upon which such a monopoly depended.

Enterprising Americans made all kinds of ingenious attempts to smuggle drawings for the most modern machines out of England, but it was an Englishman, Samuel Slater, who finally succeeded.

Although textile workers were forbidden to emigrate, Slater traveled to the United States in secret. Determined to take nothing in writing, he memorized the intricate designs for all the machines in an English textile mill, and in partnership with Moses Brown, a Quaker merchant, recreated the mill in Rhode Island.

Forty-five years later, in part as a result of the initial model by Slater and Brown, America had changed from a country of small farmers and craftsmen to an industrial nation in competition with England.

> Now get ready to answer the questions

Audio

22. Who is the speaker?

Answer

(B) Because the speaker is introduced as a professor of history and discusses trade during the eighteenth century, it must be concluded that she is a professor of history. It is not as probable that the lecturers mentioned in Choices (A), (C), and (D) would discuss this topic.

Audio

23. According to the speaker, how did England control trade in the eighteenth century?

Answer

(C) "To maintain this favorable balance of trade, England went to fantastic lengths to keep secret the advanced manufacturing processes. . . ." Choice (D) is not correct because the colony [America], not England, stole the plans. Choices (A) and (B) are not mentioned and may not be concluded from information in the talk.

Audio

24. What did Samuel Slater do?

Answer

(C) "Determined to take nothing in writing, he [Slater] memorized the intricate designs for all the machines in an English textile mill. . . ." Choices (A) and (B) are not correct because Slater, in partnership with Brown, opened a mill in the United

States in the state of Rhode Island. Choice (D) is not correct because he took nothing in writing.

Audio
25. What happened as a result of the Slater-Brown partnership?

Answer
(A) ". . . in part as a result of Slater and Brown, America had changed from a country of small farmers and craftsmen to an industrial nation. . . ." Choices (B), (C), and (D) are not mentioned and may not be concluded from information in the talk.

Audio Conversation

Narrator:	Listen to part of a conversation between a student and an employee in the bookstore on campus.
Man:	Hi. I understand that I can reserve textbooks for next semester.
Woman:	That's right. If you know what courses you will be taking, we can have your order waiting for you the week before classes start.
Man:	Great! This semester I couldn't get two of my books until three weeks into the semester because you ran out of them before I made it to the bookstore.
Woman:	That has been a problem for a lot of students, and that's why we are trying this system. If we know that you want them, we can order books right away instead of waiting until faculty members place their orders for the whole class.
Man:	What do I have to do?
Woman:	Just fill out one of these forms. Be sure that you include both the course number and the section number for each course because different instructors may not be using the same books. Then pay for your books at the register, and we'll place the order.
Man:	Then do I just stop by the bookstore at the beginning of the semester?
Woman:	There's a space for your phone number on the form. We'll call you as soon as they come in. Sometimes we get them before the end of the current semester.
Man:	That would be great. Then I could take them home with me over the break to get a head start on the reading.
Woman:	Quite a few students do that now.

Now get ready to answer the questions

Audio
26. What is the purpose of this conversation?

Answer
(A) "I understand that I can reserve textbooks for next semester." Choice (B) is true, but it is a comment, not the purpose of the conversation. Choice (C) is not correct because the faculty member, not the woman, orders books for the whole class. Choice (D) is not mentioned and may not be concluded from information in the conversation.

Audio

27. What was the man's problem last semester?

Answer

(B) "This semester I couldn't get two of my books until three weeks into the semester. . . ." Choice (C) is not correct because he received his books three weeks after the semester started. Choice (D) refers to this semester, not last semester. Choice (A) is not mentioned and may not be concluded from information in the conversation.

Audio

28. How can the man order books?

Answer

(B) "Just fill out one of these forms. . . . Then pay for your books . . . and we'll place the order." Choice (A) is true but refers to ordering books for the whole class. Choices (C) and (D) are not mentioned and may not be concluded from information in the conversation.

Audio

29. How will the man know that the books have arrived?

Answer

(B) "We'll call you as soon as they [the books] come in." Choice (C) refers to the student's question about receiving his books, not how he will know when the books arrive. The word *form* in Choice (A) refers to the system for ordering books, not to the way to know that books have arrived. Choice (D) is not mentioned and may not be concluded from information in the conversation.

Audio Talk

Narrator: Listen to a talk by a college instructor in an English class.

So many different kinds of writing have been called essays, it is difficult to define exactly what an essay is. Perhaps the best way is to point out four characteristics that are true of most essays. First, an essay is about one topic. It does not start with one subject and digress to another and another. Second, although a few essays are long enough to be considered a small book, most essays are short. Five hundred words is the most common length for an essay. Third, an essay is written in prose, not poetry. True, Alexander Pope did call two of his poems essays, but that word is part of a title, and after all, the "Essay on Man" and the "Essay on Criticism" really are not essays at all. They are long poems. Fourth, and probably most important, an essay is personal. It is the work of one person whose purpose is to share a thought, idea, or point of view. Let me also state here that since an essay is always personal, the term "personal essay" is redundant. Now, taking into consideration all of these characteristics, perhaps we can now define an essay as a short, prose composition that has a personal viewpoint that discusses one topic. With that in mind, let's brainstorm some topics for your first essay assignment.

Now get ready to answer the questions

Audio
30. What is the instructor defining?

Answer
(A) "So many different kinds of writing have been called essays, it is difficult to define exactly what an essay is." Choices (B), (C), and (D) are secondary themes used to develop a definition of the essay.

Audio
31. What is the main point of the talk?

Answer
(C) ". . . four characteristics that are true of most essays." Choices (A), (B), and (D) are secondary themes used to develop the main theme of the talk.

Audio
32. According to the talk, which of the characteristics are NOT true of an essay?

Answer
(B) ". . . an essay [is] a short, prose composition with a personal viewpoint that discusses one topic." Choice (B) is not correct because an essay is written in prose, not poetry. Choices (A), (C), and (D) are all included in the definition.

Audio
33. What will the students probably do as an assignment?

Answer
(B) ". . . let's brainstorm some topics for your first essay assignment." Choices (A), (C), and (D) are not mentioned and may not be concluded from information in the conversation.

Audio Talk
Narrator: Listen to a talk by a guest speaker in a history class.

Thomas Jefferson was a statesman, a dipomat, an author, and an architect. Not a gifted public speaker, Thomas Jefferson was most talented as a literary draftsman. Sent to Congress by the Virginia Convention in 1775, he was elected to the committee to draft a declaration of independence from England. Although John Adams and Benjamin Franklin also served on the committee, the composition of the Declaration of Independence belongs indisputably to Jefferson. In 1779, Jefferson was elected governor of the state of Virginia, an office he held until Congress appointed him to succeed Franklin as U.S. minister to France. Upon returning to Washington, he accepted the position of secretary of state.

Although Jefferson was a Republican, he at first tried to cooperate with Alexander Hamilton, a Federalist who was first among President Washington's advisors. When he concluded that Hamilton was really in favor of a monarchy, hostility between the two men sharpened.

Having served as vice-president in John Adams' administration, Jefferson ran for president in the election of 1800. He and Federalist Aaron Burr received an identical vote, but the Republican Congress elected to approve Jefferson as president. The most outstanding accomplishment of his administration was the purchase of the Louisiana Territory from France in 1803. He was easily re-elected in 1804. When he left office four years later, he returned here to Monticello, where he promoted the formation of a liberal university for Virginia.

> Now get ready to answer the questions

Audio
34. What is the main purpose of this talk?

Answer
(D) The main purpose of this talk is to summarize Jefferson's life. Choices (A), (B), and (C) are secondary themes in the life of Jefferson.

Audio
35. Jefferson was a member of which political group?

Answer
(C) "Although Jefferson was a Republican, he at first tried to cooperate with Alexander Hamilton, a Federalist. . . ." Choice (A) refers to Jefferson's opinion of Hamilton's political affiliation. Choice (B) refers to Hamilton, not Jefferson. Choice (D) is not mentioned and may not be concluded from information in the talk.

Audio
36. How did Jefferson become president?

Answer
(B) "He [Jefferson] and Federalist Aaron Burr received an identical vote, but the Republican Congress elected to approve Jefferson as president." Choice (A) is not correct because Jefferson and Burr received an identical vote. Choices (C) and (D) are not mentioned and may not be concluded from information in the conversation.

Audio
37. According to the lecturer, what was it that Jefferson was NOT?

Answer
(A) "Thomas Jefferson was a statesman, a diplomat, an author, and an architect. . . . Not a gifted public speaker, he was most talented as a literary draftsman." Choices (B), (C), and (D) are all mentioned as attributes of Jefferson.

Audio Lecture
Narrator: Listen to part of a lecture on geology.

Fossils are the remains of organisms that have been preserved. Some of the most common fossils are shells, skeletons, leaves, and insects. They are occasionally preserved in ice, but most have been buried in mud or sand that collects at the bottom of bodies of water, especially lakes, swamps, and oceans. In order for fossils to form, the animals and plants must be buried quickly; otherwise, the organisms will disintegrate. If they are buried in loose sediment, the soft tissues will begin to decay. But the harder structures such as bones and shells will remain intact for much longer. After years of pressure from the layers of sediment above them, the lower layers of sediment turn into rock, encapsulating the organisms.

There are several different mineral processes that continue the fossilization of organisms in the sedimentary rocks. A few plants and animals become fossilized after mineral-rich water soaks into the pores and openings in the hard tissues of the plant or animal. In these fossils, the original body of the organism is strengthened by the infusion of mineral deposits, and every detail of the organism is preserved. But in most fossils, the minerals in the water dissolve the original organism, leaving a fossil mold. Minerals continue to be deposited in the mold at the same time, a process that results in the replacement of the living organism by a mineral deposit of exactly the same shape. In the casts of these molds, the internal features of the organism are not preserved, but the outer structure is accurate in every detail. Sometimes the fine shapes of even very fragile feathers and fur are preserved by mineral replacement.

Although the fossil record is incomplete, the composite of fossil findings chronicles the forms of life that existed at various periods in the past. In a sense, the fossil record is a history of life. The location of fossils in layers of undisturbed sedimentary rock shows not only which groups of organisms lived at approximately the same time but also indicates the order in which they were buried, that is, their relative ages. Plants and animals on the lower layers are presumed to be older than those buried after them in the layers above.

> Now get ready to answer the questions

Audio
38. What are the two most common places where fossils may be found?

Answer
(B) (C) "They [fossils] are occasionally preserved in ice, but most have been buried in mud or sand . . . at the bottom . . . of water. . . . " Choice (A) refers to a place where fossils are occasionally preserved, not the most usual place. Choice (D) refers to the location of the mud and sand, under water.

Audio
39. The professor briefly explains a process. Summarize the process by putting the events in order.

Answer
(C) (B) (D) (A) ". . . animals and plants must be buried quickly . . . mineral-rich water soaks into the . . . plant or animal. . . . Minerals in the water dissolve the original organism, leaving a fossil mold."

Audio
40. What is lost in the process of replacement?

Answer
(B) ". . . the internal features of the organism are not preserved. . . ." Choice (A) is not correct because the shapes of fragile feathers and fur are preserved. The word

minerals in Choice (C) refers to a part of the process, not to what is lost in the process. Choice (D) is not correct because the mold is left.

Audio

41. Why are the layers of sedimentary rock important to the fossil record?

Answer

(A) "The location of fossils in layers of . . . sedimentary rock shows . . . the order in which they were buried, that is, their relative ages." Choice (B) is true, but it is not the reason that the layers are important to the fossil record. Choice (C) is not correct because the mineral water dissolves the organisms. Choice (D) is not correct because plants and animals buried in the same layers of rock lived at approximately the same time.

Audio Conversation

Narrator: Listen to part of a conversation between a student and a secretary on campus.

Woman: Let me see if I understand this. You have completed all of your course work for graduation.

Man: Right.

Woman: But you didn't apply to graduate.

Man: Right.

Woman: But you want to graduate this semester.

Man: Yes, and I thought I would, automatically. I mean, I didn't understand that I had to do anything.

Woman: Who is your advisor?

Man: I'm not sure. I have been sort of advising myself.

Woman: You have?

Man: It's not that hard. The requirements are all spelled out in the catalog, and I have just been taking the required courses, and keeping track of all my grades. Here's my latest transcript, and as you can see, I've got all the credits I need.

Woman: So you don't even have a signed program of study.

Man: Not signed, no. But I have a program of study. I used the program in the catalog.

Woman: I know. But I am talking about a form that is filed by your advisor.

Man: No, I don't have that.

Woman: Okay. The first thing we need to do is to assign you an advisor to go over all your transcripts and help you create a program of study.

Man: How long will that take?

Woman: We'll try to get you in to see someone today. If you really have been able to take all the requirements, then there shouldn't be anything missing from the program and your advisor can sign it and also help you apply for graduation. But if you have misread the catalog or failed to take a critical course, then you may not be eligible for graduation. All I can tell you right now is that you have enough hours to graduate, but only an academic advisor can verify that you have completed the correct course work.

Man:	Oh no. You mean I might not graduate?
Woman:	I don't know. Let's make that appointment and go from there.

> Now get ready to answer the questions

Audio

42. Why didn't the man apply for graduation?

Answer

(D) ". . . I thought I would, [graduate] automatically." Choice (A) is not correct because the student believes he has completed all of the course work for graduation. Choice (B) is not correct because he has enough hours to graduate. Choice (C) is true but does not explain why the man did not apply for graduation.

Audio

43. How did the man select his courses?

Answer

(A) "The requirements are . . . in the catalog. . . ." Choice (B) is not correct because the man has to explain how he selected his courses. Choice (C) is not correct because the man did not have a program of study. Choice (D) is not correct because the man did not have an advisor.

Audio

44. What does the woman suggest?

Answer

(B) "The first thing we need to do is to assign you an advisor. . . ." Choice (A) is not correct because the man may have taken the required courses. Choice (C) is not correct because the man referred to the requirements in the catalog. Choice (D) is not correct because the man has his latest transcript with him.

Audio

45. What is the man's problem?

Answer

(B) ". . . if you . . . failed to take a critical course, then you may not be eligible for graduation." Choice (A) is not correct because the man is told that he has enough hours to graduate. Choice (C) is not correct because the woman will try to get the man in to see someone that day. Choice (D) is not mentioned and may not be concluded from information in the conversation.

Audio Discussion

Narrator:	Listen to part of a class discussion about American English.
Dr. Wilson:	Because the United States is so large, and has such a diverse population, several major dialect regions have been identified. The question is whether there is one universally acceptable standard of American English. Any thoughts?
Laura:	Dr. Wilson? I know that the two articles we read both argued that no dialect is inherently better than any other. Isn't that right?

Dr. Wilson:	Yes, I would say so. Since this is a linguistics class, the articles were written by linguists, and from a linguistic point of view, all dialects of a language are of equal value.
Laura:	Okay. And that is because all dialects can express everything that is necessary for a language community to communicate.
Dr. Wilson:	Precisely. But, I think you are going somewhere with this argument.
Laura:	I am. All dialects are linguistically equal, but are they equal socially? In other words, aren't some dialects more well-respected than others?
Dr. Wilson:	Interesting observation. In fact, your comment anticipates our assignment for the next class period when we will discuss standard dialects. For now, let me just say that, although there are several definitions of a standard dialect, the definition that we will use for our class is this: A standard dialect is the dialect that is selected as the educational model.
Laura:	Does that mean that the dialect of the schools is the standard?
Dr. Wilson:	Exactly.
Vicki:	Now I have a question.
Dr. Wilson:	Okay.
Vicki:	In different regions of the country, the pronunciation is very different, so the schools in each of these regions would have a different standard dialect. Isn't there a standard for the whole country?
Dr. Wilson:	Indeed, there is. Standard English has a common grammar and vocabulary. These are the basic building blocks of a dialect. The pronunciation is an accent, not a dialect. So the accent may be regional, but as long as the grammar and vocabulary are standard, the school is teaching the standard American English dialect with, let's say, a Southern accent or a New York accent.
Vicki:	So an accent is different from a dialect?
Dr. Wilson:	Technically, yes. However, certain accents tend to attach themselves to particular dialects.
Laura:	Oh, I see. So there is a standard accent, too, then.
Dr. Wilson:	Some linguists would say no, there isn't. But a number of sociologists would answer your question in a different way. Some accents are associated with a higher socioeconomic class and, therefore, tend to be the preferred standard accent in schools.
Laura:	I think I understand. There isn't anything inherently better about any dialect or accent, but the prestige of the social group that uses it makes some more desirable than others, so they are chosen for the language of the schools, and become the standard.
Dr. Wilson:	Well said.

> Now get ready to answer the questions

Audio

46. In which class would this discussion probably take place?

Answer

(C) "Since this is a linguistics class, the articles were written by linguists. . . ."
Choices (A), (B), and (D) are subjects that are referred to in the discussion, but they are not the class in which the discussion takes place.

Audio
47. According to the discussion, what is the definition of a standard dialect?

Answer
(D) "A standard dialect is the dialect that is selected as the educational model." Choice (B) is not correct because all dialects of a language are of equal value. Choice (C) is true of all dialects, but it is not the definition of a standard dialect. Choice (A) is not mentioned and may not be concluded from information in the discussion.

Audio
48. What is the linguistic perspective put forward in the articles that were assigned?

Answer
(D) ". . . from a linguistic point of view, all dialects of a language are of equal value." Choice (A) is not correct because the accents taught with a standard grammar may be regional accents. Choice (B) is not correct because the school may teach a standard dialect with a regional accent. Choice (C) is not correct because several major dialect regions have been identified.

Audio
49. Which two linguistic components are included in a dialect?

Answer
(A) (C) "Standard English has a common grammar and vocabulary. These [grammar and vocabulary] are the basic building blocks of a dialect." Choice (B) refers to accent, not dialect. Choice (D) is not mentioned and may not be concluded from information in the discussion.

Audio
50. What do sociologists tell us about accents?

Answer
(A) "Some accents are associated with a higher socioeconomic class and, therefore, tend to be the preferred standard accent in schools." Choice (B) is not correct because the prestige of a social group makes a dialect more desirable. Choice (D) refers to the linguistic perspective of accents, not the sociological perspective. Choice (C) is not mentioned and may not be concluded from information in the discussion.

Section 2: Structure

1. **(C)** *Most* is used before a noncount noun to express a quantity that is larger than half the amount. A singular verb follows the noncount noun. Choice (A) does not have a verb. In Choice (B), the verb is before, not after the noun. In Choice (D), *the* is used before *most*.

2. **(B)** An adjective is used before *enough* to express sufficiency. In Choice (A), *goodly* is ungrammatical. The adverbial form of the adjective *good* is *well*. In Choice (C), *as* is unnecessary and incorrect. In Choice (D), the adjective is used after, not before *enough*.

3. **(A)** *Responsible for* is a prepositional idiom. *Responsible the* should be *responsible for the*.

4. **(B)** A form of BE is used with the participle in passive sentences. *Practice* should be *practiced*.

5. **(B)** There must be agreement between pronoun and antecedent. *Which* should be *who* to refer to the antecedent *Shirley Temple Black*. *Which* refers to things. *Who* refers to persons.

6. **(A)** *The* can be used before a noncount noun that is followed by a qualifying phrase. *Population* should be *the population* before the qualifying phrase *of the Americas*.

7. **(C)** An adjective clause modifies a noun in the main clause. *That the earliest cultures evolved* modifies *the way*. Choice (A) is a clause marker *that* and a noun. Choice (B) is a verb and a noun. Choice (D) is a clause marker *which* and a noun.

8. **(D)** Comparative forms are usually followed by *than*. After the comparative *more reasonable, as* should be *than*.

9. **(C)** *There* introduces inverted order, but there must still be agreement between subject and verb. *Has been* should be *have been* to agree with the plural subject *two major factions*.

10. **(A)** In order to refer to occupying a place on the battlefields, *lain* should be used. *To lay* means to put in a place, and the participle is *laid*. *To lie* means to occupy a place, and the participle is *lain*.

11. **(C)** A sentence has a subject and a verb. Choice (A) is redundant because the subject pronoun *it* is used consecutively with the subject *calculus*. Choice (B) has the marker *that* to introduce a main clause. Choice (D) is redundant because it has a verb that replaces the main verb *can reduce*.

12. **(B)** Subject-verb order and a negative verb with *either* expresses negative agreement. Negative agreement with *neither* requires verb-subject order and an affirmative verb. In Choice (A), verb-subject order is reversed. In Choice (C), verb-subject order is reversed, and *neither* is used at the beginning, not at the end of the clause. In Choice (D) *either*, not *neither*, is used with verb-subject order and an affirmative verb. "Neither does Mexico" would also be correct.

13. **(B)** *Large* should be *largest*. Because there were more than two ethnic groups, a superlative form must be used.

14. **(B)** The determiner *a* is used before a singular count noun. *Results* should be *result*.

15. **(D)** A sentence has a subject and a verb. Choice (A) does not have a verb. Choices (B) and (C) introduce a main clause subject and verb.

16. **(C)** The anticipatory clause *it is accepted that* introduces a subject and verb, *the formation...began*. Choices (A), (B), and (D) are incomplete and ungrammatical.

17. **(B)** When the degree of one quality, *the heat,* is dependent upon the degree of another quality, *the humidity,* two comparatives are used, each preceded by *the*. *The worst* should be *the worse* because it is a comparative.

18. **(B)** A dependent clause modifies an independent clause. *Which are* should be *are* to provide a verb for the subject *statistical data,* of the independent clause.

19. **(A)** The word order for a passive sentence is a form of BE followed by a participle. Only Choice (A) has the correct word order. Choice (B) does not have a BE form. Choice (C) has a HAVE, not a BE form. Choice (D) is a present tense verb, not BE followed by a participle.

20. **(A)** *Despite of* is a combination of *despite* and *in spite of.* Either *despite* or *in spite of* should be used.

21. **(C)** Subject-verb order is used in the clause after a question word connector such as *how much.* In Choice (A), subject-verb order is reversed. In Choice (B), the auxiliary *does* is unnecessary and incorrect. In Choice (D), the verb *are* is repetitive. "The Consumer Price Index lists how much every car *is*" would also be correct.

22. **(A)** Because it is a prepositional phrase, in a comparison *as every nation* should be *like every nation. As* functions as a conjunction. *Like* functions as a preposition.

23. **(C)** A logical conclusion about the past is expressed by *must have* and a participle. Choices (A), (B), and (D) are not logical because they imply that the theater will act to restore itself.

24. **(A)** The verb *thought* establishes a point of view in the past. *Will* should be *would* in order to maintain the point of view.

25. **(D)** Ideas in a series should be expressed by parallel structures. *To plant* should be *planting* to provide for parallelism with the *-ing* forms *plowing* and *rotating.*

Section 3: Reading

1. **(A)** "Webster's Work" is the best title because it states the main idea of the passage. Choice (B) is not correct because Webster's dictionaries represent only part of the work referred to in the passage. Choices (C) and (D) are mentioned briefly in the discussion, but are not the most important topics.

2. **(D)** In the context of this passage, inadequate could best be replaced by unsatisfactory. Choices (A), (B), and (C) are not accepted definitions of the word.

3. **(C)** "…he discovered how inadequate the available schoolbooks were for the children of a new and independent nation…. In response to the need for truly American textbooks, Webster published *A Grammatical Institute of the English Language.*" Choice (A) is a result of having written *A Grammatical Institute,* not a reason for writing it. Choice (B) is not correct because British books were available, but not appropriate. Choice (D) is not mentioned and may not be concluded from information in the passage.

4. **(D)** "…*The American Spelling Book*…provided him with a considerable income for the rest of his life." Choices (A), (B), and (C) are all publications by Webster, but the income afforded by each is not mentioned and may not be concluded from information in the passage.

5. In the context of this passage, popular is closest in meaning to the phrase very successful. No other words or phrases in the **bold** text are close to the meaning of the word popular.

6. **(A)** In the context of this passage, considerable is closest in meaning to large. Choices (B), (C), and (D) are not accepted definitions of the word.

7. **(C)** "Published…in 1828, *An American Dictionary of the English Language* has become the recognized authority for usage…." Choice (A)

refers to the date that Webster finished his study of English and began writing the dictionary. Choice (B) refers to the date that Webster began work on the dictionary. Choice (D) refers to the date that Webster finished writing the dictionary, not to the date that it was published.

8. **(D)** "Webster's purpose in writing it [the dictionary] was to demonstrate that the American language was developing distinct meanings, pronunciations, and spellings from those of British English." Choices (A), (B), and (C) would change the meaning of the sentence.

9. "Webster's purpose in writing it [an American dictionary] was to demonstrate that the American language was developing distinct meanings, pronunciations, and spellings from those of British English." Quotation from sentence 4, paragraph 2.

10. **(C)** In the context of this passage, distinct is closest in meaning to different. Choices (A), (B), and (D) are not accepted definitions.

11. **(C)** "He [Webster] is responsible for advancing the form color...instead of colour." Choices (A), (B), and (D) are British English spellings.

12. **(A)** Choice (A) is the author's main purpose because the passage refers to the San Andreas Fault specifically. The general information referred to in Choices (B), (C), and (D) is not mentioned and may not be concluded from information in the passage.

13. **(B)** "The San Andreas Fault is a fracture at the congruence of two major plates of the Earth's crust." Choice (A) refers to the plates, not to the fracture. Choices (C) and (D) refer to the results of the movement along the fracture, not to the fault.

14. **(C)** In the context of this passage, originates could best be replaced by begins. Choices (A), (B), and (D) are not accepted definitions of the word.

15. **(C)** "Its western side always moves north in relation to its eastern side." Choices (A), (B), and (D) are not correct because the western side always moves north, not in any other direction.

16. **(D)** "The total net slip along the San Andreas Fault and the length of time it [the fault] has been active..." Choices (A), (B), and (C) would change the meaning of the sentence.

17. **(D)** Intermittent means occasional. Choices (A), (B), and (C) are not accepted definitions of the word.

18. **(C)** "Tremors are not unusual along the San Andreas Fault...." Choice (B) is not correct because tremors are not unusual. Choices (A) and (D) are not mentioned and may not be concluded from information in the passage.

19. **(A)** "Californians have long anticipated the recurrence of what they refer to as the 'Big One,' a chain reaction of destructive earthquakes...." Choices (B), (C), or (D) would change the meaning of the sentence.

20. In the context of this passage, devastating is closest in meaning to destructive. No other words or phrases in the **bold** text are close to the meaning of the word destructive.

21. "Californians have long anticipated the recurrence of what they refer to as the 'Big One,' a chain reaction of destructive earthquakes that would measure near 8 on the Richter scale, similar in intensity to those [earthquakes] that occurred in 1857 and 1906." Other choices would change the meaning of the sentence.

22. **(D)** "...the San Andreas Fault...runs north in an irregular line...." The word uneven in Choice (D) means irregular. Choice (A) is not correct because the line is irregular. Choices (B) and (C) are not mentioned and may not be concluded from information in the passage.

23. **(B)** "The Structure of an Insect" is the best title because it states the main idea of the passage. Choice (C) is a

secondary idea that is used to develop the main idea. Choices (A) and (D) are not mentioned and may not be concluded from information in the passage.

24. In the context of this passage, the word segmented is closest in meaning to subdivided . No other words or phrases in the **bold** text are close to the meaning of the word subdivided .

25. **(C)** "Features of the mouth parts are very helpful in classifying the many kinds of insects." Choices (A), (B), and (D) are discussed, but not as a basis for classification.

26. **(A)** In the context of this passage, the word normal is closest in meaning to common . Choices (B), (C), and (D) are not accepted definitions of the word.

27. **(A)** "A labrum above and a labium below are similar to an upper and lower lip." Choice (B) is compared to Choice (D). Choice (C) is discussed, but not compared to anything.

28. **(B)** "…the coiled drinking tube… called the proboscis…[is] composed…of modified maxillae." Choice (A) refers to food, not to the proboscis that is used in reaching it. Choices (C) and (D) are not mentioned and may not be concluded from information in the passage.

29. **(C)** "In a mosquito or an aphid, mandibles and maxillae are modified to sharp stylets." The insect referred to in choice (A) has mandibles similar to jaws, not sharp stylets. The insect referred to in Choice (B) has a proboscis. The insect referred to in Choice (D) has a spongelike mouth pad.

30. **(A)** In the context of this passage, drill through could best be replaced by penetrate . Choices (B), (C), and (D) are not accepted definitions of the phrase.

31. **(C)** "In a housefly, the expanding labium forms a spongelike mouth pad that it [the housefly] can use to stamp over the surface of food." Choices (A), (B), and (D) would change the meaning of the sentence.

32. "An active part of the natural food cycle, insects provide nutrition for animals and devour waste products of other life forms. Although some insects, like the cockroach, have remained essentially unchanged for eons, most insects adapt readily to changing environmental conditions." The connection between the two sentences occurs on the paragraph level. The first sentence in the paragraph introduces the idea that insects are adaptable, and the four sentences that follow provide examples. The inserted sentence is a conclusion that reinforces the first sentence.

33. **(D)** Because the passage is a statement of scientific facts written from an objective point of view, it must be concluded that the purpose is to inform. Choices (A) and (B) are improbable because the passage is not written from a subjective point of view. Choice (C) is improbable because of the scientific content.

34. **(D)** The primary topic is the characteristics of protozoans. Choices (A), (B), and (C) are important to the discussion and provide details that support the primary topic.

35. **(D)** In the context of this passage, minute could best be replaced by very small . Choices (A), (B), and (C) are not accepted definitions of the word.

36. **(B)** "The protozoans…[consist] of a single cell of protoplasm…." Choices (A), (C), and (D) are not correct because the cell of a protozoan is composed of protoplasm.

37. In the context of this passage, locomotion is closest in meaning to motility . No other words or phrases in the **bold** text are close to the meaning of the word motility .

38. **(C)** Choice (C) is a restatement of the sentence referred to in the passage. *Motility* means the manner of movement. Choices (A), (B), and (D) would change the meaning of the original sentence.

39. **(C)** "The Sarcodina, which include amoebae...." Choices (A) and (B) refer to two other groups of protozoans that do not include amoebae. Choice (D) refers to the basis of classification for the three major groups of protozoans.

40. **(C)** "...a large nucleus that regulates growth but decomposes during reproduction..." Choice (A) refers to the small, not the large, nucleus. Choice (B) is not correct because the small nucleus contains the genetic code for the large nucleus. Choice (D) is not correct because the large nucleus decomposes during reproduction.

41. **(A)** "Protozoans are considered animals because...they do not live on simple organic compounds." Choices (B) and (C) refer to characteristics of some protozoans, not to a reason why they are considered animals. Choice (D) is not correct because they have only one cell, although current research is calling that into question.

42. **(A)** "They [protozoans] are fantastically diverse, but three major groups may be identified on the basis of their motility." Choices (B), (C), and (D) would change the meaning of the sentence.

43. "Current research into this phenomenon along with investigations carried out with advanced microscopes may necessitate a redefinition of what constitutes a protozoan, even calling into question the basic premise that they [protozoans] have only one cell." Quotation from sentence 2, paragraph 4.

44. **(A)** In the context of this passage, uniformly is closest in meaning to in the same way . Choices (B), (C), and (D) are not accepted definitions of the word.

45. **(C)** Choice (A) is mentioned in sentence 3, paragraph 4. Choice (B) is mentioned in sentence 1, paragraph 1. Choice (D) is mentioned in sentence 4, paragraph 4. Protozoans consist of a single cell, although in the case of Ciliata, the cell may have a larger nucleus and a smaller nucleus.

Writing Section

Question:
Many people have learned a foreign language in their own country; others have learned a foreign language in the country in which it is spoken. Which is better? Give the advantages of each and support your viewpoint.

Outline
Advantages own country
• Teacher has similar experience—can use L1
• Cheaper than foreign travel
• Less stressful

Advantages foreign country
• Natural speech—accent + idioms
• Cultural context—behaviors
• Opportunities

My opinion—intermediate proficiency own country + advanced abroad

Map

Intermediate own country
Advanced abroad

Example Essay

There are many advantages to learning a language in your own country. In the first place, it is quite a lot cheaper than it would be to travel to the country where the language is spoken. The cost of airfare, living accommodations, food, and tuition at a foreign school can be prohibitively high. In addition, there is less stress involved in learning in a familiar environment. Studying abroad requires that you speak the foreign language all the time to accomplish basic activities. Although it is an opportunity to use the language daily in a real setting, it can be very wearing. Finally, it is advantageous to have teachers who speak your native language because they have gone through the same stages of learning the foreign language that you are experiencing, and they know how to explain the new language by relating it to the native language.

Nevertheless, an argument can be made for learning a language in the country in which it is spoken. Only there can you truly hear the accent and idioms of natural speech. Being surrounded by the foreign language allows you to acquire nuances that elude the classroom. It is also beneficial to learn the language within the context of the culture so that you can learn the behaviors that accompany language. For example, learning how to order in a restaurant when you are right there with native speakers will also let you see how to behave in a restaurant in the foreign country. Finally, there are often opportunities that occur while you are in another country. Friendships can result in invitations to spend time with native speakers in their homes, and possibilities can present themselves for work or study in the foreign country.

In my opinion, the best way to learn a language is to achieve an intermediate level of proficiency in your own country and then to travel to the country where the language is spoken to make progress from the intermediate to the advanced level. By using this plan, you can benefit from the advantages of both options.

Model Test 4—Next Generation TOEFL

Listening Section

This is the Listening Section of the Next Generation TOEFL Model Test. This section tests your ability to understand campus conversations and academic lectures. During the test, you will respond to two conversations and four lectures. You will hear each conversation and lecture one time. You may take notes while you listen. You may use your notes to answer the questions. After each conversation or lecture, you will have five or six questions to answer. Choose the best answer for multiple-choice questions. Follow the directions on the page or on the screen for computer-assisted questions. Click on **OK** and **Next** to go to the next question. You cannot return to previous questions. You have 25 minutes to answer all of the questions. A clock on the screen will show you how much time you have to complete your answers for the section. The clock does not count the time you are listening to the conversations and lectures.

Independent Listening 1: "Career Counseling"

Audio Conversation

Narrator: Now get ready to listen to a conversation and take notes about it.
Listen to a conversation on campus between two students. They are both in their last year of college.

Man: I wish I were as sure about my future as you seem to be. I . . . I really don't know what I want to do after I graduate.

Woman: Well, have you talked with a counselor over at the Office of Career Development?

Man: No. . . . I talked to my academic advisor, though.

Woman: That's good, but it's really better to see someone who specializes in helping people make career decisions. You see, an academic advisor is there to help you work out your academic program. You know, figure out what your major is going to be and which courses to take and all that. But a career counselor has a lot of experience and resources to help you decide what you want to do in the work world.

Man: Did you see a career counselor?

Woman: I sure did. Last semester. I was . . . well, I didn't even know what I would be good at, for a career, I mean. So I made an appointment at the Office of Career Development, and I talked with a counselor.

Man: Do you remember who it was?

Woman: Sure. It was Ruth Jackson.

Man: Oh, but since I'm interested in careers for math majors, probably I should see someone else.

Woman: Not really. Any of the counselors can help you. Look, first I took some aptitude tests and something called a . . . uh . . . I think it was called a *career inventory*. Anyway, I took several tests, and then the counselor gave me some ideas about different careers. I even went to some group sessions with some other students for a few weeks. Mrs. Jackson was the group leader, so um that's how I met her, and then I just sort of naturally started making my appointments with her when I needed some advice.

Man: It sounds like it took a lot of time. I'm so busy already.

Woman: Well, it did take time. Probably three hours for the tests, and I think I went to maybe four group sessions, and then I saw Ruth a couple of times. I guess about nine or ten hours probably. But it was worth it.

Man: So, is that why you decided to go into library science? Because of the tests and everything?

Woman: In part. But, mostly it was because of the internship. You see, I also got my internship through the Office of Career Development. And when I was working as an intern in the public library, it all sort of came together for me. I really liked what I was doing, and I realized that I didn't want the internship to end.

Man: And you get paid for working there in the library too, don't you?

Woman: I get paid, and I get credit toward my degree. But even better, I have a job offer from the library where I'm doing my internship.

Man: Wow! Are you going to take it?

Woman:	I think so. I have to let them know next week. If I do take the job, I'll have to go to graduate school to get a degree in library science, but I can do that part-time while I'm working, and I had thought about graduate school anyway. So, I'm leaning toward taking the job.
Man:	That's great, Anne. I'm glad for you. So uh I guess I'd better make an appointment with Ruth Jackson. Maybe she can find me an internship.
Woman:	Maybe.

> Now get ready to answer the questions. You may use your notes.

Audio
1. What are the students mainly discussing?

Answer
(B) Because the woman shares her positive experience at the Office of Career Development and recommends career counseling to the man, it may be concluded that the main topic is the advantages of career counseling for the man. Choices (A) and (C) are mentioned in reference to the main topic, "the advantages of career counseling for the man." Choice (D) is not mentioned and may not be concluded from information in the conversation.

Audio
2. What is the man's problem?

Answer
(C) "I wish I were as sure about my future as you seem to be. I . . . I really don't know what I want to do after I graduate." Choice (A) is not correct because it is a concern that the man expresses when the woman suggests career counseling, but it is not the main problem that the man brings up at the beginning of the conversation. Choice (B) is not correct because the internship is an idea that occurs to him after he hears about the woman's internship. Choice (D) is not mentioned and may not be concluded from information in the conversation.

Audio
3. Why does the woman tell the man about her experience?

Answer
(A) Because the woman's experience at the Office of Career Development was positive, it may be concluded that she told the man about it in order to demonstrate the benefits. Choice (B) is not correct because the woman encourages the man to talk to a counselor about a career choice, not an internship. Choice (C) is not correct because the woman does not suggest that the man change his major to library science, the major field that she is pursuing. Choice (D) is not correct because the man has not made a career decision.

Audio
4. What is the woman's attitude toward her internship?

Answer

(C) "I really liked what I was doing, and I realized that I didn't want the internship to end." Because the woman doesn't want the internship to end, it must be a very positive experience. Choice (A) is not correct because she is thinking about going to graduate school part-time, but she does mention that she would rather go to graduate school than continue her internship. Choice (B) is not correct because the woman is already interning. Choice (D) is not correct because she does not want the internship to end.

Audio

5. What will the man probably do?

Answer

(B) "So uh I guess I'd better make an appointment with Ruth Jackson." Choice (A) is not correct because Ruth Jackson is a career counselor at the Office of Career Development, not an academic advisor. Choices (C) and (D) are not mentioned and may not be concluded from information in the conversation.

Independent Listening 2: "Admission"

Audio Conversation

Narrator:	Now get ready to listen to a conversation and take notes about it. Listen to a conversation on campus between a student and an admissions officer.
Student:	Excuse me, but the secretary referred me to your office.
Assistant:	Yes?
Student:	I'm a new student . . . well, actually, I'm not enrolled yet, but I'm trying to get all my admissions applications turned in today.
Assistant:	What's your name?
Student:	Robert Franklin.
Assistant:	Middle initial?
Student:	T.
Assistant:	Oh, I see. Wait a minute and we'll see what you have to do. . . . Well, according to the records here, you have your admissions form, a financial aid application, three letters of recommendation, transcripts from Regional College . . . so that's everything you need except a transcript from County Community College.
Student:	That's what I thought. You see, I took a couple of courses there during the summer because it's close to my parent's house. Anyway, almost all of my first two years is from Regional College, and uh that's where I'm transferring from. In fact, the credit for the community college courses appears on the transcript from Regional College as transfer credit, but uh it doesn't show my final grades in the courses.
Assistant:	Oh, and you haven't been able to register for your courses here at State University because the computer shows that you are missing some of your application materials. Is that it?
Student:	Exactly. What I was wondering is whether you have like a policy for this kind of situation so I could go ahead and register for this first semester while we wait for the transcript to get here. It should be here

now. I requested it the same time that I requested a transcript from Regional College, but they're just slow at County Community.

Assistant: That happens sometimes. . . . Do you have a copy of your transcript from County Community College?

Student: Yes, I do. It's right here. Of course, it isn't an official copy. It's stamped "unofficial copy."

Assistant: But I can use this one until the official copy gets here. Here's the best way to handle this. We can give you a provisional admission. That means that you're admitted contingent upon the receipt of your official transcript. That will allow you to register for your courses this semester. When County Community College sends us your official transcript, then I can change your status from provisional admission to regular admission.

Student: Oh, that's great!

Assistant: Is this the only copy you have of your transcript?

Student: No. I have another one.

Assistant: Good. Then I'll just keep this in your file.

Student: Okay.

Assistant: Now the only problem is you can't register for next semester without regular admission status, and you need the official transcript for me to do that, so you still need to keep after them to get everything sent to us as soon as possible.

Student: Right. Well, I'll do that. But at least I have some time to get it done . . . . Um . . . what do I need to do now . . . to get registered, I mean.

Assistant: Just wait here while I enter everything into the computer, and then you can take the copy of your provisional admission along with you to the Office for Transfer Students. They'll assign you an advisor and help you get registered later today.

Now get ready to answer the questions. You may use your notes.

Audio

6. Why does the student go to the admissions office?

Answer

(D) ". . . I'm not enrolled yet, but I'm trying to get all my admissions applications turned in today." Choice (A) is not correct because his financial aid form is already on file. Choice (B) is not correct because he has requested an official transcript from another college to include in his admissions applications. Choice (C) is not correct because he is transferring from another college, not to another college.

Audio

7. What is missing from the student's file?

Answer

(B) ". . so that's everything you need except a transcript from County Community College." Choice (A) is not correct because the woman confirms that the financial aid application is already on file. Choice (C) is not correct because the grades from Regional College would be on the transcript that is in the man's file. Choice (D) is not correct because the admissions form is the official copy of the application.

Audio
8. Listen again to part of the conversation. Then answer the question.

"Oh, and you haven't been able to register for your courses here at State University because the computer shows that you are missing some of your application materials. Is that it?"

Why does the woman say, "Is that it?"

Answer
(B) The woman paraphrases the problem and then asks for confirmation that she has understood. *Is that it* means "Is that your problem?" Choice (A) is not correct because the woman has already paraphrased the situation. Choice (C) is not correct because the woman's tone is helpful, not impatient. Choice (D) is not correct because the man has explained a problem but he has not asked a question yet.

Audio
9. What does the woman suggest that the man do?

Answer
(D) ". . . you still need to keep after them to get everything [the official transcript from County Community College] sent to us as soon as possible." Choice (A) is not correct because he already has an unofficial copy of his transcripts. Choice (B) is not correct because, according to their records, the admission form is already on file. Choice (C) is not correct because he must have his official transcript before he can change his provisional status to regular status next semester and because he will register this semester with provisional status.

Audio
10. What will the student most probably do now?

Answer
(B) ". . . you can take a copy of your provisional admission along with you to the Office for Transfer Students. They'll assign you an advisor and help you get registered. . . . " Choice (A) is not correct because the man will see an advisor, not the woman, later today. Choice (C) is not correct because it refers to what the woman, not the man, will do. Choice (D) is not correct because the woman is assigning the provisional status to the man without her superior's approval.

Independent Listening 3: "Groups"

Audio Lecture
Narrator: Now get ready to listen to a lecture and take notes about it.
             Listen to part of a lecture in a sociology class.

Professor:
Social influence involves the changes in behavior influenced by the actions of other people. Social influence can come about for a variety of reasons, on a continuum from mere suggestion to, in the more severe form, well, to torture. How does social influence work? Well, first we must become aware of a difference between ourselves

and the values or behaviors of other people. There are a great many studies of social influence that demonstrate how the presence of others can cause us to change our attitudes or actions. Studies show that people eat more when dining with others than, and I'm talking about dining out here, so they eat more in the company of others than they do when they're alone. They also run faster when others are running with them. There's even some interesting research on social influence among animals with similar results to . . . to those of human studies.

Probably one of the most interesting aspects of social influence is the pressure for conformity. Conformity is a process by which an individual's opinion or behavior moves toward the norms of the group. In a classic study by Solomon Asch, seven people were shown cards with three lines drawn on them. Here's an example:

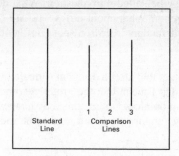

So, they were shown the lines, and then they were asked to select the line among the three that matched the uh . . . the uh . . . standard line. Here's the standard. So there's no question as to the comparison. This has to be easy, right? Wrong. You see, Asch enlisted the cooperation of six of the seven participants in the experiment. On the first card, the six respond correctly—they . . . they identify the lines of the same length—so the seventh person, who is the only real subject in the experiment, well, the seventh person answers correctly, in agreement with the others. But on the next card, four of the cooperating participants choose an incorrect answer, but they're in agreement, so the problem for the subject is whether to conform to the opinion of the peer group, even though the answer um . . . is in conflict with the answer that the subject knows to be correct.

So what do you think happened? Well, subjects who were tested alone made errors in answers fewer than 1 percent of the time. This was the control group. But of those tested in groups of seven, let's see um, 75 percent yielded at least once to conform to a group answer that was clearly incorrect, and on average, subjects conformed to the group in about 37 percent of the critical trials. This means that they were bringing their behavior into agreement with group norms in . . . in spite of what they were seeing.

Later Asch manipulated the size of the control group . . . I'm sorry, the experimental group . . . to see whether group size would affect pressure, and it did, but probably less than you might expect. Um . . . groups of four demonstrated about the same results as groups of eight. Interestingly enough, a unanimous agreement by the group was more important than the number. In other words, a unanimous opinion by three exerted more pressure to conform than a majority of seven with a dissenting opinion in a group of eight.

Similar experiments have been performed in various countries, among diverse cultural groups, with um comparable results. Of course, people in cultures that emphasize group cooperation tended to be more willing to conform, but remember that many of the original studies were done in the United States where there's a high value placed on individualism. In an interesting variation on the study, Abrams found that conformity is especially strong when the group is selected from among those people that the subject clearly identifies with, either because, um...they have characteristics in common or . . . or they know each other and interact in a peer group outside of the experimental situation.

So what does all of this mean in the real world? Well, since group members can influence one another to conform to the opinion of the group, the group . . . decisions of a group uh may be called into question. What about decisions by political committees or parliaments? What about juries who are charged with convicting or acquitting an accused defendant? Clearly, social influence will play a part in these critical group decisions.

Also interesting is the fact that after a decision is made by a group, there's a tendency to solidify, and by that I mean that the group becomes even more convinced of the validity of the group opinion. Um . . . this may happen because individual group members who strongly support the group tend to be more popular with the group members.

Now get ready to answer the questions. You may use your notes.

Audio

11. What is the main topic of the talk?

Answer

(C) "Social influence involves the changes in behavior influenced by the actions of other people." Choices (A), (B), and (D) are all mentioned as secondary topics that are used to develop the main topic of the lecture, "the influence of groups on individual behavior."

Audio

12. According to the professor, what two results were reported in the Asch and Abrams studies?

Answer

(B) (C) ". . . subjects conformed to the group in about 37 percent of the critical trials. . . . Abrams found that conformity is especially strong when the group is selected from among those people . . . [who] interact in a peer group outside of the experimental situation." Choice (A) is not correct because a larger group of eight demonstrated about the same results as a smaller group of four. Choice (D) is not correct because a unanimous opinion by three exerted more pressure to conform than a majority of seven with a dissenting opinion in a group of eight.

Audio
13. Listen again to part of the lecture. Then answer the question.

"Later Asch manipulated the size of the control group . . . I'm sorry . . . the experimental group . . . to see whether group size would affect pressure, and it did, but probably less than you might expect."

Why does the professor say this: "I'm sorry . . . the experimental group . . ."

Answer
(C) Professors occasionally misspeak and must correct themselves. The professor is talking about the experimental group, and incorrectly refers to the control group. Choice (D) is not correct because she is providing the facts in logical sequence. She is not returning to a previous point in the lecture to add important facts. Choices (A) and (B) are not mentioned and may not be concluded from information in the lecture.

Audio
14. What generally happens after a group makes a decision?

Answer
(C) ". . . after a decision is made by a group, there's a tendency to solidify . . . the group becomes even more convinced of the validity of the group opinion." Choice (D) refers to the fact that those who support the group most strongly tend to be more popular with the group, but competition for leadership is not mentioned and may not be concluded from information in the lecture. Choices (A) and (B) are not mentioned and may not be concluded from information in the lecture.

Audio
15. Based on information in the lecture, indicate whether the statements describe the Asch study. For each sentence, click in the YES or NO column.

Answer
(A) is YES. ". . . the seventh person . . . is the only real subject in the experiment. . . . "
(B) is NO. ". . . there's no question as to the comparison." **(C)** is YES. " . . . Asch enlisted the cooperation of six of the seven participants in the experiment."

Independent Listening 4: "Photography"

Audio Lecture
Narrator: Now get ready to listen to a lecture and take notes about it.
             Listen to part of a lecture in an art history class.

Professor:
We know that the Chinese had been aware of basic photographic principles as early as the fifth century B.C., and Leonardo da Vinci had experimented with a dark room in the 1500s, but it was a number of discoveries in chemistry during the eighteenth century that uh . . . accelerated the development of modern photography. The discovery that silver salts were light sensitive led to . . . experimentation with images of light on a . . . surface that had been coated with silver. Often glass was used in the early images. But the problem was that these images were ephemeral—fading

after only a short time. Some of the chemists who worked with them called them fairy pictures, and considered them uh . . . that they were only momentary creations uh . . . that they would disappear.

Okay. How to fix the image permanently was one of the most important uh . . . challenges . . . of the early photographer chemists. In France, in about 1820, Nicephore Niepce discovered a method for fixing the image after a long exposure time, oh, probably eight hours. So, although his work was considered interesting, it was uh . . . uh . . . largely dismissed for . . . as impractical. Nevertheless, one of his associates, Louis Daguerre, managed to find a way to uh . . . reduce . . . the exposure time to less than twenty minutes. So the story goes, in 1835, Daguerre was experimenting with some exposed plates, and he put a couple of them into his chemical cupboard, so a few days later, he opened the cupboard, and uh . . . to his surprise, the latent images on the plates had developed. At first, he couldn't figure out why, but eventually, he concluded that this must have occurred as a result of mercury vapor . . . from a broken thermometer that was also in the . . . uh . . . enclosed in the cupboard. Supposedly, from this fortunate accident, he was able to invent a process for developing latent images on . . . on exposed plates.

The process itself was somewhat complicated. First, he exposed copper plates to iodine which released fumes of uh . . . of light-sensitive silver iodide. These copper plates were used to capture the image, and by the way, they had to be used almost immediately after their exposure to the iodine. So, the image on the plate was then exposed to light for ten to twenty minutes. The plate was developed over mercury heated to about 75 degrees centigrade, which . . . that caused the mercury to amalgamate with the silver. Now here's the ingenious part—he then fixed the image in a warm solution of common salt, but later he began using sodium sulphite. Anyway, after he rinsed the plate in hot distilled water, a white image was left permanently on the plate. And the quality was really quite amazing.

But, um . . . the process had its limitations. First, the images couldn't be reproduced, so each one was a unique piece, and that uh greatly increased the cost of photography. Second, the image was reversed, so the subjects would actually see themselves as though they were looking in a mirror, although, uh . . . in the case of portraits, the fact that people were accustomed to seeing themselves in a mirror made this less . . . this problem less urgent than some of the others. Nevertheless, some photographers did point their cameras at a mirrored reflection of the image that they wanted to capture so that the reflection would be reversed, and a true image could be produced. Okay. Third, the chemicals and the fumes that they released were highly toxic, so photography was a very dangerous occupation. Fourth, the surface of the image was extremely fragile and . . . had to be protected, often under glass, so they didn't disintegrate from being . . . from handling. The beautiful cases that were made to hold the early images became popular not only for aesthetic purposes but uh . . . but also for very practical reasons. And finally, although the exposure time had been radically reduced, it was still . . . inconveniently long . . . at twenty minutes, especially for portraits, since people would have to sit still in the sun for that length of time. Elaborate headrests were constructed to keep the subjects from moving so that the image wouldn't be ruined, and uh . . . many people simply didn't want to endure the discomfort.

But, by the mid 1800s, improvements in chemistry and optics had resolved most of these issues. Bromide as well as iodine sensitized the plates, and some photographers were even using chlorine in an effort to decrease exposure time. The . . . the portrait lens was also improved by reducing the size of the opening, and limiting the amount of light that could enter, so the exposure time was about twenty seconds instead of twenty minutes. And negative film had been introduced in France, sorry, in England, and negatives permitted the production of multiple copies from a single image. So, photography was on its way to becoming a popular profession and pastime.

Now get ready to answer the questions. You may use your notes.

Audio

16. What is the main topic of this lecture?

Answer

(D) The lecture begins with historical background information and then focuses on the history of early photography in the 1800s when it was evolving into modern photography. Choices (A), (B), and (C) are all mentioned as secondary topics that are used to develop the main topic of the lecture, "the history of early photography."

Audio

17. According to the professor, what two limitations were noted in Daguerre's process for developing and fixing latent images?

Answer

(B) (C) "But . . . the process had its limitations. First, the images couldn't be reproduced, so each one was a unique piece. . . . Fourth, the surfaces of the image were extremely fragile and . . . had to be protected . . . so they didn't disintegrate . . . from handling." Choice (A) is not correct because Daguerre had resolved the problem of fixing the image in his process. Choice (D) is not correct because Daguerre's process had reduced the exposure time to twenty minutes.

Audio

18. Listen again to part of the lecture. Then answer the question.

"At first, he couldn't figure out why, . . . but eventually, he concluded that this must have occurred as a result of mercury vapor from a broken thermometer that was also in the uh . . . enclosed in the cupboard. Supposedly, from this fortunate accident, he was able to invent a process for developing latent images on . . . on exposed plates."

Why does the professor say this:
"Supposedly, from this fortunate accident, he was able to invent a process for developing latent images on . . . on exposed plates."

Answer

(C) The word *supposedly* implies that the speaker is not sure about the information. Choice (A) is not correct because she would not use such a neutral tone if she were trying to draw students into the story. Choice (D) is not correct because she does not invite them to use their imaginations while she is recounting the story. Choice (B) is not correct because the origin of the story is not mentioned.

Audio

19. What substance was first used to fix the images?

Answer

(B) "Now here's the ingenious part—he then fixed the image in a warm solution of common salt. . . . " Choice (A) is not correct because copper was the substance used for sensitizing the plates, not for fixing the images. Choice (C) is not correct because mercury vapor was the substance used to develop the plates, not to fix the images. Choice (D) is not correct because hot water was the substance used to rinse the plates after the images were fixed.

Audio

20. What can we assume about photographers in the 1800s?

Answer

(D) Because "the chemicals and the fumes that they released were highly toxic" and photography was "a very dangerous occupation," it may be concluded that some photographers must have experienced health problems as a result of their laboratory work. Choice (B) is not correct because many people didn't want to endure the discomfort associated with sitting still for a long time in order to have a portrait done. Choices (A) and (C) are not mentioned and may not be concluded from information in the lecture.

Independent Listening 5: "Authority"

Audio Lecture

Narrator: Now get ready to listen to a lecture and take notes about it.
             Listen to part of a lecture in an anthropology class.

Professor:
The concepts of power and authority are related, but they're not the same. Power is the ability to exercise influence . . . and control over others. And this can be observed on every level of society, from, well . . . the relationships within a family to the relationships among nations. Power is usually structured by customs and . . . and social institutions or laws and tends to be exerted by persuasive arguments or coercion or . . . or even brute force. In general, groups with the greatest uh . . . resources tend to have the advantage in power struggles. So, is power always legitimate? Is it viewed by members of society as justified? Well, no. Power can be realized by individuals or groups . . . even when it involves the resistance of others if . . . as long as . . . as long as they're in a position to impose their will. But what about power that is accepted by members of society as right and just, that is, legitimate power? Now we're talking about authority. And that is what I want to focus on today.

Okay. When individuals or institutions possess authority, they have um . . . a recognized and established right . . . to determine policies, with the acceptance of those over . . . over . . . whom they exercise control. Max Weber, the German classical sociologist, proposed three types of authority in society: traditional, charismatic, and rational or legal authority. In all three types, he uh . . . he acknowledged the right of those in positions of power to lead . . . with the consent of the governed. So, how did Weber differentiate among the three types of authority? Well, he divided them according to how the right to lead and the duty to follow are uh interpreted. In traditional authority, power resides in customs and conventions that provide certain people or groups with legitimate power in their societies. Often their origin is found in sacred traditions. The example that most often comes to mind is a monarchy in which kings or queens rule . . . uh . . . by birthright, not because of any particular . . . quality of leadership or political election, just because they have a claim to authority, based on traditional acceptance of their position, and in some cases, their uh their uh . . . unique relationship with and uh responsibility in religious practices. The royal families in Europe or the emperors in Asia are . . . come to mind as examples of traditional authority.

Okay. This contrasts sharply with charismatic authority, which is . . . uh . . . derived . . . because of personal attributes that inspire admiration, loyalty, and . . . and even devotion. Leaders who exercise this type of authority may be the founders of religious movements or political parties, but it's not their traditional right to lead. What's important here is that their followers are mobilized more by . . . by the force of the leader's personality than by the tradition or the law. So when we think of "charismatic" leaders in the United States, perhaps John Kennedy would be an example because he was able to project a youthful and energetic image that people were proud to identify with, or, if you prefer Republicans, you may argue that Ronald Reagan was able to exercise authority by virtue of his charismatic appeal. In any case, going back to Weber, to qualify for charismatic authority, a leader must be able to enlist others in the service of a . . . a cause that transforms the social structure in some way.

Which leaves us with legal rational authority, or power that is legitimized by rules, uh laws, and procedures. In such a system, leaders gain authority not by traditional birthrights or by charismatic appeal but . . . but rather because they're elected or appointed in accordance with the law, and power is delegated to layers of officials who owe their allegiance to the uh . . . principles that are agreed upon rationally, and because they accept the ideal that the law is supreme. In a legal rational society, people accept the legitimacy of authority as a government of laws, not of leaders. So, an example of this type of authority might be a president, like Richard Nixon, who was threatened with uh impeachment because he was perceived as not governing within the law.

Some sociologists have postulated that the three types of authority represent stages of evolution in society. That preindustrial societies tend to respect traditional authority, but um . . . as societies move into an industrial age, the importance of tradition . . . wanes . . . in favor of charismatic authority, with a natural rise of charismatic leaders. Then, as . . . as the modern era evolves, the rational legal authority, embodied by rules and regulations, replaces the loyalty to leaders in favor of . . . a respect for law. Of course, other sociologists argue that in practice, authority may be represented by a combination of several of these ideal types at any one time.

Now get ready to answer the questions. You may use your notes.

Audio

21. What is the main purpose of this lecture?

Answer

(A) "Max Weber, the German classical sociologist, proposed three types of authority in society: traditional, charismatic, and rational or legal authority." Choice (B) refers to the introduction, not to the main purpose of the lecture. Choices (C) and (D) are not mentioned and may not be concluded from information in the lecture.

Audio

22. According to the professor, what two factors are associated with charismatic authority?

Answer

(B) (C) ". . . charismatic authority, which is . . . derived . . . because of personal attributes that inspire admiration . . . . [A] leader must be able to enlist others in the service of a . . . cause that transforms the social structure in some way." Choice (A) refers to traditional authority, not to charismatic authority. Choice (D) refers to rational or legal authority, not to charismatic authority.

Audio

23. Listen again to part of the lecture. Then answer the question.

"But what about power that is accepted by members of society as right and just, that is, legitimate power? Now we're talking about authority. And that is what I want to focus on today."

Why does the professor say this:
"But what about power that is accepted by members of society as right and just, that is, legitimate power?"

Answer

(B) Professors often ask questions to introduce a topic. After the question, he continues, "Now we're talking about authority. And that is what I want to focus on today." Choice (A) is not correct because the professor doesn't pause long enough to invite answers. Choice (C) is not correct because he doesn't express an opinion after the question. Choice (D) is not correct because the previous point is about power, not authority.

Audio

24. In an evolutionary model, how is rational legal authority viewed?

Answer

(A) "Then, as . . . the modern era evolves, the rational legal authority, embodied by rules and regulations, replaces the loyalty to leaders in favor of . . . a respect for the law." Choice (B) refers to charismatic authority, not to rational legal authority. Choice (C) refers to the preindustrial age. Choice (D) is not correct because rational legal authority is one of the three ideal types, not a replacement for the three.

Audio

25. What does the professor imply about the three types of authority?

Answer

(B) Because the professor presents both an evolutionary model and an argument for an inclusive model that combines several types of authority, it must be concluded that sociologists do not agree. Choice (A) is not correct because the professor defines authority as "legitimate power." Choice (C) is not correct because at least some sociologists believe that societies evolve from one type of authority structure to another. Choice (D) is not mentioned and may not be concluded from information in the lecture.

Independent Listening 6: "Mineral Exploitation"

Audio Lecture

Narrator:	Now get ready to listen to a lecture and take notes about it. Listen to part of a discussion in an environmental science class.
Professor:	The exploitation of minerals involves five steps. First, you have to explore and locate the mineral deposits, then you set up a mining operation, next, you must refine the raw minerals and transport the refined minerals to the manufacturer.
Student 1:	Excuse me. Sorry. I only have four steps. Could you . . . ?
Professor:	Sure. That's exploration, mining, refining, transportation, and manufacturing.
Student 1:	Thanks.
Professor:	So, each of these activities involves costs, there are costs associated with them, and the costs can be economic, but not necessarily so. Mineral exploitation also has environmental costs associated with it. For example, the exploration stage will clearly have a high economic cost because of . . . of personnel and technology, but the environmental cost will probably be quite low. Why would that be, do you think?
Student 2:	Because you aren't actually disturbing the environment. You're just looking, I mean, after you find a mineral deposit, you don't do anything about it at that stage.
Professor:	Right. So the environmental costs would be low. But what happens when you use up all the resources that are easy to find? Then what?
Student 2:	Then the costs go up for exploration.
Professor:	Which costs?
Student 2:	Well, probably both of them, but I can see where the economic costs would increase.
Professor:	Okay. Let's say, for example, that some areas such as national parks or historic reserves have been . . . off-limits to exploration. What will happen when we use up the minerals outside of these areas? Remember now that these are uh . . . nonrenewable resources that we're looking for.
Student 1:	Then there will be a lot of pressure . . . you know . . . to open up these areas to exploration and exploitation.

Professor:	Probably so. And that means that there could be a high environmental cost. Any other options?
Student 1:	Find an alternative.
Professor:	Yes. You're on the right track.
Student 1:	Okay. Find an alternative, I mean a substitute, something that will substitute for the mineral. Maybe something man-made?
Professor:	Good. That will involve a different kind of exploration, again with economic costs. I'm talking about basic research here to find synthetics. But uh...let's go on to the other steps, and we'll see if we can pull this all together. How about mining? Now, we're looking at high environmental costs because of the destruction of the landscape and . . . and the accumulation . . . of waste products that have to be dealt with. Air and water pollution is almost always a problem. . . . Any ideas on refining?
Student 2:	Wouldn't it be the same as mining? I mean, you would have high costs because of labor and equipment, and there would be problems of waste and pollution, like you said.
Professor:	True. True. And in refining, well that often involves the separation of a small amount of a valuable mineral from a large amount of surrounding rock. So that means that . . . that uh . . . refining also carries the additional cost of cleanup. And don't forget that it's often difficult to get vegetation to grow on piles of waste. In fact, some of it, the waste piles I mean, they can even be dangerous to living creatures, including people. Not to mention the appearance of the area. So the environmental costs can be extremely high. Isn't it sad and ironic that so much of the mining and refining must take place in areas of great natural beauty?
Student 1:	So you're saying that both mining and refining have heavy costs . . . heavy economic and environmental costs.
Professor:	Right. And in both mining and refining, you would need transportation to support the movement of supplies, equipment, and personnel. But, after the minerals are mined and refined, then transportation becomes even more essential.
Student 2:	And I was just thinking that in addition to the economic costs of the transportation for trucks and fuel and labor and everything, there could be, there might be some construction too, if there aren't any roads in and out of the area.
Professor:	And that would mean . . .
Student 2:	That would mean that the landscape and even the ecosystem for the plants and animal life could be altered, so . . . so that's an environmental cost.
Professor:	It is indeed. Good point. That leaves us with manufacturing. After we find it, mine it, refine it, and transport it, we still have to manufacture it. What are the costs associated with that? Well, construction again, for factories, then there would be energy costs, technology, and labor.
Student 1:	So all that's economic. No environmental costs in manufacturing then.
Professor:	Well, yes there are actually. Pollution is often a costly problem for uh . . . manufacturing plants.
Student 1:	Oh right. I was thinking of the natural landscape, and the manufacturing is often positioned near cities to take advantage of the labor

pool. But, um . . . cities have the environmental problems associated with pollution. So, every step has both economic and environmental costs then.

Professor: Right.

Now get ready to answer the questions. You may use your notes.

Audio

26. What is the main topic of this lecture?

Answer

(D) "So, each of these activities involves costs . . . [that] can be economic, but . . . also environmental. . . ." Choices (A), (B), and (C) are all mentioned as secondary topics that are used to develop the main topic of the lecture, "the economic and environmental costs of mineral exploitation."

Audio

27. According to the professor, what are two problems that can be anticipated when roads are cut into an area for mining?

Answer

(B) (D) ". . . the landscape and even the ecosystem for the plants and animal life could be altered, . . . so that's an environmental cost." Choice (C) refers to the waste piles that are created in mining, but they are not mentioned in reference to the roadbeds. Choice (A) is not mentioned and may not be concluded from information in the lecture.

Audio

28. Listen again to part of the lecture. Then answer the question.

"And I was just thinking that in addition to the economic costs of the transportation for trucks and fuel and labor and everything, there could be, there might be some construction too, if there aren't any roads in and out of the area." "And that would mean. . . ."

Why does the professor say this, "And that would mean..."

Answer

(A) Professors often begin a sentence and then wait for the student to complete it. In this case, the professor is encouraging the student to continue by adding information to the answer that she gave initially. Choice (B) is not correct because the professor does not tell the student that he doesn't understand and does not ask the student to explain the answer that she gave initially. Choice (C) is not correct because the professor continues to direct his comments to the same student who has been speaking, not to another student. Choice (D) is not correct because the professor does not offer praise.

Audio

29. What option is proposed as an alternative when all of the mineral resources in easily accessible locations have been depleted?

Answer

(C) "Find an alternative. . . . Maybe something man-made . . . . I'm talking about basic research here to find synthetics." Choice (A) is not correct because minerals are *nonrenewable* resources, but converting to nonrenewable resources would imply that minerals are renewable. Choices (B) and (D) are not mentioned and may not be concluded from information in the lecture.

Audio

30. What does the professor imply about the environmental costs of mineral exploitation?

Answer

(B) Because the professor comments that it is "sad and ironic that so much of the mining and refining must take place in areas of great natural beauty," it may be concluded that he regrets that the environment is damaged during mineral exploitation. Choice (A) is not correct because the professor does not compare the costs. Choice (C) is not correct because the professor agrees with a student's view regarding the problems of pollution in cities, but the professor does not say that he opposes mineral exploitation near urban areas. Choice (D) is not correct because the professor poses the question but does not give his opinion about exploiting minerals in national parks and historic reserves.

Speaking Section

This is the Speaking Section of the Next Generation TOEFL Model Test. This section tests your ability to communicate in English in an academic context. During the test, you will respond to six speaking questions. You may take notes as you listen. You may use your notes to answer the questions. The reading passages and the questions are printed in the book, but most of the directions will be spoken. Your speaking will be evaluated on both the fluency of the language and the accuracy of the content. A clock on the screen will show you how much time you have to prepare your answer and how much time you have to record it.

Independent Speaking Question 1: "A Book"

Narrator 2:   Number 1. Listen for a question about a familiar topic. After you hear the question, you have 15 seconds to prepare and 45 seconds to record your answer.

Narrator 1:   Think about a book that you have enjoyed reading. Why did you like it? What was especially interesting about the book? Use specific details and examples to support your response.

Narrator 2:   Please prepare your answer after the beep.

Beep

[Preparation time: 15 seconds]

Narrator 2:   Please begin speaking after the beep.

Beep

[Recording time: 45 seconds]

Beep

Narrator 1:   Now listen to an example answer.

Example Answer
The Power of Positive Thinking by Dr. Norman Vincent Peale is one of my favorite books. Um . . . according to Dr. Peale, a positive outlook is essential to a happy, successful life. But what is especially interesting about the book are the practical strategies that help maintain an optimistic approach to living, even when uh things don't happen to be going well. He recommends reflection on all the aspects of life that are positive, and cultivating an "attitude of gratitude." He also recommends positive statements and mental pictures to encourage and motivate and . . . and to replace negative thoughts that come to mind.

Beep

Independent Speaking Question 2: "Foreign Travel"

Narrator 2:   Number 2. Listen for a question that asks your opinion about a familiar topic. After you hear the question, you have 15 seconds to prepare and 45 seconds to record your answer.

Narrator 1:   Some people think that it is better to travel as part of a tour group when they are visiting a foreign country. Other people prefer to make their own travel plans so that they can travel independently. Which approach do you think is better and why? Use specific reasons and examples to support your opinion.

Narrator 2:   Please prepare your answer after the beep.

Beep

[Preparation time: 15 seconds]

Narrator 2:   Please begin speaking after the beep.

Beep

[Recording time: 45 seconds]

Beep

Narrator 1:   Now listen to an example answer.

Example Answer

I've taken several tours, but I prefer to make my own travel plans because . . . I don't want to spend a lot of time at tourist hotels. In my experience, large hotels insulate travelers from the foreign culture. Instead of eating typical food, they prepare special meals for the tourists. And when I'm with groups of tourists, it's less likely that local people will approach me to talk. On my own, I've had some wonderful conversations with locals. Another reason that I like to travel independently is because I'm kind of a . . . a spontaneous person, so I like to take advantage of opportunities that present themselves on the trip.

Beep

Integrated Speaking Question 3: "Old Main"

Narrator 2:	Number 3. Read a short passage and listen to a talk on the same topic. Then listen for a question about them. After you hear the question, you have 30 seconds to prepare and 60 seconds to record your answer.
Narrator 1:	A public meeting is planned to discuss alternatives for renovating the original building on campus. Read the notice from the college newspaper [printed on page 353]. You have 45 seconds to complete it. Please begin reading now.

[Reading time: 45 seconds]

Narrator 1:	Now listen to a faculty member who is speaking at the meeting. She is expressing her opinion about the proposals.
Woman professor:	Although there may be some practical reasons for tearing down the structure surrounding the clock tower, I urge the committee to consider the historical importance of Old Main and opt for renovation of the original structure. I think we all agree that the brick structure is quite beautiful and basically sound. Only a few minor repairs would be necessary to preserve it. The cost of new electrical and plumbing systems for the old structure would be less than the cost of a new building with the same systems. And if a new building were to be erected, the clock tower would seem out of place somehow.
Narrator 1:	The professor expresses her opinion of the plan for the renovation of Old Main. Report her opinion and explain the reasons that she gives for having that opinion.
Narrator 2:	Please prepare your answer after the beep.

Beep

[Preparation time: 30 seconds]

Narrator 2:	Please begin speaking after the beep.

Beep

[Recording time: 60 seconds]

Beep

Narrator 1:   Now listen to an example answer.

Example Answer
The professor doesn't support the plan to demolish the main structure of Old Main and build a new structure around the original clock tower. She presents three arguments. Um . . . first, she says that the brick structure now standing is strong and it would require only minor repairs. And second, she points out that the electrical and plumbing problems in the old building could be repaired for less than the . . . the expenditure for a new building. Finally, she opposes the construction of a new building around the original clock tower because she thinks that the tower would be . . . would look odd in the new setting. She would probably support the alternative plan, which is um . . . to repair the original building.

Beep

Integrated Speaking Question 4: "Communication with Primates"

Narrator 2:   Number 4. Read a short passage and then listen to a lecture on the same topic. Then listen for a question about them. After you hear the question, you have 30 seconds to prepare and 60 seconds to record your answer.

Narrator 1:   Now read the passage about communication with primates [printed on page 353]. You have 45 seconds to complete it. Please begin reading now.

[Reading time: 45 seconds]

Narrator 1:   Now listen to part of a lecture in a zoology class. The professor is talking about a primate experiment.

Professor: Let me tell you about an experiment that didn't turn out quite like the researcher had expected. Dr. Sue Savage-Rumbaugh had been trying to train a chimpanzee to use a keyboard adapted with symbols. But no luck. What is interesting about the experiment is that the chimpanzee's adopted son Kanzi, also a bonobo Chimpanzee, well, Kanzi had been observing the lessons and had acquired a rather impressive vocabulary. After that, Kanzi was not given structured training, but he was taught language while walking through the forest or in other informal settings with his trainers. By six years of age, Kanzi had acquired a vocabulary of more than 200 words and was able to form sentences by combining words with gestures or with other words. So, the question is this: should we proceed by trying to teach language to primates in a classroom environment, or should we simply live with them and interact informally like we do with beginning learners of language in our own species? I tend to side with those who elect to support language acquisition in natural settings.

Narrator 1:   Explain the importance of the Kanzi experiment in the context of research on primate communication.

Narrator 2:   Please prepare your answer after the beep.

Beep

[Preparation time: 30 seconds]

Narrator 2:   Please begin speaking after the beep.

Beep

[Recording time: 60 seconds]

Beep

Narrator 1:   Now listen to an example answer.

Example Answer
The experiment with Kanzi is important because it supports the theory that language should be acquired in natural settings instead of in a formal classroom. Previous research to teach primates to communicate included direct instruction in American Sign Language and uh also plastic shapes that could be arranged on a magnetic board. Earlier research . . . I think it was with Kanzi's mother . . . it replicated this formal approach. But when Kanzi learned vocabulary by observing the lessons, the direction of the experiment changed. In informal settings with trainers, Kanzi acquired a vocabulary of about 200 words, and began to create sentences with words and gestures to . . . to communicate with human uh companions. Children of our own species learn by informal interaction with adults. The Kanzi experiment suggests that this may be a better way to teach language to primates.

Beep

Integrated Speaking Question 5: "Headaches"

Narrator 2:   Number 5. Listen to a short conversation. Then listen for a question about it. After you hear the question, you have 20 seconds to prepare and 60 seconds to record your answer.

Narrator 1:   Now listen to a conversation between a student and her friend.

Friend: Are you still having headaches?
Student: Yeah. I'm taking Tylenol every day.
Friend: That doesn't sound good. Why don't you go over to the Health Center?
Student: I keep thinking it'll go away. Probably just a tension headache. I feel really stressed out this semester.

Friend:	Well, you're probably right, but it still wouldn't hurt to get a check-up. Maybe the doctor will refer you for an eye exam. I used to get headaches from eyestrain, especially when I was using my computer a lot. And guess what? I needed to get my glasses changed.
Student:	No kidding? I hadn't thought about that, but I do notice that it gets worse after I've been using my computer.
Friend:	Well, then. That's important to mention when you see the doctor at the Health Center.
Student:	You think I should still go to the Health Center? I mean, if it's my eyes, I . . . I could just make an appointment with the eye doctor.
Friend:	You could, but you really aren't sure what it is. I'd go to the doctor at the Health Center, and I'd ask for a referral to the eye doctor. Besides, if you get referred, I think your student health insurance will pay most of the cost of new glasses.
Narrator 1:	Describe the woman's problem, and the two suggestions that her friend makes about how to handle it. What do you think the woman should do, and why?
Narrator 2:	Please prepare your answer after the beep.

Beep

[Preparation time: 20 seconds]

Narrator 2:	Please begin speaking after the beep.

Beep

[Recording time: 60 seconds]

Beep

Narrator 1:	Now listen to an example answer.

Example Answer
The woman's suffering from daily headaches, and she's controlling the pain by taking Tylenol. The man suggests that she make an appointment with a doctor at the Health Center because the problem should be diagnosed by a professional, but he also mentions the possibility that the doctor might refer her for an eye exam. Apparently, the problem's worse when she's been staring at the computer for long periods of time. Um . . . he reminds her that if the doctor at the Health Center refers her for the eye exam, the student health insurance may pay a large percentage of the cost for glasses. So . . . I think the woman should take the man's advice because eyestrain's a common problem for college students, and she probably does need an eye appointment, but by going to the doctor at the Health Center first, she can be certain that there isn't something more serious going on, and if she needs glasses, the referral will probably allow her to use her insurance benefit.

Beep

Integrated Speaking Question 6: "Fax Machines"

Narrator 2: Number 6. Listen to part of a lecture. Then listen for a question about it. After you hear the question, you have 20 seconds to prepare, and 60 seconds to record your answer.

Narrator 1: Now listen to part of a lecture in an engineering class. The professor is discussing the way that a fax machine transmits and receives data.

Professor: Okay, to illustrate my point that many new machines are simply combinations of machines that are already available, let's talk about the fax machine. To understand how a fax machine works, I'd like you to think of it as three machines—a copier, a modem, and a printer. First, the data is copied. How does that happen? Well, when you load paper into the fax machine, a light shines on it and optical sensors read whether a specific point on the paper is black or white. These sensors communicate the digital information into a microprocessor, where a copy of the page is made of black or white dots. Thus, you see that in the first step, the fax machine functions like a copier. Next, the fax machine works like a modem. Remember, a modem takes a black-and-white image and converts this digital data into an analog signal, that is, electronic impulses that can be sent over a phone line. The fax machine calls another fax machine to transmit, using two different types of tones to represent the black and white dots in the document. For example, it might send an 800-Hertz tone for white and a 1,300-Hertz tone for black. The last part of a fax machine is the printer. After the receiving fax machine answers the sending fax machine, it begins to accept the electronic impulses, and then it converts them back to the black-and-white dots in a digital image. Finally, it prints the image out on paper just like any other printer.

Narrator 1: Using the main points and examples from the lecture, describe the three parts of a fax machine and then explain how the fax process works.

Narrator 2: Please prepare your answer after the beep.

Beep

[Preparation time: 20 seconds]

Narrator 2: Please begin speaking after the beep.

Beep

[Recording time: 60 seconds]

Beep

Narrator 1: Now listen to an example answer.

Example Answer

A fax machine has three parts. The fax that's sending text and images has sensors to read black-and-white points on paper and communicate the patterns digitally to a microprocessor, and the microprocessor . . . it recreates the images in black-and-white dots. So this part of the process is like a copy machine. So then the digital information . . . I mean the image in black-and-white dots . . . is converted into an analog signal that's made up of electronic impulses. The impulses are sent over a phone line, like a modem. Then the fax machine that's sending the information connects with another fax machine that's receiving the information. They communicate with two tones, one that signals a black dot and another that signals a white dot. And the fax machine that receives the tones begins to print the dots on paper in the same way that any printer produces an image. So a fax is really a combination copier, modem, and printer.

Beep

Reading Section

This is the Reading Section of the Next Generation TOEFL Model Test. This section tests your ability to understand reading passages like those in college textbooks. There are three passages. After each passage, you will answer twelve or thirteen questions about it. Most questions are worth one point, but one question in each passage is worth more than one point. You will have 25 minutes to read each passage and answer the comprehension questions. You may take notes while you read. You may use your notes to answer the questions. Choose the best answer for multiple-choice questions. Follow the directions on the page or on the screen for computer-assisted questions. Click on **Next** to go to the next question. Click on **Back** to return to the previous question. You may return to previous questions in the same reading passage, but after you go to the next passage, you may not return to a previous passage. A clock on the screen will show you how much time you have to complete each passage.

Independent Reading 1: "Symbiotic Relationships"

1. **(C)** In the context of this passage, *derives* means "obtains." Choices (A), (B), and (D) are not accepted meanings of the word *derives*.

2. **(C)** "Parasitism is a relationship in which one organism, known as the parasite, lives in or on another organism, known as the host, from which it [the parasite] derives nourishment." The pronoun *it* does not refer to Choices (A), (B), or (D).

3. **(A)** In the context of this passage, *relatively* means "comparatively." Choices (B), (C), and (D) are not accepted meanings of the word *relatively*.

4. **(A)** Choice (A) is a paraphrase of the statement. Choices (B), (C), and (D) change the meaning of the statement.

5. **(A)** In the context of this passage, *tolerate* means "permit." Choices (B), (C), and (D) are not accepted meanings of the word *tolerate*.

6. **(D)** "Parasites that live on the surface of their hosts are known as **ectoparasites**." Choice (A) is not correct because mold and mildew are examples of ectoparasites, not a description of the way they survive. Choice (B) is not correct because it refers to endoparasites, not ectoparasites. Choice (C) is not correct because bacteria are an example of endoparasites.

7. **(A)** "There are many examples of commensal relationships. Many

orchids use trees as a surface upon which to grow." Choice (B) refers to a parasite, not a member of a commensal relationship. Choice (C) refers to a member of a mutualistic relationship. Choice (D) refers to a parasite.

8. **(C)** In the context of this passage, *actually* means "really." Choices (A), (B), and (D) are not accepted meanings of the word *actually*.

9. **(B)** ". . . the species can exist separately but are more successful when they are involved in a mutualistic relationship. Some species of *Acacia*. . . . " Choice (A) is not correct because the ants could exist separately but they are more successful living in the *Acacia* trees. Choice (C) is not correct because the example refers to a specific plant [*Acacia*] and animal [ant], not to all plants and animals. Choice (D) is not correct because mutualism is a solution, not a problem.

10. **(C)** ". . . have bacteria that live in their roots. . . . The bacteria do not cause disease but provide the plants with nitrogen-containing molecules that the plants can use for growth." Choice (B) is not correct because the plants use the nitrogen supplied by bacteria for growth. Choice (D) is not correct because the nodules are helpful, not harmful. Choice (A) is not mentioned and may not be concluded from information in the passage.

11. **(B)** Pronoun reference is a transitional device that connects the insert sentence with the previous sentence. The two sentences are related by the reference to "molds" and "mildews" in the previous sentence and the pronoun "they" in the insert sentence.

12. **(A)** Because the passage is about the relationship between organisms, it may be concluded that the passage would most probably appear in the chapter, "Environment and Organisms." Choices (B), (C), and (D) would probably not include a passage on symbiosis.

13. **(A) (C) (E)** summarize the lecture. Choice (B) is true, but it is a minor point mentioned as an example of a parasitic relationship. Choice (D) is true, but it is a minor point mentioned as an example of a mutalistic relationship. Choice (F) is true, but it is a minor point mentioned as an example of a commensal relationship.

Independent Reading 2: "Civilization"

1. **(B)** "...Neolithic settlements were hardly more than villages. But as their inhabitants mastered the art of farming, they gradually began to give birth to more complex human societies [civilizations]." Choice (A) is not correct because the Neolithic settlements preceded civilizations. Choice (C) is not correct because agriculture is mentioned as a cause of the rise in complex cultures, not as a definition of civilization. Choice (D) is not correct because the population centers increased in size as civilizations grew, but other basic characteristics had to be present as well.

2. **(B)** "Although copper was the first metal to be utilized in producing tools, after 4000 B.C., craftspeople in western Asia discovered that a combination of copper and tin produced bronze, a much harder and more durable metal than copper. Its [bronze's] widespread use has led historians to speak of a Bronze Age. . . ." The pronoun *its* does not refer to Choices (A), (C), or (D).

3. **(B)** "As wealth increased, such societies began to develop armies and to build walled cities." Choices (A), (C), and (D) may be logical, but they are not mentioned and may not be concluded from information in the passage.

4. **(C)** In the context of this passage, *hardly* means "barely." Choices (A), (B), and (D) are not accepted meanings of the word *hardly*.

5. **(D)** Because the author states that

Neolithic towns were transformed, it may be concluded that they are mentioned to contrast them with the civilizations that evolved. Choice (A) is not correct because a Neolithic town does not qualify as a civilization. Choice (B) is not correct because writing systems were not part of Neolithic settlements. Choice (C) is not correct because Neolithic settlements were referred to as villages, and no argument was made for the classification.

6. **(B)** ". . . . a new social structure . . . [included] kings and an upper class . . . free people . . . and a class of slaves. . . . " Choice (A) is not correct because it does not include free people. Choice (C) is not correct because it does not include free people. Choice (D) is not mentioned and may not be concluded from information in the passage. The new structure described is based on economics, not education.

7. **(A)** Choice (A) is a paraphrase of the statement. Choices (B), (C), and (D) change the meaning of the statement.

8. **(A)** In the context of this passage, *crucial* means "fundamental." Choices (B), (C), and (D) are not accepted meanings of the word *crucial*.

9. **(B)** In the context of this passage, *prominent* means "important." Choices (A), (C), and (D) are not accepted meanings of the word *prominent*.

10. **(B)** "A number of possible explanations of the beginning of civilization have been suggested." Choice (A) is not correct because scholars do not agree on one explanation. Choice (C) is not correct because trade routes are not mentioned in paragraph 4. Choice (D) is not correct because coincidence is not mentioned as one of the possible explanations.

11. **(C)** Choice (A) is mentioned in paragraph 4, sentence 9. Choice (B) is mentioned in paragraph 4, sentence 8. Choice (D) is mentioned in paragraph 4, sentence 6.

12. **(B)** A rhetorical question is a question that is asked and answered by the same speaker. Response is a transitional device that connects the insert sentence with the previous rhetorical question. Choices (A), (C), and (D) do not include transitional devices that connect the insert sentence with the sentences marked in the passage.

13. **(B) (E) (F)** summarize the passage. Choice (A) is true, but it is a minor point that is mentioned as an example in the characteristic of a class structure. Choice (C) is not mentioned in the passage. Choice (D) is not mentioned in the passage.

Independent Reading 3: "The Scientific Method"

1. **(B)** In the context of this passage, *obvious* means "clear." Choices (A), (C), and (D) are not accepted meanings of the word *obvious*.

2. **(B)** " . . . our interpretations of facts often are based on beliefs about the world that others might not share. For example . . . that the Sun rises . . . [is] an idea that might not have been accepted by ancient Egyptians. . . . " Choice (A) is not correct because the rotation might not have been accepted by ancient Egyptians. Choices (C) and (D) are not mentioned and may not be concluded from information in the passage.

3. **(C)** In the context of this passage, *essentially* means "basically." Choices (A), (B), and (D) are not accepted meanings of the word *essentially*.

4. **(A)** In the context of this passage, *flawed* means "not perfect." Choices (B), (C), and (D) are not accepted meanings of the word *flawed*.

5. **(B)** Choice (B) is a paraphrase of the statement. Choices (A), (C), and (D) change the meaning of the statement.

6. **(B)** ". . . its [the Ptolemaic model's] predictions didn't quite match actual observations—a key reason why the Earth-centered model of the universe finally was discarded." The pronoun *its* does not refer to Choices (A), (C), or (D).

7. **(A)** "Therefore, even well-established theories must be subject to continuing challenges through further observations and experiments." Choice (C) is not correct because a theory that is generally accepted by the scientific community would have to be subject to scientific observation and experimentation. Choices (B) and (D) are not mentioned and may not be concluded from information in the passage.

8. **(C)** ". . . Kepler . . . tested his model against observations that had been made previously, rather than verifying new predictions. . . ." Choice (A) is not correct because the predictions do not verify a model. Predictions must be verified by the model. Choices (B) and (D) are not mentioned and may not be concluded from information in the passage.

9. **(D)** In the context of this passage, *plenty* means "numerous." Choices (A), (B), and (C) are not accepted meanings of the word *plenty*.

10. **(D)** Choice (A) is mentioned in paragraph 2, sentence 2. Choice (B) is mentioned in paragraph 2, sentence 8. Choice (C) is mentioned in paragraph 2, sentence 5.

11. **(A)** Because the Ptolemaic model "didn't quite match actual observations. . . . " it may be concluded that a model does not always reflect observations. Choice (B) is not correct because theories are more firmly established than models. Choice (C) is not correct because a theory can never be "true beyond all doubt." Choice (D) is not correct because "a model must be continually challenged with new observations or experiments."

12. **(C)** Paraphrase is a transitional device that connects the insert sentence with a previous sentence. " . . . our [cultural] interpretations of facts" in a previous sentence is a paraphrase of "cultural orientation" in the insert sentence. Choices (A), (B), and (D) do not include transitional devices that connect the insert sentence with the sentences marked in the passage.

13. **(A) (C) (E)** summarize the lecture. Choice (B) is true, but it is a minor point mentioned in reference to the fourth and final step of the method. Choice (D) is true, but it is mentioned after the discussion of the steps in the scientific method. Choice (F) is not mentioned in the passage.

Writing Section

This is the Writing Section of the Next Generation TOEFL Model Test. This section tests your ability to write essays in English. During the test, you will write two essays. The independent essay usually asks for your opinion about a familiar topic. The integrated essay asks for your response to an academic reading passage, a lecture, or both. You may take notes as you read and listen. You may use your notes to write the essays. If a lecture is included, it will be spoken, but the directions and the questions will be written. A clock on the screen will show you how much time you have to complete each essay.

Independent Writing: *"Study in the United States"*
Question:
You are planning to study in the United States. What do you think you will like and dislike about this experience? Why? Use specific reasons and details to support your answer.

Outline
Like
• Improve language proficiency
• Participate in culture
• College courses

Dislike
- Miss family
- Rely on fast food
- Compete with Americans

Map

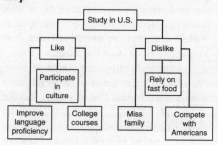

Example Essay

Living abroad provides many opportunities and challenges. When I study in the United States, I look forward to making friends with Americans. By getting to know people, I will be able to improve my English language proficiency. There are idioms and words that are best learned within the context of real conversations with native speakers. I also look forward to being a participant in a new culture. At the end of my stay in the United States, I hope that I will understand American culture in a different and deeper way than is possible when the information is derived from only movies and books. In addition, I am excited about studying on an American campus. I expect the college courses to be challenging, and I am eager to learn about the latest technological advances in my field of study.

I am realistic about the disadvantages of foreign study, however. I know that I will miss my family very much. It will be too expensive to return to my country to spend holidays with them, and I will be very lonely during the times when I know that they are gathered for special celebrations. Another aspect of the experience that I do not look forward to is the reliance on fast food that is so typical of American college students. Pizza, hamburgers, and other junk foods are easier to find and prepare than the meals that I enjoy in my country, but they aren't as good, and they probably aren't as healthy. Finally, I imagine that my life will be very stressful because I will be competing with students who know the language of the classroom and are accustomed to the expectations that American professors have for their students. I am a competitive person by nature, and I am apprehensive about my ability to compete with my classmates.

Once I am in the United States, I will no doubt find many other opportunities to take advantage of and many challenges that I must confront. Nevertheless, I expect my experience to be overwhelmingly positive, and I intend to see the lessons in both adventures and adversity.

Integrated Writing: "Problem Solving"
Audio

Narrator: Now listen to a lecture on the same topic as the reading passage [on page 373].

Professor:

Now that you've read the article on problem solving, let's talk about the role of breaks. We all know that taking a break is a good strategy for solving a problem, but how does a break really influence the solution? Well, some researchers feel that rest allows the brain to analyze the problem more clearly. We're advised to "sleep on it" when a problem is difficult to solve. Okay, but what if there's some type of *incubation effect* during sleep that allows the brain to continue working on a solution? Here's what I mean. F. A. Kekule was puzzled by the structure of benzene. One night, he dreamed about a snake biting its tail while whirling around in a circle. And when he awoke, it occurred to him that the carbon atoms of benzene might be arranged in a ring. He attributed the solution of the problem directly to the dream. But Kekule's experience and others like it present researchers with a dilemma because there's disagreement about whether unconscious mental activity exists. Were the dreamers really asleep or were they relaxed but awake when they solved the problem?

Two explanations have been proposed to explain why a break supports problem solving while we're awake. One possibility is that during the break, information may appear that provides a solution. For example, Buckminster Fuller was looking at a triangle when he saw the structure of multiple triangles as the solution for constructing a geodesic dome. Of course, another possibility is much more simplistic. It could be that the value of taking a break is as basic as interfering with an ineffective pattern of thinking. By focusing on something else, we may return to the problem in a different frame of mind and think about it in a different, and more productive, way.

Question:
Summarize the main points in the lecture, referring to the way that they relate to the reading passage [on page 373].

Outline
Sleeping
- Rest to function at higher capacity
- "Incubation effect"—Kekule structure benzene
- "Functional fixedness" released

Waking
- Input during break—Fuller geodesic dome
- Interruption unsuccessful process
- Different "mental set"

Map

Example Essay
Although researchers do not agree about the way that a break contributes to problem solving, it is clear that breaks during sleeping hours and those that we take during waking hours are both helpful. The value of sleep may be related to the brain's requirement for rest in order to function at a higher capacity. On the other hand, it is possible that there is an "incubation effect," that is, that the brain continues to problem solve at a different level of consciousness during a sleep break. For example, Kekule had insight into the structure of benzene during a dream. Although researchers are not in agreement as to the level of unconscious activity of dreamers, and some argue that dreamers who solve problems are not really asleep, it remains that the sleep break was helpful. It may even be that "functional fixedness" described in the text is somehow released in sleep so that preconceived notions are less limiting.

In contrast, breaks during waking hours appear to be more straightforward. Sometimes input during the break period will contribute to the solution. For example, Fuller's inspiration for the geodesic dome occurred while he was looking at a triangle during a break. However, merely interrupting an unsuccessful problem-solving process could be helpful. By taking a break, we may be more willing to abandon a strategy that is not working, or, as the text states, we return to the problem with a different "mental set."

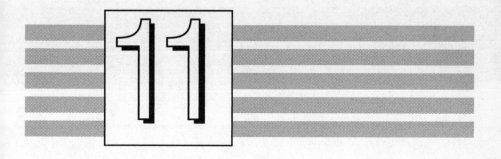

SCORE ESTIMATES

Important Background Information

It is not possible for you to determine the exact score that you will receive on the TOEFL. There are three reasons why this is true. First, the testing conditions on the day of your official TOEFL will affect your score. If you are in an uncomfortable room, if there are noisy distractions, if you are upset because you almost arrived late for the test, or if you are very nervous, then these factors can affect your score. The administration of a Model Test is more controlled. You will probably not be as stressed when you take one of the tests in this book. Second, the Model Tests in the book are designed to help you practice the most frequently tested item types on the official TOEFL. Because they are constructed to teach as well as to test, there is more repetition in Model Tests than there is on official TOEFL tests. Tests that are not constructed for exactly the same purposes are not exactly comparable. Third, the TOEFL scores received by the same student will vary from one official Computer-Based TOEFL examination to another official Computer-Based TOEFL examination by as many as 20 points, even when the examinations are taken on the same day. In testing and assessment, this is called a standard error of measurement. Therefore, a TOEFL score cannot be predicted precisely even when two official tests are used.

But, of course, you would like to know how close you are to your goal. To do that, you can use the following procedure to estimate your TOEFL score. An estimate is an approximation. In this case, it is a range of scores.

Score Correspondence Procedure

1. Use the charts on the following pages to determine your percentage scores for each section of the TOEFL.
2. Determine the total percentage score for the TOEFL.
   Listening Section = one third the total
   Structure Section = one sixth the total
   Reading Section = one third the total
   Writing Section = one sixth the total
3. Use the Score Correspondence Table to estimate an official TOEFL score.

Listening Section

Number Correct	Percentage Score
50	100
49	98
48	96
47	94
46	92
45	90
44	88
43	86
42	84
41	82
40	80
39	78
38	76
37	74
36	72
35	70
34	68
33	66
32	64
31	62
30	60
29	58
28	56
27	54
26	52
25	50
24	48
23	46
22	44
21	42
20	40
19	38
18	36
17	34
16	32
15	30
14	28
13	26
12	24
11	22
10	20
9	18
8	16
7	14
6	12
5	10
4	8
3	6
2	4
1	2
0	0

Structure Section

Number Correct	Percentage Score
25	100
24	96
23	92
22	88
21	84
20	80
19	76
18	72
17	68
16	64
15	60
14	56
13	52
12	48
11	44
10	40
9	36
8	32
7	28
6	24
5	20
4	16
3	12
2	8
1	4
0	0

Reading Section

Number Correct	Percentage Score
45	100
44	98
43	96
42	93
41	91
40	89
39	87
38	84
37	82
36	80
35	78
34	76
33	73
32	71
31	69
30	67
29	64
28	62
27	60
26	58
25	56
24	53
23	51
22	49
21	47
20	44
19	42
18	40
17	38
16	36
15	33
14	31
13	29
12	27
11	24
10	22
9	20
8	18
7	16
6	13
5	11
4	9
3	7
2	4
1	2
0	0

Writing Section

Scaled Score	Percentage Score
6.0	100
5.5	92
5.0	84
4.5	76
4.0	68
3.5	60
3.0	52
2.5	44
2.0	36
1.5	28
1.0	20
0	0

Score Correspondence Table

Model Test Percentage Scores	Computer-Based TOEFL Score Ranges	Paper-Based TOEFL Score Ranges
100	287–300	660–677
95	273–283	640–657
90	260–270	620–637
85	250–260	600–617
80	237–247	580–597
75	220–233	560–577
70	207–220	540–557
65	190–203	520–537
60	173–187	500–517
55	157–170	480–497
50	140–153	460–477
45	123–137	440–457
40	110–123	420–437
35	97–107	400–417
30	83–93	380–397
25	70–80	360–377
20	60–70	340–357
15	47–57	320–337
10	40–47	310–317
5		
0		

Progress Chart   Percentage Scores

Model Test	Listening $\frac{1}{3}$	Structure $\frac{1}{6}$	Reading $\frac{1}{3}$	Writing $\frac{1}{6}$	= Total =	Score Ranges
One						
Two						
Three						

Scores for the Next Generation TOEFL

The Next Generation TOEFL will have section scores for each of the four sections. The range for the section scores will be 0–30. Then the scores for the four sections will be added together. Although final scoring has not been determined, the total score range for the Next Generation TOEFL will probably be 0–120. To estimate your score on Model Test 4, the Next Generation TOEFL Model Test, determine your percentage of correct answers on each section and divide by four. Then multiply by 1.2. This is a very rough estimate, but until a more refined scoring scale is published, it will give you a general idea of how you would score. Continue to watch the TOEFL web site at *www.toefl.org* for the latest information about the official scoring scale.

Barron's TOEFL
Compact Disks

The compact disks in the back of this book can be used in your compact disk player to provide the audio for two of the TOEFL model tests and the Next Generation model test. You should hear audio only. If you want to simulate the Computer-Based TOEFL, with both audio and visuals, you need a CD-ROM, not a compact disk. The CD-ROM is available from Barron's Educational Series, Inc. The CD-ROM has nine model tests on it.

Telephone: 800-645-3476
FAX: 631-434-3723
E-mail: customer.service@barronseduc.com
Web site: http://www.barronseduc.com